The Role of SMEs in National Economies in East Asia

STUDIES OF SMALL AND MEDIUM SIZED ENTERPRISES IN EAST ASIA SERIES

Series Editors: Charles Harvie and Boon-Chye Lee, *University of Wollongong, Australia*

This series incorporates both theoretical and empirical studies of various aspects of small and medium sized enterprises in East Asia, focusing on a number of key issues, problems and their survival in the wake of the regional financial and economic crisis. It examines the contribution of SMEs to national economies and how best to sustain their growth and performance. Selected geographic regions and/or industrial sectors are studied in greater depth for additional insight.

These enterprises are distinct in many ways from SMEs in other parts of the world. The studies will therefore contribute to an improved understanding of the roles played by East Asian SMEs in their domestic economies as well as within one of the most dynamic and rapidly developing regions of the global economy.

Titles in the series are:

1. Globalisation and SMEs in East Asia
   edited by Charles Harvie and Boon-Chye Lee

2. The Role of SMEs in National Economies in East Asia
   edited by Charles Harvie and Boon-Chye Lee

3. Sustaining Growth and Performance in East Asia
   The Role of Small and Medium Sized Enterprises
   edited by Charles Harvie and Boon-Chye Lee

4. Small and Medium Sized Enterprises in East Asia
   Sectoral and Regional Dimensions
   edited by Charles Harvie and Boon-Chye Lee

The Role of SMEs in National Economies in East Asia

Edited by

Charles Harvie and Boon-Chye Lee

University of Wollongong, Australia

STUDIES OF SMALL AND MEDIUM SIZED ENTERPRISES IN EAST ASIA

Edward Elgar

Cheltenham, UK • Northampton, MA, USA

Published by
Edward Elgar Publishing Limited
Glensanda House
Montpellier Parade
Cheltenham
Glos GL50 1UA
UK

Edward Elgar Publishing, Inc.
136 West Street
Suite 202
Northampton
Massachusetts 01060
USA

A catalogue record for this book
is available from the British Library

Library of Congress Cataloguing in Publication Data

The role of SMEs in national economies in East Asia / Harvie, Charles,
Lee, Boon-Chye (editors).
  p. cm.— (Studies of small and medium sized enterprises series ; 2)
  Includes index
  1. Small business—East Asia—Case studies. 2. Small business—Asia,
Southeastern—Case studies. 3. Small business—Australia. I. Harvie, Charles,
1954- II. Lee, Boon-Chye. III. Series.

338.6'42'095—dc21   2002021007

ISBN 1 84064 324 2

Printed and bound in Great Britain by MPG Books Ltd, Bodmin, Cornwall

To Margaret and Alan
(Charles Harvie)

To Mei Sean
(Boon-Chye Lee)

Other books published by Charles Harvie

Contemporary Developments and Issues in China's Economic Transition (editor)
Causes and Impact of the Asian Financial Crisis (editor with Tran Van Hoa)
Vietnam's Reforms and Economic Growth (co-author with Tran Van Hoa)

Other books published by Boon-Chye Lee

The Economics of International Debt Renegotiation: The Role of Bargaining and Information

Contents

List of Tables

List of Figures

Notes on Contributors

Moha Asri Abdullah is Deputy Director and Associate Professor at the Centre for Policy Research, University Science Malaysia, Penang, and is currently a Visiting Scholar at the School of Economics, Nagoya University, Japan. He holds a PhD from the University of London. He teaches small business management and his research focus is mainly on development economics, specifically the development of small and medium enterprises. He has published more than 14 books, more than 20 papers in renowned journals and presented a number of papers in international conferences/fora. His recent books include *Foreign Workers in Malaysia* (co-author), Utusan, 1999, *Foreign Labour in Asia* (co-author), Nova Science, 1999, *Small and Medium Enterprises in Malaysia, Management of Small Enterprises, Small and Medium Enterprises in Asian Pacific Countries* (main editor), Ashgate, 1999, *Asian Small and Medium Enterprises: Challenges in the 21st Century* (editor), Wisdom House, 2001, and *Small and Medium Enterprises in the Information Age: Asian Perspectives* (editor), Wisdom House, 2001.

Albert Berry is a full professor in the Department of Economics and Director of the Centre for International Studies at the University of Toronto, Canada. He obtained his PhD from Princeton University. His areas of specialisation are in economic development and international economics. His recent publications include 'Agrarian Reform, Land Distribution, and Small-Farm Policy as Preventive of Humanitarian Emergencies', in E. Wayne Nafziger and Raaimo Vayrynen (eds), *The Political Economy of Humanitarian Emergencies*, Oxford University Press, 2000, and *Fulfilling the Export Potential of Small and Medium Firms*, with Brian Levy and Jeffrey B. Nugent, Kluwer Academic Publishers, 1999.

Peter Brimble is President, Policy Research Division of The Brooker Group plc, and has been based in Thailand for more than 15 years. He has carried out research on industrial and technological development and government policy issues in Thailand and the region – for the Asian Development Bank, the World Bank, the United Nations, the Thai Board of Investment and many other Thai government agencies/institutions. He has assisted numerous multinationals with corporate strategy work. Dr Brimble is an Economics graduate of the London School of Economics, Georgetown University, the University of Sussex, and Johns Hopkins University. His PhD thesis examined the productivity performance of Thai manufacturing firms.

Gary D. Gregory is a Senior Lecturer in the Department of Marketing at the University of Wollongong, Australia. He received his PhD from the University of Texas. Dr Gregory's areas of interest and research include small and medium sized enterprises (SMEs), internationalisation of business, cross-cultural marketing and market entry strategies. His publications have appeared in such journals as *Journal of Business Research, Psychology and Marketing, Journal of Brand Management, Journal of the Academy of Marketing Studies, Journal of Transnational Management Development, International Business Teaching, Advances in Consumer Research* and *Nursing Management.* Currently, Dr Gregory is involved in a cross-national study of factors affecting the internationalisation of SMEs in East and Southeast Asia.

Chris Hall is the MBA Director at the Macquarie Graduate School of Management in Sydney, Australia. His main research interest is in the economic and strategic issues of internationalisation, particularly in relation to small and medium sized enterprises (SMEs). He has coordinated major projects for the OECD, APEC and UNCTAD. For the OECD he led the project on SME globalisation which encompassed teams in 18 member economies plus teams in five non-member Asian economies. For UNCTAD he coordinated a major project on the facilitation of foreign direct investment in SMEs as a means of development in Asia. He is regularly an invited expert at APEC and the OECD, is the Pacific Economic Cooperation Council (PECC) SME expert and representative at APEC, and has worked with the Canadian, Japanese, Taiwanese, Philippine and French governments on related projects. He is also a leading expert on competitive intelligence, or the methods that firms use to remain informed and internationally competitive.

Charles Harvie is an Associate Professor in the Department of Economics at the University of Wollongong, Australia. He is currently Deputy Director of his faculty's International Business Research Institute and Director of the Centre for SME Research and Development based at the University of Wollongong. He obtained his PhD in economics from the University of Warwick in 1986. He has taught in the UK, Australia, Thailand, Singapore and Vietnam in the areas of macroeconomics, international economics, monetary economics and transition economics. More recently his research interests have focused upon the Asian financial crisis, China's economic reforms, and the significance of innovation for SME export performance. Dr Harvie has published his research results in the form of numerous journal articles, books and book chapters.

Nigel Haworth is Professor of International Business at the University of Auckland, New Zealand. An economist by training, his research interests include international labour market issues, the impact of internationalisation on regional integration and the HRD dimensions of regional integration. He serves on a number of APEC committees, in which one of his interests is the development of the APEC SME agenda.

Hal Hill is the H.W. Arndt Professor of the Southeast Asian Economies at the Australian National University, Canberra, Australia. His main research interests are the economies of ASEAN, especially Indonesia and the Philippines; industrialisation and foreign investment in East Asia; and Australia's economic relations with the Asia-Pacific region. He has authored/edited 12 books on these subjects, in addition to about 110 academic papers and book chapters. He is also an occasional contributor to several Australian and Asian newspapers and magazines, and has worked as a consultant for the Australian government, the Indonesian government, the World Bank, the Asian Development Bank, and several United Nations agencies. He has held visiting appointments at Gadjah Mada University, the University of the Philippines, the Institute of Southeast Asian Studies, the University of Oxford, and Columbia University.

Boon-Chye Lee is a Senior Lecturer in the Department of Economics at the University of Wollongong, Australia, where he also coordinates the International Economic and Business Integration program of the International Business Research Institute. He is a graduate of the Australian Graduate School of Management, University of New South Wales. His doctoral thesis, 'The Economics of International Debt Renegotiation', was subsequently published by Westview Press (1993). His more recent research interests have focused on SMEs, electronic money, and trust in Internet commerce. His research has been published in international journals including the *Asia-Pacific Journal of Management, Journal of International Financial Markets, Institutions and Money, Applied Economics Letters* and *Netnomics*, and as book chapters.

Manusavee Monsakul is a researcher, Policy Research Division of the Brooker Group, where she has worked on a number of projects dealing with small and medium enterprises, industry associations, and industrial competitiveness. She is a graduate of Chulalongkorn University in Bangkok, Warwick University in the United Kingdom, and the University of Auckland in New Zealand.

Matt Ngui is a Lecturer in Management and a Research Manager at the Centre for Research Policy and Innovation at the University of Wollongong, Australia; an Associate Member of the Centre for Asia Pacific Studies in Social Transformation (CAPSTRANS), Centre for Small and Medium Enterprises Research and Development and the International Business Research Institute (IBRI). In addition, he manages the Research Office for International Collaboration (ROIC), University of Wollongong, in Jakarta, Indonesia. He is writing his doctoral thesis on international organisational networks in the Asia–Pacific region. He has represented Australia in the Asia–Pacific Economic Cooperation (APEC) Forum's Human Resource Development in Industrial Technology Network.

Ha Nguyen is currently a Lecturer in the Hanoi School of Business, Vietnam National University, Hanoi, Vietnam. He was formerly employed by the Vietnamese Ministry of Trade and has participated in a number of technical assistance projects designed to promote SME development in Vietnam.

James Nguyen is currently the Head Tutor for Macroeconomics at the Department of Economics, University of Wollongong, Australia. He is currently finishing his last year of a law degree after having completed his BCom degree with Honours in economics in 2000. His honours thesis addresses the role of export-oriented SMEs in the Australian economy, focusing upon SMEs in the Illawarra region. He has special interests in monetary economics, macroeconomics and international economics.

Nguyen Van Lan is a Lecturer in the Business School, National Economic University, Hanoi Vietnam. He is currently completing his PhD at Sunderland Business School, University of Sunderland, UK. His thesis focuses on culture, institutions and management in Vietnam during the age of reform.

David Oldfield is Senior Vice-President, Policy Research Division and Head of the Greater Mekong Subregion (GMS) Unit of The Brooker Group plc. He has a diverse professional background in consulting, government advisory and academia. He manages public sector projects, in particular GMS projects supported by governments and international agencies in the fields of private sector strengthening and human resource development, and serves as an advisor to a local government in Cambodia. Dr Oldfield's current research projects include subregional economic growth areas and health policy in Indochina. He received his PhD in political science from Northern Illinois University (USA).

David Richards is currently Professor of International Business and Cross-Cultural Management in the Sunderland Business School, University of Sunderland, UK. He arrived in Sunderland in February 1998 from Darwin, Australia, where he was Associate Professor in International Management in the Graduate School of Business at Northern Territory University (NTU). Until 1986 he worked in higher education in the UK and, prior to going to NTU in 1990, was Head of Business and Management at the Brunei Institute of Technology, in Brunei, Southeast Asia. From October 1995 until June 1996 he was a Visiting Professor at the National Economics University in Hanoi, Vietnam, working on the MBA Project at the Centre for Management Learning. His research and teaching interests centre on international management, culture and organisational behaviour, with a special interest in cross-cultural and expatriate management and management learning. These interests currently focus on cross-cultural effectiveness, especially among expatriate managers and on the means by which it may be learned and enhanced. He has published two books and a number of articles in refereed journals.

Edgard Rodriguez is an economist at the Financial Sector and Industry Division (East) at the Asian Development Bank in Manila. He holds a PhD in economics from the University of Toronto, Canada. His recent publications include 'Technical Efficiency Indicators in the Philippine Manufacturing Sector' (with F. Mini), *International Review of Applied Economics* (October 2000) and 'Liberalisation and

Small Industry: Have Manufacturing Philippine SMEs benefited?' (with G. Tecson) and *Small Enterprise Development* (December 1998).

Keishi Sugiura is a consultant with Watson Wyatt in Tokyo where he specialises in technology policy. Prior to this he was a Research Fellow at the Fujitsu Research Institute Economic Research Centre where he was researching APEC economic and technical cooperation and principal–agent analysis of rural irrigation projects. He holds a DPhil in Technology and Development from the Science Policy Research Unit (SPRU), University of Sussex, UK.

Wee Liang Tan is an Associate Professor of Entrepreneurship and Law at the Singapore Management University. His involvements in entrepreneurship include: managing editor of the *Journal of Enterprising Culture*; an editorial adviser for the *Journal of Small Business Management*; and Senior Vice-President (Economic Development) of the International Council for Small Business (1994–96). His publications include articles in the *Journal of International Business Studies, Journal of Business Research, International Business Review* and *Family Business Review*, and chapters in numerous books. He serves as the National SME expert for the Asian Productivity Organisation (APO) and as an international expert for the Asia–Pacific Economic Cooperation forum (APEC).

Heather Wilson is a Lecturer in the Department of International Business at the University of Auckland, New Zealand. Formerly a lecturer in strategic management at Heriot-Watt University in Edinburgh, UK, her current teaching and research interests are focused on entrepreneurial and small and medium sized firms. Specifically, she is interested in entrepreneurial and innovative decision making, and the use of networks to support high growth strategies. Since joining the International Business Department, she has extended this focus to include the international strategies of SMEs and entrepreneurial firms.

Acknowledgements

This book is a collection of invited papers by renowned international scholars concerned with identifying and analysing the impact of the 1997 Asian financial and economic crisis on the small and medium enterprise sector in a number of East Asian countries. Each provides an invaluable, comprehensive, and fascinating insight into the contribution and composition of national SME sectors, as well as the significant role that SMEs will play in bringing about a sustainable recovery in these regional economies. Most of the chapters in this volume were initially presented, before final draft stage, at an international conference on SMEs in a Global Economy, organised by the International Business Research Institute of the University of Wollongong, Australia, held in Wollongong on 16–17 June 2000.

We would like to extend our appreciation and gratitude first and foremost to the contributors to this book, without whose dedicated, timely and scholarly contributions this volume would not have been possible. We are grateful to numerous colleagues who commented on earlier drafts of each chapter. In particular, we wish to thank Gary Gregory, Maree Murray, Matt Ngui, David Richards, Keishi Sugiura, Wee Liang Tan and Heather Wilson. We are also indebted to Robert Hood for his unrivalled skills in formatting the final drafts of each chapter, and Nadyne Smith and Priscilla Kendall for excellent administrative and typing assistance provided in getting the individual chapters to camera-ready stage.

We also wish to express our thanks to the International Business Research Institute, Faculty of Commerce, University of Wollongong, the University of Wollongong itself, and AusAid, for financial and administrative assistance provided during the completion of this project.

At Edward Elgar Publishing, we wish to thank Edward Elgar himself for his encouragement of and support for this book initiative from a very early stage, which provided the necessary impetus for its completion. In addition we would like to thank Francine O'Sullivan for her patience and highly professional assistance during the completion of this book.

Last, but not least, we would like to thank our respective families for their support and patience during the period of this project.

Charles Harvie and Boon-Chye Lee
Wollongong
May 2001

1 East Asian SMEs: Contemporary Issues and Developments – An Overview

Charles Harvie and Boon-Chye Lee

1.1 INTRODUCTION

The Asian financial and economic crisis had widespread effects, many of which are still in the process of being resolved. While the region consists of many diverse, although closely integrated, economies, a common characteristic is the significance of a sizeable and rapidly expanding small and medium sized enterprise (SME) sector. However, given such diversity, it can be reasonably expected that the SMEs in these economies are at different stages of development, their contributions to the respective economies are different, and policies adopted in these economies as a means of encouraging their development will also diverge. While they may face similar general difficulties, discussed at length in a companion volume (Harvie and Lee 2002), such as access to finance, access to technology, development of human resources, and access to market information, it is unlikely that these difficulties are inherently identical and appropriate policies to stimulate their recovery are also unlikely to be identical across these varying economies. As a consequence, emphasis in this book is placed upon identifying the characteristics of the SME sector across a number of East Asian economies, and to conduct a comparative analysis involving the identification of: common components as well as disparities; differences in priorities, appropriate policy responses and needs; the role of government; the impact of globalisation; future prospects and problems; and the impact of the financial and economic crisis. In doing so the economies analysed are classified on the basis of their stage of economic development.

The book therefore focuses upon an in-depth analysis of the SME sector across a number of East Asian economies. Emphasis is placed upon identifying issues relating to: the significance of this sector within each economy; access to finance; the role and significance of networking in the conduct of business; the contribution of culture to business acumen and entrepreneurialism; human resource development constraints and issues; technology transfer processes; utilisation and application of information technology; impact of electronic commerce and business opportunities arising; the policy framework to stimulate the growth of this sector; extent of globalisation of this sector; and the specific impact of the Asian crisis upon this sector. From this it will then be possible to conduct an international comparative analysis of the SME sector across the region, thereby enabling substantive lessons to be derived and policy measures to be identified.[1]

This chapter proceeds as follows. Section 1.2 briefly identifies a number of broad issues of relevance to the SME sector across the region as well as the importance of SMEs to countries within the East Asian region, and the APEC region more generally. Section 1.3 conducts an overview of the book, while Section 1.4 outlines the structure of the remainder of the book.

1.2   BROAD ISSUES AND THE SIGNIFICANCE OF THE SME SECTOR IN EAST ASIA[2]

SMEs have been recognised as a priority area for the East Asian economies, and more generally within the context of the Asia–Pacific Economic Cooperation forum (APEC), since the 1993 APEC leaders' meeting in Seattle. Despite being seen as a priority, and the centre of considerable discussion, a clearly enunciated APEC agenda and program of action for SMEs in the region before the onset of the financial and economic crisis of 1997–98 remained elusive. However, the crisis resulted in many of the countries of East Asia: re-evaluating their industrial policies; placing greater emphasis on improving corporate governance; improving the efficiency and competitiveness of their enterprises; and developing business sectors more able to overcome the vicissitudes of domestic, but more importantly global, market developments. The latter is of particular importance in the context of increased economic interdependence and open regionalism. The need to develop more adaptable and flexible economies, and business sectors, has resulted in more emphasis on the development of the SME sector, particularly given the relative resilience of the Taiwanese economy, an economy dominated by SMEs, and the potential platform they provided for the sustained recovery, as well as employment potential and poverty alleviation, of regional economies.

1.2.1   What Is an SME?

There is no regional, or indeed global, consensus on the definition of an SME. SMEs' definitions differ widely among the East Asian economies, and APEC more generally, depending on the phase of economic development as well as prevailing social conditions. A number of indexes are traditionally utilised to define SMEs: number of employees; invested capital; total amount of assets; sales volume; and production capability. The most commonly used index, however, is the number of employees. A summary of the alternative definitions of SMEs used in selected APEC member countries is contained in Table 1.1.[3] As can be observed from this table, in practice, the actual definition used in a number of countries is often quite complex. This is particularly so for Japan, Malaysia, Taiwan and Thailand. In Taiwan, for example, an enterprise may be regarded as an SME for the purpose of receiving government assistance, even though it may not presently meet the general criteria, provided it did meet the criteria in the immediately preceding years. Statistics on SMEs often exclude cottage and micro enterprises. In addition, some economies distinguish between different types of SMEs. For example, China distinguishes between township and village enterprises (TVEs) and SMEs, and Singapore distinguishes between local and overseas SMEs. Although some economies use the same measure to define SMEs, it may result in a different classification in different economies. A medium sized manufacturing enterprise in Australia may be viewed as a large enterprise in another country. Ideally, from an international comparative analysis perspective it would be desirable to have one common definition for SMEs. Although the definitions differ they have one thing in common; the vast majority of SMEs are relatively small and over 95 per cent of SMEs in the region employ fewer than 100 people. This still enables, therefore, broad comparisons of the role of SMEs across countries despite the differing definitions. In addition, while different definitions are adopted they do not fundamentally affect the key issues pertinent to SMEs.

1.2.2   Role and Importance of SMEs to the Region

SMEs have played, and are increasingly playing, an important economic role in the individual economies of East Asia, in the broader regional economy including that of APEC and, more generally still, the global economy. This is especially so from the point of view of creating employment, as a source of innovation, generating exporting opportunities, and as the source of future successful medium and large enterprises. Developments in information technology and movement towards greater global trade and financial integration, implies even greater opportunities for further expansion of regional SMEs. Before the onset of the financial and economic crisis they made up well over 90 per cent of regional enterprises and were variously estimated to contribute between 40 to 85 per cent of the total employment in individual regional economies (see Table 1.2, APEC 1994; Hall 1995, 2000). Consequently, SMEs have the potential to make a major impact on workforce training (Hall 2000, p. 2). The contribution of SMEs to employment growth is even higher, if somewhat contentious. Figures for Asia are not available, but in more mature economies, and where reasonably reliable studies are available, as much as 70 per cent or more of net employment creation was attributable to SMEs in the 1990s. Estimates of SME contribution to GDP are difficult to obtain for the East Asian region, but have been typically estimated to contribute somewhere between 30 per cent and 60 per cent of GDP (Hall 1995). SME wage

Table 1.1
Summary of Main Definitions of SMEs in Selected APEC Economies

Country	Definition of SME	Measure

Australia	Small enterprises:
	    Manufacturing, < 100 employees
	    Services, < 20 employees
	Medium enterprises:
	    Manufacturing, 100–499 employees
	    Services, 20–499 employees
		Employment

Canada	Manufacturing:
	    Small enterprises, < 100 employees
	    and < CDN$5 million in sales
	    Medium enterprises, 100–500 employees
	    and CDN$5–20 million in sales
	Services:
	    Small enterprises, < 50
	    employees and < CDN$5 million in sales
	    Medium enterprises, 50–500 employees and
	    CDN$5–20 million in sales
		Employment
		Sales

PR China	In general: small enterprises, 50–100 employees; medium enterprises, 101–500 employees	Employment
Indonesia	< 100 employees.	Employment

Japan[a]	A. SMEs:
	    Mining, manufacturing, transportation,
	      construction industries: < 300 employees,
	      or < ¥100 million invested capital
	    Wholesalers: < 100 employees, or less
	      than ¥30 million invested capital
	    Retailers, services: < 50 employees, or
	      < ¥10 million invested capital
	B. Small-scale enterprises:
	    Manufacturing and other industries:
	      < 20 employees
	    Commerce and services: < 5 employees
		Employment
		Assets

Korea	Manufacturing: < 300 employees,
	    won 20–80 billion of capital (assets)
	Mining, transportation: < 300 employees
	Construction: < 200 employees
	Commerce and other service business: < 20
	    employees
		Employment
		Assets

Country	Definition of SME	Measure
Malaysia	Varies Manufacturing: up to 150 full time employees, annual sales turnover not exceeding RM25 million. Definitions are for SMIs[b] Different for Bumiputera enterprises	Employment Sales Shareholders Funds
New Zealand	Up to 50 employees	Employment
Philippines	Small enterprises: 10–99 employees, and P1.5–15 million in assets Medium enterprises: 100–199 employees, and P15–60 million in assets	Employment Assets
Singapore	Manufacturing: < S$15 million in fixed assets Services: < 200 employees, and fixed assets < S$15 million	Employment Fixed assets
Taiwan	Mining, quarrying, manufacturing and construction industries: < 200 employees, < NT$60 million of invested capital Service industries and others: < 50 employees, < NT$80 million of sales volume	Employment Capital Sales
Thailand[c]	Manufacturing: Small enterprises, < 50 employees, < 20 mill. baht of investment capital (not including fixed assets) Medium enterprises, 50–200 employees, 20–100 million baht of fixed assets, 20–100 million of invested capital (not including fixed assets)	Employment Capital Fixed assets
USA	Manufacturing: < 500 employees Non-manufacturing: < US$5 million in sales	Employment Sales
Vietnam	Manufacturing and non-manufacturing: Small enterprises: < 30 employees and < 1 billion dong in capital Medium enterprises: 30–200 employees and 1–4 billion dong in capital	Employment Capital

Notes:
a   In accordance with the Small and Medium Enterprise Basic Law.
b   Small and medium industries.
c   Manufacturing enterprises only.

Source: APEC website <http://www.actetsme.org>, Hall (1995).

Table 1.2
The Relative Importance of SMEs in Selected APEC Economies

	Average GDP growth 1992–99 (%)	GNP US$billion 1998	Exports[a] as % of GDP 1999	Number of SMEs '000s	SMEs as % of all enterprises	% workforce employed by SMEs	% of SME sales in total sales volume	% of SME exports in total exports	% of GDP
USA	3.6	7 921.3	10.8	4 311[b]	96.0[c]	69.0[c]	50.0[c]	33.3[d]	50.0[c]
Japan	1.0	4 089.9	10.4	6 450[b]	98.8[c]	77.6[c]	76.8[c]	13.5[b,e]	na
Canada	3.1	612.2	43.3	2 200[c]	98.0[c]	66.0[b]	na	na	na
PRC	10.5	928.9	20.0	4 980[b]	99.0[c]	70.0[b,f]	na	40–60[b,e]	na
Australia	4.2	380.6	18.7	530[b]	97.0[b]	46.0[b]	na	50[g]	na
Korea	5.5	369.9	42.1	2 400[c]	99.0[c,h]	69.0[c]	50.0[i]	43.0[c]	50.0[i,c]
Taiwan	6.1	268.6	42.1	155[b,h]	97.8[c]	78.4[c]	32.1[c]	56.0[b,e]	na
Indonesia	3.8	138.5	35.0	105[b]	97.0[b]	42.0[b]	na	10.6[b,e]	na
Thailand	4.1	134.4	57.0	102[b]	95.8[c]	18.1[c,j]	na	10.0[b,e]	na
Malaysia	6.7	79.8	121.7	20[b,h]	84.0[c,k]	40.0[b]	19.1[l]	15.0[b,e]	na
Singapore	7.5	95.1	135.0	69[b]	91.5[c]	51.8[c]	34.7[m]	16.0[b,e]	34.7
Philippines	3.2	78.9	51.3	78[b]	99.5[c]	66.2[c]	30.8[c]	na	32.2
New Zealand	3.1	55.8	30.7[m]	na	98.9[c]	52.9[c]	35.0[c]	23.0[o]	na
Vietnam	7.5	25.6	40.1	14[b]	83.0[b]	85.0[c]	65.0[p]	20.0[b,e]	65.0[c]

Notes:

a   Goods and services;
b   From Hall (1995);
c   From APEC (available at http://www.actetsme.org – SME profile);
d   Merchandise exports share only;
e   OECD Country Studies;
f   Manufacturing only (estimate);
g   Australian Bureau of Statistics;
h   Manufacturing enterprises only;
i   Contribution to total value added of the economy;
j   Industrial workforce share only;
k   Small and medium industries;
l   Contribution to manufacturing value added (17.5 per cent of total output);
m   Contribution to net value added;
n   Figure is for 1998;
o   Wilson and Haworth (this volume Chapter 13);
p   Contribution to overall GDP;
na = not available.

Sources: World Bank (2001), *World Development Report 1999/2000*, Table 1, pp. 230–31; IMF, *International Financial Statistics*, various; Hall (1995); and APEC (1998).

payments typically make up over half of GDP in regional economies, and hence are important for domestic demand expansion, and for the generation of savings funds (Hall 2000, p. 2). In Asia, SMEs contribute as much as 35 per cent of direct exports, and the indirect contribution is even higher. The weighted[4] contribution of international SME exports to GDP is about 12 per cent, almost double the contribution in Organisation for Economic Cooperation and Development (OECD) economies. SME foreign direct investment (FDI) is usually export oriented, thereby adding further to the potential for regional exports and technology transfer (Hall 2000, p. 2).

Although SMEs are important across the region there are considerable differences in the role of SMEs in the various economies. For example, SMEs play a larger structural role in Taiwan, China, Japan, Thailand and Vietnam where they contribute over 70 per cent of employment, than they do in Indonesia or Malaysia where they contribute only around 40 per cent. In addition, the contribution of the SME sector to exports, and hence the extent of their global integration, also varies widely. They are relatively more export oriented in China, Korea and Taiwan than they are in Japan, Indonesia, Thailand, Malaysia and Singapore. Similarly, the dynamic role that SMEs play varies widely. For example in Singapore, even though SMEs are not as significant in terms of numbers and employment, they are important in providing a flexible skilled production base that attracts larger multinational corporations (MNCs). The dynamic role that SMEs have played has varied between the various countries. More recently in the case of China, and somewhat reluctantly in the case of Vietnam, entrepreneurial private SMEs and rural enterprises,[5] during the early part of the reform process, have been pivotal in the transition process from a planned to market-oriented economy. They have contributed to more efficient resource allocation, the marketisation of these economies, and are increasingly important in creating new jobs and in expanding exports. In the case of Taiwan, SMEs have played a pivotal role in the country's economic development from the beginning. More recently, however, they have been facing increased competition from SMEs in China and Vietnam, because their traditional low-cost base is rapidly being eroded. As a consequence they have had to move up the high-technology ladder in order to remain globally competitive. Recognising this requirement, the government has been actively assisting in this process. In addition, these SMEs have been engaging in FDI in Mainland China.

Table 1.3 shows the diversity of SME intensity across a number of APEC economies, measured in terms of the number of non-agricultural SMEs per 1000 people, and people per SME. Even allowing for the difficulties in getting reasonably accurate figures for the numbers of SMEs in some economies, it is clear that there is a very wide gap. In the developed economies there is about one SME for every 20 people, while in Asia, where the start-up rates and numbers of SMEs are much less,[6] it is estimated that for every SME there are 100 people.[7] This suggests that there should be around four to five times as many SMEs in the region as there are now. Table 1.3 suggests that there is considerable room for advancement in the development of SMEs in countries such as Indonesia and Thailand, two of the three most adversely

Table 1.3
SME Intensity in Selected APEC Economies

Economy	Population (million)	SMEs ('000)	SMEs per 1000 people	People per SME
USA	260	14 800	56.9	17.6
Japan	122	6 500	53.3	18.7
Australia	17	840	49.4	20.2
Taiwan	20	743	37.1	26.9
Singapore	3	69	23.0	43.5
Thailand	58	102	1.7	568.0
Indonesia	189	105	0.6	1 800.0

Source: Hall (1995).

afflicted economies during the period of the financial and economic crisis. Not surprisingly, these countries have given increased emphasis to SME sector development, with the objective of providing a firm base for sustainable economic recovery, an expansion in employment opportunities, and as a means of alleviating poverty particularly in some of the more adversely affected regions in these countries. This situation is also similar to that in China and Vietnam, where, for historical, political, and cultural reasons, the development of the SME sector has also been retarded. Hence, the sheer potential for SME start-ups in countries such as China, Indonesia and Vietnam could be a major source of job creation and growth for these economies in the future.

There is very little information on SMEs that export and import goods and services. Hence reliable estimates of the proportion of exports generated by SMEs are traditionally difficult to obtain. The proportion of exports produced by SMEs in Asia is, however, large by OECD and world standards. Table 1.4 draws upon figures presented in Hall (1995, 2000) which show that, for the East Asian countries identified, SMEs generally contribute about 35 per cent of exports. Export growth rates are generally higher than GDP growth rates, and, where figures are available, the rate of growth of SME exports is higher than the growth of overall exports. This points to SMEs in Asia already being significantly internationalised, and becoming more so. It is difficult to gauge the importance of SMEs in this sense because few countries keep export statistics broken down by size of firm. Further, many SME exports are made indirectly via a larger firm or an agent, and are difficult to attribute to SMEs even when statistics are kept. Despite these difficulties it is clear from Table 1.4 that SMEs make an important contribution to exports, although this varies widely between countries.

Weighted by GDP, for the selected OECD economies where estimates and statistics were available, SMEs made up around 26 per cent of direct manufactured exports,

Table 1.4
Structural Contribution of SMEs to Exports

	GDP US$ millions	Exports as per cent of GDP	Share of SMEs in total exports (%)
Selected OECD economies			
Denmark	121 695	27	M ~46
Finland	121 982	19	M 23
France	1 167 749	18	M 26
Greece	65 504	12	19
Italy	1 072 198	15	53
Japan	3 337 191	12	13.5
Netherlands	278 839	47	26
Sweden	280 000	25	30
Weighted contribution (%)		*4.3*	*26.1*
East Asian economies			
PR China	435 000	21	40–60
Korea	285 000	27	40
Indonesia	128 000	23	10.6
Taiwan	210 000	44	56
Thailand	108 000	29	10
Malaysia	60 000	72	15
Singapore	46 000	138	16
Vietnam	14 000	7	20
Weighted contribution (%)		*11.7*	*35.2*

Notes:
~ indicates estimate only; M = manufacturing only. Exports are direct exports by SMEs. This understates the true contribution of SMEs to exports.
Weighted contribution. For exports is the sum of GDP multiplied by the percentage of exports multiplied by the percentage of direct SME exports expressed as a percentage of total exports. For GDP is the same figure expressed as a percentage of total GDP.

Sources: SME export contribution – OECD Country Studies.
              Exports as per cent of GDP – UN Country Statistics.

and about 35 per cent from the selected East Asian economies where similar data was available. The indirect contribution is larger, and is probably closer to 50 per cent for APEC Asian economies. The contribution by international SMEs to the national income of those economies for which export figures are available is about 4 per cent for the OECD countries (6 per cent if indirect exports are included), and about 12 per cent for the Asian economies (see Table 1.4). These figures are indicative only. They assume, for example, that where only manufacturing SME export figures are available, that these are representative of exports generally in that economy. Similarly, the estimates use the indirect export figure for SMEs where this is available, but for most economies it is not. Hence the overall contribution of SMEs to exports is likely to have been understated.

The international role for SMEs in the East Asian region, however, remains volatile, for three reasons. First, export markets are inherently subject to volatility via currency and exchange rate movements. This was amply demonstrated by the 1997–98 crisis. Second, export markets are affected by general economic conditions in both the exporting and the destination economies. Third, structural competitive shifts occur that render SMEs in one economy uncompetitive with those in another in supplying global markets. These variations can lead to shifts in demand of ± 50 per cent at least over two to three years, and more in the longer term as structural changes flow through. This volatility has important implications for the stability of the SME sectors and for the continued growth of the regional economies. Hence the financial crisis of 1997–98 could be expected to have had important implications for the growth of this sector.

1.2.3   Difficulties Encountered by SMEs

The difficulties encountered by SMEs differ considerably in the aspects of exporting, investing abroad, industrial upgrading, industrial structure change, and developing and expanding. SMEs in some economies, specifically the more technologically advanced, have concerns about intellectual property rights protection, particularly copyright and patenting in exporting. Other countries, such as Indonesia, have concerns with a lack of information, orientation and experience in SMEs trading and investing abroad. Shortage of skilled labour and lack of access to loans reduce the ability of SMEs to ensure or upgrade quality production in Malaysia and New Zealand. Despite these differences the difficulties faced by SMEs have several things in common with respect to exporting and investing abroad, namely: a lack of information on overseas markets; shortage of funds for setting up business channels abroad; lack of experience in international business practice; and difficulties in managing workers employed abroad.

1.2.4   Assistance Provided to SMEs in the Region

Though the definition of SMEs varies with each economy, governments in the East Asian region, and APEC more generally, recognise the important role of SMEs in the development of their economies and especially in providing employment opportunities and in increasing and upgrading indigenous enterprises. Hence, SME development has been included as part of economic development plans, and most economies have adopted some specific policies and implementation measures relevant to SMEs. These policies and measures, by their nature, cover a very wide range of issues, for example: finance; taxation; market promotion; research and development (R&D); export strategies; and technology transfer among others. It should be stressed that policies utilised in one economy are not necessarily directly applicable to another economy, and may need further adaptation to suit local conditions and circumstances. Therefore, policies for SME development can differ widely across the regional economies. Most economies have financial assistance policies of some sort; these include export loans, financial instruments, reinsurance and lending institutions and so on. Many economies also encourage their SMEs to export, although some are more active in this area than others. For example, Taiwan has not only established a comprehensive system encompassing eight areas (financing; management; production technology; research and development; information management guidance; industrial safety; pollution prevention; and market guidance marketing), it also has established certain key supporting systems and organisations, including: a credit guarantee fund for SMEs; specialised export-processing zones; a central-satellite plants system and an SME development company and an SME development fund.

Besides government policies and measures, most economies have designed a number of private agencies or organisations to improve and support existing government policies involved in providing assistance of one kind or another to SMEs. These supporting organisations provide various services to SMEs that include consulting, market or technology information, training courses and so on. For instance, many Australian SMEs are members of a number of industry associations, which meet regularly and submit their views to the Australian government. In Thailand the Department of Industrial Promotion encourages entrepreneurs to set up SME associations, with a major aim to bring about cooperation among SMEs themselves and to provide assistance and beneficial activities to members such as specific training courses, study tours, subcontracting and joint ventures promotion, technical assistance, loans and other privileges.

1.2.5 Impact of the Financial Crisis on Regional SMEs

Regional SMEs could not avoid being adversely affected by the deterioration in the domestic and regional macroeconomic environment arising from the financial and economic crisis of 1997–98. Sales volume declined in both domestic and export markets, product prices weakened in the face of intensified competition for business and weakened demand, and production and purchasing were consequently affected. Profit margins and overall profitability were squeezed due to higher costs of inputs arising from higher domestic inflation and higher costs of imported inputs from a collapse of domestic currencies, in conjunction with a decline in sales revenue. Liquidity and cash-flow difficulties followed arising from customer bankruptcies and bad debts, difficulties in getting paid from similarly cash-constrained customers, and suppliers wishing to be paid as quickly as possible. Increased domestic interest rates on outstanding debt further intensified SME difficulties, and the availability of temporary or long-term finance from financially stricken banks or other financial institutions simply dried up. Such financial difficulties adversely affected investment, particularly in R&D, and the need to cut costs by downsizing business activities resulted in the loss of key personnel. SMEs needed to put in place, either through their own initiatives and/or with the assistance of government, measures that would minimise risk arising from the impact of market, interest and exchange rate volatility, so as to ensure their long-run development. This required improved corporate governance in the areas of risk avoidance, risk management strategies, market diversification, and improved access to information and finance. Progress made in these areas across the region has varied.

The recent experience of the aftermath of economic crises demonstrates that interest rates and exchange rates can have a major impact on SME production, sales, cash flow and profits. The question of how to conduct risk avoidance operations in the midst of a financial crisis is thus an important issue. Under current economic and financial circumstances in Asia a key issue is how corporate governance of SMEs can be maintained, or enhanced, to a point where risk can be controlled, and where the relationship between cost and profit is stable and predictable thus mitigating as much as possible the impact of future financial crises. This can prevent excessive fluctuations from affecting the long-term development of SMEs. If SMEs are able to make effective use of risk avoidance strategies, tools and methods, they should be able to keep the impact of financial crises down to a minimum. Particular emphasis needs to be placed upon risk avoidance, risk management and market diversification.

The strategic importance of SMEs for the recovery and sustained economic growth, development, and restructuring of the crisis-afflicted economies in East Asia, is widely accepted. SMEs are acknowledged to be strategically important: for industry restructuring; for employment growth; as a source of competition for large enterprises; for improving skills, flexibility and innovation; for their potential to contribute to the promotion of regional trade, investment and technology transfer; and for the attainment of social objectives such as that of poverty alleviation and regional development. Problems remain, however, in terms of access to markets, technology, human resources, financing and information. However, with improved and more effective government strategies and programs supporting SMEs in the region, there is reason to believe that these can be overcome.

1.3   OVERVIEW OF THE BOOK

The objective of this book is to discuss in more country-specific detail key developments in the SME sector, their contribution to national developments, key policy issues, and the impact on their development arising from the crisis of 1997–98. In doing so the book is divided into four parts, based upon the level of economic development of the countries analysed. The first part focuses upon a case-study analysis of the SME sector in the most underdeveloped nations of the East Asian region, focusing upon the People's Republic of China, Vietnam and the Philippines. China and Vietnam are classified as economies in transition, moving from planned to market-oriented economies. In this regard the SME sector is playing a pivotal role in the transformation of these economies to market-oriented systems. The Philippine economy has traditionally lagged behind other regional economies. The second part focuses on the newly industrialising economies of Southeast Asia (Indonesia, Malaysia and Thailand), which have tended to be most seriously affected, along with Korea, by the financial and economic crisis. From this, it will be possible to focus upon the role of the SME sector in these countries and to identify their importance to the sustained recovery of these economies. Given their current relatively small contribution to their respective economies, they can provide the foundations for a sustained recovery with suitably implemented policies. The third part focuses on the newly industrialised economies of Korea and Taiwan. An interesting contrast in the development strategies adopted by these two economies can be identified. Korea, for many years, placed the development of large industrial conglomerates at the cornerstone of its economic development. The crisis, however, encouraged the government to take stronger actions to foster the development of the SME sector. Taiwan on the other hand has placed the development of international-oriented SMEs at the cornerstone of its economic development approach. This has resulted in a rapid development of the economy, and, as witnessed by the recent regional crisis, a robust domestic economy. However, increasing domestic costs have created an incentive for many of its labour-intensive SMEs to consider locating overseas, particularly to China.

The fourth part focuses on the development of the SME sector in the most advanced of the regional economies – Australia, Japan, New Zealand and Singapore. The Japanese economy has remained moribund during the period of the 1990s, and much will depend upon the ability of its authorities to put in place growth-sustaining policies including a considerable restructuring of both its financial and corporate sectors. The role of SMEs will be important in regard to the latter. Singapore has proved to possess a remarkably resilient economy in the wake of the crisis. However, even for it there is a need to increasingly promote its SME sector so that they will remain globally competitive. Finally, the SME sectors in Australia and New Zealand are discussed. Their distinctly different cultural background sets them apart from the other East Asian economies. However, the region remains important as a market for these countries. Important policy lessons can be learned by comparing the structure, priorities, business policies and operations of SMEs in Australia and New Zealand (as two Western-style economies) with those in East Asia. A comparison of how this sector has evolved in these economies is therefore of considerable contemporary interest.

1.4   STRUCTURE OF THE BOOK

In Chapter 2, Chris Hall provides a profile of SMEs in the economies of East Asia. Painting a 'big picture' of these SMEs is problematic, according to Hall, since they are so diverse. A comparative analysis of the country-specific performance of regional

SMEs is also made difficult by the lack of a consistent definition of an SME throughout the region, as alluded to earlier in this chapter. However, he does conclude that there are four key lessons to be obtained from the performance of SMEs in the region. First, they are an important source of sustainable economic growth. The second lesson relates to their job-creating potential. SMEs in developing East Asia tend to employ far more employees than those in the developed economies. The ability to create jobs by SME start-ups is greater in East Asia, although the pool of SMEs from which fast-growth SMEs emerge is smaller. Third, regional SMEs are under-performing in terms of their contribution to exports, contributing about the same percentage of exports by the end of the 1990s as they did at the beginning of the 1990s, despite the increase in international opportunities. Finally, SMEs have become more important economically and politically, with many becoming more internationalised and consequently more footloose. This requires policy makers to recognise the significance of SMEs for longer-term economic growth, and to build an attractive and conducive entrepreneurial business environment that will nurture them and retain their presence.

In Chapter 3 Charles Harvie analyses the evolution and future prospects of China's SMEs in the context of the country's rapidly evolving market economy. He finds that China's period of economic reform has resulted in the rapid development of the country's non-state sector, and in multiple types of ownership including urban and rural private businesses, township enterprises, foreign invested enterprises and joint-stock companies. The non-state sector is increasingly replacing the state sector in the supply and distribution of goods and services. The legal and political recognition of the status of the sector was formalised by the March 1999 amendment to the country's constitution, signalling a readiness by the authorities to accept further reductions in the role of state-owned enterprises in the economy and significant expansion of the role of the private sector. The country's membership of the World Trade Organisation (WTO) will provide additional impetus as a result of the entry of foreign firms and intense competition in those industries that are currently dominated by state-owned enterprises.

Harvie argues that China's township and village enterprises, the source of economic growth during the 1980s, are being required to go through organisational and ownership change to continue to succeed in the context of the rapidly developing market economy. During the 1990s and into the new millennium, however, China's private SMEs will increasingly make a significant contribution to the growth of the economy. True private businesses already account for half of total output and will account for a much higher proportion a decade hence. Further liberalisation and institutional reform hold the key for producing a vibrant and dynamic private sector in the economy. The construction of the right policy, legal and regulatory framework will have a large pay-off in terms of more rapid development of the private sector.

In Chapter 4, David Richards, Charles Harvie, Ha Nguyen and Nguyen Van Lan discuss contemporary problems that Vietnam's SMEs have been experiencing during the country's transition to a market economy. While there has been reform of the legislative framework, the implementation of change has been very slow and inconsistent, after an initial spurt in the late 1980s and early 1990s. As a result, the growth of private sector SMEs has lagged behind the overall growth of the economy. The authors argue that SMEs in Vietnam are more efficient users of capital, and have considerable potential to provide a second wave of economic growth for the economy based upon labour-intensive manufactures and exports. To date, however, registered private SMEs have played a minor role in industrial production, although household micro enterprises have played a much larger role.

The role of private sector SMEs, in particular, is argued to be crucial for Vietnam's future economic growth and employment generation, given the need for reform of state-owned enterprises and of fundamental restructuring of the economy. However, unlike in China where there is a clear commitment from the government to bring about the necessary structural transformation of the economy focusing upon the private sector, in Vietnam the authorities have demonstrated considerable ambiguity towards such a transformation. Unless Vietnam is able to engage in similar restructuring it is likely to fall further behind its regional neighbours.

In Chapter 5, Edgard Rodriguez and Albert Berry analyse SME developments in the Philippines. The Philippine economy came through the regional crisis better than anticipated, although its economic growth still lags behind the rapid economic recovery experienced by other countries in the region. The authors argue that while part of the explanation for the relatively good Philippine experience comes from sound macroeconomic management, part also stems from changes in its manufacturing structure. The emergence of a growing information technology sector dominated by multinational companies, but also comprising some small production units, has resulted in a persistent growth pattern via exports. During the recent crisis, modern manufacturing dominated the recovery through increased exports of high-end products which helped to offset other negative impacts on Philippine manufacturing, while at the same time establishing a new, but small, breed of SMEs in electronics.

In Chapter 6, Hal Hill discusses the policy challenges for SME development facing the authorities in Indonesia. He argues that SMEs are important in Indonesia for a number of reasons. First, SMEs play a pivotal role in the country's economic development, employing 60 per cent or more of the country's industrial workforce and generating up to half of the sector's output. Second, SMEs are a clearly enunciated priority for the Indonesian government. Third, SMEs are important in Indonesia owing to their link to equity issues, by promoting *pribumi* business, and therefore as a means of asset redistribution along ethnic lines. Fourth, policies drawn up for larger industrial units will not necessarily apply to SMEs, and therefore they require their own specific policies. Fifth, international experience suggests that an efficient SME sector is conducive to rapid industrial growth and a flexible industrial structure. Finally, there is particular current interest in SMEs in Indonesia since these firms appear to have weathered the economic crisis better than larger industrial units.

The major conclusions from this chapter are that SMEs will continue to receive policy emphasis in Indonesia, requiring government intervention to focus on genuine market failures so as to achieve a more efficient SME sector and to facilitate the employment creation objectives and to provide a broad-based industrial sector. In the process it will be important to guard against 'overloading' the SME policy program with equity objectives.

In Chapter 7, Moha Asri Abdullah analyses the contribution of SMEs to the Malaysian economy. This contribution is shown to be crucial in a number of areas, and they remain an integral part of the economic development of the country. The author finds that Malaysian SMEs need to adapt and amend their mode of operations and management. In an increasingly borderless and frictionless world economy, offering both opportunities and risks, only SMEs that are capable of meeting the new challenges can survive. Creating and nurturing viable, resilient and forward-looking SMEs is, therefore, the major challenge for Malaysia. The country's further industrialisation will see SMEs becoming even more strategically important, and consequently they will receive even greater priority than that presently assigned to them by the government. Indeed, to become an industrialised country adequate attention must be paid to the development of SMEs, and a widening and strengthening of the Malaysian domestic-industrial structure. Faced with the current global business environment and a high level of business competition, SMEs will need to be more adaptable, especially towards the use of information technology, to maintain their present contribution to the Malaysian economy. While SMEs will need new strategic direction and planning and outward-looking managers and entrepreneurs with knowledge and skills, the author argues that continued efforts and support of the government in enhancing the development of SMEs remains crucial.

In Chapter 8, Peter Brimble, David Oldfield and Manusavee Monsakul consider policies for SME recovery in Thailand in the wake of the financial crisis. Since the emergence of the financial and economic crisis, the Thai government has shifted its industrial policy priority towards the promotion and development of the SME sector. A number of government policies and assistance measures were initiated to rescue SMEs from bankruptcy in the wake of the crisis, and the emphasis of industrial policy was shifted towards industrial upgrading and improving the competitiveness of local companies. The major emphasis of this chapter is on the SME policies that were altered and created to manage the crisis, the critical issues currently facing SMEs, and the effectiveness of current policies in order to provide implications for future policy in order to improve the growth and competitiveness of this sector.

The authors conclude that the growth and development of the SME sector will be a critical element of Thailand's future growth process. With policy makers having realised the importance of, and subsequently considerably improved, the business environment for SMEs, both in terms of the legislative environment and support programs and institutions. However, there is still significant scope for improved policy coordination and better integration of the various support initiatives for SMEs in Thailand. In order for SMEs to play a greater role in maintaining Thailand's competitiveness, the authors suggest several key issues that need to be addressed. First, SMEs require long-term access to finance and to financial institutions, and the provision of this access must be an integral part of the reforms in the finance and banking sector since the financial crisis. Second, SMEs need to break through the low-technology threshold and begin to undertake much greater efforts to improve their capacities for technological development. Third, most government programs have not succeeded in providing SME clients with a clear 'benchmark' of where they are strong and where they are weak. The effective provision of such benchmarks will be a critical success factor in the future implementation of programs to support SMEs. Fourth, SMEs need to be integrated more effectively into the various industry value chains or clusters. Finally, SMEs need more supportive networks.

In Chapter 9, Gary D. Gregory focuses on the promotion of Korean SMEs and the contribution of the government in this process. He finds that, while SMEs are the mainstay of the national economy and the driving force behind sustained economic growth and a balanced economic structure, they face a number of critical issues. First, many SMEs are facing financial and manpower shortages and decreasing sales. One of the major government initiatives to initiate economic recovery in Korea is the policy program to revitalise SMEs and venture business, with the objective of creating a business environment that will help SMEs exploit competitive advantages such as flexibility and rapid adaptability. Second, one of the principal constraints faced by a majority of the country's SMEs has been a lack of access to financial resources. Recently, however, the government's SME policy has shifted focus to guaranteeing SMEs greater access to loans from financial institutions with sufficiently liberalised interest rates. Third, manpower shortages have also plagued SMEs. A key role for the government will be to develop an educational system that corresponds to the long-term manpower needs of industry and businesses. Fourth, SMEs face difficulties in their sales. Consequently, the government plans to reform the procurement system and to provide SMEs with more opportunities to provide their goods and services to a global marketplace. Fifth, cooperation between large and small companies in Korea is seen as another means of promoting competitiveness in the economy. To encourage such partnerships the government has improved the subcontracting practice between large firms and SMEs, and encouraged and fostered collaborative partnerships in trade, investment, production and training.

The author indicates that Korean SMEs and venture enterprises will be an important part of Korea's new economy, requiring government support of venture enterprises and of those firms involved in knowledge-intensive industries.

In Chapter 10, Matt Ngui reviews government policies and programs for SMEs in Taiwan. The country has long been admired for its stable economic development, a core ingredient of which has been the resilience of its SMEs as exemplified by their resilience to the recent financial and economic crisis. The steady growth of SMEs has been one of the distinctive characteristics of Taiwan's economy. The major conclusions from this chapter are that the policies and programs initiated by the Taiwanese government have contributed to creating a robust SME sector enabling it to withstand the adverse impacts of the 1997 financial crisis. While growth in the number of SMEs has slowed, growth in employment and in the total value of sales has continued although exports have been marginally adversely affected. A number of other factors enhanced the strength of the SME sector during the crisis: the Taiwanese technique of a networked industrial production system; the country's integration into the economy of China; the country's business culture of low entry costs, low-cost production, thrift and relatively low-cost labour.

In Chapter 11, James Nguyen, Gary Gregory, Charles Harvie, Boon-Chye Lee and Matt Ngui focus on SME developments in Australia. They emphasise that a key ingredient for the future success of the Australian economy, will increasingly depend, because of the limited size of the domestic market, on the ability of its domestic businesses to greatly expand export capabilities. SMEs have the greatest potential in this regard. Australian SMEs have the potential to take advantage of niche markets for high-quality, high-tech products in particular.

The recent re-direction of exports away from the markets of East Asia towards the USA and the European Union (EU), as a result of the economic and financial crisis, is indicative of the degree of adaptability of Australian exporters in general, a strength that should not be underestimated given the volatility of international markets, as well as the commodities they produce. This adaptability resulted in a relatively limited impact of the regional crisis on the Australian economy.

The authors identify a number of important issues and developments with regard to the immediate and long-term prospects of the SME sector. The first relates to the recently introduced Goods and Services Tax, which has placed a disproportionately heavy burden on small businesses. A second issue concerns the role of R&D expenditure. Although there was a reduction in R&D concession rates in 1996, the data indicates that SMEs are now playing a greater role in R&D expenditure. A third issue relates to the trend towards globalisation. With the decrease in trade barriers and increased capital mobility that is associated with globalisation, Australian SMEs have an unprecedented potential to enter and expand into new and existing international markets. It will be essential that SMEs take advantage of this development given the limited size of the domestic market. Fourth, SMEs face considerable resource constraints in terms of access to finance and information technology (IT). Such resource constraints limit the ability of SMEs to play a more dominant role in the economy. A worrying sign for Australian SMEs is the fact that the problem of limited resources appears not to have been effectively addressed by the government, whose programs are utilised relatively more often by large enterprises. The authors suggest that it is imperative that public policies realise the potential that Australian SMEs possess and assist them in reaching this, by making its programs more relevant to the specific needs of SMEs.

In Chapter 12, Keishi Sugiura discusses the role of SMEs in the Japanese economy. As with the country's large enterprises, Japanese SMEs have been facing structural problems since the early 1990s. Recognising the significance of SMEs, industrial policy is now placing more importance on SMEs to provide the innovative drive necessary to deliver the Japanese economy from its current state of economic malaise.

The author concludes, however, that the imminent future prospects for Japanese SMEs are not encouraging. He suggests that the sector's difficulties are not based on the Asian financial crisis and the recent domestic credit crunch, nor such cyclical factors as business trends. Rather, SMEs are confronted with challenges arising from long-term changes – the rapid ageing of the population and the global integration of business activities – and it is not clear that they will be able to adapt successfully to these developments. The author presents evidence to suggest that the problems faced by SMEs is compounded by the loss of entrepreneurial 'spirit' and an inability to cope well with e-commerce. Despite this, expectations about the longer-term role of SMEs remain high.

In Chapter 13, Heather Wilson and Nigel Haworth analyse developments in SMEs in New Zealand. The major findings are as follows. First, in terms of financing, significant deficiencies are found in the areas of loan guarantees and informal equity provision. Second, the business environment faced by SMEs needs to be improved by reducing the regulatory burden on them, and improving the information services available to them. Third, management and innovation capacity building in the country's SMEs is an area of concern. While New Zealand policy in relation to management capacity building is considered to be generally strong, innovation capacity building, on the other hand, is seen as being weak in both the public and private sectors. The authors point out that New Zealand does not have a national system of innovation, and policy is, at best, haphazard. This is compounded by the lack of value placed in basic research versus applied research. In addition, New Zealanders, while highly inventive, do not have a history of invention commercialisation. Finally, progress has been made in terms of access to government procurement and international trade, with the government committing itself to review the award of government contracts in relation to SMEs and an export credits guarantee scheme being put in place to facilitate SME international trade. The authors also point out that the improved international competitiveness of the country, including that of SMEs, will take time, since many of the issues lie at the cultural level and may not be easily solved in the short term or even resolved by policy.

Finally, in Chapter 14, Boon-Chye Lee and Wee-Liang Tan discuss SMEs in Singapore in the context of the New Economy. The authors note that Singapore has traditionally relied heavily on its position as an entrepôt-trading centre for its economic survival, with economic strategy focusing heavily on building infrastructure, attracting foreign direct investment and export-led growth. This, in conjunction with a political commitment to openness in trade, capital and, more recently, labour, has resulted in remarkable economic outcomes. Until recently, however, the role of SMEs in this strategy has been secondary. They were primarily the local links of the supply chains of the multinational corporations that had set up operations in the country, benefiting from assured demand for their products and technology transfer. Since the late 1980s the country's economic strategy has undergone a significant shift, with the role of SMEs becoming pivotal. In the wake of the financial crisis a new element was added to this strategy: to gear the skills base and infrastructure of the economy into the 'knowledge-based economy', also known as the New Economy. The knowledge-based economy is perceived as bringing with it a fundamental change driven by two main forces: globalisation and technology. Consistent with this, technology-based entrepreneurs and enterprises are to be nurtured by the government for the 21st century.

The authors conclude that the role and development of SMEs in Singapore cannot be fully understood without referral to the pervasive influence of the government. What sets the country apart from most others is the scale of its government's ambition and the thoroughness and single-mindedness with which it pursues it. In recent years official attention has increasingly turned to the need to develop a more entrepreneurial culture as a prerequisite if the country is to reap the benefits offered by the New Economy. The government has highlighted certain industries that it hopes to foster in the next ten years in the area of e-commerce and life sciences. SMEs are the logical entities to meet this challenge. The extent to which they are able to do so will critically shape the future of the country and may well determine its economic survival.

NOTES

1   While an extensive survey of regional SMEs has already been conducted by APEC (1994 and 1998) for individual member countries, a rigorous comparative analysis of regional SME developments both before and after the financial crisis of 1997–98 is still lacking.

2   This section draws extensively upon Hall (1995).

3   See APEC (1998). This is discussed in more detail in Chapter 2.

4   By country.

5   The so-called township and village enterprises (TVEs).

6   Estimates for the number of start-ups and number of SMEs are difficult to obtain.

7   Hall (2000, p. 3) estimates that there are about 20 million SMEs in Asia, mainly small TVEs in China, suggesting 100 people per SME.

REFERENCES

APEC (1994), 'The APEC Survey on Small and Medium Enterprises', available at <www.actetsme.org>.

APEC (1998), 'SME Profile', available at <www.actetsme.org>.

Hall, C. (1995), 'APEC and SME Policy: Suggestions for an Action Plan', available at <www.arts.monash.edu.au/ausapec/smepolic.html>.

Hall, C. (2000), 'E-commerce and SMEs in APEC – HRD Implications and the Role of PECC', paper presented to the ninth annual meeting of PECC – HRD, Pacific Economic Cooperation Council Human Resource Development Task Force, Hua, Taiwan, 21–22 October.

Harvie, C. and B.C. Lee (eds) (2002), *Globalisation and Small and Medium Enterprises in East Asia*, Cheltenham, UK and Northampton, MA, USA: Edward Elgar.

2 Profile of SMEs and SME Issues in East Asia

Chris Hall

2.1 INTRODUCTION

At the turn of the new millennium there were about 2 billion people in East Asia, and about 20 million to 30 million SMEs. These SMEs made up over 95 per cent of all enterprises, they employed well over half the workforce, they contributed about half the output, about 30 per cent or so of the exports were SME exports, and about 70 per cent of net employment growth came from SMEs. SMEs are economically and politically important. The purpose of this chapter is to develop an overall profile, or 'big picture' of the state of SMEs in the economies of East Asia. Section 2.2 identifies the alternative definitions of SMEs used in the region. Section 2.3 develops a static 'snapshot' of SMEs, comparing the contribution of SMEs in East Asian economies to employment, output, exports and foreign direct investment FDI. Section 2.4 focuses more on the dynamic aspects, and especially on the contribution of SMEs to growth and to the *potential* for SMEs to contribute to growth and to the internationalisation of the region. Finally Section 2.5 brings all of this together and briefly examines the policy issues and implications.

Painting a 'big picture' of these SMEs is not easy, because SMEs are a widely diversified species. They may range from a part-time business with no employees, for example, exchanging money or selling handicrafts in Indonesia, to a semiconductor manufacturer employing hundreds of people in Japan and China. They may range from fast-growing firms, such as a small publicly listed Korean e-commerce start-up that is growing by more than 100 per cent each year, to private family firms that have not changed much for decades. They range from SMEs which are independent or stand-alone businesses, to SMEs which are inextricably part of a group, such as those which are part of an international subcontracting network, or to those with technology and investment partners based abroad, or to those which are part of a family-based *nanyang* society or cluster.

2.2   WHAT IS AN SME?

With such diversity, what are the defining or common characteristics of an SME? All but a few of the Asian economies have a definition for SMEs for statistical purposes. Most also have definitions for policy purposes, and to complicate matters further these definitions often differ from the definition used for statistical purposes, and also differ by industry and by policy program. As Table 2.1 illustrates, there is considerable diversity in the definitions even for statistical purposes. The number of employees is the most common measure, though many definitions also use a monetary measure (capitalisation, sales and so on). Even with the number employed there is considerable diversity; in most economies an SME is defined as having fewer than 100 employees (and even fewer in specific industries such as services or retail), but in some of the larger economies this ceiling is raised to 300 or even 500 employees. The only really common characteristic of SMEs is that they are 'not large'; that is, whether a firm is really an SME or not is a question of relativities.

Does this lack of precision matter? In some circumstances it is a real problem, but it depends on the reasons for defining an SME. Obviously a firm with only one or two employees is not the same as a firm with 499, and this is important when it comes to the specifics of finance, or training programs, for example. However, for many purposes it is convenient to split the economy into small, medium and large so as to get a better idea of the 'big picture'. If we recognise that this distinction is somewhat arbitrary, then the real issues are that we are conscious of the limitations of the definitions, and that we are comparing equals with equals. Making comparisons therefore really requires some reasonably comparable size classes. Unfortunately the size classes used differ across countries. Even though most statistical agencies in Asia gather SME data in such a way that the data can be presented in common size classes (for example, >5, 5–9, 10–19 and so on), it takes time and money to present it in a common format, and thus it is usually not done. APEC, for example, has not put a high priority on this, and so comparisons across countries have to be made with some caution. However, most SMEs are actually very small, and over 80 per cent of them employ fewer than five people (Table 2.2). There is only a very small percentage of firms which have more than 100 employees, typically ranging from about 1 per cent to about 4 per cent. As a rough rule of thumb then, it is useful to see the vast bulk of SMEs as having fewer than 100 employees, and most have fewer than 20 employees. Where does small finish and medium begin? Again, this is a rather arbitrary matter. In Table 2.4 the distinction is based on employees; micro is up to five employees (sometimes called cottage), small is between 5 and 20 employees, and medium is between 20 and 100, or more if the economy happens to define it that way.

Table 2.1
Main Elements of the Definitions of SMEs in APEC

	Employ	*n*	Capital	Assets	Sales	Production capacity
Australia	200	yes				
Brunei Darussalam	100	ns				
Canada	499	yes			✓	
Chile		ns				
China[a]	500	no		✓		✓
Hong Kong China	100	yes				
Indonesia	100	yes		✓	✓	
Japan[b]	300	yes	✓			
Korea	300	yes				
Malaysia	150	ns			✓	
Mexico		ns			✓	
New Zealand		yes				
Papua New Guinea		ns				
Philippines	200	yes		✓	✓	
Singapore	100	yes		✓		
Chinese Taipei[c]		yes	✓	✓	✓	
Thailand	200	ns	✓			
USA	499	yes				
Vietnam	200	yes	✓			

Notes:
Employ: figures indicate the maximum number of employees in a firm defined as an SME.
n: 'yes' means that information on the actual number of employees is collected, so it is relatively easy to stratify by employment size.
ns: indicates that those economies were not surveyed.
a China uses a number of different definitions which are usually industry specific.
b Japan changed its definitions in 1999 to reduce the criteria for SMEs in services from 100 to 50 employees.
c Chinese Taipei relaxed the definition of SMEs in 2000.

Sources: APEC (1994, 1998); individual country sources; and Hall (1998a).

2.3   A SNAPSHOT OF SMES IN EAST ASIA

A snapshot is just a means of capturing the 'family' of East Asian SMEs at a particular point in time. This allows us to make some comparisons, subject to the quality of our 'camera'. Our camera is the statistical data available in different countries, so our picture is more of a collage, made up of different snapshots. Some of the cameras used to take the snapshot are more fuzzy, less sophisticated and less precise than others. Because it takes a while for the 'pictures' to be processed, I have chosen to compare statistics around the 1996–97 period. Data after that period are not yet readily available in all economies, and the 1997 Asian crisis tends to create distorting effects which make it harder to make legitimate comparisons.

2.3.1   SMEs Make Up 95 Per Cent of Enterprises, and There Are About 20 People Per SME in Developed East Asia

Table 2.2 shows that SMEs make up well over 95 per cent of businesses in all but a few economies. Definitional artefacts or structural reasons explain the economies where SMEs appear to be less important. For example, Malaysia (84 per cent) does not define SMEs, but instead focuses on SMIs or small and medium industries – and for planning purposes these have tended to emphasise certain types of industry, mostly in manufacturing. In Singapore (91 per cent) much of development in the past few decades has been based on the encouragement of subsidiaries of multinationals, and these have tended to be larger. This emphasis is now changing to the growth of more indigenous SMEs, and so the number and percentage of SMEs will probably increase.

Table 2.2 also provides a rough idea of the number of SMEs in East Asia. There are about 2 billion people in East Asia, and about 22 million to 30 million SMEs. The figures for the number of SMEs are difficult to arrive at with any precision. Many small SMEs are usually non-employing part-time businesses and are not even counted by some statistical agencies. However, even allowing for this, there is an average of about 86 people per SME. One interesting part of the picture is that there are about 20 people for every SME in most of the developed economies, but in the less-developed economies (China, Indonesia, the Philippines, Thailand) the figure is usually much greater – closer to 100 people per SME. For example, China has about 65 per cent of the people of the region, but officially has only one-third of the SMEs, and thus has about 155 people per SME on official figures. Even allowing for official figures understating the number of SMEs in China by about 7 to 8 million, the ratio would still be about 75 people per SME.

2.3.2   SMEs and Employment

There is less commonality in the percentage of the population employed by SMEs, but typically it is above 50 per cent, and if we exclude anomalies like Malaysia and

Table 2.2
SME Profile by Economy

	Population millions[a]	Approx. number of SMEs millions[b]	% of all businesses[c]	% employed[c]	People per SME
Australia	18.3	1.00	97	50	18
China	1 244.2	8.00	99	78	155
Hong Kong	6.5	0.29	98	61	22
Indonesia	203.4	[16.00] 2.00	98	88	[13] 92[d]
Japan	126.0	5.08	99	78	25
Korea	45.7	2.67	99	73	17
Malaysia	21.0	na	84	12	na
New Zealand	3.8	0.30	98	52	13
Philippines	71.4	0.50	99	66	142[e]
Singapore	3.4	0.96	91	52	35
Chinese Taipei	21.7	1.02	98	78	21
Thailand	59.7	0.67	96	18	89
Vietnam	76.5	na	na	85	na
Total	1 901.6	22.2			

Notes:
a   Source: APEC and *The Economist*. Figures are for 1998–99.
b   Estimates only except for Australia, Japan, New Zealand.
c   APEC (1998). Figures depend on definitions for SMEs which distorts Malaysian and Thai figures. Malaysia defines SMIs – or small medium industries, so it emphasises mostly SMEs in manufacturing industries.
d   Figures based on establishments and from the BPS (Central Bureau of Statistics) Industrial Census of 1996 in [ ]. Note that estimates by the Department of Commerce and Industry suggest that there were only about 2.2 million SMEs in Indonesia in 1996, which translates into 92 people per SME.
e   Figures based on establishments.

Thailand, SME employment ranges from about 50 per cent to 80 per cent of the workforce. Except for Japan, Thailand and Malaysia, the more developed an economy, the lower the percentage of employment attributable to SMEs. This is illustrated in Figure 2.1. Malaysia is an anomaly because of its focus on industries (explained above) rather than firms. Thailand has not collected SME statistics until recently, and the figures may simply not yet be an accurate reflection of the real level of SME employment.

Table 2.3 serves to emphasise that usually over 80 per cent of SMEs are micro enterprises employing fewer than five people. Table 2.4 provides the definitions of the size classes used to distinguish 'micro', 'small', 'medium' and 'large'. Note that

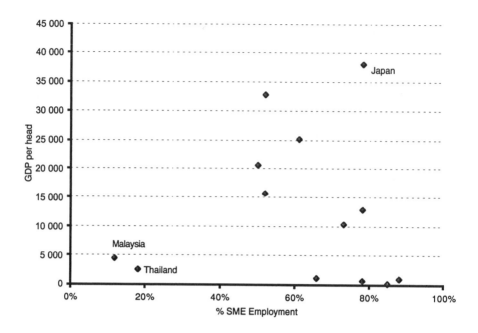

Sources: GDP per head – APEC, SME employment – see Table 2.2.

Figure 2.1   Relationship between Development and % SME employment

these are not necessarily the definitions of micro, small, medium and so on that are used in the respective economies. They are defined here on a common basis to assist in comparison. It is difficult to get breakdowns by size classes across all SMEs, and considerable caution needs to be used in interpreting this. Most data are only available for specific industries. Usually manufacturing is the best documented, and manufacturing SMEs are typically larger than service SMEs. Note that micro and small are bundled together in some economies, such as China and Chinese Taipei.

Table 2.5 makes an attempt to further compare the employment contribution of SMEs by size classes across the East Asian economies. Detailed breakdowns by size are hard to get, and even harder to compare. The size class definitions used are set out in Table 2.4. SMEs generally contribute between 50 per cent and 80 per cent of all employment, but the contribution is disproportionately more from medium sized businesses, defined as those which employ between 20 and 99 people. Medium sized enterprises typically make up only about 4 per cent of all SMEs (or about 20 per cent of manufacturing SMEs), but they employ about 20 per cent of the workforce (or about 30 per cent of the manufacturing workforce). Although there are a lot of SMEs, and around 80 per cent of those SMEs are micro businesses, micro business does not

Table 2.3
Enterprises by Size Class (%)

	Micro	Small	Medium	Large	
Australia	80.0	15.8	3.3	0.5	1996
China		96.1	2.8	1.1	1996 census
Hong Kong				na	
Indonesia	95.6	3.8	0.5	0.06	
Japan		73.5	22.2	4.3	Manufacturing
Korea		73.2	22.9	3.9	Manufacturing
	85.0	8.4	6.2	0.3	Services
Malaysia				na	
New Zealand	84.0	12.0	2.0	2.0	1999
Philippines	88.4	9.8	0.8	1.0	1996
Singapore		40.7	42.2	17.1	Manufacturing
Chinese Taipei		70.00	28.07	2.4	1996
Thailand	79.4	18.5	2.0	0.01	
Vietnam				na	

Sources: Australia – ABS, *Small Business in Australia*.
China – *Statistical Yearbook*.
Indonesia – BPS (Central Bureau of Statistics).
Japan – JSBRI/MITI, *White Paper on SMEs in Japan*.
Korea – Hong et al. (1999).
New Zealand – Ministry of Commerce (2000).
Philippines – statistics provided by National Census and Statistics Bureau (NCSB) and Bureau of Small and Medium Business Development (BSMBD).
Singapore – Census of Industrial Production.
Chinese Taipei – *White Paper on SMEs* (2000), SMEA
Thailand – Statistics Thailand – Industrial Census.

contribute much to overall employment – typically only about 10 to 20 per cent. Table 2.5 and Table 2.3 also hint at the 'missing middle', the concept that many developing economies have a lot of very small SMEs, and a dominant large firm sector, but not much in between. Contrast this 'missing middle' with the more developed economies, where medium sized firms contribute significantly to employment and are a major source of high growth firms which contribute much to employment growth. Unfortunately data broken down by size is hard to get from developing economies.

2.3.3   SME Contribution to Sales, Output, Value Added

Breakdowns by size of the contribution of SMEs to economic value added, sales, or output are even harder to get, and more difficult to interpret in comparable terms.

Table 2.4
Definitions of Size Classes

	Micro	Small	Medium	Large	
Australia	<5	5–19	20–99	100+	1995–6
China		nd	nd	nd	1996 industrial
only					
Hong Kong				na	
Indonesia	<5	5–19	20–99	100+	1996 census
Japan		4–19	20–99	100+	Manufacturing 1997
Korea	<5	5–19	20–100	100+	Manufacturing
	<5	5–9	10–100	100+	Services 1996
Malaysia				na	
New Zealand	<5	5–19	20–100	100+	1999
Philippines	<P1.5m	1.5–15m	15m–60m	above 60m	1997
Singapore		10–19	20–100	100+	
Chinese Taipei		1–9	10–99	100+	1996
Thailand	<5	5–19	20–99	100+	
Vietnam				na	

Note: These definitions are not necessarily the definitions used in the economies concerned; na – not available; nd – not defined.

Table 2.6 makes an attempt, and shows that SMEs contribute about 50 per cent of value added or sales on average, but that this ranges from about 30 to 70 per cent. Small and micro firms contribute a lot in developing economies (about 50 per cent of output in China and the Philippines, for example), but less in the more-developed economies.

2.3.4   SME Exports and FDI

How important are SMEs internationally? We have seen that SMEs make up more than half of most national economies, in terms of employment, and about half when it comes to output, sales or value added. In terms of exports, SMEs contribute less than proportionally, and even less when it comes to foreign direct investment or FDI. Statistics which break exports and FDI down by size of firm are difficult to get in most economies, and only Chinese Taipei and Korea keep reliable figures. For example, Japan, the largest economy in the region and the largest exporter, does not directly measure the proportion of SME exports, but instead estimates the figure based on the

Table 2.5
Employment by Size Class (%)

	Micro	Small	Medium	All SMEs	
Australia	14.3	22.3	22.5	68.15	1996/7[a]
China	na	na	na	78.0	na
Hong Kong	na	na	na	61.0	
Indonesia	na	na	na	88.0	
Japan	11.2	10.1	31.2	71.9	Manufacturing 1997
				78.0	1996 all
Korea	10.5	11.7	30.5	69.3	Manufacturing Services
Malaysia	na	na	na	12.0	
New Zealand	23	18	19	60.0	1999
Philippines	25.5	17.7	8.2	51.6	Manufacturing
	53.2	27.4	5.5	86.3	Services 1995
Singapore		5.2	20.6	25.8	Manufacturing
Chinese Taipei	na	na	na	na	
Thailand	na	na	na		
Vietnam	na	na	na		

Note:
a   ABS 1321.0 (1999), p.31, Table 2.5 private sector only.

Sources: As for Table 2.3, unless otherwise noted.

proportion of SME shipments (that is, goods leaving the factory gate) in an industry relative to industry total; if 70 per cent of shipments in value terms are from SMEs then all the exports of that industry are allocated to SMEs. Considerable caution needs to be exercised in interpreting SME export figures.

The best available figures suggest that SMEs contribute about 30 to 35 per cent by value of trade in Asia. Table 2.7 provides figures from nearly a decade ago, and are based on a jigsaw of information collected by the author for OECD (1997).

KOTRA (1999) provides some more recent estimates and these are summarised in Table 2.8. These broadly confirm the rough picture of about 30 per cent of exports in the region being directly attributable to SMEs. Because SME subcontractors often indirectly export via their contracting principal organisation, the figure of 30 per cent probably underestimates the real contribution.

Interestingly enough, the percentage of exports by Chinese Taipei's SMEs has fallen from a high of about 70 per cent in the early 1980s to around 50 per cent in 1997. This reflects partly a move by Chinese Taipei's SMEs to internationalise, so

Table 2.6
Contribution to Output, Sales, or Value Added (%)

	Micro	Small	Medium	All SMEs	
Australia	na	na	na	30	1997/8 Sales all sectors
China		49.4	16.7	66	Industrial only 1996 gross output
Hong Kong				~63	all sectors
Indonesia				na	
Japan	4.1	5.1	22.0	50.8	Manufacturing 1997
				42.5	all SMEs – sales
				56.6	all SMEs value added
Korea		9.6	20.2	46.3	Manufacturing
	16.5	8.4	38.4	63.2	Services
Malaysia				na	
New Zealand	19.0	16.0	20.0	55.0	Sales 1998
Philippines	35.8	12.0	10.8	26.5	Manufacturing
	24.0	30.1	8.4	62.7	Services value added 1995
Singapore		2.7	11.8	14.5	Manufacturing
Chinese Taipei		na	na	32.0	Sales 1997
Thailand				na	
Vietnam				na	

Note: ~ indicates estimate only.
Sources: As for Table 2.3 unless otherwise noted.

that they have established production facilities in China, and in other East Asian economies. It also reflects the changing and maturing nature of Chinese Taipei industry.

SME foreign direct investment is even harder to gauge than exports. FDI by SMEs is probably about 50 per cent or more of cases of FDI, but only about 10 per cent to 5 per cent or less of actual value. In principle, FDI can be monitored when it is received (for example, approvals for incoming investment), or when it is made (for example, approvals for money to be sent out of a country). No economies monitor incoming investment flows to see what size of firm they are coming from and going to, and even if they did, it would be hard to interpret (for example, if the FDI is coming from an SME to an SME it is clearly SME investment, but it can also be coming from a major multinational corporation (MNC) and going to an SME). Estimates made by

Table 2.7
Structural Contribution of SMEs to Exports, 1991–92

	GDP US$ millions	Exports as % of GDP	Share of SMEs in total exports %
Japan	3 337 191	12	13.5
China	435 000	21	40–60
Korea	285 000	27	40
Indonesia	128 000	23	10.6
Chinese Taipei	210 000	44	~56
Thailand	108 000	29	10
Malaysia	60 000	72	15
Singapore	46 000	138	16
Vietnam	14 000	7	20
Weighted contribution	11.7		30–35%

Notes:
~ indicates estimate only. Exports are direct exports by SMEs. This understates the true contribution of SMEs to exports.
Weighted contribution. For exports is the sum of GDP multiplied by the percentage of exports multiplied by the percentage of direct SME exports expressed as a percentage of total exports.

Source: Adapted from OECD (1997).

the author for UNCTAD are summarised in Tables 2.9 and 2.10. Table 2.9 is an approximation, by measuring 'small package' approvals – that is, approvals for investments of less than US$1 million are *assumed* to be indicative of investments in SMEs.

Korea actually identifies outward FDI by size of firm. These data show that FDI by SMEs amounts to about 20 per cent by value (though this dropped off abruptly in the aftermath of the 1997 Asian crisis), and about 67 per cent to 54 per cent of cases. SME FDI over the period from 1993 to 1998 has grown, or shrunk, at about the same rate as total FDI. The average amount of investment by Korean SMEs abroad was about US$600 000 in 1995.

Japan also collects some information on the number of cases of SME investment abroad. The Ministry of Finance collects information based on notifications, and the Ministry of International Trade and Industry (MITI) collects additional information on SME FDI based on survey data. The figures are not directly comparable; there are numerous discontinuities in the series, and the figures do not include the value of that investment. However it seems that SMEs make up about 50 per cent of cases of FDI. The proportion rose as high as 60 per cent in 1988 when the Yen was rising steeply,

Table 2.8
SME Exports as a Percentage of Total Exports: Selected Economies

	SME exports as % of all exports	
Australia	na	
China	60	1997
Hong Kong	na	
Indonesia	5	1996
Japan	15	1996[a]
Korea	42	1996–98
Malaysia	na	
New Zealand	na	
Philippines	na	
Singapore	13.5	1996
Chinese Taipei	50	1996
Thailand	na	
Vietnam	na	

Note:
a   The Small and Medium Enterprise Agency of Japan estimates the exports of typical SME products
     to be only 7.3 per cent in 1997 (JSBRI 1999, p. 7).

Source: KOTRA (1999).

then dropped back to around 40 per cent in 1992 and in 1996 had risen again to about 52 per cent (JSBRI 1997, p. 36). About 13 per cent of Japan's manufacturing output was produced abroad in 1997 although the proportion attributable to SMEs is not known (JSBRI 1999, p. 8).

2.4   THE MOVIE – THE DYNAMICS OF SMES IN EAST ASIA AND THEIR CONTRIBUTION TO GROWTH

What are the dynamics and longer-term trends, and where might SMEs in East Asia be heading if they get the right environment to develop? Piecing together a big picture movie of SMEs in Asia over four decades is a bit like making a movie out of offcuts from numerous other movies off the editing room floor; the end product is not very elegant, and we need to be a bit patient if we are to see the real story. Two key points emerge:

1. SMEs have generally become more important, and SMEs make a major contribution to economic growth and employment growth in particular, though this is clouded by structural and policy shifts in the region.

Table 2.9

Trends in Inward Small Package FDI in Developing Economies in Asia, 1989–95 (US$ m current and as % of total approvals)

	1989	1990	1991	1992	1993	1994	1995
Philippines							
$ 'SME' FDI	–	–	–	–	–	–	–
% $ approvals	17	8	8	11	7	2	2
% cases	86	83	80	85	73	62	63
Vietnam							
$ 'SME' FDI	–	–	12	13	24	28	29
% $ approvals	–	–	0.9	0.6	0.8	0.6	0.4
% cases	–	–	18	15	22	14	13

Notes:

Philippines: Figures are based on approvals for projects of less than peso 60 million (about US$2 000 000 at the time).

Vietnam: Figures are estimates based on published information on smaller projects, and probably underestimate slightly the role of SME FDI. FDI figures used are the official approvals, not the UNCTAD figures in tables above which are based on estimates only.

Source: UNCTAD (1998).

Table 2.10

Republic of Korea – Total Outward FDI and SME FDI (US$ m)

	1993	1994	1995	1996	1997	1998
Value of FDI						
Total	5 411	7 477	10 225	–	–	–
SMEs	1 026	1 519	2 054	–	–	–
% $ SMEs	19	20	20	21	18	8
Cases of FDI						
Total	2 726	4 133	5 326	–	–	–
SMEs	1 603	2 722	3 593	–	–	–
% SMEs	60	66	67	55	57	54

Source: UNCTAD and national statistical sources. KOTRA (1999) for figures post-1995.

2. SMEs have the potential to make a much more important contribution than they are making at present in the East Asian economy. To do this they need to be provided with a more conducive business environment, especially one with fewer barriers to growth and internationalisation. To some extent this is occurring naturally, as the business environment evolves around the Web, but governments could do more to facilitate the entrepreneurial engine.

2.4.1 SMEs Have Become More Important ...

Tables 2.11 and 2.12 give some roughly comparable figures on the role of SMEs over a two- to four-decade period for manufacturing. These provide a tenuous suggestion that SMEs became more important in their contribution to economic activity over the last two decades, especially in regard to employment. Over the last two decades, in all economies for which data is available, the output contribution increased, except for Japan (where it remained steady) and Chinese Taipei (where it fell from 46 per cent to 39 per cent). Similarly, over the last two decades the percentage of the workforce employed by SMEs grew in all economies except Indonesia. The effect of policy

Table 2.11
The Changing Role of SMEs – SME Contribution to Output
Percentages of Total (manufacturing unless otherwise stated)

	1960s	1970s	1980s	1990s	
Indonesia	–	–	23	30	
Japan	–	–	52	52	
Korea	43	34	33	44	
Singapore	53	19	18	19	
Chinese Taipei	na	37	46	39	
Philippines	–	–	24	27	value added
Vietnam	na	na	na	40–70	

Sources: Adapted from UNCTAD (1998)
Notes:
For definitions of SMEs in respective economies, see Table 2.1.
Japan: JSBRI (1994), *Small Business in Japan.*
Singapore: *Report on the Census of Industrial Production.*
Chinese Taipei: *White Paper on SMEs*. Figures are for sales, not output.
Korea: (Seong 1995, p. 125). Korean policies changed in the 1980s to increase the importance of SMEs. Data for 1960s is from 1963 to 1969. Sourced from Korea Development Bank 1963/66, Economic Planning Board thereafter.
Indonesia: Central Bureau of Statistics, *Industrial Statistics and Small Enterprises Survey*, various years.
Philippines: Small and Medium Enterprise Development (SMED) Council research.

Table 2.12
The Changing Role of SMEs – SME Contribution to Employment
Percentages of Total (manufacturing unless otherwise stated)

	1960s	1970s	1980s	1990s	
Australia	–	–	21	29	manufacturing
			45	47	all SMEs
Indonesia	–	–	48	42	
Japan	–	70	76	85	
Korea	58	46	61	63	
Singapore	55	29	31	35	
Chinese Taipei	43	46	63	80	
Philippines	–	45	47	50	

Sources: See Table 2.11. Adapted from UNCTAD (1998).
Australia: ABS 1321.0 (2000), Table 2.3.
Indonesia: Figures are for 1986–89 and 1990–93.

shifts can be seen over the longer term. For example, Korea adopted policies in the 1960s and 1970s that tended to downplay the role of SMEs, and only reversed these policies to actively support SMEs in the 1980s. Singapore's policy has been aimed more at major MNCs and their subsidiaries for several decades, and only in the last decade has changed to give more emphasis to the growth of SMEs as such.

2.4.2   The Contribution of SMEs to Growth

SMEs make a major contribution to economic growth, and particularly to employment growth. Most of the available evidence suggest that SMEs contribute about 60 per cent to 70 per cent of net employment growth, so they are an important 'entrepreneurial engine'. This contribution has two main aspects:

1. *Net start-ups* – The net addition of new firms generates economic growth. About 80 per cent to 90 per cent of SMEs are micro enterprises, and they 'churn'; that is, a significant proportion (between about 5 per cent and 20 per cent) 'die' each year, while a similar proportion are 'born' each year. If there is a net gain of births over deaths then this tends to add to overall economic growth, even though the average micro firm itself does not grow much in size.

2. *Fast-growth SMEs* – It seems to be the sustained growth of a relatively small group of successful (or high-growth) firms that contributes a lot to economic growth. These firms typically survive for more than eight years, and often experience growth rates exceeding 30 per cent per annum. It is only a relatively

small percentage of SMEs (perhaps 5 per cent or less) that contribute significantly to overall growth in this way, but their contribution can be quite large.

Detailed analysis of the contribution of SMEs to growth is a difficult statistical exercise, and is subject to some dispute. For example, the most common argument is about the way size classes are used to attribute employment changes. Many firms start as SMEs, but it is distorting to allocate employment growth to the 'small' category when a firm starts small, but finishes 'large'. Much of the dispute on the topic seems to have missed a key point; it is not so much an issue of small versus large, but rather the process which is going on between the two, and which firms make the biggest contribution. Some of the dispute (for example, Davis et al. 1993) is based on cross-sectional analysis which cannot resolve the issue. What is contended here is that much of the job growth comes from firms which start off being small, but contribute most as they become larger. The only way to really assess this is by longitudinal studies, and these are relatively limited, especially in Asia. There are no comparable figures for the region. However, what we can do is build up a mosaic of evidence from those economies that have carried out some analysis, which looks at net start-up rates and the contribution of SMEs to growth.

- *Australia* – SMEs in Australia have contributed between 63 per cent and 78 per cent of net employment growth (see Table 2.13). Preliminary analysis of the longitudinal GAPS (Growth and Performance Survey) data shows that in 1993/4 78 per cent of job growth came from SMEs (36 per cent from medium sized firms), and in 1994/5 63 per cent came from SMEs. In later years, the contribution has remained at about 67 per cent. Start-up rates for SMEs in Australia range between about 9 per cent (BIE AIT October 1993, p. 51, 1992–93), and 16 per cent (BIE AIT October 1994, p. 103, 1993, Registrations only). Exit rates are about 7 per cent to 10 per cent (ABS, Exit Rates 1997, 8144.0).

- *Japan* – Exit rates and entry rates for Japan are shown in Table 2.14. Two things stand out clearly. One is that Japan has much lower entry and exit rates than other developed economies; the rates are less than half the rates common in the US or most of Europe. Second, the closure or exit rate has exceeded the start-up rate for the last decade, so what growth there has been from Japanese SMEs it has not come from net start-ups. Note that Japanese SMEs have still been starting up, but not in Japan; they have been moving business to the rest of East Asia, and particularly to China. This is part of the symptom of Japan's economic malaise that has hindered it since the early 1990s, but it is also part of the internationalisation of the entrepreneurial engine in the region.

- *Korea* – Table 2.15 and Table 2.16 show that over the last two decades SMEs have generally contributed more to growth than larger firms, reversing the situation prevailing before the 1980s. This reflects a shift in government policy

Table 2.13
Australia – Contribution to Total Net Employment Growth
by Size of Firm (%)

	Australia 93/4	Australia 94/5	96/97	97/98
Micro	4	20	na	na
Small	37	14	57	50
Medium	36	28	11	17
SME	78	63	68	67
Large	22	37	32	33
Growth rate %pa	4.28	3.74	na	na

Sources: For 1993/4 and 94/5 preliminary statistics from GAPS, for later period ABS 8141.0, 1997–98, p. 30.

Table 2.14
Japan Entry and Exit Rates – Enterprise Data (%)

	75/8	78/81	81/86	86/91	91/96
Start-up	5.9	5.9	4.3	3.5	2.7
Closure	3.8	3.7	4.0	4.0	3.2

Source: JSBRI (2000).

to encourage SMEs, but it also reflects the latent potential of the 'entrepreneurial engine' that the policy was aimed at facilitating.

- *Chinese Taipei* – Start-up rates are about 6 to 8 per cent, while exit rates are about 4 to 5 per cent. The number of registered new business start-ups in 1997 totalled 75 995, relative to about 1.1 million SMEs, while firm closures in that period reached about 50 000. Table 2.17 provides further details. These rates are also fairly low when compared with the USA and Europe.

- *New Zealand* – In New Zealand (New Zealand 1998) about 80 per cent of net employment gain between 1995 and 1997 was from micro firms (with fewer than 5 employees), and firms that were internationally active tended to add more to employment than those that were not. Start-up and exit rates were about equal in 1998/9 at about 15 per cent of all enterprises.

- *Singapore* – A longitudinal study of SMEs in Singapore (unpublished, Department of Statistics 1997) from 1984 to 1994 showed that those SMEs

Table 2.15
Korea – Growth Rates by Firm Size: 1960s–1990s (unit: %)

Items		Growth rate[a]			
		1960s (63–69)	1970s (70–79)	1980s (80–89)	1990s (90–97)
No. of establishments	SMEs[b]	3.4	3.1	9.0	4.4
	Large firms	11.8	5.1	1.9	−5.3
No. of employees	SMEs	5.4	10.2	7.3	0.0
	Large firms	12.8	10.8	2.0	−4.7
Gross output	SMEs	14.5	40.4	20.7	15.0
	Large firms	29.7	39.1	14.8	12.6
Value of shipments	SMEs	14.7	40.1	20.8	15.1
	Large firms	29.7	38.9	15.0	12.6
Value added	SMEs	16.3	40.0	21.9	15.1
	Large firms	29.6	35.3	16.4	13.7

Notes:
a   Annual average rate.
b   5–299 employees.

Sources: From Hong et al. (1999) and sourced from Korea Federation of Small Business (KFSB), *Economic Development and Contribution of SMEs*, 1998.

which grew in employment and output or sales over the period made up about 29 per cent of the surviving businesses (or about 13 per cent of the original enterprises). These growth SMEs increased their employment from 78 000 to 184 000 over the period, while that of other non-growing SMEs declined from 149 000 to 105 000. This suggests it is a relatively small proportion of surviving, growing, SMEs that provide the bulk of job growth.

What does all this fragmentary evidence suggest about the role of SMEs in the entrepreneurial engine of East Asia?

First, it is clear that SMEs do provide the lion's share of growth. Typically, in the economies for which there are reliable data, about 70 per cent of employment growth comes from SMEs. Anecdotally, even in economies for which there are no data, SMEs play a major role; for example, almost all net employment creation in China, Vietnam and Indonesia in the last five to ten years has been in SMEs. In China and Indonesia, for example, large firms have been net job destroyers as they downsize – a phenomenon also common in Europe and the US.

Second, the entrepreneurial engine is underpowered in much of East Asia, especially in the less-developed economies of China, Indonesia, the Philippines,

Table 2.16
Korea – Contribution Ratios to Economic Growth by Firm Size (unit: %)

Items		Contribution rate[a]			
		1960s (63–69)	1970s (70–79)	1980s (80–89)	1990s (90–97)
No. of establishments	SMEs[b]	94.0	93.1	99.6	101.6
	Large firms	6.0	6.9	0.4	−1.6
No. of employees	SMEs	38.1	45.3	89.2	−3.4
	Large firms	61.9	54.7	10.8	−96.6
Gross output	SMEs	26.5	32.1	44.6	48.4
	Large firms	73.5	67.9	55.4	51.6
Value of shipments	SMEs	26.7	32.2	44.5	48.4
	Large firms	73.3	67.8	55.5	51.6
Value added	SMEs	25.7	35.5	46.9	47.1
	Large firms	73.3	64.5	53.1	52.9

Notes:
a   The contribution ratio is the percentage share of each enterprise to total increasing quantity.
b   5–299 employees.

Sources: From Hong et al (1999) and sourced from Korea Federation of Small Business (KFSB), *Economic Development and Contribution of SMEs*, 1998.

Table 2.17
Chinese Taipei Business Start-ups and Closures of Registered Firms
(unit: enterprise, NT$ m)

	Number of enterprises			Capital volume		
	Start-ups	Closures	Net increase	Start-ups	Closures	Net increase
1996	67 592	48 136	19 456	517 527	176 088	341 439
1997	75 995	50 274	25 721	585 348	173 452	411 896
1998.1	4 967	3 556	1 411	87 959	11 873	76 086
1998.2	4 844	6 025	−1 181	18 635	14 506	4 129
1998.3	7 145	5 252	1 893	41 149	18 608	22 541
1998.4	7 374	4 076	3 298	96 862	16 290	80 572

Source: MOEA, *White Paper on SMEs*, Statistics Department, Ministry of Economic Affairs (MOEA).

Table 2.18
Estimated Benchmark SME Numbers in Developing East Asia (millions)

	Population	Estimated number of SMEs now	Benchmark SMEs if ratio is 20 people per SME	Additional SMEs needed to meet benchmark
China	1 244.2	8.0	62.2	54.2
Indonesia	203.4	2.0	10.2	8.2
Philippines	71.4	0.5	3.6	3.1
Thailand	59.7	0.7	3.0	2.3
Vietnam	76.5	0.5	3.8	3.3
Totals	1 655.2	11.7	82.8	71.1

Source: Author's calculations and Table 2.2.

Thailand and Vietnam. In these economies there are simply fewer SMEs than might be expected. Table 2.18 shows that the number of people per SME in these economies is much higher than in the more developed economies. This means that there are fewer start-ups, and the pool of SMEs from which high-growth SMEs can emerge is much smaller. Consequently there is less growth than there would otherwise be. In a very rough order of magnitude calculation, for these economies to achieve a benchmark level of 20 people per SME, there would have to be about 70 million new SMEs created (see Table 2.18). This needs to be compared with the 20 million or so SMEs in all of East Asia at present. This means 70 million or more people will need managerial skills and training. Most of these are in China. Even in economies like Vietnam and the Philippines, there need to be about 3 million or more additional managers. In the past this would be seen as a government responsibility, and the task is just too enormous to even contemplate for most governments. Changing technology (notably the World Wide Web (www), and especially Wireless Application Protocol (WAP) access to the www) are changing this, and making it more feasible for the private sector to train large numbers of managers in a relatively short period of time, but it will still need public–private cooperation to achieve the sort of growth that is needed.

Third, in developing East Asia the bulk of the SME contribution to growth will probably come from net start-ups, while in developed East Asia the growth contribution will tend to come more from high-growth firms. Start-up rates tend to be relatively low, especially in Japan, which is the largest economy in the region. Japan's net start-up rate (domestically at least) has been negative for some time. Part of this is the economic downturn, and part of it is cultural and institutional inhibitions to taking risk and starting a business. These cultural and institutional factors need to be actively addressed if East Asia is to really make use of the potential of its entrepreneurial engine.

Fourth, the entrepreneurial engine is being internationalised. For example, a small but significant proportion of SMEs in Japan, Korea and Chinese Taipei have already expanded operations abroad; about 13 per cent of Japan's manufacturing output is now sourced abroad. It is becoming easier for SMEs to operate across borders. This is partly as a result of efforts to reduce trade and non-trade impediments by the World Trade Organisation (WTO), APEC and the Association of South East Asian Nations (ASEAN). It is also part of the general globalisation of business occurring as a result of improved communications (particularly e-commerce and the Web) and other technological and social changes. This SME internationalisation is not limited to specific regions, such as East Asia, but is more global. It is to this last aspect of the potential of SMEs to contribute more to the international economy that we now turn.

2.4.3 International SME Dynamics and Growth Potential

Because internationalisation is taking place at a higher level than just East Asia, it makes some sense to look at this aspect from a broader APEC-wide perspective. The potential for fast-growing internationalised SMEs to add to the APEC economy is quite large. Estimates below suggest that greater structural integration of APEC economies (offered by e-commerce and reduction of tariff and non-tariff barriers) will allow SMEs to increase their contribution to the APEC economy *relative* to larger firms, and bring it more in line with that typically found in the more integrated national economies. Available evidence suggests that there is the potential for SMEs to add about US$1 trillion in trade and about US$150 billion in FDI per annum to the APEC economy if structural changes allow a simpler, more business-friendly, more integrated APEC economy to emerge.

How much SME trade and investment *could* there be in APEC? This question is impossible to answer except in some very broad-brush terms. Two aspects need to be distinguished:

- The first is growth of international activity by SMEs as a result of economic growth. UNCTAD evidence generally suggests that, as a rough proxy, trade grows at about double the rate of GDP growth, and FDI grows at about double the rate of trade. Other things equal, and even if SMEs remain relatively under-represented in international activity, we can expect the growth of SME trade and investment to outstrip GDP growth. This will necessarily mean that internationalised SMEs will contribute proportionally more to national economic growth. This is the 'rising tide' effect. As APEC reduces trade and non-trade impediments, all enterprises, large and small, will benefit and rise on the rising tide.

- The second is a structural change in the relative importance of SMEs versus larger firms in international activity. The potential for gains here is much larger.

SMEs make up only about 30 per cent of trade and about 10 per cent of FDI, whereas they have the potential to contribute nearly 50 per cent of each if the international economy becomes more integrated.

Table 2.19 suggests that trade in APEC is likely to be about US$3 trillion per year in 2000. If GDP in APEC grows at about 4 per cent per annum, then growth in trade can be expected to be about 8 per cent per annum, and SMEs should add about 30 per cent of this, or about US$80 billion per year.

Table 2.20 shows FDI flows in APEC. SMEs probably make up only about 10 per cent of these (or about US$20 billion). If GDP in APEC grows at 4 per cent then FDI is likely to grow at about 16 per cent, so the growth of SME contributions to FDI is likely to be about US$3.2 billion.

How much *could* SMEs contribute to trade under ideal conditions? In a fully integrated economy SMEs typically make up about 50 per cent of economic activity; that is SMEs contribute about 50 per cent of GDP and about 50 per cent of investment. At present SMEs seem to make up only about 30 per cent or so of trade. If APEC exports are expected to be about US$3 trillion in 2000 (see Table 2.19), then SMEs would make up only US$1 trillion of the total (or about 30 per cent). If SMEs were to realise their full potential, then they should contribute roughly the same as larger firms (that is about 50 per cent, or about what they contribute in a fully integrated economy), or about US$2 trillion. This implies that if SMEs reach their full economic potential, SME exports would double, from US$1 trillion to US$2 trillion, and total export trade in APEC would expand by 30 per cent, from US$3 trillion to US$4

Table 2.19
Imports and Exports, 1990–97 – APEC and the World

	World imports US$ trillion	APEC imports US$ trillion	% APEC	World exports US$ trillion	APEC exports US$ trillion	% APEC
1997	5.4	2.4	44	5.3	2.3	42
1996	5.3	2.3	43	5.2	2.1	40
1995	5.1	2.1	43	4.9	2.1	41
1994	4.2	1.9	44	4.1	1.8	42
1993	3.7	1.6	43	3.6	1.5	42
1992	3.8	1.5	39	3.7	1.4	39
1991	3.5	1.4	38	3.4	1.3	38
1990	3.6	1.3	37	3.4	1.2	35

Source: APEC, drawn from UN, *Monthly Bulletin of Statistics*, July 1998.

Table 2.20
FDI Flows in APEC, 1996

	FDI inflows 1996 US$m	FDI outflows 1996 US$m
Australia	6 403	1 343
Brunei Darussalam	9	0
Canada	6 681	7 543
Chile	3 140	956
China	42 300	2 200
Hong Kong China	2 500	27 000
Indonesia	7 960	512
Japan	220	23 440
Korea	2 308	4 188
Malaysia	5 300	1 906
Mexico	7 535	553
New Zealand	2 928	−157
Papua New Guinea	230	0
Philippines	1 408	182
Singapore	9 440	4 800
Chinese Taipei	1 402	3 096
Thailand	2 426	1 740
USA	84 629	84 902
Vietnam	2 156	1 740
Total	188 975	165 944

Source: UNCTAD, *World Investment Report 1997*, Table B.

trillion. To put this in perspective, an extra US$1 trillion in trade each year is more than the combined economies of Canada and Australia, and about double the equivalent of all of ASEAN. It would be a significant addition to the APEC economy.

How much *could* SMEs contribute to increased FDI in APEC under ideal conditions? SMEs typically make up about half of all investment in an economy, but across borders it is much less; SME FDI usually only makes up about 10 per cent of FDI. Table 2.20 shows that in 1996, FDI flows in APEC amounted to about US$189 billion in inflows and US$166 billion in outflows. (Seen in perspective, FDI flows are less than one-tenth of trade flows in APEC, but typically trade flows are growing at about double GDP growth, and FDI is typically growing at about double the growth in trade flows.) About 90 per cent of this FDI (or about US$166 billion in outflows) is probably attributable to large firms (US$149 billion), and only 10 per cent, or about US$20 billion in outflows, is attributable to SMEs. In a more integrated world, SMEs would be contributing about as much as the large firms. This would suggest that the potential is there for SMEs to increase FDI in APEC by about US$150 billion per year. To put this in rough perspective, US$150 billion is about the same as the GDP of Hong Kong or Indonesia. In itself it would be a significant addition to the APEC economy, but FDI has strong multiplier and technology transfer benefits as well.

In summary, we should expect that if commitments to reduced trade and investment barriers are maintained then we can expect SMEs to add:

- about US$80 billion a year to trade in APEC; and

- about US$3.2 billion in FDI.

Similarly, were the APEC economies to achieve a level of integration where SMEs can move as easily across borders as large firms (in effect achieving an almost borderless economy) it would be possible for SMEs to add as much as about:

- US$1 trillion each year in additional economic trade; and

- US$150 billion each year in additional investment.

Clearly the main gains will come from a structural shift which would enable SMEs to operate in a more integrated APEC economy. How realistic is this? On the one hand, it is unlikely that APEC will become a fully integrated economy in the next 20 years, at least in the sense of the moves of the European Union to full monetary union. The target might thus be discounted to reflect the political reality that even with the best will in the world, and even by 2020, economic union in APEC will be a long way off. Even so, even if the figures above are halved, they still reflect a very large potential gain which at present is being almost ignored. On the other hand the rapid changes brought forth by e-commerce and globalisation mean that the potential for SMEs to contribute to the growth of the global or regional economy is greater than ever before. It would be particularly shortsighted to ignore this potential, and to not address any impediments that can be identified. The potential gains tend to be largest in East Asia, simply because there are more SMEs there, and the entrepreneurial engine there is underpowered.

2.5   PUTTING THE PIECES TOGETHER ...

Table 2.21 summarises the nine key common features, and the differences, of the profile of SMEs in East Asia.

What does all this tell us about the directors' role in orchestrating the shape of the future picture of SMEs in East Asia? There are four main messages for the policy makers:

1. SMEs (generally those enterprises with fewer than 100 employees) are important to economic growth, and are especially important to jobs and job creation. SMEs

already contribute over half the jobs in the East Asian region, and about 70 per cent of new job creation seems to be coming from SMEs. In developing economies the contribution of SMEs to employment tends to be higher, around 70 per cent of the workforce, but as economies develop to higher income per head levels, the contribution to employment by SMEs tends to decline to around 50 per cent. In developing economies the jobs tend to be created more by start-ups, but in the developed economies jobs seem to be created more by high-growth SMEs. It is important for policy makers to understand and to foster the way this entrepreneurial engine works and evolves.

2. The entrepreneurial engine in developing East Asia seems to be underpowered. This means that the job creating potential of SMEs is less than it could be. There are about 2 billion people in East Asia, and about 20 million SMEs. In most of the developed economies there are about 20 people per SME, but in developing East Asia, there are about 100 people per SME. This means that the ability to create jobs by start-ups is more, and the pool of SMEs from which fast-growth SMEs emerge is smaller. This is largely due to historical and political reasons; for example, China and Vietnam have only followed policies to stimulate SME growth in the last decade or so, and there is a lot of catching up to do. Policy makers in both the developing and developed economies need to work with the private sector to address this aspect of catch-up.

3. Internationally, SMEs have more opportunities than ever before, but they seem to be growing only at about the same rate as the international economy. SMEs contribute about 30 per cent or so of direct exports, which is about what they seemed to contribute at the start of the 1990s, and it is less than might be expected in an increasingly globalised economy. That is to say, SMEs are rising on the rising tide of trade liberalisation, but they are not surfing the wave of future globalisation. Part of the problem here is the paucity of statistics on SME international activity. Part of it is that the trade barriers that *have* been addressed so far by APEC and the WTO tend to favour larger trading firms, and do not address the more specific non-border non-trade impediments that SMEs tend to be obstructed by when operating across borders. These impediments need to be identified and addressed more aggressively.

4. SMEs have tended to become more important economically and politically. SMEs are given political recognition by most national and provincial governments because they employ so many people. However, politically, SMEs have tended to be taken for granted by many national governments because they were essentially a relatively weak domestic political force. It is only in the last decade that SMEs have had the real choice of being able to internationalise, just as larger enterprises did in the 1950s and 1960s. SMEs, especially those fast-growth SMEs which contribute much to economic and employment growth, can increasingly decide where to locate their business activity. This is very much a two-edged sword for

Table 2.21
Summary of the Profile of SMEs in East Asia

	Common features ...	... and differences
Numbers of Enterprises	1. There are about 20 to 30 million SMEs in East Asia. 2. On average there are about 85 people for every SME.	1. Most of the SMEs are in China (8 million) and Japan (5 million) and Korea (2.6 million) which together have 70 per cent of the SMEs in East Asia. 2. In developed economies there are only about 20 people per SME, but the ratio is above 100 in the developing economies, especially in China, Vietnam, the Philippines and Indonesia.
Employment	3. SMEs employ over 50 per cent of the workforce. 4. Over 95 per cent of enterprises employ fewer than 100 people, and over 80 per cent employ fewer than 5 people. 5. SMEs seem to contribute about 70 per cent of net employment growth.	3. In developing economies (below about US$15 000 per capita income) SMEs employ about 75 per cent of people, above US$15 000 the level is closer to 50 per cent. Japan is a major exception – Japan's SMEs employ around 80 per cent of the workforce. 4. More-developed economies seem to have more medium sized SMEs and they play a greater role. Developing economies seem more likely to have a 'missing middle'. 5. In developed economies most of this growth probably comes from fast growth firms, in developing economies a higher proportion probably comes from net start-ups.

	Common features ...	... and differences
Output measures (sales, value added etc.)	6. SMEs contribute about 50 per cent of sales, value added or output.	6. The contribution varies from lows of 15 per cent (Singapore) and 30 per cent (Australia) to about 60 per cent for most other economies.
Exports	7. SMEs generate about 30 per cent of exports, much less than the SME contribution to employment (about 60 per cent to 70 per cent) or output (about 50 per cent).	7. SME export figures are difficult to verify, but they range from about 5 per cent or less (Indonesia) to around 40 per cent (Korea) of total exports.
FDI	8. SMEs generate about 50 per cent of cases of FDI, but only less than 10 per cent of value of FDI.	8. Korean, Japanese and Chinese Taipei SMEs contribute most FDI originating in the East Asian region.
Entrepreneurial engine and international potential	9. SMEs already contribute the bulk of growth, and SMEs could make a much bigger contribution to the Asian regional economy if efforts were made to address impediments to SME internationalisation. This could add as much as US$1 trillion per year in trade.	9. The developing economies need to create about 50 to 70 million more SMEs if they are to achieve 'benchmark' levels of SME activity.

policy makers, but they need to see that as much as 70 per cent of the longer-term growth for their economies comes from SMEs, and they need to work together to build an attractive and conducive entrepreneurial business environment in the region, and in their own economies.

REFERENCES

APEC (1994), *The APEC Survey on Small and Medium Enterprises*, Chinese Taipei: APEC.

APEC (1998), *Profile of SMEs in Asia*, Malaysia: APEC.

Australia, Australian Bureau of Statistics (1997), 'Analysing the Business Growth and Performance Survey (GAPS) – Employment Analysis', preliminary working paper, Canberra: AGPS.

Australia, Bureau of Industry Economics (BIE) (1993), *Australian Industry Trends*, No. 19, October, Canberra: AGPS.

Australia, Bureau of Industry Economics (BIE) (1994), *Australian Industry Trends*, No. 20, April, AGPS, Canberra.

Chinese Taipei (2000), *White Paper on SMEs*, Taipei: SMEA.

Davis, S.J., J. Haltiwanger, and S. Schuh (1993), 'Small Business and Job Creation: Dissecting the Myth and Reassessing the Facts', National Bureau of Economic Research, Working Paper No. 4992, Cambridge, MA.

Hall, C. (1998a), *APEC SME Indicators – A Feasibility Study*, Sydney: APEC.

Hall, C. (1998b), 'Squeezing the Asian Entrepreneurial Engine: The Impact of the Credit Squeeze on Sustainable Entrepreneurial Job Creation in Asia', paper presented to the International Council of Small Business (ICSB) 43rd World Conference Singapore, 8–10 June.

Hall, C. (1999a), 'Using the International Entrepreneurial Engine to Restart Asian Growth', in Leo Paul Dana (ed.), *International Entrepreneurship, an Anthology*, Singapore: National Technological University (NTU) Entrepreneurship Development Centre, pp. 229–40.

Hall, C. (1999b), 'The Challenges and the Opportunities of E-commerce and International SMEs; implications for HRM in APEC', paper presented to the APEC Human Resource Management Symposium, Kaohsiung, 29–31 October.

Hong Soon-Yeong, Jang-Hyuk Park and Jong-Young Park (1999), *Status and Prospects of Small & Medium Enterprises (SMEs) in Korea*, Seoul: Korea Small Business Institute.

Japan Small Business Research Institute (JSBRI), various years, *White Paper on SMEs in Japan*, Tokyo: MITI.

Korean External Trade Organisation (KOTRA) (1999), *A Strategy for Internationalization of SMEs in the Asia Pacific Region: Lessons From the Empirical Study on Korean and Other APEC Member Economies*, Singapore: APEC.

New Zealand, Ministry of Commerce (2000), *SMEs in New Zealand, Structure and Dynamics*, Wellington: Ministry of Commerce.

New Zealand, Statistics New Zealand (1998), *Business Activity Statistics – Part 2: Business Demography 1998*, Wellington: Statistics New Zealand.

Organisation for Economic Cooperation and Development (OECD) (1997), *Globalisation and SMEs*, vols 1 and 2, Paris: OECD.

Seong, S. (1995), 'Korean Country Paper', in Eul Yong Park(1995), *Small and Medium Sized Enterprises and Economic Development*, Seoul: KDI, pp. 116–39.

United Nations Conference on Trade and Development (UNCTAD) (1998), *Handbook on Foreign Direct Investment by SMEs – Lessons From Asia*, Geneva: UNCTAD.

3 China's SMEs: Their Evolution and Future Prospects in an Evolving Market Economy

Charles Harvie

3.1 INTRODUCTION

China has experienced a prolonged and impressive period of economic growth and development during its twenty-odd years of economic reform that started in 1978. The most fundamental change that this reform has brought about has been the development of the non-state sector, which has resulted in multiple types of ownership including urban and rural private businesses, township enterprises, foreign-invested enterprises and joint-stock companies. The non-state sector is increasingly replacing the state sector in the supply and distribution of goods and services. In view of this contribution to rising living standards in China, the status of the sector was recognised politically and legally as a significant component of the 'socialist market system' in the March 1999 amendment to the constitution. With this recognition the authorities have indicated a readiness to accept a renewed phase of further reducing the role of state-owned enterprises (SOEs) in the economy, and to accept a further significant expansion, in particular, of the role of the private sector. The country's membership of the World Trade Organisation (WTO) will result in the entry of foreign firms and intense competition in those industries that are currently dominated by SOEs. This will contribute to a further reduction in the role of the state in the economy and provide sustained impetus to the development of the domestic private sector and fundamental changes in China's ownership landscape.

Compared with the state sector, the non-state sector is primarily composed of SMEs engaged in labour intensive lower-value-added activities. The domestic private sector has insufficient access to financial resources to make the large-scale investments required to become established in capital-intensive industries. The underdeveloped banking sector, dominated by the four state-owned banks, with its traditional focus upon providing credit to the state sector, has become a bottleneck to continued high growth as it fails to channel resources to the most productive sector in the economy – the private and so-called township and village enterprises (TVEs). The extent of the distortion of resource allocation is exemplified by the fact that the non-state sector contributes more than 70 per cent of output but uses less than 30 per cent of total bank credits. This severe misallocation of investment resources across different ownership groups and across industries is making the prospects of China's economic growth unclear. A serious policy mistake during the period of reform has been the lack of development of non-state financial institutions that would more adequately serve the growth of the non-state sector. The fundamental process of replacing SOEs with enterprises of other types of ownership and reforming the banking system by introducing competition, can lead to better utilisation of economic resources in China and therefore lead to higher economic growth. Introducing competition into the banking industry is particularly important so that resources are channelled to the most productive sectors of the economy. With foreign banks handling renminbi (RMB) business soon after China's membership of the WTO, there is greater potential for private enterprises in China to obtain finance from the banking sector.

The remainder of this chapter proceeds as follows. Section 3.2 conducts a brief review of the rise and significance of the non-state sector and its key constituents. Section 3.3 focuses upon the small and rural-based TVEs in terms of: their development; their unique organisational form; the issue of property rights and the TVE performance paradox; and the prospects for their sustainable development. Section 3.4 discusses TVEs' contribution to the economy in terms of output, employment and exports as well as their performance in terms of profitability, total factor productivity and upgrading of technology. Section 3.5 identifies the reasons behind their success. Section 3.6 focuses upon evolving business alliances involving TVEs, including those with publicly funded research institutes and universities, as well as organisational and ownership changes that will be required if the TVEs are to sustain their development within China's rapidly evolving market economy. Section 3.7 focuses upon the economic contribution, growth and major constraints currently facing the rapidly developing private sector. Section 3.8 discusses the policies essential for the future sustainable growth and development of SMEs in China and for the private sector more generally. Section 3.9 identifies the impact of the Asian financial crisis upon China's SMEs. Finally, Section 3.10 presents a summary of the major conclusions from this chapter.

3.2   DEVELOPMENT OF THE NON-STATE SECTOR

One of the most striking outcomes during China's period of economic reform since 1978 has been the rapid growth of the non-state sector. This consists of four broad types of business entities: township and village enterprises (TVEs); urban collectives; private and individual enterprises; and joint ventures and wholly foreign-owned enterprises, which together are called foreign funded enterprises (FFEs). The sector has attained major outcomes in terms of output, employment, and export growth as well as in technology upgrading, profitability and gains in total factor productivity. By 1998 the non-state sector produced 72 per cent of the gross value of industry output, which compared with 24 per cent in 1980 and 45 per cent in 1990 (State Statistical Bureau, *China Statistical Yearbook* 1999).[1] The industrial output share of SOEs and urban collectives has dropped, while that of the more dynamic TVEs and local private and foreign enterprises has grown rapidly. Indeed the highest growth rates during the 1990s have been recorded by the privately owned enterprises and FFEs. A similarly radical shift has occurred in industrial employment patterns. While in 1980 SOEs employed more people than all other ownership forms of industrial enterprises combined,[2] by the late 1990s the non-state sector's contribution had increased substantially, to 43 per cent of the urban population, and the TVEs had become the single largest source of employment for industrial workers. TVE employment, overall, more than quadrupled between 1980 and 1996.[3]

The non-state sector dominates light industry and has generated about three-quarters of total export growth since 1978. It also produces over 80 per cent of industrial output in the coastal provinces. In fact the pre-eminence of the non-state sector in these provinces is one of the main sources of dynamism of the coastal region. In the past the non-state sector confronted discriminatory tax and other policies, and, until recent developments in the late 1990s,[4] still had some concerns regarding security of property rights. Difficulties remain in accessing bank finance, upgrading technology, obtaining access to skilled labour and management personnel, dealing with government interference in the management of some enterprises, and securing product transport and distribution. However, legal and regulatory reforms and political developments in the 1990s have greatly improved the position of non-state sector firms, contributing to the sector's dramatic growth.

The dynamism of the industrial sector during the latter half of the 1980s was primarily provided by the TVEs. Their output increased by 25 per cent a year from the mid-1980s to the mid-1990s, resulting in their share of GDP increasing from 13 per cent in 1985 to over 30 per cent by the mid-1990s (World Bank 1996, p. 51). During the period from 1980 to 1995 they created over 100 million new rural jobs. A comparison of their performance with that of the SOEs is also remarkable. Although the capital–output ratio in collective industry, of which the TVEs are a crucial component, in China is only 25 per cent of that in the state sector, labour productivity (output per capita) is close to 80 per cent of that in state enterprises and rising at more than 10 per cent a year (World Bank 1996, p. 51). Total factor productivity in TVEs was also considerably higher than in the state sector, growing at 5 per cent a year, more than twice the rate in state enterprises (World Bank 1996, p. 51). Since 1996, however, the major momentum for growth has increasingly shifted towards the private sector.[5]

During the period of economic reform the non-state sector has made major strides. A small proportion of the labour force in 1980, some 6 per cent, was employed by urban collectively owned factories at the beginning of the reform program. Only a negligible percentage of people were engaged in self-employed business, such as bicycle and shoe repairs.[6] In 1980 the state sector employed 19 per cent of the working population, while the non-state sector, including agriculture, accounted for the remaining 81 per cent. By 1998, in the urban sector, the contribution of the non-state sector to employment stood at 43 per cent. Hence the state sector still dominates in the towns and cities. In the rural area private and township enterprises developed into a major source of employment, contributing nearly 34 per cent of total rural employment in 1998, with the remainder working in agriculture. The growth of non-state-owned businesses, plus the dissolution of the commune system in the rural sector, reduced the overall employment contribution of the state sector to 13 per cent by 1998. In addition to expanded employment in the non-state sector, this sector has also seen an expansion in its share of total fixed assets to 45 per cent by 1998 in comparison to the state's share of 55 per cent.

The performance of the non-state sector in manufacturing industries is most noteworthy. The share of the non-state sector in manufacturing increased from 25 per cent in 1980 to 72 per cent in 1998 in terms of total output, from 43 per cent in 1993 to 53 per cent in 1997 in terms of value added, from 34 per cent in 1986 to 43 per cent in 1998 in terms of employment, and from 28 per cent in 1993 to 37 per cent in 1997 in terms of total fixed assets (State Statistical Bureau, *China Statistical Yearbook* 1999). While the non-state sector has assumed an increasingly important role in the production of manufactured goods, SOEs are still major players. Contributing some 47 per cent of manufacturing value added in 1997. This higher share of SOEs in industrial value added than in output suggests that the non-state sector is composed of SMEs engaged in lower-value-added activities. SOEs dominate the more-capital-intensive industries, since the domestic private sector has insufficient access to financial resources to make the large-scale investment in capital-intensive industries. The underdeveloped banking sector, dominated by the state-owned banks, favours the SOEs, and therefore fails to channel resources to the most-productive sectors, the private and township enterprises, of the economy. This has contributed to the recent growth slowdown of the economy.

A similar pattern of ownership structure can be observed in the services industries as for the manufacturing industries. There has been increasing significance of the non-state sector in the smaller services industries, with the dominance of SOEs in key and more-capital-intensive services sectors. In catering, leasing, recreation, information and consulting, computer application, tourism and commercial brokerage, the non-state sector has started to play an important role alongside SOEs. In three of the largest services industries, hotel, construction and retail services, the non-state sector has also taken a considerable share. In the retail industry, SOEs accounted for only 21 per cent of retail sales of consumer goods in 1998. However, in other large services sectors, such as electricity, gas and water; transport and storage; post and telecommunications; and wholesale; SOEs dominate (see State Statistical Bureau, *China Statistical Yearbook* 1999). Such is also the case in the banking industry. About

85 per cent of the total assets of the banking sector are in the hands of the four large state-owned commercial banks and the three state policy banks. Another 13 per cent are joint stock banks with SOEs as major shareholders. Less than 2 per cent of banking sector assets are held by foreign invested banks and private individuals are not allowed to start a banking business (see Mai 2000).

3.3   TVE BACKGROUND

This section focuses upon the development of small rural manufacturing enterprises that have contained the embryonic source of entrepreneurialism in the Chinese economy. The success of these small rural enterprises provided the launching pad for the later development of private enterprises in both the rural and urban economies, as well as the major source of growth in the Chinese economy during the second half of the 1980s and early 1990s.

3.3.1   Background

The origins of the TVEs can be traced to the agricultural collectives, or communes, established at the time of the Great Leap Forward in 1958, and which were held responsible for establishing and promoting rural industry.[7] So-called 'commune- and brigade-run enterprises' were the outcome of this process. These remained in place until the end of the 1970s when the household contract responsibility system gradually replaced the people's commune system, and commune- and brigade-run enterprises began to enjoy greater autonomy. In this new environment they had an incentive to increase production, improve productivity, and develop new businesses. In addition, the central government implemented various policies encouraging their development such as loans on favourable terms, tax reduction or exemption, and technical assistance. All these measures laid the foundations for the further development of rural industries.

With the effective demise of the agricultural collectives by 1983 the responsibility for the commune- and brigade-run enterprises was transferred to local government industrial departments, which contributed start-up funds, appointed managers, and were ultimately involved in strategic decision making (see Naughton 1994). In 1984 commune- and brigade-run enterprises, of which there were approximately 1.4 million, were officially renamed as township and village enterprises (TVEs),[8] but it was decided that the label would also apply to individual rural enterprises and those based on farm cooperatives. This meant that the number of TVEs suddenly increased five-fold to about 6.1 million in 1984. Hence four types of ownership structures involving TVEs, as defined by a government document in 1984, existed: county- and township-run enterprises; village-run enterprises; farmers' cooperatives; and individual or family-run businesses.[9] The first two categories were owned collectively by townships (formerly communes) and villages (formerly brigades). The cooperatives were owned by households/farmers who pooled their resources together for production. The last category consisted of enterprises owned by individuals. Many of the first two types, that is county, township or village-run enterprises, followed on from the commune and brigade enterprises. The additional farmers' TVEs were mostly very small. Because of the family quota contract system, farmers produced an agricultural surplus and found themselves with some free time. They were encouraged and supported by the government to use this time to develop certain new businesses. Unlike SOEs, TVEs' finance, supplies, sales, production and personnel were not subject to state planning, however they became intimately linked with local government.

3.3.2   TVEs and Their Contribution to Promoting Rural Industrial Development

The impetus for the initial growth of the TVEs arose from the success of China's agricultural reforms of the late 1970s and early 1980s, which greatly expanded rural savings, freed millions of workers to seek non-farm employment and increased rural demand for consumer goods, as well as the decentralisation of fiscal revenue raising in the mid-1980s. The importance of the TVE form of industrial enterprise in the context of promoting rural industrial development in China has been due to the following features. First, the TVEs allowed rural communities to translate control over assets and resources into income, despite the absence of asset markets. The growth of product markets provided rural communities with the opportunity to realise value from locally controlled resources.

Second, TVEs provided a way to convert assets into income without solving the difficult problem of privatisation. The Chinese government then, and reconfirmed in 1993, was unwilling on ideological grounds to permit mass privatisation. The administrative difficulties involved with privatisation would have been immense due to the sheer size of China and the lack of administrative apparatus. The difficult problems associated with privatisation were probably insoluble in China during the 1980s. Hence the TVEs circumvented this difficulty while contributing importantly to competition and the opening up of markets.

Third, with well-functioning markets, urban firms would have purchased land and hired suburban labour. In the absence of such institutions TVEs represented an alternative solution. Urban SOEs could subcontract to TVEs, providing in the process technology and equipment, or rural governments could take the initiative in this regard themselves. Many TVEs grew up as complements to state-run industry, consequently the majority of TVE growth was concentrated in advanced periphery–urban regions. For example, in 1988, in the three provinces of Jiangsu, Zhejiang and Shandong, producing half of all TVE output, linkages with urban firms were central to TVE growth.

Finally, TVEs facilitated access to capital on the part of start-up firms. In China, local government ownership played a key role in the process of financial intermediation. Local governments could better assess the risks of start-up businesses under their control, and were diversified and able to act as guarantors of loans to individual TVEs. By underwriting a portion of the risk of entry, local governments enabled start-up firms to enter production with a larger size, starting with some mechanisation, and exploiting economies of scale. With local governments playing an important role in the flow of capital to rural enterprises, such firms were able to take advantage of China's relatively abundant household savings. In return the profitable opportunities and reasonable risk levels in the TVE sector kept real returns high and contributed to the maintenance of high savings rates.

3.3.3   TVEs and Local Government

Township and village leaders are typically appointed from above by county administrators, who in turn designate the managers of TVEs. They in effect possess all the key components of property rights: control of residual income; the right to dispose of assets; the right to appoint and dismiss managers; and assume direct control if necessary. Local residents possess no 'right of membership' in the TVEs, nor do TVE workers possess any rights to participate in TVE management. Township and village officials' compensation is determined by a 'managerial contract' with explicit success indicators covering economic and social objectives. TVE output and sales value, profits and taxes enter into the compensation schedule, as well as family planning, maintenance of public order and education. However, there are strong pressures to stress profits since the township or village as a unit is subject to a fairly strong hard budget constraint. The successful township official maximises his/her own career prospects by producing economic growth during his/her term as a community leader, and this is likely to crucially depend upon maximising net revenue from the TVEs. Managers of TVEs not performing in a satisfactory fashion in accordance with such criteria can be dismissed. Without doubt, local governments viewed the TVEs as an important potential source of revenue for local budgets (Zweig 1991; Oi 1992, 1995).

The role of China's TVEs is unique in the context of an economy in transition. In no other such economy has public ownership played such a dynamic role. However, the collective ownership form, which TVEs are classified as being, does not have a precise definition in the country, leading to uncertainty about ultimate ownership rights. The literature would suggest that public ownership combined with vague ownership rights would present a recipe for economic disaster (Weitzman and Xu 1994). However, the performance of the TVEs in terms of output growth, employment creation, profit rate and growth of total factor productivity (TFP), indicates to the contrary that the TVEs have accomplished a good record in comparison to its private counterparts and much better than that of the SOEs (Svejnar 1990; Pitt and Putterman 1992). Under a collective ownership, with an unclear delineation of property rights, the success of TVEs therefore seems to pose a paradox for the standard property rights theory, which states that a well-defined private property rights system is a precondition for eliminating disincentive and free-rider problems as well as other opportunistic behaviour (see Demsetz 1967; Alchian and Demsetz 1972; Furubotn and Pejovich 1974; and Cheung 1982). Weitzman and Xu (1994) attempt to reconcile this by arguing that the success of the TVEs has arisen from their internal institutional form, which facilitates cooperation through implicit contracts among community members.

Naughton (1994) argues, on the other hand, that the success of the TVEs was largely due to a set of external conditions to which they were an effective adaptation. They were a response to a distinctive feature of the Chinese transition process that saw the early development of product markets, without well-developed markets for factors of production and assets. The latter in fact only developing gradually, such that even in the 1990s it was still at a very early stage of development. Naughton therefore argues that the TVEs were a flexible and effective but basically ordinary adaptation to this environment. Such a view would suggest that TVEs may not represent an enduring organisational form, and that as underlying economic conditions change, rural industry will lose ground to large domestic firms, enterprise groups, and joint-venture companies during the course of the 1990s and beyond. Such a difficulty would be compounded by foreign competition arising from China's membership of the WTO.

However, although predominantly owned by local government, many TVEs were effectively privately operated, and the proportion of true collectives to privately owned TVEs was about equal by the late 1990s. Many of the TVEs became involved in joint ventures with SOEs and foreign companies and a high proportion incorporated a complex network of affiliations and alliances involving scientists, engineers, academics and business entrepreneurs. This enabled them to gain access to technology and to become competitive. These evolving alliances will be essential to the sustainability of the TVE form of enterprise, and are discussed further below.

3.4   TVES' PERFORMANCE AND CONTRIBUTION TO THE ECONOMY

Greater autonomy, financial support, freedom from bureaucracy and entrepreneurial drive resulted in a stunning rate of growth for the TVEs during the period of economic reform, which contributed significantly to the rapid growth of the Chinese economy. The TVEs made major progress on a number of fronts including that of output, employment, export growth, as well as improvements in efficiency as measured by both labour productivity and total factor productivity, an upgrading of technology, and sustained profitability.

3.4.1   Output

Table 3.1 shows the output value, number of establishments and employment level of the TVEs during the period of economic reform. The output value of TVEs increased from 49.3 to 6 891.5 billion yuan over the period from 1978 to 1995. In line with this rapid expansion in output, TVE numbers also increased rapidly from over 1.5 million in 1978 to 22 million by 1995, almost 3 million less than for 1994, declining to 20 million by 1998. By the mid-1990s, TVEs accounted for 25.5 per cent of GDP and over 30 per cent of gross industrial output, or close to 40 per cent if urban collectives are included (Table 3.2), which compares with a figure of 22 per cent in 1978. In conjunction with these developments the SOE share of industrial production fell steadily during the period of reform, from 78 per cent in 1978 to less than 30 per cent by 1998 (see Table 3.2). There has also been a rapid expansion in the contribution of privately owned and foreign funded enterprises, whose joint share of industrial

Table 3.1
Basic Statistics of China's TVEs, 1978–98

Year	Number of enterprises (million)	Workers employed (million)	Gross output value (billion yuan)
1978	1.52	28.27	49.3
1980	1.43	30.00	65.7
1984	6.07	52.08	171.0
1985	12.23	69.79	272.8
1986	15.15	79.37	345.1
1987	17.50	88.05	476.4
1988	18.88	95.45	649.6
1989	18.68	93.66	742.8
1990	18.50	92.65	846.2
1991	19.09	96.09	1 162.2
1992	20.79	105.81	1 797.5
1993	24.53	123.45	3 154.1
1994	24.95	120.18	4 258.9
1995	22.03	128.62	6 891.5
1996	–	135.08	–
1997	20.15	130.50	–
1998	20.04	125.37	–

Sources: State Statistical Bureau, *China Statistical Yearbook*, 1996, Tables 11-29, 11-30, 11-31, pp. 387–9; State Statistical Bureau, *China Statistical Yearbook*, 1999.

Table 3.2
Gross Industrial Output by Business Type, 1990–98 (million yuan)

Year	1990	1991	1992	1993	1994	1995	1996	1997	1998
Total	23 924	26 625	34 599	48 402	70 176	91 894	99 595	113 733	119 048
SOEs	13 064	14 955	17 824	22 725	26 201	31 220	36 173	35 968	33 621
Per cent	54.6	56.1	51.5	47.0	37.3	34.0	36.3	31.6	28.2
Collectives	8 523	8 783	12 135	16 464	26 472	33 623	39 232	43 347	45 730
Per cent	35.6	33.0	35.1	34.0	37.7	36.6	39.4	38.1	38.4
Individual-owned enterprises[a]	1 290	1 287	2 006	3 861	7 082	11 821	15 420	20 376	20 372
Per cent	5.4	4.8	5.8	8.0	10.1	12.9	15.5	17.9	17.1
Other[b]	1 047	1 600	2 634	5 352	10 421	15 231	16 582	20 982	27 270
Per cent	4.4	6.0	7.6	11.1	14.8	16.6	16.6	18.4	22.9

Notes:
a   In both the urban and rural areas.
b   Mainly FFEs.

Source: State Statistical Bureau, *Chinese Statistical Yearbook*, 1999, Table 13.

production increased from being negligible in 1978 to over 25 per cent by the mid-1990s. The latter represents a rise almost as spectacular as that of the TVEs themselves, and has important implications for the future evolution of the TVEs in terms of their organisational as well as ownership form. Although growth of the TVEs continued apace during the 1990s (see Table 3.1), developments during the latter half of the 1990s indicated a slowdown in their growth. The reasons for this are discussed in more detail below.

3.4.2   Employment

In terms of employment creation the contribution of TVEs to the rural economy has been truly spectacular. They employed some 28.3 million workers in 1978, rising to a peak of 135 million by 1996 (see Table 3.1). This made a major contribution to the employment of surplus labour in rural China, in a cost-efficient way, as well as raising rural incomes. These are two essential tasks in the development of China's rural economy. Table 3.3 indicates that the TVEs are the largest employers of industrial labour. Indeed over the 1978–96 period they provided an additional 100 million jobs in the rural sector.

While the output growth of TVEs has remained at a high rate concern has, more recently, arisen from the fact that expanded TVE employment has increased at a much slower rate (see Table 3.4). For example, the net output of TVEs increased by

Table 3.3
Employees by Business Type ('000 people)

Year	SOEs	Urban collectives	FFEs	TVEs	Private[a]	Individ-ual[b]
1980	80 190	24 250	–	30 000	–	810
1985	89 900	33 240	60	69 790	–	4 500
1990	103 460	35 490	620	92 650	1 700	21 050
1995	112 610	31 470	2 410	128 620	9 560	46 140
1998	90 580	19 630	2 930	125 370	17 100	61 140

Notes:
a   Urban and rural sectors.
b   Self-employed in the urban and rural sectors.

Source: State Statistical Bureau, *China Statistical Yearbook*, 1999, Table 5.5, pp. 136–7.

Table 3.4
Employment Growth by Business Type 1990–98 (per cent)

Year	SOEs	Urban collectives	FFEs	TVEs	Private[a]	Individ-ual[b]
1990	2.4	1.4	50.0	−1.1	na	na
1991	3.0	3.3	66.7	3.7	11.8	10.0
1992	2.2	−0.3	40.0	10.6	21.1	6.9
1993	0.3	−6.3	−7.1	6.8	65.2	19.0
1994	2.7	−2.9	53.8	−2.7	71.1	28.6
1995	0.4	−4.3	20.0	7.0	47.7	22.0
1996	-0.2	−4.1	16.7	5.1	21.9	8.9
1997	−1.8	−4.6	7.1	−3.4	15.4	8.4
1998	−17.9	−32.6	−3.1	−3.9	26.7	12.5

Notes:
a   Urban and rural sectors.
b   Self employed in the urban and rural sectors.

Source: State Statistical Bureau, *China Statistical Yearbook*, 1999, Table 5.5, pp. 136–7.

125 per cent at fixed prices from 1991 to 1995 but employment expanded by only 27 per cent. There is a general concern by the authorities that the TVEs alone may not be able to expand sufficiently to absorb unemployed labour in both the rural and urban economies. Hence the increasing importance of the private sector is recognised in this regard. As Table 3.4 indicates, the major source of employment growth has come from the private sector. The major shedding of jobs has occurred in the state sector and from the urban collectives.

3.4.3 Exports

Until 1984 exports from TVEs were negligible, but starting from 1985 they increased rapidly. In 1986 TVEs' exports of US$5 billion accounted for one-sixth of China's total exports. In the same year about 20 000 TVEs specialised in production for export, 2 400 TVEs were involved in equity and cooperative joint ventures, and about 10 000 were engaged in compensation trade and production according to clients' requirements or samples. In 1987 China's new policy of accelerating the economic development of coastal regions gave 14 cities the status of coastal open cities, with extra freedoms and tax breaks for foreign trade and investment and gave a further impetus to the development of TVEs. In this year TVEs were allowed to participate directly in international trade, rather than just indirectly as subcontractors to state trading companies and SOEs, and the result was a dramatic increase in TVE exports (Sachs and Woo 1997). From the second half of 1988 to 1991 both central and local governments put great emphasis on the development of export-oriented businesses to acquire capital, technology and raw materials from Western companies and international markets. Although during the same period the central government was tightening money supply and controlling investment in domestic markets, export-oriented TVEs began to take off. They succeeded because of their operating flexibility and customer-oriented approach. The position of TVEs in China's foreign trade became increasingly important thereafter (see Table 3.5). From 1987 through 1992 TVEs' exports and imports grew by an average of 60 per cent per year. Their exports of 468 billion yuan (US$20 billion) in 1992 accounted for a quarter of China's total exports (US$85 billion). By the mid-1990s about 80 000 TVEs were engaged in export-oriented production, accounting for over 30 per cent of China's total exports and over 25 per cent of China's GDP. The share of overall exports accounted for by TVEs increased from 9.2 per cent in 1986 to more than 40 per cent, at its peak, in 1996.

3.4.4 Profitability

Table 3.6 compares the profit rates between TVEs and state-owned industrial enterprises (SOIEs) during the period of economic reform. This suggests that for most of the years from 1978 to 1994 the pre-tax and after-tax profit rates of the TVEs have been higher than those of the SOIEs, except for the years from 1986 to 1989. However, to obtain a more accurate picture of their respective performances, the

Table 3.5
Share of TVEs in Total Exports

Year	Total exports billion yuan	TVEs' exports % of total exports	Total exports % of GDP
1987	147	10.9	12
1988	177	15.3	13
1989	196	18.9	12
1990	299	16.4	17
1991	383	17.5	19
1992	468	25.4	19
1993	529	44.4	17
1994	1 042	32.6	23

Source: Sachs and Woo (1997, Table 5).

profit rates of the SOIEs must be discounted by the subsidies provided by the central government. These budget subsidies increased from 11.7 billion yuan in 1978 to 36.6 billion yuan in 1994, and for most of the years this accounted for a share of more than 10 per cent of total government revenue. Therefore if the profit rates of the SOIEs recorded in Table 3.6 are discounted by this factor, their performance has lagged considerably further behind that of the TVEs which operate in the absence of government subsidy.

3.4.5   Upgrading of Technology

During the period from 1991 to 1995, the capital stock of TVEs increased by 142 per cent, and was the primary factor behind the rapid growth in TVE output during this period. This expansion of capital intensity of TVE production is confirmed from Table 3.7, which clearly indicates an upgrading of the technology employed by TVEs. The vast majority of the funds for which came from bank loans and retained earnings, with the latter becoming of increasing significance during the period of the 1990s (see Table 3.8). While this is of benefit to some TVEs, as they move to increasingly higher-value products, it does present a strange paradox in a labour surplus economy, and explains the slowdown in labour absorption in rural China as previously indicated. Why has labour been substituted for capital in this way? Recent research (see Liu 1997) suggests that in the coastal provinces the reason for this is that most of the surplus labour has already been absorbed, and that further production is being achieved by increasing relatively cheap capital for increasingly costly labour. In the poorer inland provinces with surplus labour, the marginal productivity of labour is already low, and hence expanded production could come about more easily through an

Table 3.6
Profit Rates of TVEs and SOIEs, 1978–94 (%)

Year	TVE		SOIE	
	Pre-tax	After-tax	Pre-tax	After-tax
1978	39.8	31.8	24.2	15.5
1979	35.4	29.1	24.8	16.1
1980	32.5	26.7	24.8	16.0
1981	29.1	22.3	23.8	15.0
1982	28.0	20.2	23.4	14.4
1983	27.8	18.5	23.2	14.4
1984	24.6	15.2	24.2	14.9
1985	23.7	14.5	23.8	13.2
1986	19.7	10.6	20.7	10.6
1987	17.0	9.0	20.3	10.6
1988	17.9	9.3	20.6	10.4
1989	15.2	7.1	17.2	7.2
1990	13.0	5.9	12.4	3.2
1991	12.7	5.8	11.8	2.9
1992	14.3	4.8	9.7	2.7
1993	19.0	11.6	9.7	3.2
1994	14.8	9.0	9.8	2.8

Note: Profit Rate = Pre- or After-tax Profit/(Fixed Capital + Working Capital).

Source: State Statistical Bureau, *China Statistical Yearbook* (1992: pp. 391, 431; 1993: pp. 436–7; 1994: pp. 366: 1995: pp. 403–406).

expansion of capital rather than labour. This, Liu concludes, has important policy implications for labour migration and training, and for the allocation of capital, to improve labour absorption in rural China across its provinces. Labour should be encouraged to move to the coastal provinces, and capital to the poorer inland provinces.

3.4.6   Efficiency

Strong empirical evidence exists supporting the proposition that TVEs have been more efficient than SOEs. For example, Weitzman and Xu (1994) compared the growth rates of output, capital, labour and total factor productivity (TFP) of the SOIEs and the TVEs from 1979 to 1991. They found that the growth rates associated with the TVEs was much higher than that of the SOIEs. It is particularly evident for the growth of TFP, which grew three times faster for the TVEs in comparison to that of the SOIEs. Similar results were derived by Jefferson and Rawski (1994), who found that

Table 3.7
Capital Intensity of TVEs and SOEs

Year	TVEs' capital to labour ratio	SOEs' capital to labour ratio
1985	1 362.8	10 434.6
1986	1 636.5	11 488.7
1987	2 034.2	12 830.2
1988	2 522.5	14 283.3
1989	3 148.6	16 459.6
1990	3 633.6	18 529.9
1991	4 110.1	21 259.4
1992	5 022.3	24 292.6
1993	6 532.9	29 571.9
1994	8 808.9	35 867.1
1995	11 780.9	39 741.0
1985–95 % p.a. (nominal)	24.1	14.3
1985–95 % p.a. (deflated)	12.2	2.4

Source: TVE *Statistical Yearbook* (1995 and previous years).

the collective form of enterprise performed better than that of the state sector both in terms of labour productivity and more importantly in terms of TFP. These results reflect the fact that TVEs achieved considerable technological progress as previously mentioned, and particularly relative to both the SOIEs and collective industries in urban areas.

The reasons behind the phenomenal success of the TVEs during the period of the late 1980s and early 1990s, as well as outstanding problems, are discussed in the following section.

3.5   REASONS FOR THE SUCCESS OF THE TVES

A number of reasons have been advanced in the literature (see, for example, World Bank 1996, p. 51; Harvie and Turpin 1997; Kwong 1997; Sachs and Woo 1997, p. 39) to explain the phenomenal growth and impressive efficiency record of TVEs relative to that of the SOEs in particular. The major ones include the following:

- *Small, flexible and market driven*. From the outset TVEs had to rely on markets for sourcing supplies and selling products. Many TVEs positioned their business in areas where there were severe shortages, or where SOEs were

Table 3.8
Sources of Enterprises' Investment Finance, 1980–93

	SOEs	Urban collectives	TVEs	Joint ventures	WFOEs*
Plan allocation					
1980–84	12	0	0	0	0
1985–89	9	0	0	0	0
1990–93	12	0	0	0	0
Bank loans					
1980–84	82	80	na	25	na
1985–89	72	67	81	24	37
1990–93	76	78	53	47	27
Retained earnings					
1980–84	6	20	na	75	na
1985–89	18	33	19	74	63
1990–93	9	22	47	47	73
Share/bond issues					
1980–84	0	0	na	0	na
1985–89	1	0	0	0	0
1990–93	3	0	0	6	0

Note: * = Wholly foreign owned enterprises.

Source: Perkins and Raiser (1994, Table 12) from a survey of 300 coastal province enterprises.

weak. Most were small and autonomous compared with SOEs, and thus had flexibility to respond to market changes quickly. Their management was also more market oriented.

- *Appropriate production technology.* The TVEs faced cheap labour and expensive capital and natural resources, causing them to choose appropriate production technologies. As the reform process progressed and prices were gradually liberalised to reflect relative scarcity values, the SOEs found themselves at a competitive disadvantage because of inappropriate capital and resource-intensive technologies.

- *Distortions, market opportunities and rural saving.* The TVEs were highly profitable because of the distortions carried over from the formerly planned system. At the beginning of the reform process in 1978, the average rate of profit on TVE capital was 32 per cent.[10] Most of the new TVEs were in manufacturing where initial state price controls kept profitability high so that the state could obtain high revenues from the SOEs. In addition, due to past biases in the planned system against light industry and services, the TVEs could enter market niches for which the SOEs had either failed to produce or failed to innovate and improve quality control. The resulting high profits achieved by TVEs attracted further investment and rapid growth. This was further strengthened by high rural saving and demand following the agricultural reforms of 1978, in conjunction with the limited scope for emigration from rural areas.

- *Low taxation.* Taxes on TVEs were low, requiring them to pay only 6 per cent of profits as tax in 1980, climbing to 20 per cent after 1985. Such low tax rates in China were primarily due to a policy-driven desire to foster rural industrialisation.

- *Decision making.* Information channels between the TVE managers and local government authorities tended to be both shorter and simpler compared to those for the SOEs, encouraging greater efficiency. Further, this greater flexibility and autonomy in management has meant that inter-firm alliances and technological alliances with universities and research institutes has produced a 'networked' approach to innovation and industrial production. Such institutional innovations could be implemented without the approval of the central government. Recent locally initiated transformation of TVEs into 'shareholding cooperatives' is a case in point. This feature has enabled the TVEs to move closer to best international practices in corporate governance.

- *Decentralisation plus financial discipline.* In 1984 a decentralisation of fiscal power took place in China which allowed lower levels of government to retain locally generated revenues, creating a strong incentive for the development of local industry. A non-performing TVE in this system would become a drain on limited resources. Local government officials and TVE managers, therefore, had to focus more upon financial objectives, profit plus local tax revenues, since local governments lacked the borrowing capacity of higher levels of government, and TVEs could not automatically turn to banks for a bailout. Hence the TVE enterprises under their jurisdiction faced harder budget constraints than SOEs, and were more likely to fall into bankruptcy if persistent losses were made. This focused upon the need for TVEs to be efficient, competitive and profitable in a period of a rapid opening up of markets. Meanwhile managers of SOEs, having responsibility for housing and other social services as well as industrial operations, faced a more complex set of objectives and state obligations.

- *Kinship and implicit property rights.* A number of researchers have suggested that, despite the absence of well-defined property rights, the demographic stability of China's rural communities promoted the emergence of 'invisible institutions' to provide a 'moral framework for rights' or a 'cooperative culture' that served to reduce problems of shirking and monitoring found in most public enterprises (see Byrd and Lin 1990; Yusuf 1993a, 1993b; and Weitzman and Xu 1994). The incentives facing TVEs are similar to those facing private firms in that residual profits are dispersed among a small group, consisting of a stable local community and in particular its local government and TVE manager. Studies have shown the importance of TVE profits in local government budgets and the close links between local economic performance and the status, income and career prospects of local officials.

- *Links with the state enterprise sector.* The state sector also represented an important, and not sufficiently recognised, component in the successful development of TVEs and other non-state firms. The TVEs and collectives in general relied on the state sector as a source of capital, materials, equipment, specialised personnel, technology, subcontracting arrangements and sales revenue. For example, in southern Jiangsu province more than two-thirds of TVEs established various forms of economic and technical cooperation arrangements with industrial enterprises, research units, and higher educational institutions in larger cities. Local government officials attempting to develop industry in poor localities are encouraged to pursue joint operations with scientific research organisations or large and medium-scale state enterprises.

- *Market entry and competition.* The continual reduction of entry barriers associated with China's industrial reform created a domestic product cycle in which new products, materials and processes introduced by innovative state firms were adopted by TVEs and other non-state enterprises.[11] They could then use their cost advantages to erode state sector profits and force state industry toward fresh innovations. In addition there was intense competition for investment, including that for foreign investment, among communities with TVEs. The ability to attract such investment is strongly influenced by the reputation of the TVEs, as well as local economic performance. TVEs themselves are being increasingly subject to competition from the even more dynamic but smaller private and foreign invested sectors. An issue discussed further in a later section of this chapter.

- *Improvement in human resources, innovation and quality.* Many TVEs put special emphasis on human resources, innovation and product quality. With their autonomous and flexible systems it is their usual practice to recruit highly competent engineers and technicians from SOEs, to pay them attractive salaries and actively pursue innovation. At the beginning of the 1980s they mainly targeted and sought retired technicians and engineers from urban areas. Since the mid-1980s their attention shifted to scientists and technicians working in research institutes and SOEs, who were discontented with their working conditions. More recently they have been competing with large and medium-sized SOEs for talented staff and trying to attract foreign experts. TVEs maintain close links with research institutes. About 60 per cent of inventions and innovations developed by China's scientific and technological institutions have been put into production by TVEs.

- *International orientation.* Many TVEs, particularly those in coastal provinces, actively pursued cooperation and joint ventures with SOEs, with other TVEs, and with foreign companies. Joint ventures between TVEs and foreign companies having grown rapidly during the 1990s. By developing joint ventures and subcontracts with foreign firms, TVEs gradually upgraded their technology, became involved in foreign direct investment (FDI), and expanded the quality of their produce for overseas markets.

- *Lower cost structure.* TVEs possessed lower cost structures than SOEs, and paid less tax. Because their managers historically had to rely on retained earnings and loans instead of government grants, they constantly pressured local authorities to give them tax breaks. Wages in rural areas are also significantly lower than in cities where most SOEs are found. They do not have thousands of retirees for whom they are liable for pension payments, they do not have to offer welfare benefits like healthcare and social security insurance to their workforce, and they do not have to provide housing for their workers. TVE workers work long hours, and the quality of their production has improved. Where simple technology is required this represents a big advantage, particularly in light industries like textiles and electrical appliances,

Despite these favourable characteristics, many TVEs still suffer from a number of difficulties, including the following:

- *Limited funds and supplies.* Although the Chinese government implemented favourable loan and taxation policies to support TVEs, it did not directly invest in TVEs as it did with SOEs. The growth of TVE investment to sustain their rapid development during the latter half of the 1980s depended primarily upon bank loans, and increasingly upon retained earnings during the early part of the 1990s (Table 3.8). Another difference between TVEs and SOEs is that the former never benefited from supplies, at low cost, through the central plan.

- *Obsolete technology.* Many TVEs are still using obsolete technology, partly because their businesses are small and newly established and partly because their managers and employees have only recently stopped working on the land. In fact, some worked part time as employees and part time as farmers. Hence, they are incapable of pursuing R&D activities and developing new products. Apart from some TVEs in the southern coastal provinces, most relied on mechanical or semi-mechanical technology and quite a few on manual work. Many are too small to invest in research and development (R&D) and keep up with the latest technology, making them vulnerable to competition from financially stronger foreign invested ventures.

* *Low level of employees' education.* One of the major problems in TVEs is the employees' very low level of education. In the early 1990s only about 200 000 employees in TVEs had a degree or higher education, and only 420 000 held a medium level technical qualification. These two figures come to less than 1 per cent of their employees.

* *Profitability not clear.* Many foreign investors partnering TVEs sometimes discovered that much of their profitability was based purely on preferential tax policies.

* *Vague property rights.* Growing conflicts of interest may arise from their historically vague ownership status. Because employees theoretically own everything collectively and nothing individually, they often act more like employees than owners seeking to increase their salaries rather than cut costs and maximise company profit. Vague ownership rights and reliance on special privileges have clouded their future. In response to this, the authorities passed the Law of Township and Village Owned Enterprises in October 1996 with the objective of clarifying TVE property rights.

3.6 EVOLVING BUSINESS ALLIANCES, ORGANISATIONAL AND OWNERSHIP CHANGE AMONG TVES

For the TVEs to maintain their remarkable performance they will be required to evolve into enterprises capable of being competitive within the context of China's increasingly market-oriented economy. This will require making further advances in a number of key areas, including: management control; clarification of property rights; expanding access to finance; gaining access to developments in science and technology; enhancing the human capital of its employees and managers; ensuring access to input supply; and improving the efficiency of their distribution and marketing systems. Those TVEs unable to make such advances are unlikely to survive within the new economic environment rapidly evolving in China. This has been given further impetus with China's membership of the WTO. Successful TVEs are likely to be those able to develop into new organisational forms based upon business alliances with other enterprises, involving cooperation and joint ventures between TVEs, SOEs, private domestic and foreign enterprises, and also with research institutes and universities in order to gain access to advances in science and technology. This will enable them to compete in both domestic and international markets, as well as to invest overseas.

The gap between the developed coastal and backward inland regions is likely to widen since TVEs in the coastal region attract and introduce far more FDI than inland regions. This process will encourage more and more TVEs to turn to exports, including processing and manufacturing based on clients' samples and specifications, processing clients' raw materials, and direct export. Joint ventures between TVEs and foreign firms will increase. TVEs in the coastal region will gradually develop their own R&D capacity. More and more capable technicians will be attracted to TVEs in the coastal region, where they enjoy a higher living standard than inland areas and have autonomy and funds to pursue research. Additionally, the intensification of competition, particularly from the rapidly developing private sector and foreign enterprises, is likely to result in the traditional collective ownership structure of the TVEs no longer being viable. Some of these key issues are now discussed.

3.6.1   Evolving Business Alliances and Partnerships Involving TVEs

For foreign firms, TVEs can be appropriate business partners or subcontractors to pursue a global sourcing strategy and to penetrate China's domestic market. This process can also bring major benefits to the TVEs in the form of access to finance, technology, managerial expertise and international markets. The development of joint ventures with TVEs, in comparison with joint ventures involving SOEs, can bring numerous benefits to foreign companies:

- TVEs can provide greater commercial focus and more flexibility in comparison with SOEs, and hence they can respond rapidly to changing market circumstances;

- they are more sensitive to market signals and are more conscious of the need for efficiency;

- joint ventures with ailing SOEs, even in more dynamic provinces, may be unprofitable, as many of the better ones already have business links with foreign companies. Foreign companies may find that those available have poor potential. Such SOE joint ventures may require excessive investment by foreign partners with long pay-back periods;

- TVEs operate much more independently from state bureaucracy. Such bureaucracy may wish to participate in SOE joint-venture hiring and pricing policies;

- there is a willingness of local party officials at the village level, who sometimes see themselves as patrons of TVEs, to help a TVE/foreign company joint venture with daily problem solving;

- TVEs have the ability to hire labour as needed without being required to hire unnecessary or unsuitable workers;

- in most cases TVEs face an absence of financial burdens, such as surplus labour, weak distribution systems, excessive factory space, obsolete equipment, high welfare benefit obligations to current and retired workers;

- many TVEs are now able to produce goods which are of an acceptable standard in international markets;

- TVEs are eager to develop partnerships with foreign enterprises;

- in many cases local governments encourage, support, and reward those TVEs which have developed cooperation or joint ventures with foreign firms;

- land and labour costs are lower for the TVEs than in urban areas. Salaries in TVEs can be 20–30 per cent lower than in the urban-based SOEs. Thus by developing a partnership with TVEs, foreign firms' products are able to achieve competitive cost advantages in China and in international markets. TVEs have also attained improvements in productivity relative to SOEs;

- the sense of pressure to make profits is felt more by TVE managers and employees than by those in SOEs, and thus hard work and greater entrepreneurship are often the norm.

For these reasons foreign companies wishing to have products manufactured to their own designs and specifications, and to source supplies/components, may find TVEs ideal partners. Products which require frequent changes in design and specifications, and whose product batches are relatively small, are particularly suitable for TVEs.

However, a large number of TVEs may not be suitable for the establishment of a business alliance with a foreign company, for a number of reasons:

- they may have limited financial, technological and human resources;

- they may be in locations away from major urban areas and without essential amenities. This is particularly the case for TVEs located in the poorer inland and western provinces;

- they may receive less support from senior political leaders in provincial or central governments, possibly leading to problems of resource allocation and utilities supply,

- there is the possibility of weaker legal protection for a TVE partner if the political climate of the non-state sector deteriorates. Membership of the WTO, however, significantly reduces such a likelihood in the country.

3.6.2 Technology

In order to maintain their competitiveness TVEs have not only been developing relationships with industrial partners but also R&D relationships with research institutes, universities and government agencies. As indicated previously a number of TVEs are rapidly upgrading their technology, relying heavily on retained earnings to do so. It is this horizontal connection between TVEs and science-based institutions that is likely to provide the organisational capabilities for their sustainable development. There appear to have been three important areas of reform that have contributed to these developments. First, state-driven economic reforms have contributed to an environment that has encouraged TVEs to move into new areas of industrial production and trading. Second, science policy reforms have steered technological alliances with public research institutions towards TVEs rather than towards SOEs. Third, reform at the local government level created an environment conducive to the formation of horizontal alliances among TVEs and other enterprises. As future reforms in the state-owned sector deepen, it is likely that the long-term survival of the TVE sector will rest even more on their capacity to build and maintain scientific and industrial organisational networks.

These cooperative arrangements between TVEs and other firms, as well as science-based institutions, have produced organisational alliances with the capability to compete successfully with the larger and more powerful SOEs. However a major issue is whether this development will also enable the TVEs to compete successfully with the rapidly developing and highly efficient private sector in the future, as well as from an opening up of the economy to foreign competitors. This may require a change in ownership structure from the collective to private form. This option has been given major impetus arising from decisions made at the 15th Communist Party Congress during September 1997, which encouraged an expansion of other ownership types including that of private ownership. The issue of privatisation has therefore clearly appeared on the agenda for China's small and medium sized urban SOEs, and is increasingly being applied to TVEs under rural local government control.

3.6.3   Privatisation

TVEs started their fast growth in 1984. Many of those that developed thereafter were effectively owned and operated by private individuals, but it was to their advantage for their businesses to be classified as a 'collective' rather than as a private enterprise. Growing official acceptance and recognition of the importance of the non-state sector for growth and economic development, including that of the private sector, has led to a reappraisal of the benefits of being a collective enterprise. In 1996, after the Law of Township and Village Owned Enterprises of the People's Republic of China was passed in October, many TVEs started to get rid of their 'red hats'[12] and became private. The TVE law legitimates TVEs, regardless of ownership, as a legal enterprise entity and an important component in the national economy. More importantly, the TVE law clearly stipulates that the property rights of private TVEs belong to their investors. It provides private TVEs equal treatment to that of collective TVEs in the legal protection of their property rights, their property, their managers and their autonomy in management. Ideological objections to private ownership have been further relaxed over the past few years, and this was formally sanctioned at the Party Congress in September of 1997. Many rural local governments have taken advantage of such a development by privatising their own TVEs. In 1997, private TVEs surpassed collective TVEs in terms of number of units, total number of employment and total value added, although collective TVEs still contributed more to industrial value added.

For many TVEs low-skilled labour, unsophisticated management, capital shortages, and inability to attract business partners and to engage in alliances with research institutes have made it difficult to upgrade quality, move into higher-value types of manufacturing, and increase their scale of production. At the same time, local government ownership can make it hard for company managers to make their own decisions. On the other hand, many managers of local government-owned TVEs are not held responsible for failures. During periods where profits are being made this may be acceptable, but during periods of declining profits and possible losses, as has occurred more recently, local governments are left with the debts, unsold inventories and workers who need jobs. This is one reason why some township and village governments began privatising their companies, selling them wholly or partially to private citizens consisting of former factory managers or outsiders. If such enterprises go bankrupt, thereafter, it then no longer becomes a problem for the local government. Shrinking tax receipts for local government has also been another motivation for privatisation. Without good TVE results, the local governments cannot collect enough tax revenue to build more roads, schools, houses and other community services.

Privatising TVEs, however, has become popular not just for loss-making TVEs. Increasingly local government officials appear to be convinced, and particularly in the richer coastal provinces where most of the successful TVEs are located, that private ownership is the appropriate form of ownership to ensure that organisational and structural developments, essential for sustained competitiveness, take place even for profitable TVEs. The ideological acceptance of private ownership in the late 1990s has paved the way for further privatisation of TVEs.

The issue of the survival of many TVEs in the near future when a large number of foreign enterprises compete in China's domestic market with advanced technology and management knowledge, and are free to choose their locations according to economic principles, is a critical problem facing the country. China's entry into the WTO will lead to employment opportunities in both the old and the newly establishing urban areas where the infrastructure is much better than the rural areas, where most of the TVEs are presently located. Then, there will be demand for a large amount of rural labour migration to these areas. The pressure for restructuring and the relocation of many TVEs will be inevitable for survival.

Finally, private TVEs will not only lead to the development of employment opportunities and greater efficiency in manufacturing industry, but can also promote the development of urban private enterprises. Domestic private enterprises are usually small in size due to capital constraints. If private TVEs can be treated equally with collective TVEs in capital financing, the enlargement of private TVEs would speed up the capital accumulation of private entities and promote the growth of the whole private sector. Many private TVEs have performed well after they got rid of their 'red hats'. By 1997, the TVEs produced 27 per cent of GDP and contributed 41 per cent to the gross domestic product in secondary, manufacturing, industry.

A diminishing role for the collective form of TVEs has been advanced by many analysts (see, for example, Naughton 1994; Putterman 1995; and Sachs and Woo 1997). The basis of which is that it would be better for China to move from the half-way house of collective ownership to the next step of real private ownership of small rural enterprises. Sachs and Woo (1997, p. 40) advocate expanded private ownership due to four basic problems with the TVEs. First, collective ownership invites political intervention by local government in the workings of local enterprises, resulting in inefficiency and inequity. Second, collective ownership results in a lack of wealth diversification. A community that puts its wealth only into a narrow range of enterprises runs the risk of losing everything – jobs and saving. Third, collective ownership limits the scale of operations of the enterprise. A TVE can grow as a result of new investments by the community, including reinvestment of profits or through bank loans. However, it is difficult to get outsiders to invest in a TVE since the property rights of the outside investors would not be well defined or protected. Fourth, collective ownership limits the market's ability to influence managerial control and behaviour. Bad managers may remain in control due to political contacts with local government. In a normal market setting an outside buyer could approach the owners of the business and make a takeover bid, replacing the existing manager. This is unlikely to occur with the collective ownership of TVEs.

In addition, recent developments have increased the pressure on TVEs to clarify their property rights. The rapid expansion of output by many TVEs in the coastal provinces of southern China has increased their dependence on labour migrants from the poorer inland provinces. The original inhabitants in these richer provinces wish to protect against new residents having an automatic share in the dividends of the collective-owned enterprises. Consequently, in some areas, collective TVEs have been converted into 'shareholding cooperatives' by corporatising the TVEs and dividing the shares among the existing residents. Since the government has not prevented such de-collectivisation of TVEs this has been taken as implicit approval, accelerating the conversion of many TVEs to shareholding cooperatives.

As discussed in the next section there have been significant developments since 1992, and particularly during the second half of the 1990s, that have legitimised and resulted in the protection of, and reduced discrimination against, private ownership. Consequently, many TVEs have taken off their red hats, feeling that there is no need to register as 'red hat', or collectively owned ventures, because the difference in preferential treatment between private and public units has been considerably narrowed. This has contributed to the rapid growth of the private sector, as discussed in the following section.

3.7 GROWTH OF CHINA'S PRIVATE SECTOR

3.7.1 Rapid Growth of Private Enterprises

The private sector in China was suppressed during the period of central planning, but re-emerged with the initiation of reforms in 1978.[13] The sector grew rapidly over the next 20 years and by 1998, including household agricultural production, accounted for approximately 50 per cent of GDP,[14] although there is no clear dividing line between genuinely private and collective enterprises. A more favourable attitude of the authorities towards private ownership in China contributed to growth in the number of registered private firms, employment in these firms and increased share in total GDP.

Individual private enterprises, in particular, developed rapidly during the 1980s. From 1981 to 1988, the gross industrial output value of the individual sector grew at an average annual growth rate of 87 per cent. The growth trend of formally registered private enterprises, including single industrial and commercial proprietor enterprises called *getihu*, can be seen from Table 3.9. The average growth rate of formally

Table 3.9
Growth Trend of Private and Other Categories of Enterprise in China, 1989–98 (average growth rate, %)

	Average	State	Collective	FDI	*Getihu*	Private[a]
Number of firms	na	5.37	0.27	34.40	8.48	33.27
Employment	2.64	−0.01	−0.06	22.55	13.60	29.76
Registered capital	na	12.89	11.56	36.94	27.64	63.97
Tax revenue	17.55	14.83	11.80	30.37[b]	60.79	73.15
Fixed capital investment[c]	24.20	21.60	28.20	11.73[d]	16.00	33.80
Gross value of output (industrial)	16.61	5.39	18.30	27.84[c]	32.95	51.85
Retail sales	13.20	5.32	4.64	na	22.35	57.24

Notes:
na – not available.
a   Private refers to formally registered private enterprises.
b   1994–97.
c   1990–98.
d   1994–98.

Source: Garnaut and Song (2000, p. 3).

registered private enterprises far exceeded that of both state and collective enterprises over 1989–98 in all measurements listed, most noticeably employment, registered capital, tax revenue, gross value of industrial output and retail sales. From the early 1990s many small and medium sized SOEs were taken over by, or merged with, private enterprises.

Most individual businesses are located in industrial retail sectors and in service industries. The fast development of individual enterprises provided an outlet of self-employment for people who could not get into the SOEs and the collectives, or who were not satisfied with their situation in the SOEs or the collectives. However, rural private enterprises have not been overshadowed by urban private enterprises. There appears to be a division of labour between the urban and the rural private sectors. The rural private sector concentrates upon the primary and the secondary sectors,[15] while the urban private sector is dominant in the tertiary sector.[16] Because both types are subject to capital constraints these individual enterprises tend to be small in size.

The success of the private sector in a regulatory environment overwhelmingly geared to the requirements of the state-owned enterprises is remarkable. The recent reform of the regulatory and institutional framework provides more beneficial conditions for the private sector, which is the most dynamic, and now the larger, part of the Chinese economy. This has the potential to provide new impetus for economic growth. In particular, the component of the collective sector that is in reality private will now grow rapidly, as the regulatory and ideological advantages of a real or nominal 'red hat' disappear. This will be beneficial to the economy overall as this sector is likely to use resources more effectively than the state sector.

3.7.2   Contribution of the Private Sector to the Economy

The growth of the private sector has played an important role in the development of the economy, particularly during the period of the 1990s, in a number of areas. Its contribution in terms of growth of employment, tax revenue, fixed capital investment, industrial output and retail sales for the 1989–98 period is summarised in Table 3.9. Its contribution to increased employment has enhanced labour productivity, by recruiting new workers into the non-farm economy as well as absorbing laid-off workers from reformed SOEs.[17] The private sector has increased competition in those sectors where it has been allowed to compete, as well as nurturing competition and initiating innovation. It has helped to channel an increasing part of investment into more efficient uses and hence increased the overall efficiency of the economy. In meeting the demands of the private sector a regulatory and institutional framework more compatible with a market system can be established, which will also assist in improving the performance of state-owned and collective enterprises. An expanding private sector can also accelerate growth with less risk to macroeconomic stability than the expansion of state-owned enterprises, since private firms are subject to a hard budget constraint.

Before 1985 the share of formally registered private enterprises in national industrial output was negligible, although its share of employment was already around 2 per cent of the national non-agricultural force in 1981. By 1997, the sector's share in national industrial employment reached more than 18 per cent. Its share of national industrial output rose from below 2 per cent in 1985 to 12.2 per cent in 1993 and 34.3 per cent in 1997. In absolute terms, formally registered private enterprises' industrial output has experienced substantial and rapid growth in the last 20 years to reach 3.8 trillion yuan in 1997. Employment expansion in the private industrial sector experienced a major downturn from 1989 to 1991,[18] but thereafter recovered rapidly (see Table 3.10). By 1998, the total number of workers employed in the private sector had reached 78.3 million.

The private sector's share in GDP, outside agriculture, reached 33 per cent in 1998, which was still smaller than the state sector's share of 37 per cent. If agriculture, a sector comprising mainly individual farmers, is regarded as mainly private, the share of the private sector rises to 50 per cent (Garnaut and Song 2000). The true private sector and true collectives together contribute a non-state sector share of 62 per cent in 1998. The fast growth of the private sector in the 1990s was mainly within the formally registered private firms, as distinct from non-incorporated enterprises. The disproportion between its performance share and resource shares is a major feature of China's private sector development in the 1990s.

3.7.3 Major Constraints

The extraordinary growth of the private sector occurred despite an initially highly unfavourable environment. In a country whose production and commercial activities have been dominated by large state-owned enterprises for decades, there is still much discrimination against smaller and private enterprises in areas such as business registration, taxation, financing and foreign trading rights. It therefore remains a big task to develop the regulatory framework to allow a wider and more direct participation by private firms in developing China's economy (Garnaut and Song 2000).

Among the most important areas where reform is required are: improving the operation of markets for goods, services and factors of production; strengthening the rule of law, specifically in relation to property and contract rights; streamlining and raising the efficiency of government; removal of rent-seeking behaviour by government in its dealings with business; and the development of fiscal and other measures by government to alleviate unfavourable income distribution effects that may be associated with sustained and rapid private sector development. Measures aimed at encouraging private sector development have been gradually introduced. Of these, the most important has been the recognition of the sector in the constitution and state policy at the March 1999 meeting of the National People's Congress. Within this context a large number of small and medium sized SOEs are currently being restructured based on market conditions in which private firms are allowed to play an important role.

State commercial banks have been asked to assist in the development of small firms, including private enterprises, by charging flexible interest rates, capable of being varied in response to market conditions including perceptions of risk on loans made to these firms. From the beginning of 1999, for the first time since 1957, a number of private enterprises were granted licences to conduct foreign trade on their own, and more sectors, including infrastructure and financial services, have been opened to foreign competition.

Private sector enterprises face a number of constraints which require urgent attention if they are to face a level playing field with state-owned and collective enterprises. These include the following: the imposition of arbitrary fees and taxes on private enterprises by local governments; unequal access to business finance particularly from state financial institutions; the absence of efficient and transparent bank lending systems to small and medium sized enterprises in general, and, more particularly, to private enterprises; a weak skill base at both the managerial and employee levels, and particularly that facing small and medium sized enterprises; weak and non-transparent accounting and auditing practices; insufficient support to private enterprises by different levels of government in registration, land use, finance, market entry and law enforcement; a weak legal and regulatory environment; weak markets particularly in the financial and labour markets; and the absence of a competitive environment in which all types of firms are competing on an equal footing.

3.8   POLICIES FOR FURTHER DEVELOPMENT OF THE PRIVATE SECTOR

If the private sector, and small businesses in particular, is to be further developed, a number of areas, therefore, require further urgent reform. These include: reform of the financial system; reforming the government tax and revenue system; enhancing the technical innovation system; improving legal protection of property rights; improving education and training; and opening up more sectors for private investment and competition.

3.8.1   Financial System

An uneven distribution of bank loans between the state and non-state sectors represents a major constraint on the further development of the non-state sector, particularly for small sized private enterprises. The result has also been an inefficient use of bank funds. In 1998, the non-state sector contributed 71 per cent of industrial gross output value but its share of total bank loans was only 30 per cent. Small private enterprises, in particular, find it difficult to get a bank loan. It may be that loans extended to small enterprises are perceived as being more risky than those to larger enterprises. This

Table 3.10
Employment in the Private Sector, 1990–98 (million)

Year	Urban		Rural		Total private sector[b]	% of total employment
	Private	Individual[a]	Private	Individual		
1990	0.6	6.1	1.1	14.9	22.7	4.0
1991	0.7	6.9	1.2	16.2	25.0	4.3
1992	1.0	7.4	1.3	17.3	26.7	4.5
1993	1.9	9.3	1.9	20.1	33.2	5.5
1994	3.3	12.3	3.2	25.5	44.3	6.6
1995	4.9	15.6	4.7	30.5	55.7	8.5
1996	6.2	17.1	5.5	33.1	61.9	9.0
1997	7.5	19.2	6.0	35.2	67.9	9.8
1998	9.7	22.6	7.4	38.2	78.3	11.2

Notes:
a Self-employed individuals.
b Urban and rural sectors
Source: State Statistical Bureau, *China Statistical Yearbook*, 1999, Table 5.5, pp. 136–7.

financial constraint on small private enterprises seriously restricts their development and growth and requires urgent attention from the authorities.

A number of policy changes will be required if these problems are to be overcome. First, a more even-handed treatment of state and non-state enterprises by the state banks is required. Second, there is also the need to develop non-state financial institutions that would more adequately serve the growth of the non-state sector. China's membership of the WTO will eventually offer opportunities for foreign banks based in China to engage in domestic currency lending, and this will have an important impact upon the further development of the private sector. Third, the current policy of zero risk lending by state banks, applied mainly to non-state enterprises, should be replaced by portfolio management. With this a bank branch or an employee would be evaluated by the profitability of the resources allocated to them in a certain period, not simply by whether one or two loans had been lost. They would not be evaluated differently according to whether the borrower was a state or a private enterprise. This outcome would be achieved naturally by requiring state banks to operate competitively and profitably within a rational system of prudential supervision, which systematically discounted non-performing assets independently of the identity of the borrower, and which required maintenance of minimum ratios of capital to assets, all within a transparent accounting framework.

To give incentives to banks to extend loans to small enterprises, to cover their perceived risk of losses, and to eliminate rent seeking behaviour, a flexible interest rate is needed. As the first step, controls on lending rates can be eased to allow banks to charge different rates according to different risks of loans. To finance small and medium sized enterprises, there is a need to develop new non-state financial institutions. A new policy should allow non-state financial institutions to grow, but under the supervision of the state. A total ban on all new financial institutions is inappropriate. Small business would also potentially benefit from the removal of current impediments to the provision of venture capital. Carefully designed loan guarantee funds or systems could usefully be used to resolve financing problems facing private enterprise at the moment. From this perspective, it seems that firm-managed guarantee funds may be a solution to small and medium firms' financing problems (Garnaut and Song 2000).

3.8.2   Government Taxation and Revenue System

Although the tax burden on private enterprises is relatively low compared with other countries, there are considerable irregular fees, fines and involuntary 'donations' collected by various government departments at the different administrative levels. In addition, the actual tax burden among firms is uneven. Small firms have been known to pay a higher proportion of their sales revenue in the form of taxation. This reflects the fact that large firms have more opportunity for tax privileges.

The current tax system discourages investment and technical innovation by enterprises. This is mainly because investment in capital assets and R&D does not attract deductions in assessment of value-added tax and income tax. The tax system therefore needs to be made more transparent and more equitable in its application across firms. For fairness and equity in tax collection, efforts are required to help small enterprises to improve management and accounting systems. Accounting and auditing services are also required to meet the increasing needs of private firms, especially small ones.

3.8.3   Technical Innovation, Property Rights and Human Capital

Although private enterprises are found to be very active in technical innovation, there have been several major constraints to their investment in R&D and other activities conducive to the development of technological capabilities. These constraints include shortages and weaknesses in human capital, financial resources, information and effective protection of intellectual property rights.

China also lacks financial institutions dealing with investments in R&D, and venture capital more generally, which have high risk but high potential returns. The government intends establishing various kinds of funds for the purpose of research and development. Again, non-government institutions should also be allowed and encouraged to participate in these efforts. It is important that information services systems of importance to private and especially small business are improved, in order to effectively provide information on international and domestic goods, services and factor markets as well as technology and management. This can be best achieved by facilitating the emergence of new businesses providing these services on a market basis. It would be helped by a more competitive telecommunications system, providing basic services at international prices.

An important measure for technical innovation is to improve and strengthen the system of legal protection for intellectual property rights. This will give more incentives to enterprises for increased R&D expenditures and other innovation activities. Protection of property rights should be legislated more clearly and should be protected more effectively. The legal system needs to be further improved and law enforcement to be strengthened to curb irregularities and to reduce transaction costs.

During the past two decades of economic growth government and business alike have paid insufficient attention to education and other investments in human capital, partly due to the lack of funds. Based upon the experiences of other countries it can be suggested that rapid economic growth is unlikely to be sustainable without a significant improvement in the rate of investment in human capital. Consequently, the government needs to invest heavily in education as well as expenditure on R&D. The government could also reduce its financial burden on developing a sound education system by allowing private investors, including overseas investors, to invest in education. Of particular importance currently to the private sector is investment in education in relevant business skills including: business law; accounting; auditing; business and public administration; as well as specialised areas including finance and economics.

3.8.4   Opening Up More Sectors for Private Investment

China's accession to the WTO will require rapid liberalisation and opening of its economy to foreign traders and investors, and consequently will require considerable adjustments to its regulatory framework. However, such changes and adjustments are quite consistent with the current policy shift towards accommodating the development of the private sector in the economy. One area that needs further action by government is the opening of more areas for private investment and trade. All sectors except the small number in which the state has indicated an intention to maintain predominant control should be open to private investment. The Law on Protection Against Unfair Competition, enacted in December 1993, to create a fair and competitive business and investment environment needs to be strictly implemented. Preferential policies towards SOEs and foreign investments need to be gradually phased out and a policy of national treatment to enable domestic private enterprises to compete with SOEs and foreign firms, on an equal footing, needs to be adopted. Foreign trading rights for all qualified private enterprises need to be extended to allow direct and wider participation by private enterprises in China's foreign trade.

3.9   IMPACT OF THE FINANCIAL CRISIS UPON CHINA'S SMES

During the 1993–96 period, the Chinese authorities implemented an austerity program with the objective of reducing inflationary pressure within the economy while maintaining a high, but more sustainable, rate of economic growth. With a so-called soft landing[19] achieved in 1996, it was anticipated that the economy's growth rate would once again pick up. However, in 1997 the economy slowed further to a GDP growth rate of 8.8 per cent, largely due to the collective sector's sluggish 11.7 per cent expansion in 1997 which was down from 17.7 per cent in 1996. During 1998, Premier Zhu Rongji's commitment to further reform the SOEs and state administration resulted in considerable uncertainty of employment for workers in this sector, as well as creating the expectation of higher housing and other expenditures. Consumer spending consequently remained weak and was compounded by the Asian financial crisis which resulted in a stagnation in the country's exports. The latter resulted from the weakness of markets in East Asia and the loss of competitiveness of the renminbi, which was tied to the US dollar, relative to currencies of the crisis-afflicted economies. This general slowdown in the economy resulted in GDP growth slowing to 7.8 per cent in 1998 and further to 7.1 per cent in 1999. Weakening domestic and international demand contributed to excess capacity and production in most sectors of the economy. Rural unemployment pressure has also been increasing, with surplus rural labour totalling approximately 130 million people at the end of 1997. Slowing labour absorption and prospective lay-offs by TVEs could result in rural dissatisfaction, and workers migrating to China's cities in search of jobs.

In response to these recent developments, as well as increasing competition from the private sector, there have been many cases of privatisation of TVEs, as alluded to earlier, with the objective of reviving sluggish rural industry. The success or failure of these efforts will have important implications for the Chinese economy. In response to the further slowdown in the economy, and concern over social unrest with rising unemployment, the authorities initiated a stimulatory infrastructure policy in mid-1998 and a further infrastructure spending package in the latter half of 1999. The latter in particular proving to be quite effective.

Against this background of weak demand and a relatively strong renminbi, many SMEs experienced a decline in profitability, rising stocks, reduced revenue and a loss of international competitiveness. The TVEs have experienced a decline in market share and profits. The slowing economy and excess capacity, arising from many domestic and foreign companies expanding production in the first half of the 1990s, has resulted in a surplus of many commodities and especially the low-value-added labour-intensive items that TVEs produce. In this intensely competitive environment, only the best-managed and most efficient companies will survive. While some TVEs have made the necessary changes to remain contenders, as identified previously, many have not. This highlights the limitations of the TVE form of business entity. The response of the authorities to the slowing demand in the form of an expansionary publics works program financed by bond issues primarily, and for the state banks to give priority credit to hard-pressed SOEs and exporters, could consequently further adversely affect the prospects of SMEs gaining access to more finance. The need to allocate more finance as a policy priority to SMEs, as discussed in the previous section, appears to have been put on hold in the face of the current economic difficulties facing the economy. What adverse consequences this will have for the future longer-term growth of the economy can only be speculated upon at present. However, it can be suggested that this effect is likely to be a negative one.

These difficulties will be further intensified with China's membership of the WTO, and the latter's requirement that members open their economies to foreign competitors. These competitors are likely to possess superior technology, access to international markets, managerial expertise and marketing know-how, and able to locate where markets are most developed and infrastructure provision most advanced. This will exert major competitive pressure on indigenous small businesses, requiring them to adapt to the evolving Chinese market economy at an even more rapid pace.

3.10 SUMMARY AND CONCLUSIONS

The success of China's rural small businesses, the TVEs, was largely an unanticipated outcome of the process of economic reform. They were able to attain a major market niche in the production of consumer goods for both domestic and international markets – a legacy of the central planning system and the SOEs' lack of consumer goods production. Their rapid rate of growth during the reform era contributed significantly to: the absorption of surplus rural labour; higher labour productivity; the generation of higher rural incomes and saving; the economic development of local rural communities; and the generation of revenue for local governments. These developments contributed to reducing the extent of migration to urban areas.

While there are many aspects of the TVEs that are specific to China, they can still provide important lessons for other economies in transition. These include, most notably, the significance of liberal market entry, the benefits of competition, the need for enterprises to operate under a hard budget constraint, the benefits of appropriate fiscal incentives for local governments, and the gains to be had from access to science and technology. However, to maintain competitiveness in China's rapidly developing market economy will require changes in their organisational form, through the development of both business and scientific alliances. The rapid rise of China's privately owned and foreign funded enterprises suggests that the major source of future competition will no longer simply be with the SOEs, over which the TVEs' performance has been impressive, but rather with these alternative forms of business entities. The pressure for change on TVEs will be intense, and even more so with greater openness of the economy arising from membership of the WTO, and may ultimately require a change of ownership form of the TVEs themselves as well as their location. The former has already been under way since the mid-1990s.

While the literature in general suggests that the longer-term growth of TVEs in their present form is unsustainable, there is much evidence to suggest that many TVEs are already transforming themselves into complex interconnected networks involving science, industry and local government. The status of firms in China is highly dynamic in the present environment. Hence the key issue is not whether the TVEs will be able to maintain their industrial momentum, in the light of deepening reforms, but rather whether they will be able to develop appropriate organisational and ownership forms that will enable them to do so.

The development of small private enterprises in China was steady during the early years of the reform and has been rapid since the early 1990s. Private firms have made, and will increasingly make, a significant contribution to the growth of the economy. True private businesses already account for half of total output and will account for a much higher proportion a decade hence. Further liberalisation and institutional reform hold the key for producing a vibrant and dynamic private sector in the economy. The construction of the right policy, legal and regulatory framework will have a large pay-off in terms of more rapid development of the private sector. SMEs will be required to absorb new and modern managerial practices, focus more on the market rather than government bureaucracies, pay more attention to technological innovation and development of new products, care more about the interests of workers, and rely more on external sources of financing.

There is growing demand by the private sector for specialised expertise and training to develop that expertise. The skill requirements include that of financing, corporate planning and governance, management skills, business strategy, marketing and technological know-how. Competitive firms in these areas, especially those from overseas, will be well placed to provide such services to domestic enterprises.

A recent significant development was the constitutional amendment acknowledging the importance of the private sector, adopted during the March 1999 sessions of the National People's Congress. It provides a legal basis to embrace private enterprise in the Chinese economy, gives official recognition that the growth in non-farm employment and output is in the private sector despite the continued tendencies for capital to be allocated disproportionately to SOEs, allows individual enterprises to take off their 'red hats', reduces uncertainty in the business environment, and allows the official policy and regulatory environment to be refocused to remove impediments to continued dynamism in this major part of the economy. This will provide the momentum necessary for this sector to make an even more important contribution to the growth and reform of the Chinese economy in the new millennium.

NOTES

1 Garnaut and Song (2000) estimated that the non-state sector's contribution to GDP, which includes the agriculture sector, reached 62 per cent in 1998.
2 Some 68 per cent of total employment was in agriculture.
3 TVE employment peaked in 1996 at 135.1 million. Since this time the numbers employed have declined.
4 In 1997 official acceptance of different ownership forms and the importance of the private sector occurred. In March 1999 this recognition was included in the country's constitution.
5 In the case of TVEs there was increased blurring between what were effectively private TVEs (so-called 'red hat enterprises') and true collective TVEs.
6 There were about 810 000 self-employed persons in 1980 in urban China (State Statistical Bureau, *China Statistical Yearbook*, 1987, p. 115).
7 At this time the official emphasis on self-reliance and the breakdown of the national distribution system caused the rural communes to expand their non-agricultural activities.
8 The TVEs represent a unique institutional form, since, at least formally, rural industry is owned by the local government or collectively by members of a village. TVEs were, and are, non-state enterprises since they operated entirely outside of the state plan, and were subject to a hard budget constraint since they received no subsidies from the state budget, state banks and only rarely from local government. At least, formally, they are not private enterprises, since they lacked clear private owners.
9 Sachs and Woo (1997, pp. 34–5) highlight three main types of TVEs. The first type is known as the Jiangsu model because of its concentration in three cities in southern Jiangsu province. Here the local authorities exercised tight controls over the TVEs in terms of participating in production and investment decisions, regulating wages and labour mobility across TVEs, and protecting their TVEs by limiting the number of partnerships and individual firms that could be set up. The second type of TVE form is known as the Zhejiang model. Local governments in Zhejiang province, although a significant shareholder in many TVEs, normally refrained from intervening in the production, dividend and personnel decisions of the TVEs, provided that the enterprise made an annual contribution to village funds. The Zhejiang TVEs resembled leased companies, with the difference that their managers could be removed by local officials. The third TVE type are true private enterprises masquerading as TVEs. Here the entire capital of the enterprise is from an individual or a small group, and the enterprise paid a fee to the local authority in order to be allowed to register as a TVE. These are referred to as TVEs that wear a 'red hat'. Disguising their true ownership led to advantages in terms of lower tax rates, easier approval procedures, fewer restrictions on the size and operation of the enterprise, and shelter against possible reversal in the political fortunes of the reformers.

10   Capital being defined as depreciated fixed capital plus all inventories.

11   However, competition in many key sectors of the economy was not permitted, and remained dominated by SOEs.

12   This expression is used to describe those enterprises that were effectively privately owned and operated, but which, due to circumstances, found it more to their advantage to remain officially classified as a collective enterprise.

13   Individual private enterprises never disappeared from China's economy in reality. They were not recorded in Chinese industrial statistics in 1978 due to their small size and lack of legitimacy in the constitution compared with the SOEs and collectives.

14   See Garnaut and Song (2000, p. 2).

15   Essentially the agriculture/resources sector and industrial sector, respectively.

16   The services sector.

17   Since 1995 over 15 million state employees have been laid off and at an accelerating rate. Many of them have been re-employed in the private sector.

18   This was a period in which a 'rectification program' was implemented by the authorities, with the objective of slowing down economic reform and growth of the overheated economy (see, for example, Bell et al. 1993, p. 3).

19   Defined as being a situation where the rate of inflation is lower than the rate of growth of the economy.

REFERENCES

Alchian, A.A. and H. Demsetz (1972), 'Production, Information Costs, and Economic Organisation', *American Economic Review*, **62** (5), 777–95.

Bell, M.W., H.E. Khor and K. Kochhar (1993), 'China at the Threshold of a Market Economy', IMF Occasional Paper 107, IMF, Washington, September.

Byrd, W.A. and Q. Lin (1990), 'China's Rural Industry: An Introduction', in W.A. Byrd and Q.-S.Lin (eds), *China's Rural Industry: Structure, Development, and Reform*, New York: Oxford University Press, pp. 3–18.

Cheung, S.N.S. (1982), 'Will China go "Capitalist"?', Hobart Paper 94, Institute of Economic Affairs, London.

China State Science and Technology Commission (1991), *White Paper on Science and Technology*, No. 4, Beijing: International Academic Publishers.

China State Science and Technology Commission (1993), *China S&T Newsletter*, No.13 December.

Christerson, B. and C. Lever-Tracy (1996), 'The Third China? China's Rural Enterprises as Dependent Subcontractors or as Dynamic Autonomous Firms?', paper presented to the Asia–Pacific Regional Conference of Sociology, Manila, 28–31 May.

Demsetz, H. (1967), 'Towards a Theory of Property Rights', *American Economic Review,* **57** (2), 347–59.

Furubotn, E.G. and S. Pejovich (1974), 'Introduction: The New Property Rights Structure', in E.G. Furubotn and S. Pejovich (eds), *The Economics of Property Rights*, Cambridge, MA: Ballinger, pp. 1–9.

Garnaut, R., and L. Song (2000), 'Private Enterprise in China', paper presented at the China: Growth Sustainability in the 21st Century conference, ANU, Canberra, Australia, September.

Harvie, C. and T. Turpin (1997), 'China's Market Reforms and its New Forms of Scientific and Business Alliances', in C.A. Tisdell and J.C.H. Chai (eds), *China's Economic Growth and Transition: Macroeconomic, Environmental and Social/Regional Dimensions*, Commack, NY: Nova Science Publishers, pp. 257–91.

Jefferson, G.H., and T.G. Rawski (1994), Enterprise Reform in Chinese Industry, *Journal of Economic Perspectives*, **8** (2), 47–70, Spring.

Jefferson, G.H., T.G. Rawski and Y. Zheng (1992a), 'Growth, Efficiency, and Convergence in China's State and Collective Industry', *Economic Development and Cultural Change*, **20** (2), 239–66.

Jefferson, G.H., T.G. Rawski and Y. Zheng (1992b), 'Innovation and Reform in Chinese Industry: A Preliminary Analysis of Survey Data (1)', paper delivered at the annual meeting of the Association for Asian Studies, Washington DC, April.

Kwong, C.C.L. (1997), 'Property Rights and Performance of China's Township-Village Enterprises', in C.A. Tisdell and J.C.H. Chai (eds), *China's Economic Growth and Transition: Macroeconomic, Environmental and Social/Regional Dimensions*, Commack, NY: Nova Science Publishers, pp. 491–512.

Liao S.-L. (1995), 'The Development of Township Enterprises in Rural Fujian Since the Early 1980s', paper presented to the International Workshop on South China, Nanyang Research Institute, Xiamen University, PRC, May 22–24th.

Liu, Y. (1997), 'Labour Absorption in China's Township and Village Enterprises', paper presented at the International Conference on the Economies of Greater China, Perth, Australia, July.

Mai, Y.H. (2000), 'China's Marketisation Process and the WTO', paper presented at the China: Growth Sustainability in the 21st Century conference, ANU, Canberra, Australia, September.

Naughton, B. (1994), 'Chinese Institutional Innovation and Privatization from Below', *American Economics Association, Papers and Proceedings*, **84** (2), May, 266–70.

Oi, J. (1992), 'Fiscal Reform and the Economic Foundations of Local State Corporations in China', *World Politics*, **45** (1), October, 99–126.

Oi, J. (1995), 'The Role of Local Government in China's Transitional Economy', *The China Quarterly*, **144**, December, 1132–49.

Perkins, D. (1994), 'Completing China's Move to the Market', *Journal of Economic Perspectives*, **8** (2), 23–46, Spring.

Perkins, F.C. and M. Raiser (1994), 'State Enterprise Reform and Macroeconomic Stability in Transition Economies', Kiel Working Paper, No. 665, Kiel University, Kiel.

Pitt, M., and L. Putterman (1992), 'Employment and Wages in Township, Village, and other Rural Enterprises', mimeo, Brown University.

Putterman, L. (1995), 'The Role of Ownership and and Property Rights in China's Economic Transition', *The China Quarterly*, **144**, December, 1047–64.

Rawski, T.G. (1994), 'Chinese Industrial Reform: Accomplishments, Prospects, and Implications', American Economics Association, *Papers and Proceedings*, **84** (2), May, 271–75.

Research Centre for Rural Economics (1995), 'Case Study on Technology Transfer and Development of Township and Village Enterprises (TVEs)', Report to UNESCO, Beijing.

Sachs, J.D. and W.T. Woo (1997), 'Understanding China's Economic Performance', NBER Working Paper, No. 5935, Cambridge, MA.

So, B.W.Y. (2000), 'Development Trends of Indigenous Private Enterprises in the 1990s', paper presented at the China: Growth Sustainability in the 21st Century conference, ANU, Canberra, Australia, September.

State Statistical Bureau (various years), *China Statistical Yearbook*, Beijing: China Statistical Publishing House.

Svejnar, J. (1990), 'Productive Efficiency and Employment', in W.W. Byrd and Q. Lin (eds) in *China's Rural Industry: Structure, Development, and Reform*, New York" Oxford University Press.

Tisdell, C.A. and J.C.H. Chai (1997), *China's Economic Growth and Transition – Macroeconomic, Environmental and Social/Regional Dimensions*, Commack, NY: Nova Science Publishers.

Tseng, W., H.E. Khor, K. Kocharm, D. Mihajek and D. Burton (1994), 'Economic Reform in China, a New Phase', IMF Occasional Paper 114, IMF, Washington, November.

Wen, M. (2000), 'Can China Sustain Fast Economic Growth? – A Perspective from Transition and Development', paper presented at the China: Growth Sustainability in the 21st Century conference, ANU, Canberra, Australia, September.

Weitzman, M. and C. Xu (1994), 'Chinese Township Village Enterprises as Vaguely Defined Cooperatives', *Journal of Comparative Economics*, **18** (2), 121–45.

World Bank (1996), *From Plan to Market – World Development Report*, New York: Oxford University Press.

Yusuf, S. (1993a), 'The Rise of China's Non-state Sector', unpublished manuscript, World Bank.

Yusuf, S. (1993b), 'Property Rights and Non-state Sector Development in China', unpublished manuscript.

Zweig, D. (1991), 'Rural Industry: Constraining the Leading Growth Sector in China's Economy', Joint Economic Committee, US Congress, *China's Economic Dilemmas in the 1990s: The Problems of Reforms, Modernisation and Interdependence*, April.

4 The Limping Tiger: Problems in Transition for Small and Medium Sized Enterprises in Vietnam

David Richards, Charles Harvie, Ha Nguyen and Nguyen Van Lan

'Everything you hear about Vietnam is true but none of it is reliable.'
(Expatriate proverb)

4.1 INTRODUCTION

Vietnam is a place of contradictions; there are many Vietnams and which one you see depends upon which one you want to see. The rate of transformation in Vietnam since 1990 has been so dramatic that one expatriate said that you could stand on the street corner and see it change in front of your eyes. Walking round the capital, Hanoi, still provokes the thought that this must have been what London or Manchester would have been like in the early 19th century, when they were undergoing such rapid economic development and social change. There are some differences, for example in Vietnam it is happening at a much faster rate and most people are so pleasant and good mannered about it (for example, there is little crime so far in Hanoi).

The immediately striking features are the activity on the street and the chaotic traffic. The traffic is so remarkable that it is initially difficult to see much else. It flows along like an endless torrent, ill-disciplined from the Western viewpoint, yet with its own logic and rules. Everywhere by the side of the road everyone seems to be selling something. People are squatting, selling or cooking or making or repairing. Bicycle repairmen are almost falling over one another, as are people selling very small amounts of petrol. Walking by are travelling street vendors, mostly women, some with baskets on their head containing mysterious things wrapped in sacks (initially mysterious at least, although one later finds that they are selling hot fresh bread, twice a day); others with sticks over their shoulders with two baskets balanced at either end, each containing tomatoes or green vegetables. Enterprise and enthusiasm is publicly evident everywhere, mostly at the individual and family group level. This energy and productivity has not, however, characterised Vietnamese small and medium sized enterprises in general, and certainly is not found in the massive state-owned enterprises.

Until late 1997 and early 1998, it had been almost a cliché to cite the huge potential for growth and consumption in new markets outside the industrialised nations such as in the former Soviet Union, China, Indonesia and Vietnam. The resulting concentration of growth within East and Southeast Asia was seen as producing one of the most vigorous zones of world economic activity. Optimism about this Asian miracle clearly diminished following the economic downturn, as many emerging economies encountered the consequences of a slowing of growth.

North Vietnam was not prepared for the collapse of South Vietnam in 1975 and appears to have had no coherent policy to manage the state or the economy after the end of the war. Recovery was also delayed by the Vietnamese military intervention to rescue Cambodia, which in turn provoked a brief war with China in 1979 (see Taylor 1983; Jamieson 1993; and Wolff 1999). The extremely rapid economic growth from 1986 under '*doi moi*', the program of economic renovation and reform and transition to a market economy, was thus embarked on nearly ten years after China's. Nevertheless, Vietnam attracted the attention of overseas investors to an economy generally seen as one of the most plausible new miracles in East Asia. For the first half of the 1990s Vietnam was proclaimed as the next great 'Asian Tiger'. There seemed to have been considerable progress in reforming and reorienting the public service and in developing the private sector. With a population of nearly 80 million, it is the second largest country in Southeast Asia and the 13th largest in the world. Vietnam has an abundant supply of natural resources, with 'young people who are well-educated, hard-working and very cheap, even by Asian standards' (*The Economist* 2000, p. 65). The country appeared to have a lot to offer the global entrepreneur and multinational company, and was thought to offer the biggest opportunity for foreign investors since China.

The effects of the Asian downturn in Vietnam were different from those in its neighbours, as were the resulting policy debates. The prevailing opinion in 1996 was that over the next few years high but unbalanced economic growth would continue, with the private sector gaining increased power and influence. Foreign business interests were predicted to play an increasingly important role in the economy, mainly through equity joint ventures (see Fforde 1991; and Fforde and Goldstone 1995). This positive view of the economy was increasingly questioned (see, for example, Edwards 1997) following evidence of a slowdown in economic growth, which predated the precipitating crises in Southeast Asia and Korea in 1997. The full extent of Vietnam's slowdown was difficult to assess, chiefly because of an absence of reliable information, but gross domestic product (GDP) growth slowed and foreign direct investment levels dropped. It was argued that the decade-old economic renovation process had reached a point of near exhaustion.[1]

The nature of the Vietnamese economy and social structure determined, and will continue to determine, the different response of the economy to world and regional economic trends (Buchanan et al. 1998). The financial crisis in Asia did not help, but since Vietnam had a rudimentary banking system, a non-convertible currency, and no stock market, it was not greatly directly affected by the processes that undermined the economies of the rest of Southeast Asia. As Malesky et al. argue, Vietnamese policy makers must simultaneously address two apparently conflicting trends – *economic downturn* and *continued movement towards a market economy* (Malesky et al. 1998, p. 3). Malesky et al. argue that 'far from being contradictory, the issues are related; the recent economic crisis among Vietnam's neighbours has been sparked in part by underlying structural weaknesses in their market systems, giving Vietnam the opportunity to address its own deficiencies, while its market institutions are still in their formative stages' (Malesky et al. 1998, p. 3).

The general conclusion from recent research is that despite many well-designed reforms in the legislative framework, the implementation of change has been very slow and inconsistent (Malesky et al. 1998; Pistor 1998; and Verbiest 1998). This is not an unusual problem in transition economies, but implementation of reform seems particularly sluggish in Vietnam and certainly in comparison to its giant regional neighbour China. It is anticipated that general political stability will continue with change unlikely despite the increased tensions resulting from rising dissatisfaction with government corruption and inefficiency, and as unemployment rises and income differentials widen.[2] Although the nominal GNP per capita of Vietnam is ranked as one of the lowest in the world[3] (US$310 in 1997,[4] UNDP 1999), its Human Development Index (HDI) in 1997, using the UNDP measure, at 0.664 points compared very favourably with that of developing economies as a whole (0.637 points) (see UNDP 1999). This gave the country a ranking of 111 in 1997, an improved ranking of 11 places in comparison to a year earlier, out of a total of 174 countries. The country has a relatively high level of educational attainment and an enviably high adult literacy rate of 91.9 per cent in 1997 (UNDP 1999). This compared very favourably with other countries in the region. Malaysia, for example, a relatively upper- or middle-income country, had an adult literacy rate of 85.7 per cent in 1997. Wages are lower in Vietnam than in China, for example, but so is productivity. Foreign investment creates five times fewer jobs in Vietnam than in China for the same amount of money, yet goods produced by that investment are more expensive. 'A Chinese farmer who earns several times more than his Vietnamese counterpart pays half the price for a motorbike', said a Vietnamese government statistician quoted by Gittings (2000).

Foreign direct investment (FDI) disbursements increased rapidly during the 1992–97 period from US$0.4 billion to US$3.3 billion. Most of this went into heavy industry, real estate and property development in the tourist sector focusing upon that of hotels, the resources sector and import substituting industries. However, since 1997 there has been a significant decline in FDI to around half its 1997 level by 1999 (Ministry of Planning and Investment 1999). Much of the blame for this fall arises from: overinvestment and saturation of the original areas for investment resulting in declining profitability; investor perceptions about the high cost of doing business in the country; the bulk of the initial inflows of FDI originated from within the East Asian region, hence the financial crisis contributed to a decline in FDI that was not offset by inflows from non-regional sources; two-thirds of FDI involved the formation of joint ventures with SOEs which have proven to be less flexible, and, with continuing difficulties in entering joint ventures with non-state enterprises, this could have caused them to reassess their investment decisions; finally, the government has been dragging its feet in regard to the implemenation of much-needed structural and other reform of the economy. For many foreign investors their initial overenthusiasm has given way to frustration and a desire to withdraw from the country. This has been compounded by excess bureaucracy and an increasingly perceived lack of commitment to reform by the authorities. 'Reforms have ... been slow and modest. They are often accompanied by capricious new rules. The years needed to negotiate and gain approval for new projects make India seem eager; corruption and inefficiency are as bad as in China. But whereas investors feel they need to be in China, they know they can avoid Vietnam' (*The Economist* 2000). Nevertheless, Vietnam remains a country of many contradictions, since, despite foreign investors' annoyance at the slow pace of reform, it can claim one of the best-performing poverty-reduction programs in the developing world (Gittings 2000).

The remainder of this chapter proceeds as follows. Section 4.2 focuses upon Vietnamese culture and its implications for the functioning of its society and the conduct of business. Section 4.3 reviews Vietnam's recent economic performance and the contribution of the private sector. Section 4.4 looks at SME promotion and private sector development. Section 4.5 identifies the effects of the Asian financial crisis on Vietnam's private sector and SMEs. Section 4.6 is concerned with identifying key issues in the promotion of Vietnam's SMEs. Section 4.7 focuses upon the key policy agenda for development of the private sector, and in particular SMEs, and the crucial role of government in this process. Finally, Section 4.8 presents a summary of the major conclusions from this chapter.

4.2   VIETNAMESE CULTURE

The present-day leaders of Vietnam have many concerns about their powerful neighbour, China, whose great economic progress both fascinates and worries them (Gittings 2000). In many ways China is Vietnam's biggest foreign-policy problem, which they have to manage by strengthening their relations with the ASEAN countries to the south. Probably this has always been so. There is little doubt that Vietnam is a society deeply influenced by China over the last two thousand years. This influence stemmed originally from conquest and colonisation, but has continued through migration from and commerce with Southwest China. China transformed the

Vietnamese language, script and vocabulary, brought a bureaucratic form of government, and influenced education, art and family life (Taylor 1983). This has resulted in a culture very different from that of the rest of Southeast Asia. Although Vietnam is intrinsically different to China, its substantial influence has meant that 'over time, beginning in the late fifteenth century and becoming most extreme in the nineteenth century, Neo-Confucianism came to be a dominant influence' (Jamieson 1993, p. 11). The teachings of Confucius emphasise a social hierarchy and a conservative protection of the status quo, so that, as everyone knows his or her place and acts accordingly, social order will be ensured. This view of social order, although criticised by the government of Vietnam, has in many ways been confirmed by it, with Communist party social order complementing, modifying and sometimes replacing, feudal social order. As Ralston et al. (1991, p. 670) say with respect to China, 'Today, age and belonging to the right group (for example, the Communist Party) are just as important as they were decades, and even centuries ago'.

Considerable research has been conducted in recent years on Chinese culture and psychology (see Bond 1996a). A review of recent work on Chinese values concludes that: 'At the cultural level, Chinese societies may be characterised as high in hierarchy and very high in discipline; at the individual level, Chinese may be characterised as placing a high value on identification with their various in-groups. Across other dimensions there is considerable variation among the results for the Chinese groups' (Bond 1996b, p. 225).

Following Hofstede's seminal work on the dimensions of culture (Hofstede 1980), the work of Bond and the Chinese Culture Connection, using the Chinese Value Survey (CVS), threw some light upon modern variants of Confucian values (Chinese Culture Connection 1987; and Bond 1988). Hofstede and Bond (1988) observed that three dimensions are common to both pieces of research (power distance; individualism/ collectivism; and masculinity/femininity). However: 'We did not find a CVS dimension related to Uncertainty Avoidance. We earlier associated this dimension with man's search for Truth: it seems that the Chinese do not believe this to be an essential issue' (Hofstede and Bond 1988, p. 16). They did, however, find another clearly marked dimension, which they called Confucian Work Dynamism, together with a preference for integration, human-heartedness, and moral discipline.

Countries that scored high on the Confucian Work Dynamism dimension (for example, Hong Kong, Taiwan, Japan and South Korea) emphasised those aspects of Confucian teaching which are more dynamic and oriented towards the future: persistence (perseverance); ordering relationships by status and observing this order; thrift; and having a sense of shame. Those countries that scored highly on this dimension did not emphasise to the same degree traditional Confucian values. The logical link between these modern Confucian values and economic growth is East Asian entrepreneurship, say Hofstede and Bond, and other studies have confirmed this view (Ralston et al. 1991).

The influence of Communism in Vietnam would seem to have created a contradictory relationship to Confucian Dynamism. Vietnam has a greater focus on traditional values, those which are oriented towards the past and present and a more static and tradition focused mentality, emphasising personal steadiness and stability; protecting your face; respect for tradition; and reciprocation of greetings, favours and gifts.

In Vietnam:

> [B]oth Neo-Confucianism and communism were primarily ethical systems, prescribing a way of life ... Many peasants and intellectuals sought ... some well defined, encompassing, and bounded framework within which to pursue their socially oriented goals and ambitions. This stress upon ideological orthodoxy and conformity to socially imposed constraints on individual behaviour on the part *of the Communists* was a return to rather than a departure from traditional Vietnamese values. (Jamieson 1993, p. 217, emphasis added)

There have been very few empirical cultural studies of Vietnam, but David Ralston has recently extended his comparative cultural values work in Asia to Vietnam. With colleagues he published an interesting comparative study that tends to confirm our discussion above (Ralston et al. 1999). Ralston et al. employed a measure that allows the assessment of the Individualism and Collectivism construct. This is the most reliable of the dimensions studied by Hofstede and 'one that has frequently been used to contrast Asian and Western cultural behaviours' (Ralston et al. 1999, p. 4). Hofstede saw the construct as a single continuum with Individualism and Collectivism as polar opposites. However in an impressive body of work, Triandis and colleagues have argued that they might be unique constructs (Triandis et al. 1988) and part of what they have come to call 'cultural syndromes' (Triandis 1993). The elements of Individualism are self-reliance, a focus on attaining personal needs and on competition, rather than cooperation. Collectivism is about being orientated to others, especially one's in-group, subordinating personal goals to those of the in-group and focusing on developing relationships.

Ralston et al. (1999) compared Vietnamese managers, both from the North and the South, with US managers and what they call 'traditional' and 'cosmopolitan' Chinese managers. They found that both North and South Vietnamese managers 'were significantly higher on collectivism than the other groups'. They say 'that the Vietnamese, as a whole, may be more "traditional" (have transitioned less) than even the traditional Chinese ... [and also find] ... a stronger adherence to eastern-culture Collectivism in Vietnam than in China' (Ralston et al. 1999, p. 11). Ralston et al. conclude 'that foreign investors from market economies need to appreciate what it means to grow up in a centrally-planned economy operating in a centuries-old Confucian culture (and that) in a country like Vietnam, the politics-economics links may be unusually strong, causing negative ramifications to citizens challenging the system' (Ralston et al. 1999, pp. 13–14).

Whatever the exact position of Vietnam within a Confucian framework of values, there is little doubt that the Vietnamese share with Chinese cultures a high potential level of entrepreneurial zeal. Also, like Chinese cultures, it seems that whether this is realised in Vietnam depends on whether it is encouraged or not by the state. Here also the influence of Communism seems negative. It is the Overseas Chinese and Vietnamese who exemplify the Confucian entrepreneurial spirit (see Redding 1990). There are several organisational and social factors that produce this spirit.

> Firstly, the close relationship between ownership and control in Chinese businesses means that talented, enthusiastic outsiders are rarely promoted to responsible positions in someone else's company. Secondly, Chinese outside China are often refugees or resented minorities. They therefore feel vulnerable, and this, combined with the Chinese drive to acquire social power, leads to a preoccupation with accumulating wealth. The result is the proliferation of small business units formed by entrepreneurs eager to exercise their own control and generate wealth for their own family. (Bond 1991, p. 80)

Bond goes on to say that 'there is a widespread hunger in Chinese culture to begin one's own business ... which fuel(s) a vigorous enterprising economy of small resourceful businesses', while depriving larger organisations of the talented individuals necessary for growth (Bond 1991, p. 81).

Certainly, specific 'Asian values' brought Vietnam very rapid growth, but, as in the rest of Asia, others may have contributed to the recent decline in growth through characteristics which emphasise high power distance and collectivism (Hofstede 1980, 1991). These are associated with a preference for indirect communication and interpersonal and social harmony (Gudykunst and Ting-Toomey 1988), which, in combination with respect for authority, leads to a reluctance to confront issues and people in powerful positions (Hofstede 1987; and Bond 1991). It has been argued (for example, by Alon and Kellerman 1999) that it is likely that these characteristics have not been helpful to sustaining market-led economic growth.

4.3   VIETNAM'S RECENT ECONOMIC PERFORMANCE AND THE CONTRIBUTION OF THE PRIVATE SECTOR

4.3.1   Vietnam's Recent Economic Performance

During the period of the 1990s Vietnam was one of the fastest-growing economies in the world, achieving an annual average GDP growth rate of 7.4 per cent. This contributed to a rapid improvement in GDP per capita (see Figure 4.1). During this period of rapid economic growth there was a noticeable change in the structure of the economy, with the contribution of the agriculture sector to GDP declining from 40.6 per cent in 1990 to 23.8 per cent in 1999, the GDP share of the industry sector increasing from 22.4 per cent in 1990 to 34.3 per cent by 1999, and the share of the services

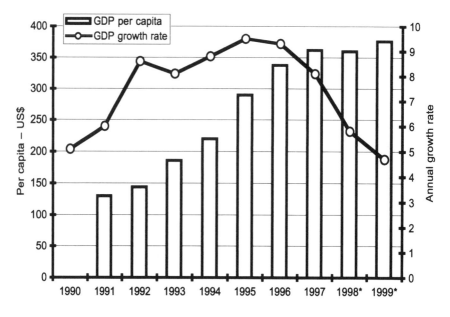

Note: * Preliminary.

Source: GSO Statistical Yearbooks, and UNDP computation.

Figure 4.1   Vietnam GDP, 1990–99

sector increasing from 36.9 per cent of GDP in 1990 to 41.9 per cent in 1999 (see Figure 4.2). Such a structural transformation is a typical and nearly universal feature accompanying economic development (see, for example, Chenery and Syrquin 1975).

On further analysis it can be found that this rapid rate of economic growth has been led by the industrial sector. Table 4.1, taken from Belser (2000), shows that the average annual growth of GDP over the high growth rate period, 1993–97, was an impressive 8.9 per cent. The major sector contributing to this growth was the industrial sector, where value added increased at an average annual rate of 13.4 per cent. The services sector also grew impressively at 9.4 per cent a year during this period, while the agriculture sector lagged behind with an average annual increase of 4.3 per cent. This accounts for the share of industry and services in GDP increasing relative to that of agriculture. The period of the 1990s has seen a rise in the importance of both the non-state sector and the foreign invested sector in industrial production (see Figure 4.3). In 1990 the state sector contributed almost 68 per cent of industrial production, falling to just over 50 per cent by 1995. However, in 1999 there was a further decline in its contribution to industrial production down to just under 44 per cent. Therefore

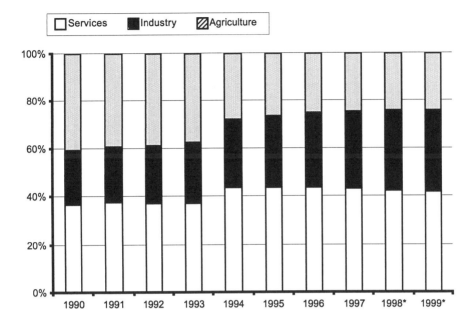

Note: * Preliminary.

Source: GSO Statistical Yearbooks.

Figure 4.2   Sectoral Shares of GDP, Vietnam, 1990–99

Table 4.1
Industrialisation of Vietnam

	Average annual real GDP growth during 1993–97 (%)	Estimated share in total output in 1992 (%)	Share in total output 1997 (%)
Total	8.9	100	100
Agriculture	4.3	31.6	25.2
Industry	13.4	27.3	33.1
Industry less construction	13.1	20.7	24.7
Services	9.4	41.1	41.7

Source: Belser (2000, p. 2).

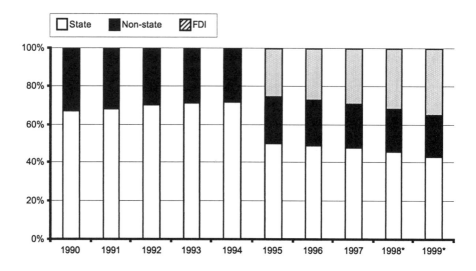

Note: * Preliminary

Source: GSO Statistical Yearbooks

Figure 4.3   Industrial Production by Ownership, Vietnam, 1990–99

over half of industrial production in 1999 was from the private domestic and foreign sectors, with the contribution of the latter, in particular, worthy of note.

The rapid growth of the industrial sector has contributed to an expansion in industrial employment. Cross-country evidence provided by Gillis et al. (1987) indicates that over the period from 1965 to 1983, developing countries experienced on average a growth elasticity of employment in industry of around 0.6. That is, industrial employment expanded at around 60 per cent of the rate of industrial growth. In the case of Vietnam, however, industrial growth has had only a moderate impact on employment. As indicated by Tables 4.2 and 4.3, the growth rate of industrial employment in Vietnam between 1992/93 and 1997/98 was 4 per cent per year. While respectable this represents less than 30 per cent of the rate of industrial output growth. Consequently, despite the rapid growth of the industrial sector the share of industrial employment in total employment has only increased from 11.8 per cent to 13.1 per cent. Interestingly, when construction is excluded from the industry sector, the record is even worse. Hence a key issue for policy makers in Vietnam is how best to benefit in terms of employment growth in the context of rapid growth in the industrial sector. In this regard the contribution of the private sector and SMEs will be of particular importance.

There are a number of reasons to explain this sluggish growth of employment, and this can be identified with the aid of Table 4.4. This shows that in industry the

Table 4.2
Industrial Employment Growth

	1992–93 (million)	1997–98 (million)	Absolute increase 1992–93 to 1997–98 (million)	% increase per year 1992–93 to 1997–98	Incremental employment distribution 1992–93 to 1997–98
Total employment	36.8	40.3	3.5	1.8	100
Agriculture	26.2	26.8	0.6	0.4	16.7
Industry	4.3	5.3	1.0	4.0	27.0
Industry less construction	3.8	4.3	0.5	2.6	14.8
Services	6.3	8.2	1.9	5.6	56.3

Note: Employment data is for people between 15 and 65.

Source: GSO, *Vietnam Living Standards Survey*, 1 and 2.

Table 4.3
Employment by Sector

	Share in total labour force 1992–93 (%)	Share in total labour force 1997–98 (%)	% Change from 1992–93 to 1997–98
Agriculture	71.2	66.4	–4.7
Industry	11.8	13.1	+1.3
Industry and construction	10.3	10.7	+0.4
Services	17.0	20.5	+3.4

Source: GSO, *Vietnam Living Standards Survey*, 1 and 2.

state and the domestic non-state sectors grew rapidly over the 1995–98 period. However, it is clear that the state sector dominates the domestic non-state sector and more specifically the private sector. In 1998 the state sector's contribution to industrial value added was more than twice that of the domestic private sector. State enterprises therefore contributed substantially to the expansion of industrial production, amounting to 37.2 per cent of Vietnam's total industrial growth between 1995 and 1998. This compared to only 16.2 per cent for domestic private companies. Foreign investment, however, was the most important single contributor to expanded industrial production.

Table 4.4
Contribution to Industrial Production and Employment by Sector

	Industrial production growth (%) 1995–98	Share in industrial production growth (%) 1995–98	Share in industrial GDP (%) 1998	Share in industrial employment 1997–98 (%)
State sector	10.2	37.2	46.2	24.2
Foreign investment	22.7	46.5	31.8	11.5
Domestic non-state sector	9.2	16.2	22.0	64.3
Of which:				
• private and mixed	21.6	11.1	7.9	25.2
• collective	8.7	0.3	0.6	1.3
• households	4.0	4.7	13.5	37.8

Sources: General Statistical Office and GSO, *Vietnam Living Standards Survey*, 2.

By comparison with its contribution to industrial production the state sector's contribution to industrial employment is considerably less. The State sector's industrial employment was less than 25 per cent of total employment in this sector. The domestic non-state sector, by contrast, although contributing only 22 per cent of industrial output employed more than 64 per cent of industrial workers. A large proportion of these workers were in household enterprises. Of particular interest is the employment contribution of the registered private and mixed companies. Although contributing only 7.9 per cent of industrial GDP in 1998 they employed more workers than that of the state-owned enterprises (SOEs).

Vietnam's slow employment growth in the industrial sector, therefore, arises from the state sector's strong growth but low labour intensity, and the private sector's still relatively small size. This poor employment performance can therefore be partially explained as a byproduct of the transition period to a market economy, in which the growth of private enterprises is rapid but their overall contribution is small as a result of starting from a much lower base. Also, state enterprises, which tend to be concentrated in import-substituting activities and are sheltered from both foreign and domestic competition, typically draw capital and other resources away from the private sector. This could have prevented higher rates of private sector growth and employment, and could be of concern for the attainment of longer-term growth.

Another important feature of Vietnam's development process has been the increasing significance of international trade. Table 4.5 indicates that between 1992

Table 4.5
Exports, Imports and the Share of Trade in GDP

Year	1992	1997	1999
Value of exports (million US$)	2 581	9 185	11 500
Value of imports (million US$)	2 540	11 592	11 600
(Exports + Imports)/ GDP (%)	51.6	85.7	58.0

Source: General Statistical Office and UNDP (available at <www.undp.org.un/fact/stat>).

Table 4.6
Export Growth by Sector

	Estimated average annual real growth 1992–97 (%)	Share in total exports in 1992 (%)	Share in total exports in 1997 (%)
Total exports	18.8	100	100
Agriculture	11.1	49.5	35.3
Heavy industry and minerals	12.3	37.0	28.0
Light industry	45.1	13.5	36.7
Of which:			
• textiles and garments			16.4
• footwear			10.6

Source: Belser (2000, p. 5).

and 1999, for example, the dollar value of imports and exports more than quadrupled, increasing the share of trade in GDP from 52 per cent to 58 per cent. In 1997 the share of trade in GDP reached a remarkable 86 per cent, a high level by international standards. Table 4.6 indicates that Vietnam's export growth was led by impressive growth in light manufacturing exports, which in real terms grew by no less than 45 per cent a year and whose share in total exports rose from 13.5 per cent in 1992 to 36.7 per cent in 1997. Also remarkable is the strong rise in the value of agriculture exports, mainly reflecting the spectacular take-off in rice and coffee production. In only a few years Vietnam turned from being a net rice importer into the world's second largest exporter with over 3.5 million tons in 1998.

The performance in manufacturing exports was supported by foreign investment. Vietnam's trade and taxation regimes now contain special provisions that allow export oriented foreign enterprises to import duty free intermediate goods from abroad and to enjoy preferential tax rates. In addition, many joint ventures are also exempted from import duties on equipment goods, machine components, spare parts and transport equipment and materials. Table 4.7 shows that the dollar value of exports by foreign invested companies, about 40 per cent of which stem from light manufacturing, grew by 80 per cent per year between 1994 and 1997. This raised the share of exports by foreign invested companies from less than 4 per cent in 1994 to almost 20 per cent of total exports in 1997.

Table 4.7
FDI and Its Contribution to Exports

	1994	1997
Total exports by foreign companies (US$ million)	161.1	1 790
Total light industrial exports by foreign companies (US$ million)	na	728
Share of FDI in total exports (%)	3.9	19.5
Share of FDI in light industry exports (%)	na	21.6

Source: Belser (2000, p. 5).

4.3.2   Contribution of the Private Sector to the Economy

The Prime Minister in his opening speech to the National Assembly in November 1999, emphasised the importance of creating a climate conducive to private sector development. Farmers, household micro enterprises, private SMEs and relatively large foreign invested enterprises comprise the private sector in Vietnam. The de-collectivisation of agriculture, together with the approval of the Domestic and Foreign Investment laws in the late 1980s, as well as the Commercial Law in the early 1990s, were extremely effective in promoting growth of the private sector from a negligible base. The economic reforms of the 1980s were remarkably effective in galvanising the energy of millions of Vietnamese individuals who diversified and expanded their agricultural production rapidly, and set up many micro household enterprises as well as domestic private registered SMEs. Foreign firms invested in majority foreign-owned joint ventures or in wholly foreign-owned enterprises. Tapping the potential of individual farmers' drive and dynamism through '*doi moi*' was key to the rapid growth and employment generation of the 1990s (see World Bank 1999). In the early part of the 21st century, unleashing the potential of the private non-farm sector, to produce and to export, is likely to be the key to restoring higher growth of income and employment during the next decade.

While systematic data on the performance of the domestic private sector is limited, what does exist suggests a significant expansion and diversification of private sector activities in the last 10 years. Five important facts about the performance of the private sector can be usefully highlighted.

First, the share of the private sector in total GDP in 1998 was about 50 per cent, see Table 4.8, which is approximately the same share as in 1993. Hence the domestic private sector's share of GDP has remained stagnant in recent years. During the 1995–98 period, the domestic private sector, despite its many constraints, grew at 9 per cent a year, only a percentage point lower than the growth of the state-owned sector.

Second, less than half of manufacturing GDP in 1998 was produced by private firms, but the share is increasing, with the domestic private sector dominating that share (see Table 4.8). The domestic private sector, especially household enterprises, has had an important role in manufacturing. Micro household enterprises and private SMEs account for 28 per cent of manufacturing GDP. As of 1999 there were around 600 000 micro household enterprises in manufacturing, contributing 18 per cent of manufacturing value added, and 5 600 private SMEs in manufacturing accounting for 10 per cent of manufacturing GDP. However, with the introduction of the Enterprise Law in 2000 the situation was changing rapidly, especially for private registered SMEs, with more than 10 000 new firms registered during the first nine months of 2000.

The period of the 1990s has seen a steady decline in the contribution of the state sector towards industrial output, from around 62 per cent in 1990 to 44 per cent by

Table 4.8
Private Sector's Share in 1998 GDP (%)

	Total GDP	Manufacturing GDP
State sector	49	54
State-owned enterprises	na	na
Private sector	51	46
Foreign invested sector	10	18
Domestic private sector	41	28
Of which:		
• Household enterprises/farmers	34	18
• Private SMEs	7	10

Source: GSO, *Statistical Yearbook*, 1999.

1999 and to just over 42 per cent in 2000 (see Table 4.9). While the domestic private (non-state) share has actually declined during this period the foreign invested enterprises' share has increased considerably. Most of this was due to very rapid growth of foreign invested enterprises in the oil and gas sector as well as in manufacturing. Household enterprise growth stagnated after the first half of the 1990s as the environment for domestic private enterprises was not sufficiently favourable to promote their rapid growth. Thus foreign invested enterprises now have a much bigger share of total private industrial output than was the case in 1990.

Third, the domestic private sector is considerably more labour intensive in comparison to the state sector and the foreign invested sector. Referring to Table 4.4 again, it can be seen that in 1998 the state sector contributed 46 per cent to industrial production but employed only 24 per cent of the industrial workforce. The foreign invested sector contributed 32 per cent of industrial production but employed only 11.5 per cent of the industrial workforce. By contrast the domestic non-state sector, household enterprises and private SMEs, contributed only 22 per cent of industrial production but employed 64 per cent of the industrial workforce. The relatively large share of the private sector in employment and in labour-intensive exports indicates that it has been outperforming other enterprises in exploiting Vietnam's comparative advantage in labour-intensive production. Indeed, private sector development in Vietnam, through its effect on growth and employment, can have a significant impact on poverty reduction.

Fourth, private SMEs in manufacturing, especially the larger ones, are highly export oriented. In Vietnam there are around 457 private manufacturers with more than 100 full time workers (see MPDF 1999) that operate mainly in labour intensive sectors like garments, footwear, plastic products, seafood and so on (see Table 4.10).

Table 4.9
Industrial Output: Growth and Share by Sector, 1990–2000

	1990	1995	1999[a]	2000[b]
Total industrial growth (%)	3.2	13.8	10.4	15.5
Per cent of industrial output				
State-owned enterprises	61.7	50.3	43.5	42.2
Domestic private (non-state) sector	29.5	24.6	21.8	22.7
Foreign invested	8.8	25.1	34.7	35.2

Notes:
a   Preliminary figure.
b   Estimate.

Source: GSO, *Statistical Yearbook*, 2001.

On average, these SMEs export around three-quarters of their production, and consequently have a greater export orientation than SOEs. By comparison foreign invested enterprises export only around a half of their output.

Finally, private foreign invested enterprises are playing an increasingly important role in the economy, accounting for about a fifth of manufacturing output, and employing 300 000 workers in 1998. There has been a slight trend away from joint ventures with state enterprises and an increase in wholly foreign-owned investments. A large share of foreign investment in industry is in the production of import competing goods in capital-intensive sectors. This is a reflection of the incentives offered to foreign investors in the form of protection to these sectors. In particular, import licensing restrictions with unlimited protection have encouraged overinvestment for the domestic market, at the cost of export markets. This structure of foreign investment partially reflects Vietnam's high barriers to heavy industrial imports which not only protect state enterprises but also attracts foreign investors into import-substituting and capital-intensive activities, often with SOEs. This form of foreign investment is generally inefficient. It creates local monopolies and raises the price of products relative to those that would have prevailed under free imports. Thus, although foreign investment has boosted local production it has done little to create employment. Improving the climate for export-oriented foreign investors would certainly assist Vietnam towards more labour-intensive export-led growth in line with its comparative advantage.

The adoption of the 1987 Law on Foreign Investment and subsequent amendment established an 'open door' policy for investors and increasingly simplified investment

Table 4.10
Private Registered Manufacturers – Export Orientation

	Number of firms	Output (%)Exports/ (unweighted average)
Garments and textiles	159	80.5
Leather products	34	85.0
Rubber and plastic products	22	75.0
Food and beverages (incl. seafood)	71	63.2
Wood products	65	75.1
Other non-metallic products	39	73.2
Basic metals	9	na
Chemical products	9	20.0
Others	49	74.4
Total	**457**	**75.3**

Source: Mekong Project Development Facility (1999).

procedures. This gradual improvement in the investment climate led to a large increase in foreign capital inflows, mainly from Asian countries. During the 1993–97 period the inflow of disbursed foreign investment increased by almost 46 per cent per annum (in terms of current US dollars), reaching nearly US$2.1 billion during 1997. Most of this foreign investment was capital intensive. Although the share of foreign direct investment (FDI) going to light industry has increased in recent years, most investment entered oil-related production, heavy industry or real estate. By the end of 1998 less than 13 per cent of the total stock of FDI was in the labour intensive light industrial sector, where about 80 per cent of production is exported (according to information from the Ministry of Planning and Investment 1999). This indicates that the amount of export-oriented and labour-intensive foreign investment attracted by Vietnam's high human capital and low labour costs has been relatively small. It is therefore not surprising that foreign investment, while accounting for 31.8 per cent of industrial production in 1998, and half of industrial growth over the 1995–98 period, employed only 11.5 per cent of all industry workers in 1997/98.

Despite a number of favourable developments the private sector remains more constrained in Vietnam than in other countries in the region, including China. The private sector continues to face various unnecessary restrictions on entry arising from the remaining business licence requirements, whose modification and rationalisation are still needed. Access to and transactions in land-use rights remain difficult despite recent changes in land law and security regulations. New institutional arrangements such as registries, and procedures for selling foreclosed land-use rights are not in place. Access to capital and credit is also more difficult for private SMEs in part because banks are in dire financial straits, and in part because lending to SOEs is viewed more favourably than lending to the private sector. But improving the climate for day-to-day operations of private investors – making interactions with the bureaucracy easier – will necessitate deep-seated behavioural changes in the way private activity is perceived by the civil service, the dominant state-owned commercial banks, and, most importantly, by the political leadership.

4.4   SME PROMOTION AND PRIVATE SECTOR DEVELOPMENT

4.4.1   SME Overview

The Central Committee of the Communist Party of Vietnam has drafted a Socio-Economic Development Strategy (SEDS) 2001–10 that is 'aimed at accelerating industrialisation and modernisation in the socialist orientation and creating a foundation for Vietnam to become an industrialised country by 2020'.[5] This envisages that GDP will double from 2000 to 2010.[6] Vietnam in 2000 faced serious challenges in employment generation with unemployment figures at more than 7 per cent, underemployment around 30 per cent and an expected growth of the workforce of 11 million people over the next 10 years. Since unemployment and underemployment are the major factors contributing to poverty, the creation of new jobs, and particularly in the rural sector, will be crucial for the reduction of poverty.

To accomplish these aims the SEDS gives particular emphasis to SMEs and private enterprises, especially given their ability to generate employment and opportunities for the poor. In 2000 overall SMEs, both state and private, generated approximately a quarter of GDP, employed around 50 per cent of the Vietnamese labour force and were the fastest-growing type of enterprise in terms of numbers (see World Bank 2001, p. 49). A flourishing private sector and a growing number of SMEs have the potential to: generate new jobs as well as absorb labour made redundant by the ongoing reform of the SOEs; provide the engine for economic growth; contribute to export growth; and play a vital role in the modernisation and industrialisation of Vietnam. Therefore the government realises that it will be essential, in order to achieve the targets set under the SEDS, to support the further development of the private sector and SMEs.

Meeting the draft strategy's investment targets will require total domestic private investment having to rise to 11–13 per cent of GDP. This is unlikely to occur without a significant improvement in the climate for the private sector, and for SMEs in particular. The climate for the private sector, however, still remains grudging rather than supportive. This contrasts markedly with China where the private sector has been recognised openly as a key partner in the country's development.[7] Despite this there are indications that the climate is improving. In mid-1998 the Law on Promotion of Domestic Investment was revised, providing new incentives for the domestic private sector. This was followed by the approval and implementation of the Enterprise Law in 1999 and 2000. Together with the elimination of more than 100 different business licences that restricted entry in different sectors, ongoing implementation of the law is improving the policy environment for domestic private SMEs significantly. The Enterprise Law 2000 substantially simplified business start-up and led to the registration of more than 10 000 additional domestic firms in the first nine months of 2000. However, domestic private registered firms (private SMEs) still number only around 30 000 and produce less than 10 per cent of GDP. Creating a level playing field for the private sector will require a shift in the social and administrative culture from one of reluctance and control towards one of active support and encouragement. The private sector will also benefit from the introduction of a transparent and predictable regulatory framework, where discretionary actions on the part of officials are minimised.

In addition, three recent government policies have gone some way to reducing the restrictions on private SMEs. First, firms are allowed to export directly. This will help small firms most of all as they were least able to bear the additional transactions costs of previous restrictions. Second, requirements to import through state enterprises, to satisfy stipulated conditions of capital and qualified personnel needed for being registered as an importer, have been removed. Third, foreign investors are now allowed to own 30 per cent of shares in existing domestic enterprises, permitting private firms to seek foreign partners.

More needs to be done in the area of finance and access to credit for SMEs, particularly for efficient enterprises in rural industry. So far, farmers, SOEs and private foreign firms have driven growth. Private small and medium enterprises have played a negligible role, especially in industry. But private SMEs have been the most efficient users of resources in other countries of the region and key to employment creation. They need to be encouraged in Vietnam. A vigorous private SME sector will need more freedom to operate and better services from a vigorous and modern banking sector, neither of which Vietnam has at present. A precondition for promoting such entrepreneurship will be to introduce reforms to reorient the country's banks towards the needs of private SMEs and to restructure, equitise and liquidate SOEs, to improve their efficiency. A more open trade regime and less import protection for heavy industry will mean more investment in labour-intensive sectors and exports (garments, footwear, travel goods, processed agricultural products, tourism), stimulating rural industry and agriculture. While registered private firms can export or import more easily, registration of private businesses, a prerequisite for trading, still remains difficult.

The most cost-effective prospect for generating off-farm employment is through promoting SMEs (that is, registered private companies with 50–300 employees). Each job generated in an SME is estimated to require a capital investment of about US$800 (VND 11 million, in book value). In contrast, one job created in an SOE requires approximately US$18 000 (VND 240 million). Empirical evidence from other countries also indicate that SMEs are more efficient users of capital under most conditions.[8]

During the early period of reform in the late 1980s agricultural growth, made possible by allowing farmers greater decision-making freedom, was the main engine for Vietnam's initial surge of growth. Eliminating the existing restrictions on SMEs has the potential to result in a second round of growth by boosting labour-intensive manufactures and processed agricultural exports, thereby protecting rural areas from the current slowdown. So far private SMEs (that is, registered corporate firms) have played a minor role in industrial production, contributing only 2 per cent of industrial output, and have grown very slowly. Household enterprises play a much larger role. This contrasts sharply with the experiences of its rapidly developing regional neighbours.

4.4.2   Vietnam's SMEs – A Profile

The Vietnamese economy is characterised by a large number of small and medium sized enterprises with little capital, total SME capital accounts for just 20 per cent of the total business capital value of all enterprises, and a small number of state-owned enterprises holding most of the capital of the whole country.[9] More than half of all SMEs are not owned by the state and are therefore, officially at least, private. In practice many companies that appear to be private are really not. 'So dominant is the state in Vietnam that the only way to survive is through a network of political patronage' (*The Economist* 1997, p. 46). Before 1988 Vietnam had no private enterprises, 'apart from family firms, which were politically above suspicion if only because, at least officially, they did not employ any wage labour' (Wolff 1999, p. 72). There were, however, some enterprises that were run virtually along market-economy lines, particularly in the south of the country. Currently, the most important organisational form of private enterprise is still the household firm, employing an average of three employees each (Wolff 1999, p. 73).[10] The next largest element of what Wolff calls *the semi-formal private sector*, are the industrial cooperatives and quasi-cooperative 'production groups' (Wolff 1999). The number of non-state enterprises has increased dramatically recently,[11] and the number of enterprises in the collective and state sectors has tended to decrease. The number of private enterprises, excluding business households or groups working below the limit of legal capital, has been increasing most quickly. Only 5.7 per cent of non-state enterprises were established before 1990.[12]

The number and structure of small and medium sized enterprises

In Vietnam, SMEs are officially defined by the government as enterprises with chartered capital of less than VND[13] 5 billion (or US$360 000) and fewer than 200 staff.[14] In 1998 there were more than 30 000 registered enterprises in Vietnam, including more than 23 000 non-state enterprises. Of these registered firms, approximately 22 000 were SMEs. SMEs in Vietnam account for 87.7 per cent of the number of state firms, 30 per cent of joint ventures, and 96 per cent of total private firms in Vietnam (CIEM 1998).

If we classify SMEs by their amount of investment capital (those enterprises with investment capital below VND 5 billion) and by their number of employees (fewer than 200), then around 90 per cent of the total number of enterprises in Vietnam are classified as small or medium sized. Despite making up the preponderance of Vietnamese enterprises the capital value of these SMEs accounts for only 20 per cent of the total business capital value of all enterprises.[15] The considerable capital value of the SOEs, particularly the large ones, accounts for this, in addition to the fact that the capital value of the non-state SMEs account for only just over half (52 per cent) of the total capital value of non-state enterprises.

Figure 4.4 indicates the growth in number of private registered SMEs over the 1994–97 period. In 1994 there were 10 859 private registered SMEs of which most were in the industry sector (4 392) and trade sector (3 894). While overall industrial growth has outstripped service sector growth, growth in the number of private SMEs has been far higher in services than industry. This reflects the bias in industrial growth in favour of capital-intensive and large sized enterprises. Trading SMEs more than tripled in number between 1994 and 1997 (Figure 4.4) while those in construction and other services more than doubled. The faster growth of service SMEs is largely because this sector is less dominated by state enterprises and thus experiences fewer restrictions on private participation. In 1997 56.5 per cent of all SMEs were in trade and repairing services; 21.2 per cent were in the industry sector; 6.9 per cent were in

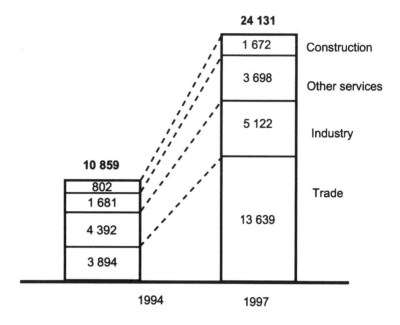

Source: GSO, *Yearbook*, 1994, 1997.

Figure 4.4   *Private Registered Small and Medium Firms*

the construction sector; and the remaining 15.3 per cent in other services. Most (90 per cent) of the more than 5 122 SME firms in industry in 1997 were in four sub-sectors: food and beverages (56 per cent); garments and shoes (9 per cent); metals and metal products (17 per cent); and wood and paper products (11 per cent). SMEs are typically well represented in sectors in which size and scale are not significant cost advantages. Such activities offer the greatest potential for future expansion of private SMEs (World Bank 1998, p. 30).

The contribution of non-state SMEs under a number of categories for various economic sectors in 1997 is contained in Table 4.11 and that for the economy as a whole in Table 4.12.

Contribution to GDP and production
In Vietnam there are almost no figures available for the contribution of SMEs to the economy. The following is an attempt to draw a general picture of the sector based on data available for economic inputs. In 1995 the share of 'value added' produced by the non-state sector to GDP was 65 per cent. The contribution of non-state enterprises, including SMEs, to GDP was approximately 36.6 per cent. The share of capital value of SMEs in the total business capital value of all non-state enterprises was

Table 4.11
Contribution of Non-state SMEs in the Main Economic Sectors, 1997 (%)

Sector	Capital	Labour	Turnover	Tax payments
Fisheries	55	80	57	87
Processing industry	15	49	22	24
Construction	22	56	33	19
Trade	21	60	42	18
Service & hospitality	19	56	43	63

Source: General Statistical Office, 1998.

Table 4.12
Contribution of Non-state SMEs in the Economy, 1998 (%)

Capital	Labour	Turnover	Tax payments
10.2	47	35	16

Source: Ministry of Planning and Investment (1999).

approximately 52 per cent.[16] It is therefore possible to assume that the proportion which SMEs provided of the total value added produced by non-state enterprises was also 52 per cent, that is 19 per cent of GDP. The share of value added produced by SOEs as a whole is equal to 25 per cent of GDP.[17] Assuming that the value added by state SMEs is equal to one-fifth of this then the contribution of state SMEs to value added is equal to approximately 5 per cent of GDP. Thus, the share of value added produced by all SMEs in the country, in all economic sectors, is estimated to be approximately equal to 24 per cent of GDP (see Table 4.13). This corresponds with the figure of 25 per cent of GDP quoted by the World Bank (2001, p. 49), suggesting that the proportion of GDP contributed by all SMEs has not changed by much during the latter half of the 1990s.

Tables 4.4 and 4.9 indicate that the state sector dominated the industrial sector during the period of the 1990s. However, by 2000 its contribution had fallen to 42 per cent of industrial production, and foreign invested enterprises, including joint ventures with SOEs, contributed a further 35 per cent of industrial production. The domestic non-state sector contributed the remaining 23 per cent of industrial production, with

Table 4.13
Contribution of Vietnamese SMEs to GDP, 1995

No.	Vietnamese SMEs by ownership	Percentage of GDP
1	Non-state SMEs	19
2	State-owned SMEs	5
Total		24

Source: Ministry of Planning and Investment (1998).

the bulk of this being produced by micro household enterprises. While private registered companies (SMEs), overall, contributed a very small proportion of industrial output, only about 2.4 per cent of industrial production in 1997 (Table 4.14), they were very important in the production of key export items including that of garments and textiles. However, the share contributed by all SMEs (including state SMEs, private local SMEs and those with foreign investment) to the total industrial gross output has been estimated by one source to be equal to 31 per cent.[18] However, compared with other countries in the region, where SMEs contribute on average 50–60 per cent of GDP,[19] the performance of Vietnamese SMEs remains modest.

Table 4.14
Distribution of Industrial Output by Ownership (%), 1997 Figures

	Total industry	Garments	Textiles
State-owned enterprises	51.4	36.0	60.0
Foreign invested enterprises	24.4	15.0	16.0
Non-state	24.2	49.0	24.0
Of which:			
Private companies	2.4	18.0	14.0

Note: Includes 100 per cent foreign-owned companies and joint ventures with SOEs; Private registered enterprises and others not in partnership with SOEs.

Source: World Bank (1998, Table 2.4, p. 30).

Contribution to industrial employment

The non-state sector contributes significantly to employment. As indicated in Table 4.15 the non-state sector contributed 76 per cent of industrial employment in 1997–98, with the domestic private sector contributing 64 per cent of total industrial employment. Private SMEs contributed 27 per cent and household enterprises contributed 37 per cent of total industrial employment in 1997/98 (see Table 4.15). The World Bank (2000, p. 49) has asserted that total SMEs for all sectors contribute 50 per cent of total labour employment.

Table 4.15
Industrial Employment by Sector (%), 1997–98

Ownership	% of workforce
State sector	24
Foreign invested	12
Private SMEs	27
Household enterprises	37

Sources: GSO, *Vietnam Living Standards Survey*, 2, 1999.

Contribution to international trade

As identified previously, Vietnam has made considerable advances in increasing the openness of its economy. Between 1991 and 1995 private firms were allowed to engage in foreign trade by obtaining a licence, tariff exemptions were introduced for imported inputs used in the production of exports, licensing procedures were simplified, an inter-bank foreign exchange market was introduced, and quotas on exports were removed except for rice. Vietnam signalled its intention to integrate with the region by joining ASEAN in 1995, and is now also seeking membership of the World Trade Organisation (WTO). Since 1998 the trade regime has been opened up further. The most significant measure was the freeing up of trading rights for firms registered in Vietnam. These firms were allowed for the first time to export and import goods directly without a license.[20] This newly provided right for domestic firms encouraged significant participation of private firms in foreign trade. Domestic private SMEs' share of non-oil exports rose from 12 per cent in 1997 to 22 per cent in mid-2000. Their share of imports increased from 4 per cent to 16 per cent over the same period (see Table 4.16). There is therefore considerable potential for an expansion of exports by SMEs, particularly given that they primarily produce labour-intensive products that are in line with the country's comparative advantage.

Table 4.16
Shares in Non-Oil Exports and Total Imports

	Non-oil 1997	Exports mid-2000	Total 1997	Imports mid-2000
State-owned enterprises	65	46	68	57
Foreign invested enterprises	23	32	28	27
Domestic private SMEs	12	22	4	16
Total	100	100	100	100

Source: Ministry of Trade.

Distribution of SMEs by location

According to Ministry of Planning and Investment calculations, see Table 4.17, more than 55 per cent of the total number of SMEs are located in the southeast and the Mekong River Delta. The figures for the Red River Delta and the North Central Coast are 18.1 per cent and 10.1 per cent, respectively. This suggests that there is considerable scope for an expansion of SMEs in the north of the country, where in the past SOEs have traditionally dominated.

Table 4.17
Distribution of SMEs by Region

Region		%
1	Southeast Coast & Mekong River Delta	55.0
2	Red River Delta	18.1
3	North Central Coast	10.1
4	Other regions	16.8
Total		100.0

Source: Ministry of Planning and Investment (1998).

4.5   EFFECTS OF THE ASIAN FINANCIAL CRISIS ON VIETNAM'S PRIVATE SECTOR AND SMES

Vietnam's neighbours were greatly affected by the regional financial crisis. They were afflicted by: dramatic declines in the value of their domestic currencies and stock markets; increased foreign debt; bankrupt corporations and businesses; structurally weak financial sectors; decreased exports; increased unemployment and poverty; and negative growth rates. While Vietnam's economy was not as highly integrated with the global trading system and international financial markets as the crisis-afflicted economies, and therefore not as directly affected by the crisis, its trade and other economic links, including that through foreign direct investment, are overwhelmingly with its East Asian neighbours. Hence lower regional output and import volume growth made Vietnam highly vulnerable. Vietnam's dependence before the crisis on Asia for exports and investment was substantial, making the impact of the regional crisis unavoidable. East Asia, including Japan, accounted for almost 80 per cent of Vietnam's exports in 1996 and 70 per cent of its foreign investment. In addition to the comparative price disadvantage of Vietnamese goods and services arising from the collapse of regional currencies, traditional buyers from neighbouring economies have been less able to pay, which has fuelled cash-flow problems and reduced the amount available for investment. Taking Japan as an example, Vietnam's largest investor, the crisis has shrunk the Southeast Asian market, the target of Japanese investors in Vietnam. Japan, once a large and rich market, now also has lowered growth and consumption. Japanese investors who take advantage of low Vietnamese labour costs to produce goods for export to Japan and the region are thus facing smaller markets.

4.5.1   Export of Commodities and Services

More than 60 per cent of the exports of Vietnam are to other Asian countries,[21] but the drastic depreciation of currencies in neighbouring countries made Vietnamese commodities less price competitive. Due to the effects of the crisis, exports to East Asia, including Japan, fell by 5 and 20 per cent in 1997 and 1998 respectively. Non-traditional exports like garments, textiles, footwear and seafood, two-fifths of total exports, were most affected by the crisis. During the period from 1997 to 1998, the price of services and of many export commodities such as rubber, crude oil and cinnamon dropped strongly, with a 20 per cent drop for garments and footwear processing.[22] East Asia and Japan's import contraction affected these items disproportionately since these countries constitute more than half of Vietnam's market for these goods. Also, these are price-sensitive exports which became relatively less competitive in the region given the large devaluations in crisis countries. At the same time, with the recovery from the crisis, these exports are also potentially the most competitive and their rapid expansion must be part of any major export drive during the recovery phase.

These are areas in which, as identified previously, the private sector, and SMEs in particular, make a significant contribution. The tourism industry was also affected, with sharp drops in the number of travellers from other countries visiting Vietnam.

The regional crisis made Vietnam less competitive for two major reasons. First, the substantial currency devaluations in the region. In Indonesia the currency at one point depreciated by nearly 80 per cent, while those of the Philippines, Thailand, Malaysia and South Korea depreciated by around 35–40 per cent in nominal terms. The VND, on the other hand, was devalued by much less and not enough to restore competitiveness to pre-crisis levels. Three exchange rate adjustments in July 1997, February 1998 and August 1998 devalued the dong by about 17 per cent, but this was insufficient to offset the gains in competitors' positions.

Vietnam's labour cost advantage was also reduced as a result of the real appreciation of the dong. Before the crisis Vietnam's labour costs were less than a fifth of its regional neighbours, except Indonesia. Since then the cost of unskilled and minimally skilled labour in Indonesia fell in dollar terms, and became almost on a par with that of Vietnam, arising from the large depreciation of the rupiah and deflation.

Second, reforms currently being implemented in crisis-afflicted economies will make them more attractive to investors and exporters than they were before. These countries have liberalised their legal framework for property ownership and foreign investment, eliminating tax disincentives to restructuring and new domestic investment, as well as lowering trade barriers. The financial sectors of such countries are also being restructured and made leaner and more efficient, even in China.

4.5.2   Capital and Production

The crisis in the region resulted in a sharp decrease in foreign direct investment, which in turn has hindered the development of local firms and especially small to medium sized businesses. Foreign investment inflows into Vietnam fell by around 40 per cent in 1998 and then by a further 22 per cent in 1999. New commitments fell even further over this same period. Much of the undisbursed licensed investment was in the real estate and tourism sectors, where demand and prices collapsed. About two-thirds of this was from East Asia and Japan where many firms were strapped for cash. This does not augur well for higher foreign investment flows in the near future. The impact of the crisis also affected the nature of foreign investment flows, with more than half of investment in 1998 coming from outside Asia. Only Japan, Taiwan, Singapore and Korea continued to invest, even if at lower levels than before. In addition the sectoral composition of investment was different in 1998. On the positive side the regional economic downturn provided the opportunity for better technology transfer from countries such as South Korea and Japan. A number of Vietnamese businesses were able to purchase equipment and material at below-market prices which provided for further expansion and operation of their businesses.[23]

In addition to these developments which have impinged upon Vietnam's domestic private sector in terms of reduced competitiveness, demand and profitability, the country's exposure to the crisis disrupted economic growth, adversely affected state banks and the profitability of SOEs, threatened fiscal and external balances, and made the country more susceptible to underlying policy weaknesses. In addition there was a significant human cost from the crisis in terms of its impact on poverty, particularly in the rural sector and poorer provinces, unemployment, erosion of informal social safety-net conditions, and reduced social spending. Falling employment in industry was partly a reflection of the high capital intensity of production that was encouraged by import protection. In terms of generating employment, policy emphasis needs to be placed on encouraging the production of labour-intensive products. This is where the role of SMEs will be very important during the period of recovery from the current economic downturn.

4.6   PROMOTING VIETNAM'S SMES

According to a recent survey by the Vietnam Chamber of Commerce and Industry (VCCI 1999), the main difficulties encountered by SMEs in Vietnam are:

- the majority (80 per cent) lack capital for production and trade;
- most have obsolete equipment and machinery;
- they lack adequate physical and human resources;
- they lack current information on technical, market and legal issues; and
- they lack support from the state, especially in technology transfer, credit guarantees and loans.

In this section, four of these issues are given particular focus: access to finance; access to technology and use of information technology; access to market information; and human capital deficiencies. Each of these is now briefly discussed in turn.

4.6.1   Access to Finance

Government policies on mobilising financial resources have been implemented through taxation, interest-rate management, and investment promotion strategies. Domestic production did develop rapidly in the first half of the 1990s as did domestic savings and gross investments. From 1991 to 1995 domestic private investment (mainly by SMEs) accounted for 30 per cent of total gross investment (approximately equal to US$6 billion). The remainder of the capital for enterprises was mobilised from formal domestic and international institutions.

Despite the increase in investment nearly all (80 per cent) of Vietnamese SMEs lack capital for production or business, according to official statistics (MPI 1999). According to a survey of SMEs conducted in 1999 by the VCCI: 55 per cent of enterprises have difficulty in obtaining capital; 67.5 per cent of enterprises have to borrow from relatives and friends; 25 per cent of enterprises have to deliver materials in advance; only 42.5 per cent of enterprises borrow from the banks; and 20 per cent of enterprises borrow from other financial organisations (VCCI 1999).

Other surveys of SMEs by government management agencies and other organisations give similar results. These surveys have also pointed out that the share of bank loans allocated to the non-state enterprises has tended to increase, but not in accord with their number and their contribution to GDP. For instance, bank loans to these enterprises, as a proportion of total loans, were: 10.3 per cent in 1990, 18.2 per cent in 1992, 33.1 per cent in 1993, and 37.1 per cent in 1994 and 50 per cent in 1995.[24] However, this has not satisfied the demand for credit by non-state enterprises. The financial system can satisfy only 25.6 per cent of the credit demand by the non-state enterprises. According to CIEM, in 1995, among 407 SMEs surveyed, 316 had to borrow from informal financial sources.

Difficulty in accessing financial resources by SMEs has partly resulted from the obstacles created by some of the policies and regulations on capital mobilisation. The effect of these policies has been as follows. First, the majority of external resources, such as foreign direct investment and official development assistance, have been allocated to the state sector. Second, there are still irrational regulations that seriously hamper the capital mobilisation of SMEs. For example, the regulations on short-term credit issued by the State Bank give preferential treatment to the state-owned enterprises, which enjoy cheaper financing in comparison to their counterparts in the private sector. Compulsory insurance is also unreasonably required for those assets financed by bank loans when such loans are in general not yet given by the banks and when the ownership documents related to the assets are not available. Collateral for bank loans is required for non-state enterprises while it is not for SOEs. There is still no guidance document available on collateral procedures. According to Decision 198/NH on 16 September 1994 by the State Bank and Decision 217 on 17 August 1996, the maximum bank loan is defined to be equal to 70 per cent of the value of the collateral written in the loan contract. However, in practice, enterprises are given loans equal to less than 50 per cent of collateral, regardless of the fact that the asset values determined by the banks are usually different from the actual values. Third, there are no special financial institutions for SMEs, except for a number of foreign funds such as the SME Development Fund, which operates through the existing commercial banks, and the Mekong Project Development Facility which mainly provides technical assistance for private sector SMEs.

4.6.2   Access to Technology and Use of Information Technology

Technology and equipment in SMEs
A draft development strategy for SMEs prepared by the Ministry of Planning and Investment (MPI 1999) indicates that their technology level as well as the nature of their equipment and machinery is in poor shape. Moreover, the rate of renovation is too low, approximately at the level of 10 per cent of annual investment. The strategy

document proposed, in order to improve conditions for the development of technology, that:

- competition should be created to encourage enterprises to adopt new technology and renovate existing technology;
- the economy should be open to access and exchange information;
- enterprises should be encouraged to improve their capacity to apply new technology.

Presently, the majority of Vietnamese enterprises, especially SMEs, are using obsolete technology that is perhaps three or four generations behind the world's average level. Their technological and technical capacity is limited, and the capital level per employee is low (only 3 per cent of the level in the large industrial enterprises).[25]

In a recent survey by the Central Institute for Economic Management, specialists in government organisations and other SME support institutions recognised that the technology level in SMEs is obsolete, that technology management skills are poor, and that product quality is low. At the same time the government has not provided supporting policies for technological advance. Among 40 enterprises surveyed only two had been able to get any technological support.[26] Policies that support the enhancement of technology for SMEs have many weaknesses. These are:

- There are no policies specific to SMEs (that is specific policies on training and improving the skills in management, technology and so on).
- No research and development organisation has been created specifically for SMEs.
- The specialised organisations in science, technology and training that exist are not strong enough to provide the supporting and consulting services required for SMEs.
- The existing promotion centres were established mainly to meet the requirements of international assistance projects rather than to satisfy the need to support SMEs.
- There is still no master plan or national strategy for the development of SMEs in the country.

Access to information technology – electronic commerce
Electronic commerce has yet to be systematically developed in Vietnam. In the country as a whole there are only four Internet Service Providers (ISPs), and fewer than 100 companies with their own registered websites. The Internet is still a luxury to most people, with high service charges (2 US cents for each minute online) and extremely limited banking infrastructure support for e-commerce.

As in many other countries e-commerce could play a vital role in Vietnam in the future. Currently however, especially in rural areas, lack of proper telecommunications, hardware and software, training, human skills and access to appropriate technology constitute major obstacles to the development of e-commerce especially for SMEs. Today only 72 000 Internet connections are registered in Vietnam. Major effort is required by the government to improve the current situation.

4.6.3   Availability of Information

One of the first steps in entering the export business is to get adequate and reliable information on market opportunities. This is a major difficulty for many SMEs. Most obtain information through the media or by personal contacts and not through formal channels. These personal contacts could be relatives or friends living overseas, or acquaintances made at trade fairs, conferences or on private trips. Only the more dynamic SMEs tend to contact formal organisations like the SME Club, the Chamber of Commerce and Industry and the various trade associations for such information. However, the average SME can neither digest nor effectively use the large quantity of statistical data and general information from the above sources, even if they manage to obtain it. The lack of reliable and useful market information often leads to a situation where local firms export their products with lower prices than the competition or miss out on good business opportunities.

The availability of specific information regarding new technology has been improved with the opening of technology centres such as the Technology Presentation House (TPH) in Ho Chi Minh City. These centres have been established with the aim of introducing new technologies and advanced products – both local and international – that can be implemented in Vietnam.

4.6.4   Human Capital – Skills and Qualifications

The skills of employees in SMEs do not meet desirable standards according to the Vietnamese government, because the majority of them, especially in small businesses, have not received any training while their educational level is low. Only about 5 per cent[27] of employees in the non-state sector have a university degree. The majority of the owners of non-state enterprises established in recent years have also not received any training, but they have a higher level of general education. Nevertheless, only 31.2 per cent of the owners of non-state enterprises have a university or higher degree,[28] and 51.8 per cent of proprietors have a management qualification. The percentage in proprietorships that have no management qualifications is 70.5 per cent and in limited liability companies 26.4 per cent.

4.7   GOVERNMENT'S ROLE AND SUPPORT FOR SMES

4.7.1   Background

Until the beginning of the 1980s in Vietnam there were only two significant institutional forms in the economy: state-owned enterprises (SOEs) and co-operatives. Private production and business units were allowed to operate but their scale and scope were negligible. Economic management during this period was based on the mechanisms of central planning. Enterprises did not have any autonomy in their production and business process since the government controlled and distributed resources and applied a monopoly policy on trade.

Economic reform started in 1986, but by 1988 inflation was increasing at an annual rate of 40 per cent with a large current account deficit. The events of 1989 convinced the Vietnamese government that it would get no further help from its previous benefactor, the Soviet Union. Starting in that year, it therefore adopted a package of measures introducing strict structural reforms and macroeconomic stabilisation, in line with International Monetary Fund (IMF) orthodoxy (Reidel and Comer 1997, pp. 195–7). The 'shock therapy' included the adoption of a policy of trade liberalisation and switching the economy to a market price mechanism that accelerated reform. The abolition of the majority of subsidies helped, and indeed forced, enterprises to operate within the market mechanism. The shift to a market focus was a key element in the policy of economic reform and contributed substantially to the development of the private sector in Vietnam. The policy of creating a market economy through the liberalisation of business activities relied on two factors: that market forces determine production and business decisions, and that the valid rights of enterprises are protected by the state (Woo 1997). One of the essential components of economic reform is defined in the policy for multisectoral development that recognises the permanent existence of a variety of forms of enterprise and provides for their equal treatment under the law.

4.7.2   Government's Long-term Vision

The draft Socio-Economic Development Strategy (SEDS) 2001–10 of the Central Committee of the Communist Party of Vietnam emphasises accelerating industrialisation and modernisation of the country and creating a foundation for Vietnam to become an industrialised country by 2020. In order to accomplish these aims the SEDS emphasises the importance of SMEs and private enterprises. A flourishing private sector and a growing number of SMEs would: absorb new workers as well as labour made redundant by the ongoing reform of the SOEs; be a key engine of economic growth; contribute to export growth; and play a vital role in the modernisation and industrialisation of Vietnam. The role of the government in supporting the further development of the private sector and SMEs will be essential, and involve levelling the playing field between SOEs and private companies and enhancing the business environment by: simplifying the tax system; streamlining administrative procedures; reducing red tape and corruption; restructuring the banking system; and strengthening existing or, when necessary, creating additional support institutions. Particular focus is required for the development of SMEs in the rural sector where non-agricultural jobs are scarce, underemployment is high and poverty widespread.

4.7.3   Achieving the Long-term Vision

Since the change to the Constitution in 1992, recognising the right of freedom of business and equality before the law for all sectors of the economy, the government has taken steps to develop the private sector and SMEs. Most recently the SEDS, the PSPAP[29] and a *draft* Governmental Decree on SME Promotion Policies Structure provide details of government plans for further action in this area. These plans focus upon the following areas: enhancing the legal environment for SMEs; strengthening existing and/or establishing new institutions; easier access to capital; trade promotion and export development of SME/private enterprises; and improving the image of the private sector. These are now discussed in turn.

Enhancing the legal environment for SMEs
Since 1986 important achievements have been made in adopting and elaborating legal measures and in creating the legal framework within which all types of enterprises can operate. Up to the end of 1996, 55 laws (codes, laws and acts), 64 decrees and 251 resolutions had been promulgated.[30] However, the soundness and validity of the fundamental reform legislation is in doubt. Significant problems are being caused by the proliferation of legal instruments, many contradictory, which are issued at every hierarchical level. This is due partly to a lack of experience in constructing the legal framework and partly because of the nature of the culture and social structure and the tensions within it. This results in an inability of the state to make any one entity accountable. The effect of this is a proliferation of state agencies with overlapping responsibilities and opposing functions (Kornai 1990).

Although the legal system is still not complete and has many imperfections, it has provided a level of protection higher than before that has helped the economy to operate on a legal basis. However, overall reforms have been slow and moderate and have often been accompanied by arbitrary new rules. A government agency (Central Institute for Economic Management (CIEM) 1998) identified the following main shortcomings:

- Legal regulations are too complex, ambiguous and contradictory.

- The legal environment for different types of enterprises is different and creates unequal grounds for enterprises to be established and operated. Many policies give priority to enterprises based on their ownership without supporting measures being linked to the scale of enterprise (so small enterprises which are officially or semi-officially owned receive more protection than larger ones which are not).

• Frequent changes in the regulations provide an unstable legal environment.

• Legal instruments are usually issued hastily, without corresponding support from supporting legislation.

• Some legal documents still lack a rational basis that causes difficulties and restrictions for enterprises, and creates gaps which they can abuse.

• Communication of the nature and implications of legal changes is still limited, and generally enterprises, especially SMEs, have limited knowledge of the regulations.

To advance the development of SMEs, Vietnam requires a rule-of-law-based regulatory framework. The current system of vague and frequently changing regulations and excessive bureaucracy has resulted in: increased risk and cost of doing business; a drain on the resources and time of private entrepreneurs that would otherwise be available for investment or for management of the business; and has created an inhospitable business environment. Evidence from other countries shows that bureaucratic stranglehold, exercised through bureaucratic discretion, has been a major drag on private sector dynamism. To establish the rule of law as the basis for government–business relationships there will also be a need for institution-building.

A transparent legal and regulatory framework for the private sector, therefore, needs to be established, to ensure a level playing field for both SOEs and the private sector. Three actions over the medium term will be required to achieve this. First, government should continue to monitor carefully and implement effectively the Enterprise Law (for example, eliminating, modifying and rationalising the remaining business licences in other sectors) and the Domestic Investment Law, since they are the key instruments for facilitating Vietnamese private entry further. In January 2000 the new Enterprise Law came into effect,[31] permitting for the first time non-discretionary registration of private firms, instead of by government approval, thereby eliminating bureaucratic steps. It also regulates the approval of establishment of a new business, which has to be decided within 15 days of the submission of the application. While this is a very important development, its implementation and enforcement is not yet consistent. Even though the government has abolished many licensing requirements a large number of licences still need to be obtained, depending on the field of business. The momentum for the elimination of unnecessary licences needs to be maintained.

The government has announced its intention to promulgate a Decree on SME Promotion Policies Structure in order to demonstrate a commitment to SME promotion and its strategy for achieving this. This will provide guidelines on support measures for private enterprises and SMEs covering areas such as encouragement policies and the set-up of support institutions. The Decree, originally planned to be promulgated in 2000, requires promulgation as soon as possible. The government also recognises the need to encourage the establishment of new SMEs, and to this end make administrative procedures simpler and more transparent. The problem concerning bureaucracy and complicated procedures in holding back the development of SMEs is acknowledged in the SEDS.[32]

Second, the revised Foreign Investment Law and Decision 24 need to be implemented in the spirit in which they were developed. Foreign investors should be encouraged, not discouraged, from engaging in joint ventures with private Vietnamese firms, to facilitate transfer of technology, and enhance marketing contacts and management expertise. Third, there is a need to make the regulatory framework for private participation in infrastructure more transparent and predictable over the medium-term and conclude some of the build–operate–transfer (BOT) transactions in the power sector in the short term. More generally, as recommended in the SEDS, implementation of equal terms for all enterprises regardless of ownership should be carried out as soon as possible in all relevant fields, for example, related to bidding for government procurement, access to land and credit and so on.

In addition, it will be important to improve the situation concerning land use rights: unclear and cumbersome procedures make it very difficult for private SMEs to acquire land. This presents a major obstacle since access to land-use rights is essential, especially to private enterprises, as collateral for accessing credit. In order to improve access to land the following steps are necessary: (i) clarify and speed up procedures for land title allocation; (ii) unify and modernise registers for land and buildings; (iii) reduce heavy fees and taxes on registration; (iv) provide clear, simple and fair procedures for resolving disputes.

Strengthening of existing and/or establishment of new relevant institutions and changing social and administrative attitudes

Ministries and agencies involved in industry, planning, education and training, such as the Ministry of Industry, Ministry of Planning and Investment, and universities, are still geared towards support of the SOEs. These organisations will be required to shift their focus towards the private sector and SMEs in order to enhance the general economic environment. This will require a fundamental change in social and administrative attitudes and a focusing upon an improvement in the image of the private sector in the country. The vital role of private companies for employment generation and modernisation of Vietnam should be acknowledged and disseminated through the media and the educational system at all levels. Given the many years of discrimination against private enterprises and private entrepreneurs, stronger and more frequent endorsement of private business by the Vietnamese leadership is required as was the case in China. Regular public exhortations by top leaders of the Party and government to the bureaucracy to provide support to private enterprises under the law, would be extremely helpful. Stories in the media of domestic private business successes and visits by top leaders to successful private exporters would help to reinforce the value of private business in Vietnam's development.

Apart from access to capital, most SME entrepreneurs consider lack of access to technical and market information and lack of skilled labour and know-how as their main business obstacles. The government needs to implement measures that will strengthen the business environment for SMEs through enhancing the performance of existing organisations and/or establishing relevant new organisations where appropriate. Measures agreed upon but still not implemented include the establishment of a national SME Agency that will coordinate consistent SME development. At the national level a Council for Private Sector Promotion has been proposed to provide a forum for a regular dialogue between relevant parties such as government agencies, local authorities, business organisations/associations and representatives of the private sector and SMEs. It will also provide advice on private sector and SME encouragement policies and programs.

Given the importance of mechanical engineering for the industrialisation and modernisation of Vietnam as well as the enhancement of technical know-how of entrepreneurs, the government decided to establish three technical assistance centres (TACs) (in North, Central and South Vietnam). The TACs not only concentrate on the enhancement of technical know-how but also support industrial sub-sectors such as textiles, ceramics, rubber/plastics, food processing and craft products, by providing engineering experts with experience in specific areas required by SMEs.

Providing an information system containing data on the latest developments for private enterprises through an Information Centre for Private Enterprises would benefit private enterprises. At the provincial and local levels the authorities should be encouraged to incorporate the private sector and SME promotion into their local development plans. In addition appropriate institutions on the provincial and local level should be established or strengthened in order to support private business activities.

Measures that include a strengthened provision of business development services (BDS) to assist the private sector and SMEs improve their access to resources, markets, new technologies and qualified labour would be beneficial. International experience shows that a growing number of private companies are the most flexible and effective providers of BDS to the diverse and fast-changing demands of the private sector. A number of public organisations, including business associations, already exist in Vietnam providing these services and they should be part of the future support to the BDS market as well. Since many SMEs are not aware of the existence of and benefits from BDS and/or are unable to pay market rates, the development of a well-functioning BDS market needs to be supported by the government and/or local authorities.

In many countries, business associations are playing a crucial role in identifying and advocating the needs and demands of the business community and in establishing a policy dialogue between the business community and relevant authorities. This has been acknowledged by the New Enterprise Law, which regulates, and the draft Decree on SME Promotion Policies Structure, which supports, the establishment and operation of private business associations.

Easier access to capital

A major constraint facing private SMEs in Vietnam is a shortage of funds. Private SMEs lack access to long-term loans, an equity financing system, and access to collateral. The strict collateral requirement by banks and the low incentives for state-owned commercial banks (SOCBs) to lend to SMEs, and on the other hand the unwillingness of private SMEs to deal with SOCBs, are serious constraints. This generates a vicious circle that prevents many SMEs from entering the formal credit sector, and forces them to rely on informal credit. Financial policies have an important impact on capital mobilisation and development of enterprises. Vietnam's banking reforms aim to address the shortages and problems of availability of credit and capital for the economy. However, the impact of these reforms on the domestic private sector will continue to remain limited if the private sector continues to experience difficulties in securing access to land-use rights, their potentially most valuable source of collateral.

The Private Sector Promotion Action Plan (PSPAP), the so-called Miyazawa Plan, agreed between Japan and Vietnam in 1999, includes more than 40 measures to diminish the constraints placed upon the growth of the private sector. It is based on three common principles: defining government policy to promote the private sector; securing equal treatment for private enterprises *vis-à-vis* SOEs; and granting private enterprises freedom to conduct business within the laws of Vietnam. A number of these include measures to improve the financial environment of SMEs. Some of these have already been implemented such as: the promulgation of the Decree on the Lending Guarantee; the Circular related to the Auction System; the Decree Liberalising Transactions involving Land Use Rights in 1999; and the establishment of the Stock Exchange Centre in 2000.

Others key steps to achieve further improvement in the financial environment for SMEs are the creation of a Two-step Loan Fund and a Credit Guarantee Fund. An agreement for a Two-step Loan Fund was signed between the Japan Bank for International Cooperation (JBIC) and the government of Vietnam in 1999. It intends to provide long-term credit to SMEs through selected participating financial institutions (PFIs), including joint-stock commercial banks. It is expected that 70 per cent of the beneficiaries from this fund will be private SMEs. The Credit Guarantee Fund for SMEs aims to further encourage financial institutions to lend to SMEs by absorbing a part of the credit risk, thereby alleviating current borrowing constraints as a result of their insufficient collateral capacity.

Other measures proposed include further improvement of the regulatory framework on lending, mortgaging, and leasing, and the pending banking sector reform will also provide SMEs with better access to credit.

Trade promotion and export development of SMEs/private enterprises

The government has applied a relaxed policy on restricting imports and exports and, as a result, the growth in the value of exports and imports from 1992 has increased rapidly. During the 1992–1999 period, the value of exports and imports has increased more than four times. However, the number of trade licences given to enterprises in the private sector only accounts for 15–20 per cent of the total number of trade licenses (Figures from Ministry of Trade 1998). A number of general trade restrictions remain. Non-state enterprises are allowed to export commodities produced by them and can import the input factors necessary to their production. However, they have to get permission from the prime minister if they want to participate in other export and import activities. At the beginning of 1997 regulations limiting licences on exported commodities were abandoned. In addition, access to domestic and international markets for some valuable trade items is severely restricted. Licences to trade in rice, petroleum, fertiliser, black cement, cars and motorcycles are only given to a few favoured enterprises. Only 19 enterprises are allowed to export rice and 25 enterprises are allowed to import fertiliser. Abandoning these regulations would greatly increase trading opportunities.

In addition to requiring export or import licences, the Ministry of Trade still has the right to require specific additional licences related to certain groups of exported or imported commodities. Furthermore, for some commodities additional export or import licences must be obtained from the line ministries. The tariff system also remains extremely complicated with many tariff lines, and nominal rates are high and the range of tariff rates is excessively wide. The system of tariff codes is not compatible with the system of product codes.

While trade procedures have gradually improved a number of problems remain. Institutional support for trade is still not available. Effective measures to prevent a large inflow of smuggled goods are not available. Some policy measures, such as the 90/CP or 91/CP decrees, which established the state-owned general corporations, and the special preferential treatment to SOEs though the credit and trade policies, are disadvantaging SMEs in the private sector.

More recently, the promulgation of three new implementing decrees related to the new Enterprise Law in 2000, and the removal of some quantitative restrictions in import management, represent a significant step forward in improving the trade and business environment for private sector development and SME support in Vietnam. Export licensing and trade management by quota is becoming less important than in the past. However some of the quotas now accessible to private enterprises need to be further opened up, and the bidding system should be more transparent. Also, special attention should be directed at the proper implementation of the new decrees, regulations and instructions of the government.

At present, the major obstacle preventing SMEs from seizing trade opportunities is their limited experience of global trade. Fragmentary knowledge and understanding of foreign markets are some of the basic trade barriers. This applies not only for information about management accounting, technical requirements, marketing skills, import regulations and consumer preferences, but also for assessing the suitability of imported goods. Limited language skills of the entrepreneurs is also a problem. Lack of these fundamental skills could be a severe problem when Vietnam further integrates into the global economy in the coming years.

Overcoming these difficulties requires not only an extended exposure of Vietnamese entrepreneurs to the world market, but also an intensive teaching and training of SMEs. Tapping into the expertise existing in neighbouring and other foreign countries would be particularly beneficial.

Beyond the information gap, the low level of competitiveness and the restricted ability to produce larger numbers of identical items of similar quality and on time are other severe trade barriers for local SMEs. Therefore, tailor-made quality management systems have to be propagated and implemented in order to enhance SMEs export opportunities.

Image of the private sector
The image of the private sector has to be improved in the country. The vital role of private companies for employment generation and modernisation of Vietnam should be acknowledged and disseminated through the media and the educational system at all levels. Negative social and administrative attitudes towards private enterprises impact adversely upon behaviour towards those engaged in private activities. They influence individual's decisions to enter the private sector and, once entered, constrain their ability to unleash their full potential. Developing one's business and increasing its visibility through success is seen as a risky proposition by many entrepreneurs in Vietnam, because private business has tended to be viewed negatively.

With greater freedom for the private sector also comes the need for improved corporate governance. There are at least three problems of corporate governance that will need to be addressed if the private sector is to grow in a transparent, accountable and effective manner. First, a key characteristic of the private SMEs is that their organisations are quite opaque. Not only is the ownership structure of most of these SMEs not known but also the way decisions are made is unclear. This is not much of a problem when firms are small, but as they become bigger and owner-managers' span of control is less adequate, absence of appropriate decision-making processes will constrain their growth. Second, most SMEs now do not maintain sufficient accounts or make any public disclosure of their accounts. Various types of restrictions and insufficient social acceptance of business success leads SMEs to misreport financial and other flows, when reporting is required. In the coming decade, it will be necessary to put in place the framework that will ensure that such enterprises act in a transparent and accountable manner.

4.8   SUMMARY AND CONCLUSIONS

The most cost-effective way of generating non-agricultural employment in Vietnam, according to the World Bank Consultative Group, is through promoting small and medium sized enterprises, that is, registered private companies with between 50 and 300 employees (World Bank 1998, p. 29). Each job generated in an SME is estimated to require a capital investment of about US$800, compared with an investment of US$18 000 in a state-owned enterprise (World Bank 1998, pp. 29–30). This conforms, says the Bank, to empirical evidence from other countries indicatings that SMEs are more efficient users of capital under most conditions.

The World Bank report observes that allowing farmers greater freedom of decision making made possible the agricultural growth that was 'the main engine for Vietnam's first great wave of growth' (World Bank 1998, p. 30). It recommends that 'unshackling SMEs from existing restrictions could unleash a second round of growth by boosting labour-intensive manufactures and processed agricultural exports, thereby protecting rural areas from the current slowdown' (World Bank 1998, p. 30). To date, however, private SMEs have, according to the Bank, 'played a minor role in industrial production, contributing only two per cent of industrial output and have grown very slowly. Household enterprises play a much larger role' (World Bank 1998, p. 30).

There are many factors which influence the development of small-firm economies – cultural, economic, financial, political and sociocultural – some of which we have been able to examine in this chapter. While agreeing with Orrù (1997) that 'No single factor, however important, can by itself account for the creation of small-firm economies' (p. 365), in Vietnam the role of the government has been and will remain crucial. The main effect of the Asian crisis on Vietnam has been to confirm the current leadership's belief that opening up to the West too quickly invites catastrophe (*The Economist* 2000, p. 67). The experience has swung the fine balance within the ruling elite between the conservative and progressive elements against a continued headlong rush into the world market. The price of slow economic growth seems one that is worth paying if the result is stability. Vietnam's more-developed neighbours, particularly Indonesia and South Korea, they argue, paid an economic and political price in instability and conflict, whereas less-reformed Vietnam was not much affected.

Real changes may follow the national party congress in 2001 when the last of the older generation of leaders will retire. The role of SMEs, particularly in the private sector, is crucial in helping development by harnessing latent entrepreneurial zeal. SME development does not provide as many of the major political and economic costs as are attached to reforming large, usually state-owned enterprises. Many of these are unprofitable and will need revitalising or privatising, which will result in the loss of jobs and the opening of Vietnam to greater foreign competition. However, giving greater emphasis to economic freedom that is necessary for releasing the energy of the SME sector runs the risk of triggering the instability that the regime is anxious to avoid. In the short term, it will also result in more unemployment and poverty. The many contradictions, new and old, evident in Vietnam, provide unenviable choices for the leadership. If they continue to reform slowly then Vietnam will probably stagnate, but if they open the country too fast then political change and internal disruption may be inevitable. Probably this is a necessary price, but it is one that currently the government of Vietnam doers not seem willing to pay.

The government has stated that it will support the development of small and medium enterprises with favourable policies and assistance in finance, market information and staff training (specified in a draft strategy to develop SMEs in Vietnam to 2010 prepared by the MPI). To support SMEs, the Vietnam Chamber of Commerce and Industry is working with relevant agencies, including the MPI, on the establishment of a credit guarantee system. It is clear that further government support is needed to help SMEs develop. It will be necessary to offer additional tax incentives, and support in funds and floor space to develop production, as well as to devise reasonable financial policies to attract money from the public and encourage effective investment by the private sector. Priority for enterprises will need to be given to trade categories focused upon traditional trades, handicraft, consumer goods, exports and hi-tech products. In addition, the state needs to reform the way it manages SMEs, so that procedures can be simplified and made easier to implement. SME development in the rural sector to expand employment and reduce poverty should also be given priority.

If the changes in policy identified in this chapter address the four key areas of: enhancing the legal environment for SMEs; strengthening existing institutions and developing new ones; enable easier access to finance; trade promotion and export development; and improvng the image of, and attitudes to, the private sector as well as its corporate governance, then the optimistic growth of the private sector outlined in the SEDS can be achieved. As China, another transition economy, has demonstrated, and as discussed in detail in Chapter 3, private firms if given the right environment can grow rapidly, from 100 000 to 1 million in just six years, and make a major contribution to the economy. In the case of China, however, there is clear commitment from the government to bring about this structural transformation, while in Vietnam the authorities have demonstrated considerable ambiguity.

Despite the capital-intensive nature of much of Vietnam's growth, there have been encouraging signs in the last few years of the emergence of a labour intensive export sector. Changes in trade policies have been an essential component of the doi moi policy adopted since 1986. Licensed private companies have been allowed to engage directly in international trade, breaking the trade monopoly of a small number of state-owned enterprises operating under central or provincial authorities. However, until very recently, private enterprises had to satisfy a number of fairly restrictive conditions to obtain the necessary licences. The recent removal of trade licensing, allowing companies to freely engage in trade within the registered scope of their business activities, should further improve the environment for export-oriented industries. In addition, over the years, most export quotas have been lifted and export taxes have been reduced to generally very low levels. These reforms, together with sound macroeconomic management, have allowed Vietnam to exploit its comparative advantage in labour-intensive manufactures, putting the country on track for export-led growth. This is a major lesson to be learned from the rapid growth of its regional neighbours.

NOTES

1   'A leading economist in Ho Chi Minh City ... called for a new wave of reforms aimed at reviving Vietnam's economy and providing for sustainable future development. Pham Xuan Ai, of the Ho Chi Minh City Economic Institute told the Thoi Bao Kinh Te Sai Gon newspaper in an interview that Vietnam's decade-old economic renovation process, known as *Doi Moi*, had reached a point of near exhaustion' (Edwards 1997, not paginated).

2   This prediction is based on the assumption that the Vietnamese Communist Party remains unambiguously in control of the government.

3   The World Bank ranked Vietnam as the twelfth poorest country in the world in 1996 on US$200 GNP per capita (World Bank 1996, p. 188).

4   If calculated on a purchasing power basis, however, per capita income was US$1 630 in 1997 (UNDP 1999).

5   Central Committee of the Communist Party 'Socio-Economic Development Strategy 2001–2010' (draft), p. 1.

6   Central Committee of the Communist Party 'Socio-Economic Development Strategy 2001–2010' (draft), p. 6.

7   See Chapter 3.

8   See World Bank (1998, pp. 29–30).

9   Vietnam had approximately 5 300 SOEs in 2000.

10   Ironically, the government of Vietnam does not consider family-owned businesses to be private companies (Vietnam News Agency 2000).

11   The size of registered capital of these newly established enterprises has been decreasing.

12   General Statistical Office (1996).

13   Vietnamese dong.

14   Ministry of Planning and Investment (1998).

15   General Statistical Office (1996).

16   Ministry of Planning and Investment (1998).

17   General Statistical Office (1998).

18   Central Institute for Economic Management (1998).

19   Ministry of Planning and Investment (1999).

20   For imports: registered domestic firms could only import products that were specified in their registration licence, and foreign invested firms could not do so until the recent revision to the Foreign Investment Law had eased those restrictions somewhat.

21   Ministry of Trade (1998).

22   Ministry of Trade (1998).

23   Obtained from interviews with directors of SMEs in Hanoi and Ho Chi Minh City by the authors.

24   Sources: State Bank of Vietnam, Ministry of Finance, Central Institute of
      Economic Management.
25   Ministry of Planning and Investment (1999).
26   Central Institute for Economic Management (1998).
27   General Statistical Office (1996, p. 97).
28   General Statistical Office (1996).
29   Private Sector Promotion Action Plan (PSPAP) agreed between Vietnam and
      Japan in 1999. Also called the Miyazawa Plan.
30   Malesky et al. (1998, pp. 10–15, 73–4) provide an excellent summary of the
      nature and significance of these legal provisions.
31   Resulting in the establishment/registration of more than 10 000 new enterprises
      during 2000.
32   Central Committee of the Communist Party 'Socio-Economic Development
      Strategy 2001–2010' (draft), p. 30.

REFERENCES

Alon, I. and E.A. Kellerman (1999), 'Internal Antecedents to the 1997 Asian Economic
    Crisis'. *Multinational Business Review*, Fall, 1–12.
Belser, P. (2000), 'Vietnam: On the Road to Labour Intensive Growth?', Background
    paper for the Vietnam Development Report 2000 'Vietnam Attacking Poverty',
    Joint Report of the Government of Vietnam–Donor–NGO Poverty Working Group.
Bond, M.H. (1988). 'Finding Universal Dimensions of Individual Variation in Multi-
    cultural Studies of Values: The Rokeach and Chinese Value Surveys', *Journal of
    Personality and Social Psychology*, **55**, 1009–15.
Bond, M.H. (1991). *Beyond the Chinese Face*, Hong Kong: Oxford University Press.
Bond, M.H. (ed.) (1996a). *The Handbook of Chinese Psychology*, Hong Kong: Oxford
    University Press.
Bond, M.H. (1996b), 'Chinese Values', in M.H.Bond (ed.), *The Handbook of Chinese
    Psychology*, Hong Kong: Oxford University Press, pp. 208–26.
Buchanan, I., C. Boulas and B. Raj Gopi (1998), 'Asian Paradox: Miracle, Myth and
    Financial Crisis', *Monash Mt Eliza Business Review*, **1** (2), 24–45.
Business Vietnam (1996), 'Direct Foreign Investment 1995', **7** (12), December 1995–
    January 1996: 31. Hanoi, Vietnam.
Central Institute for Economic Management (CIEM) (1997), *Economic Report*, Hanoi,
    Vietnam: Government of the Socialist Republic of Vietnam.
Central Institute for Economic Management (CIEM) (1998), *Report on Industrial
    Small and Medium Enterprises*, Hanoi, Vietnam: Government of the Socialist
    Republic of Vietnam.
Chenery, H. and M. Syrquin (1975), *Patterns of Development 1950–70*, New York:
    Oxford University Press.

Chinese Culture Connection (1987), 'Chinese Values and the Search for Culture-free Dimensions of Culture', *Journal of Cross-Cultural Psychology*, **18** (2), 143–64.

Economist, The (1997), 'Nothing is Really Private in Vietnam', **343** (8017), 17 May, 45–7, London.

Economist, The (2000), 'Goodnight Vietnam', **354** (8152), 65–7, 8 January, London.

Edwards, A. (1997), 'Vietnam Economist Calls For New Wave of Reforms', Hanoi, Reuter, 15 August, *Vietnam Insight* (vinsight@netcom.com), available at <www.vinsight.org/>.

Fforde, A. (1991), *Country Report – Vietnam*, Hanoi and Stockholm: Swedish International Development Authority.

Fforde, A. and A. Goldstone (1995), *Vietnam to 2005: Advancing on All Fronts*, London: Economist Intelligence Unit.

General Statistical Office (GSO) (1994), *Vietnam Living Standards Survey, 1992–93 (VLSS 1)*, Hanoi, Vietnam: The Statistical Publishing House, Government of the Socialist Republic of Vietnam.

General Statistical Office (GSO) (1996), *The Non-state Sector in the Open Period 1991–1995*, Hanoi, Vietnam: The Statistical Publishing House, Government of the Socialist Republic of Vietnam.

General Statistical Office (GSO) (1997), *Statistical Yearbook 1996 (NGTK)*, Hanoi, Vietnam: The Statistical Publishing House, Government of the Socialist Republic of Vietnam.

General Statistical Office (GSO) (1998), *Statistical Yearbook 1997 (NGTK)*, Hanoi, Vietnam: The Statistical Publishing House, Government of the Socialist Republic of Vietnam.

General Statistical Office (GSO) (1999), *Vietnam Living Standards Survey, 1997–98 (VLSS 2)*, Hanoi, Vietnam: The Statistical Publishing House, Government of the Socialist Republic of Vietnam.

Gillis, M., D. Perkins, M. Roemer and D. Snodgrass (1987), *Development Economics*, New York: Norton and Company.

Gittings, J. (2000), 'No Easy Victory in Hanoi's War on Poverty', *The Guardian*, 21 April, 20, London and Manchester.

Government of the Socialist Republic of Vietnam (1995), *Report to the Sectoral Aid Co-ordination Meeting on Education*, September, Hanoi: Government of the Socialist Republic of Vietnam.

Gudykunst, W.B. and S. Ting-Toomey (1988), *Culture and Interpersonal Communication*, Newbury Park, CA: Sage.

Hofstede, G. (1980), *Culture's Consequences: Differences in Work Related Values*, Beverly Hills and London: Sage.

Hofstede, G. (1987), 'The Applicability of McGregor's Theories in Southeast Asia', *Journal of Management Development*, **6** (3), 9–18.

Hofstede, G. (1991), *Cultures and Organizations: Software of the Mind*, London: McGraw-Hill.

Hofstede, G. and M.H. Bond (1988), 'The Confucius Connection: From Cultural Roots to Economic Growth', *Organizational Dynamics*, **16** (4), 4–21.

Jamieson, N.L. (1993), *Understanding Vietnam*, Berkeley and Los Angeles: University of California Press.

Kornai, J. (1990), *The Road to a Free Economy*, New York: W.W. Norton & Company.

Li, B. and A. Wood (1989), *Economic Management Capabilities in Vietnam: an Evaluation and Assessment of Needs with a Suggested Priority Project for UNDP's Management Development Programme*, New York: UNDP.

Malesky, E., V.T. Hung, V.T. Dieu Anh and N. Napier (1998), *The Model and the Reality: Assessment of Vietnamese SOE Reform – Implementation at the Firm Level*, Working Paper No. 154, July, Ann Arbor, MI: William Davidson Institute, University of Michigan.

McMillan, J. and C. Woodruff (1999), 'Inter-firm Relationships and Informal Credit in Vietnam', *Quarterly Journal of Economics*, **114** (4), 1243–85.

Mekong Project Development Facility (MPDF) (1999), *Vietnam's Under Sized Engine: A Survey of 95 Larger Private Manufacturers*, June, Washington, DC: International Finance Corporation.

Ministry of Labour, War Invalids and Social Affairs (1998), *Labour Forces and Jobs in Vietnam*, Hanoi, Vietnam: Government of the Socialist Republic of Vietnam.

Ministry of Planning and Investment (MPI) (1998), *Report to Government*, August, Hanoi, Vietnam: Government of the Socialist Republic of Vietnam.

Ministry of Planning and Investment (MPI) (1999), *Draft Strategy for SME Development in Vietnam*, Hanoi, Vietnam: Government of the Socialist Republic of Vietnam.

Ministry of Trade (1998), *Annual Report*, Hanoi, Vietnam: Government of the Socialist Republic of Vietnam.

Orrù, M. (1997), 'The Institutional Logic of Small-firm Economies in Italy and Taiwan', in M. Orrù, N. Biggart and G. Hamilton (eds), *The Economic Organisation of East Asian Capitalism*, Thousand Oaks, CA: Sage, pp. 340–67.

Pistor, K. (1998), 'The Implementation of Enterprise Reform in Vietnam', paper presented at OECD Conference on Enterprise Reform and Foreign Investment in Vietnam, 19–20 January, Hanoi, Vietnam.

Ralston, D.A., D.J. Gustafson, P.M. Elass, F. Cheung and R.H. Terpstra (1991), 'Eastern Values: A Comparison of Managers in the United States, Hong Kong, and the People's Republic of China', *Journal of Applied Psychology*, **77** (5), 644–71.

Ralston. D.A., N.V. Thang and N.K. Napier (1999), 'A Comparative Study of the Work Values of North and South Vietnamese Managers', *Journal of International Business Studies*, **30** (4), 655–73.

Redding, S.G. (1990), *The Spirit of Chinese Capitalism*, Berlin/New York: de Gruyter.

Reidel, J., and B. Comer (1997). 'Transition to a Market Economy in Vietnam', in W.T. Woo, S. Parker and J.D. Sachs (eds), *Economies in Transition: Comparing Asia and Europe*, Cambridge, MA: MIT Press, pp. 189–215.

Taylor, K. (1983), *The Birth of Vietnam*, Berkeley: University of California Press.

Triandis, H.C. (1993), 'Collectivism and Individualism as Cultural Syndromes', *Cross-Cultural Research*, **27** (3–4), August, 155–81.

Triandis, H.C., R. Bontempo, M.J. Villareal, M. Asai and N. Lucca (1988), 'Individualism and Collectivism: Cross-cultural Perspectives on Self-in-group Relationships', *Journal of Personality and Social Psychology*, **54**, 323–38.

United Nations Development Programme (UNDP) (1994), *Human Development Report*, New York/Oxford: Oxford University Press for UNDP.

United Nations Development Programme (UNDP) (1999), *Human Development Report*, New York/Oxford: Oxford University Press for UNDP.

Van Arkadie, B. (1993), 'Managing the Renewal Process: The Case of Vietnam', *Public Administration and Development*, **13**, 435–51.

Verbiest, J.-P. (1998), 'State Enterprise Reforms in Vietnam: Current Situation and Reform Agenda', paper presented at OECD Conference on Enterprise Reform and Foreign Investment in Vietnam, 19–20 January, Hanoi, Vietnam.

Vietnam Chamber of Commerce and Industry (VCCI) (1999), *A Survey of Private SMEs in Vietnam*, Hanoi: Vietnam Chamber of Commerce and Industry.

Vietnam Economic Times (1996), 'What it Takes', January, 14-20, Hanoi, Vietnam.

Vietnam Economic Times (1999), 'Little by Little', August, Hanoi, Vietnam.

Vietnam Investment Review (2000), 'Vietnam Income, GDP Targets Outlined', 1 March.

Vietnam News Agency (2000), 'Simplified Rules Boost Business Registrations in Vietnam', 29 March.

Wallroth, C., C. Rosvall and N. Austriaco (1990), *A Strategy for the Development of Management in Vietnamese Enterprises*, Stockholm: Swedish International Development Authority.

Wolff, P. (1999), *Vietnam – The Incomplete Transformation*, London and Portland, OR: Frank Cass.

Woo, W.T. (1997), 'Improving the Performance of Enterprises in Transition Economies', in W.T. Woo, S. Parker and J.D. Sachs (eds), *Economies in Transition: Comparing Asia and Europe*, Cambridge, MA: MIT Press, pp. 299–324.

World Bank (1996), *World Development Report – From Plan to Market*, New York: Oxford University Press for the World Bank.

World Bank (1998), *Vietnam: Rising to the Challenge*, Economic Report of the World Bank Consultative Group Meeting for Vietnam, Hanoi, 7 December, New York, World Bank.

World Bank (1999), *Vietnam: Preparing for Take-off?*, Informal Economic Report of the World Bank Consultative Group Meeting for Vietnam, Hanoi, 14–15 December, New York, World Bank.

World Bank (2001), *Vietnam Development Report 2001: Vietnam 2010: Entering the 21st Century*, Washington, DC: World Bank.

5   SMEs and the New Economy: Philippine Manufacturing in the 1990s

Edgard Rodriguez and Albert Berry

5.1   INTRODUCTION

The Philippines emerged in the early 1990s from a long period of slow growth, economic and political imbalances, and then managed to escape the 'Asian crisis' relatively unscathed. According to the International Monetary Fund (IMF),[1] this suggests that the reforms under way since the late 1980s, and intensified in the 1990s, have paid off, and are continuing to bear fruit with the help of skilful crisis management through the financial crisis. As a whole the Philippine economy fared the crisis better than anticipated, although economic growth remains unable to reverse three decades of poor economic performance or to surpass the rapid economic recovery experienced by other countries in the region. Moreover, the sustainability of the recovery will also depend in part on the solution to the recent political turbulence created by the impeachment of President Joseph Estrada.

While part of the explanation for the relatively good Philippine experience comes from sound macroeconomic management, part also stems from changes in its manufacturing structure. In particular, foreign investment in manufacturing targeted information technology products. Also, this investment is in itself correlated with a positive international attitude towards the macroeconomic management in the country. Like other technological changes in the past, information technology has the potential to affect a range of economic activities.

In the case of the Philippines, the economy has very much benefited from the growth of exports of new information technology products, such as semiconductors. In 1997, according to the OECD (2000), the Philippines produced information

Part of this work draws on Berry and Rodriguez (2001). We would like to thank Dr Thomas Africa and Ms Lourdes Homecillo at the National Statistics Office (NSO) for recent census and survey data.

technology goods (semiconductors plus a number of office and telecommunications equipment) worth US$6.6 billion, more than either India or Indonesia. This amount appears to be below Singapore or Taiwan which, according to the same source, produced on average more than US$30 billion worth of these goods. However, if one were to take into account the exports of semiconductors from the Philippine special export zones (US$15 billion in 1997 according to the Semiconductor Industries Association, see Rodlauer et al. 2000, p. 73), the Philippines produced US$21 billion worth of information and technology goods that year. A similar figure comparable to output in other Asian countries.

A large new production of information and technology goods heralds the arrival of a 'New Economy' which should also have other desirable effects for the economy and for manufacturing as a whole. For example, the 'new economy' could also bring new opportunities for SMEs because it provides them with the chance to combine their advantage of being small with the economies of scale provided by information technology.

Worldwide, it is too early to find evidence of major economic effects of information technology (IT). Most of the evidence focuses on the US, where a large share of overall productivity growth is due to productivity growth in the IT sector itself. Evidence in other OECD countries (including Canada) is just starting to appear. According to an ongoing OECD project on economic growth,[2] this is true partly because IT sectors are small and partly because it is related to the way their output is measured. Although manufacturing of computer-related equipment has been around for several years, it has not been until very recently that the use of computers has mushroomed.

The objective of this chapter is to explore recent evidence on the SME manufacturing sector in the Philippines, with emphasis on the 1990s. Section 5.2 looks at recent developments in manufacturing in terms of employment and productivity. Section 5.3 looks at selected dynamic factors affecting the survival of SMEs and their subcontracting activities, especially in sectors with traditional and modern exports such as IT exports. Section 5.4 reviews the recent policy responses and limitations of credit policies, and Section 5.5 provides concluding remarks.

5.2   RECENT DEVELOPMENTS IN MANUFACTURING SMES

Often it has been argued that an advantage of many SMEs is their flexibility. That is their capacity to weather storms, shift from product to product, expand and contract easily and so on. At the same time it is often argued that SMEs are the first victims of macroeconomic disturbances like the recent 1997–98 crisis. The regional macroeconomic crisis afflicted the Philippines less heavily than elsewhere but the slowdown has none the less been marked in the economy as a whole as well as in manufacturing, though exports were far less affected.

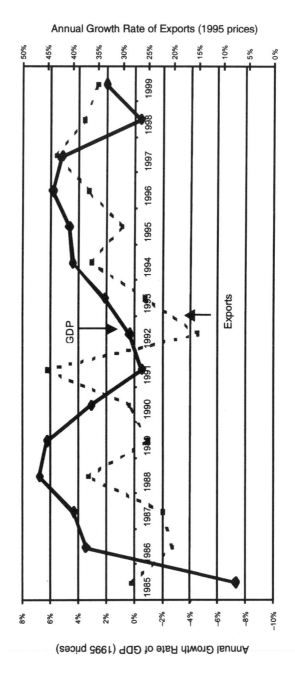

Figure 5.1 Exports and GDP Growth, The Philippines, 1985–99

The Philippines experienced two recent episodes of recovery before the recent financial crisis. One came after the Marcos administration (1986–90) and the other after the early 1990s downturn (see Figure 5.1). In 1996, GDP growth was at its highest (6 per cent). However, it decelerated over 1997, started to contract in the second quarter of 1998, and in the last quarter of 1998 finally shrank by 1.2 per cent. Manufacturing followed a similar pattern but with a more severe decline (–3.4 per cent) in the last quarter of 1998. In 1999 the economy grew around 2 per cent and in 2000 the growth rate doubled to 4 per cent, marking the start of the third recovery episode.

The recent recovery was accompanied by a continued growth in exports not present in the previous two recovery episodes. Most of the negative trends in manufacturing were not immediately, if at all, reflected in the evolution of exports during the financial crisis. During 1997 and the first quarter of 1998, these grew at double-digit levels. However, by the second quarter of 1998 export growth had slowed to 3.7 per cent. Although growth in exports slowed they did not contract.

In a clear break from the past, Philippine exports are today dominated by IT exports. Between 1996 and 1998 exports of electronics grew in every quarter, slowing down only in the third quarter of 1998. In 1999 they posted a 2-digit annual growth with respect to 1998. Electronics and components remained the top Philippine export in 1999 and the first five months of 2000. A bit more than half of these exports came from semiconductor devices, one-fifth from digital monolithic integrated units (that is, micro circuits), and the balance from other electronics and components. Most electronic exports are manufactured from imported electronic materials on consignment, which also makes electronic components the top import.

5.2.1 Recent Developments in SMEs

After the onset of the crisis a 1998 World Bank survey of firms (Lamberte et al. 1999) showed that non-exporting large firms were among the hardest hit. Most firms reported that the slowdown in their production was caused by the increase in input costs because of the devaluation, by the decline in domestic and foreign demand for goods, and by the rise in interest rates. The great majority of 385 firms surveyed were in five sectors – food products, textiles, clothing, chemical and rubber products, and electrical machinery. Most claimed to have continued access to credit, and the survey found that indeed there had been little change in the debt–equity ratio of firms after the crisis hit. About half of the respondents were SMEs (under 150 workers in 1996) with an average of 67 workers. In this survey most SMEs were more likely to have some foreign ownership than were large firms (54 per cent compared to only one-fifth of large firms), and they were also more likely to export than larger firms (74 per cent compared to only one-third of large firms).

The response to the crisis of these exporting, foreign-owned SMEs was, on average, better than that of large firms. First, according to capacity utilisation estimates, large firms were hit the hardest. Their capacity utilisation declined more (from 77 per cent to 66 per cent) between 1996 and 1998 than was the case for SMEs (from 79 per cent to 72 per cent). Second, 42 per cent of large firms cut down on hours while only 37 per cent of small firms did so. Also, large firms were more likely to use a compressed work week and forced vacation than smaller firms, while no major change in salaries occurred in either large or small firms.

Such a relatively good response to the crisis by Philippine SMEs may appear atypical. In part the response reflects the limitation of the post-crisis survey to the surviving – and perhaps more successful – firms. Moreover, there may not have been too many really small firms in the sample because SMEs were defined as having fewer than 150 workers which is a high cut-off employment level.

The next section reviews the trend in SME development over the last several decades, and portrays a less rosy, though not pessimistic, trend of Philippine SMEs. As in most developing countries the Philippines moved towards more market-friendly policies in the late 1980s after the Marcos administration ended in 1986. This shift was in part explained by the fact that policy makers concluded that the import-substituting industrialisation policy of the past either had never been very effective at

Table 5.1
Profile of Philippine Firms after the 1997–98 Crisis

	SME (fewer than 150 workers)	Large (more than 150 workers)
Total sample of firms	51%	49%
Financial Indicators		
Debt–equity ratio	11.16	4.39
Firm Characteristics		
Average number of employees	67	176
Share that export	74%	32%
Share that have foreign direct investment (FDI)	54%	20%
Response to the Crisis		
Current capacity utilisation	72%	66%
Share with fewer workers	46%	39%
Optimistic for future growth	66%	72%

Source: Survey of Philippine Industry and the Financial Crisis, World Bank, 1998.

promoting healthy growth, or was no longer so under the changing economic conditions.[3]

5.2.2   Trends in SME Development

After years of decline, the importance of manufacturing employment in SMEs[4] expanded in the late 1980s and 1990s, and so did their value added. Figure 5.2 shows the evolution of SMEs as a percentage of the reported employment in survey or census years over the 1957–97 period. Note that the use of survey data before 1972 (and in 1997) is not as reliable as census data available for years after 1972 (the next census is scheduled for 2000). Starting at 35 per cent of recorded manufacturing employment when SMEs were defined as those firms employing 20 to 99 workers, the share of SMEs declined markedly over the first period (1957–70) to about 18 per cent. Over the second period (1972–97) when the definition used was broadened to include establishments with 10 to 19 workers, SMEs 'recovered' in terms of employment share reaching almost one-quarter (at least part of the recovery must be due to the change in definition). The value-added shares show a similar pattern, and, hence, relative productivity must have changed little over the period.[5] In 1997 the value added of SMEs rose to 17 per cent of total manufacturing while their employment declined to 22 per cent of the manufacturing labour force, so that there was an improvement in overall labour productivity of SMEs before the financial crisis.

Average labour productivity of manufacturing establishments picked up in the economic censuses, the coverage of which is considerably better than that of the annual surveys. Over the intercensal period, 1975–94 (the next census was in 2000), average productivity rose by 39.3 per cent or 1.9 per cent per year (see Table 5.2). But the advance was far from continuous. Over 1975–88, there was a net decline of 5 per cent followed by a very sharp recovery in the next six years. All size groups showed this pattern, albeit to differing degrees.

In general, productivity gaps by firm size widened over time. For example, the ratio of labour productivity in establishments of 200 workers and up to that of those with 10–49 workers rose from 2.5 in 1975 to three-fold in the 1990s. More specifically the 10–49 worker group whose share of employment jumped at this time lost ground productivity-wise *vis-à-vis* each of the other categories.[6] Over the next six years, during which major reforms began to be implemented, these gaps changed much less, and the smallest category gained on the rest. Taking the whole 1975–94 period, there was a tendency for labour productivity gaps of the larger establishments in relation to the 10–49 worker category to rise despite an increase in the productivity of SMEs. Data from the 1997 annual survey of manufacturing continue to show a productivity gap between small and large firms of around 3.

Given the very choppy record of productivity growth it may be hazardous to draw much from this two-decade experience up to 1997. Over the 1975–97 period, labour productivity growth in manufacturing was only 1.1 per cent a year. Among micro enterprises and SMEs, medium firms appear to have done better, and micro enterprises

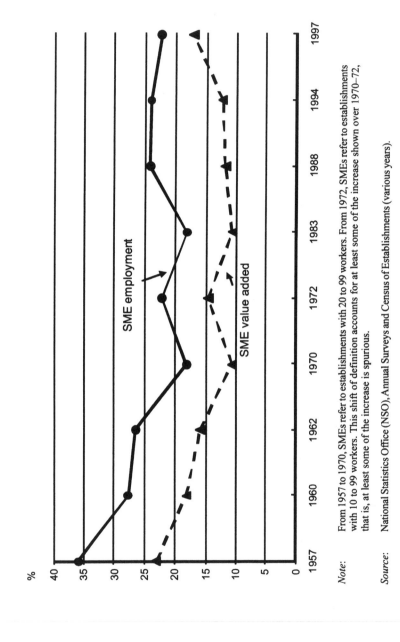

Note: From 1957 to 1970, SMEs refer to establishments with 20 to 99 workers. From 1972, SMEs refer to establishments with 10 to 99 workers. This shift of definition accounts for at least some of the increase shown over 1970–72, that is, at least some of the increase is spurious.

Source: National Statistics Office (NSO), Annual Surveys and Census of Establishments (various years).

Figure 5.2   SME Employment and Value Added in Manufacturing, the Philippines, 1957–97

worse. Over the same period, the productivity of the 50–99 category grew 2 per cent a year, while the productivity of the 10–49 category grew only 0.5 per cent. According to the 1997 survey, SMEs also appear to have posted high annual increases of productivity between 1994 and 1997 (1.9 per cent for the 10–49 category, and 8.0 per cent for the 50–99 category). In contrast the recorded growth for firms with 1–9 workers was nil over the entire period, although this figure is the least reliable.[7]

Labour productivity at the firm level rises over time due to investment and to technological change. At the level of the industry or of manufacturing as a whole it also usually rises through reallocation of resources towards firms with higher labour productivity. On the other hand, total factor productivity (TFP) rises primarily as a result of technological change in the industry. The last two censuses of establishments provide a glimpse of these two measures of productivity (labour productivity and TFP) by 2-digit manufacturing sector and size (Berry and Rodriguez 2001). Over the inter-censal period (1988–94) one tends to observe more the effects of rising capital-labour ratios – which increased on average at 10 per cent per annum in real terms – and perhaps of resource reallocation than of technological change as such (see Table 5.3). Note that the solid growth in labour productivity among all size categories over the 1988–94 period (over 6 per cent per year) shows a large variance across sectors so that no one single pattern of productivity by size emerges.

Table 5.2
Labour Productivity in Philippine Manufacturing by Size of Establishment,
1975–97 (value added per worker)

Size of establishment	1975	1988	1994	1997[a]	1975	1988	1994	1997[a]
	In 1990 thousands of pesos[b]				As % of firms with 10–49 workers			
1–9 workers	28.9	21.2	28.1	24.3	0.3	0.3	0.3	0.2
10–49 workers	100.0	71.2	103.3	111.3	1.0	1.0	1.0	1.0
50–99 workers	169.5	132.2	195.1	265.2	1.7	1.9	1.9	2.4
100–199 workers	203.9	172.9	294.9	232.2	2.0	2.4	2.9	2.1
200+ workers	254.7	234.1	341.0	346.2	2.5	3.3	3.3	3.1
Total	162.5	154.1	226.5	210.6				

Notes:
a   Data for 1997 come from the annual survey.
b   Constant pesos using the wholesale price index (1990=100): 12.8 (1975), 82.0 (1988), 126.9 (1994), and 188.4 (1997).

Sources: 1975 census tabulations from Bruch and Hiemenz (1983, Table 3–3); 1988, 1994 and 1997, special unpublished tabulations.

Table 5.3
Manufacturing Sectors with Highest Labour Productivity Growth,[a] 1988–94

	Total	1–9	10–49	50–99	100–199	200+
Machinery &						
transport	8.1	1.3	8.5	4.6	11.2	6.4
Textiles & apparel	6.8	2.6	10.1	17.7	4.6	6.4
Chemicals	6.8	14.8	−5.4	3.4	4.0	8.7
Other	6.9	0.9	11.1	4.9	−1.6	8.6
All manufacturing	6.4	4.8	6.4	6.7	9.3	6.5

Note: a   Value added in 1990 pesos per worker.

Sources: Census of Establishments, 1988 and 1994, own calculations.

5.2.3   Firm Survival in the 1990s

Developing countries value SMEs for the static and dynamic gains that these firms bring. From the static point of view SMEs on average are believed to generate relatively large amounts of employment while also achieving decent levels of productivity. From the dynamic point of view the sector is viewed as being populated by firms most of which have considerable growth potential – in contrast to micro enterprises which tend not to graduate from that size category (Leidholm and Mead 1999). Many SMEs will grow significantly without exiting that size category while others will eventually become large – the 'seed-bed for large firms' function of SMEs. Another aspect of the dynamics of SMEs that distinguishes them from larger enterprises is their high entry and exit rates. The process of rapid turnover raises a set of issues about possible impacts on the economic efficiency of the sector and about policies that may curtail such efficiency losses as are associated with it. Finally, it is often argued that one advantage of SMEs is their flexibility, relative at least to larger firms.

Data on the life cycle of firms in the Philippines are very scarce. An early study by Fajardo (1979, cited in Tecson et al. 1990, pp. 372–5) gives a glimpse of the dynamics of SMEs in the 1970s. This early study defined SMEs as firms with 5 to 199 workers. To get a richer understanding of the life pattern of SMEs, Fajardo took a sample of 501 establishments in the National Statistics Office listings for 1972, 1975 and 1977. The exercise revealed that 2 per cent of the firms operating in 1972 disappeared in the 1975 listing and reappeared in 1977 because of temporary closures. Also, the exercise showed that the median age of her sample of SMEs was seven years, but the most common age was just two years, which shows the relatively short life of most SMEs.[8] Finally, part of the study monitored a subset of 101 firms from 1972 to 1977 and found that 85 per cent of firms 'survived', that is, were still operating after five years (that is, 1977).

To our knowledge no other systematic study on firm dynamics in the Philippines has yet been undertaken. However, data based on the NSO survey listings (see Berry and Rodriguez 2001) show what seems to be the only recent evidence on survival rates of Philippine manufacturing establishments. On average 85 per cent of firms in all sectors survived their first year, and only 65 per cent survived the second year. Survival rates of around 80 per cent are not uncommon in the first years after foundation of the firm in other countries. Liu and Tybout (1996) report survival rates of 79 and 73 per cent for large Colombian and Chilean firms after the first year respectively, while Audretsch (1991) reports survival rates of 77 per cent for new German firms after the first two years in operation. In Canada survival rates for manufacturing firms are 83 per cent in the first year, and the rates drop to half by the fourth (Baldwin et al. 2000).

5.3   ELECTRONICS EXPORTS AND SMES

Large enterprises in developing countries achieve productivity increases to a considerable extent simply by borrowing from the shelf of technologies available in the world. For SMEs as a group it is not so evident that processes like foreign direct investment, technology licensing, joint ventures, and access to engineering and other advances will provide the gains needed. Yet SMEs need fairly continuous productivity increases if they are to maintain or increase their contribution to overall development as capital becomes less scarce and the range of technologies available expands in the world.

Raising productivity by technological upgrading (in the broadest sense to include not just better machinery but also improvements in workplace organisation, inventory handling, product design and so on) is achieved through a variety of mechanisms. It is accepted that most SMEs will be less able to handle this process successfully on their own in comparison to that of larger enterprises. Accordingly, much attention has been given to the possible roles of subcontracting and clustering as arrangements which make such advances more easily accessible to SMEs, and to collective support systems including those of the public sector and of private associations. The Japanese experience is viewed as the paradigm for the importance of subcontracting in creating the conditions for a major SME role in a strong and internationally competitive manufacturing sector. Italy's export-oriented clusters have become a model for the role of clusters in competitive export activities. These two phenomena (subcontracting and clustering) are of course not limited to export settings, though they may have their most impressive manifestations there. There is evidence that technical efficiency in the Philippine textile industry is positively related to exporting and to subcontracting (Mini and Rodriguez 2000). One wonders whether this link is more general.

Subcontracting appears to be low in the Philippines compared to other Asian economies. Closer observation does make it clear that there is a considerable amount of it, including that engaged in by household units. Still, it has been less prevalent than in countries like Taiwan and (recently) Korea. According to one common view this is to be expected where high levels of protection reduce incentives for cost reduction and have negative impacts on the demand for the output of smaller firms and on their learning opportunities (Hill 1985). Measured as the percentage of work carried out for others the 1994 Philippine census indicated that only 1.7 per cent of manufacturing output was carried out for others. Across firm size the percentage is the highest for small firms with 10 to 49 workers (8.5 per cent). Moreover, small firms in textiles and apparel as well as in machinery and transport undertake a large percentage of their output for other firms (31 per cent and 11 per cent, respectively).

Sector-wise a number of export-oriented industries exhibit a higher than average share of subcontracting. Industries with a high reliance on components allow more room for subcontracting activity. Where such orientation is present, exporting tends to enhance the possibility for subcontracting, which brings cost advantages and flexibility that are often crucial to success in highly competitive export markets. A good example is electrical and non-electrical machinery (PSIC 38 Machinery and Transport) with high export orientation and a higher-than-average degree of subcontracting activity for SMEs (small firms produced 11 per cent of output for other firms). Apparel also fits this mould. In general, subcontracting can be a promising route for SMEs to obtain access to export markets, provided the sector has high export orientation and can use components.[9] They are assured of (derived) demand from the assembly firms who undertake the exporting of the final products. Hence, they do not have to worry about the information bottleneck they would face in trying to export directly. It also offers the possibility for technology transfer and quality control, as well as the discipline associated with exporting (for example, compliance with delivery dates). Above all, subcontracting favours the creation of backward linkages that lead to the deepening of the industrial structure by fostering domestic production of capital goods and intermediate inputs.

Exports are concentrated among the largest firms, but in terms of share of output all size categories were in the 18–19 per cent range except those with 10–49 workers at 11.6 per cent.[10] Table 5.4 shows the tabulations of the most recent census of manufacturing (the first census with information on exports at the firm level). Across sectors there are major variations in this pattern. In many industries, medium establishments export a higher share than larger or smaller ones, for example, food, textiles, apparel, wood and furniture, and non-metallic mineral products. On the other hand, large firms in machinery and transport export much more of their output (almost half) than do smaller ones. In all industries larger firms do most of the exporting because of their weight in total output. This is especially true for 'machinery and transport' of which the major exporting subsector is electronic equipment (large firms with more than 200 workers exported almost 96 per cent of the total from this sector). But it is less so for wood and furniture manufacturers (one-fifth of all exports in this sector are done by firms with 10 to 49 workers).

The considerable subcontracting reported for very small firms of say 5–50 workers

Table 5.4

Manufactured Exports by Establishment Size, the Philippines, 1994

	As % of total output in size category					As % of all exports				
	Total	10–49	50–99	100–199	200+	Total	10–49	50–99	100–199	200+
Food	10.3	6.7	17.6	22.3	7.8	100.0	3.5	8.1	36.5	51.9
Textiles & apparel	39.1	17.9	44.9	38.9	44.7	100.0	5.2	12.8	10.4	71.5
Wood & furniture	28.7	36.6	54.8	45.2	42.7	100.0	20.5	13.9	16.2	49.4
Paper	5.5	1.4	11.1	12.6	4.2	100.0	3.3	21.8	28.7	46.2
Chemicals	5.3	7.6	5.8	9.9	4.6	100.0	5.2	4.8	18.5	71.5
Non-metallic	8.2	11.2	18.3	21.8	6.6	100.0	5.9	7.6	22.2	64.3
Iron & steel	4.4	5.4	5.2	5.0	4.0	100.0	3.8	10.9	21.7	63.7
Machinery & transport	37.8	8.6	10.9	12.5	42.7	100.0	0.9	1.1	2.0	96.0
Other	52.4	44.8	33.9	68.6	57.2	100.0	9.5	6.3	16.8	67.4
Total	17.4	11.6	18.6	18.7	18.2	100.0	3.7	5.9	12.7	77.8

Source: Census of Establishments, 1994, special tabulation.

in certain industries extends also to the household level. As of the early 1980s international subcontracting was practised in car parts, textiles, leather and leather parts, toys, handicrafts, food processing, musical instruments, paper/packing products, plastic and rubber products and metal fabrication (Ofreneo 1983, p. 37). In many of these industries, but especially in wooden furniture/wooden products and in apparel, household subcontractors have also been active (Csorgo 1994, p. 23). Csorgo's analysis of why contractors opt to work with these very small units – the average number of workers per unit was 2.4, of whom 0.7 were hired non-household members, and 86 per cent carried out their production activities in-house – highlights cost advantages on wages and production space. In addition, contractors use this system to deal with demand fluctuations. For their part these family subcontractors' reasons for engaging in such arrangements include most prominently easier marketing.

During the recent crisis, exports of electronics continued to dominate not only half of all Philippine manufactured exports but also export growth in general (Figure 5.3). Electronic and apparel exports have provided the bulk of exports since the 1980s. These sectors, especially electronics, have traditionally had more foreign direct investment (FDI) than any other branches of manufacturing in the Philippines. Between 1988 and 1995, although other branches, such as textiles, furniture and footwear, raised their exports, they only play a very small role compared to exports in electronics and apparel. Between 1995 and 1999 exports of machinery and transport have been the driving force of the entire (export) sector. Figure 5.3 shows that quarter after quarter since 1995, 'machinery and transport' (with electronics being the key actor) grew, while other more traditional manufactured exports remained quite sluggish.

Philippine manufacturing can be characterised as having two very different types of exporting clusters. On the one hand, one observes producers who export traditional manufactured goods such as footwear and furniture. On the other, much of the recent FDI in the Philippines has created a group of active exporters in less traditional more high-end products such as semiconductors and other computer-related equipment.

SMEs produce many of the more traditional exports while larger firms produce most of the more technologically advanced exports. There SMEs play a very secondary role. On the one hand, the largest foreign exchange earners among the more traditional industries are footwear and furniture, but their exports are quite small compared to those of such high-technology categories as machinery and electronic manufactures, which amount to US$8.1 billion, or more than half of all manufactured exports in 1994. Although both industries (footwear and furniture) had a long presence in the Philippines and in international markets they remain Filipino owned, and are quite fragmented into many small firms in or around Metro Manila.

On the other hand, large foreign firms were the largest foreign exchange earners in electronics. Despite the Asian crisis, 38 new electronics companies registered during 1998, according to the Board of Investment-Philippine Economic Zone Authority, bringing the total number to 462. Of these, 138 were Philippine firms (relatively small); 199 of Asian origin (Japanese, Korean or Taiwanese), and 39 American. The latter accounted for about 70 per cent of all exports.

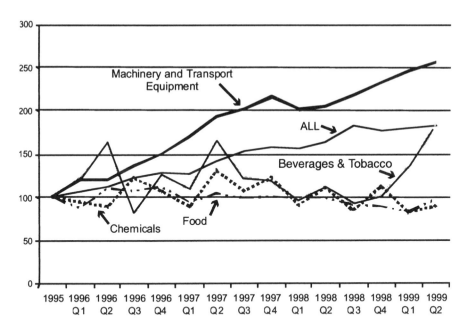

Source: NSO Statistics online (<www.census.gov.ph>).

Figure 5.3   Electronics and Other Manufactured Exports, 1995–99

The recent re-emergence of FDI in the Philippines has created a new generation of SMEs in modern industries such as electronics and cars. These sectors had been chosen in the 1970s for the encouragement of supporting industries through a local content requirement policy (see Tecson 1999a for a detailed discussion of the success of the policy). Their growth has generated the simultaneous development of supplier industries. In the case of the car industry, SMEs are the major producers of car parts. In electronics SMEs are found in the assembly of parts, while large firms dominate the production of parts themselves, such as semiconductors. The economic downturn of 1998 was less sharp in this modern manufacturing sector than elsewhere, mainly through the role of exports.

Although growth of electronics exports occurred in the 1990s, the sector has long historic roots in the Philippines. Electronics consists of four subsectors: consumer electronics, telecommunications equipment, computers and computer components (including semiconductors). Each subsector is linked to a particular period in Philippine manufacturing's recent history. The electronics industry was born in the 1950s out of the service and repair of imported electronic products. In the 1960s production of consumer electronics equipment came with the entry of multinationals, which were attracted by the size of the potential domestic market. In the 1970s the industry received a boost from the entry of producers from the US, Japan and Europe, who were in search of low-cost labour for the assembly stage in order to maintain competitive advantage in export markets. This wave included the largest semiconductor-producing firms such as Intel, Motorola, Texas Instruments, Philips, Sanyo and Fuji among others. FDI in the late 1980s and 1990s flowed into telecommunications equipment and computer peripherals. The major Japanese multinationals such as Hitachi, Fujitsu, Toshiba and NEC have recently entered the Philippines to assemble hard-disk drives (Tecson 1999b).

According to census data, SMEs dominate the assembly industry in electronics while large firms dominate the production of parts; this is the inverse of what one finds in the automotive industry where parts, not assembly, is dominated by SMEs. The number of firms in electronics assembly increased from 119 in 1983 to 163 in 1988 and 198 by the last manufacturing census of 1994. On average an electronic assembly firm employed 177 people in 1983, 132 in 1988 and 274 in 1994. Note that firms producing electronic parts were fewer than 75 over this period, and employed on average more than 600 workers each (Tecson 1999b, Tables 12a and b).

The production of hard-disk drives in the Philippines is essentially explained by Japanese FDI, and it is a very recent example of how FDI supports the development of a foreign-owned transplant of SMEs. In the late 1980s the political environment for FDI in the Philippines was far from being auspicious with the People's Revolution in full swing, causing Japanese firms to stay away from the Philippines. In the 1990s the largest hard-disk drive producers in Japan moved into the Philippines, together with their network of Japanese suppliers, and made the Philippines the only centre for the assembly of hard-disk drives. While assemblers were motivated to relocate to the Philippines because of the strategic location of the country, the relative abundance of labour and worker trainability, suppliers were motivated 'to be near the majors' (Tecson 1999b).

The crisis may have reduced domestic sales but the domestic market in electronics (and car parts) remains tiny compared to export markets, reflecting both the weak deepening of the high-technology industries in terms of backward linkages within the Philippine manufacturing sector and the small domestic consumer market. Such a weak deepening characterises economies with the sort of slow-growth record achieved by the Philippines.

But the export market has remained buoyant. As Figure 5.3 shows, after 1995, electronics (included under machinery and transport equipment) have continued to dominate the export recovery experienced in the Philippines. The sector exported almost double its 1995 level by the end of 1998, while all other sectors reported export values similar to those of 1995. Only a small part of this growth can be attributed to SMEs owned by foreign investors in joint ventures such as those described above. The crisis appears to have had little effect on domestic market-oriented production of electronics (and to a lesser extent car parts) because of the lack of linkages with the rest of the economy. Domestic production for the electronics industry is limited to indirect inputs such as carton packaging and some minor chemicals. Probably the same is true of parts headed for the country's third top export from the industry, namely input–output peripheral units. The bulk of the domestic parts production in the sector is destined for the electronic appliance industry that did show a sluggish trend during the crisis (for a discussion, see Tecson 1999a).

A modest average annual GDP growth rate of 2.5 per cent per year characterised the period from 1988 to 1994. The average productivity in manufacturing was almost nil, though it may have been better for the smaller establishments of under 50 workers. The productivity record appears to be better during the next three years of good growth (1994–97) before the downturn brought on the Asian crisis. No estimates are yet available for the period after 1998.

The evidence presented in this section suggests some grounds for optimism, both on overall performance and with respect to SMEs. As of 1994 the SME sector (censused establishments with 10–199 workers) accounted for about 23 per cent of manufacturing output and 22 per cent of direct exports (Table 5.4) plus a few additional per cent of exports indirectly through subcontracting. Over 1988–94 the most dynamic export activity was electronic equipment where, as we have seen, only a small share of exports came directly from the SME sector. Apparel, where SMEs are important as exporters was the second most dynamic, and the second largest exporter. The 1994–97 period provides an interesting test of future possibilities since growth was solid each year. Exports were again led by electronic equipment, while apparel grew more modestly. Hopefully, now that regional growth has returned, Philippine exports will continue to expand rapidly with an increasing participation by SMEs. Whether this becomes an established pattern will no doubt depend on some of the policies in place.

5.4   GOVERNMENT RESPONSE TO THE CRISIS: OLD VERSUS NEW POLICIES

After decades of targeted intervention in industry, support is moving towards a more market-friendly approach. Certain disenchantment with respect to SME-targeted policies is emerging based on the poor performance of highly interventionist policies of the past. Today, in the Philippines, the interventionist approach has lost ground in favour of a more open and market-friendly approach towards multinationals. Perhaps SMEs could also benefit from a similar hands-off approach.

The example of electronics, a sector not dominated by SMEs, illustrates how firms, which have not necessarily been targeted directly by government policies, have managed to flourish in a less bureaucratic environment with adequate infrastructure and access to international markets. Electronics, the export star in the Philippines, has benefited from the more open trade regime of the 1990s than a more regulated policy environment. The industry (mainly export oriented) must have benefited from the local content policy in the 1980s that helped to encourage growth in industries of tool and die-cast or metal and plastic injection. The trade reforms of the 1990s have reduced the bias against exports by liberalising foreign equity ownership; introduced changes to the Investment Incentives Law to provide incentives similar to those in other ASEAN countries, and created privately owned economic zones which have eliminated previous infrastructure or bureaucratic bottlenecks.

During the crisis, however, some interventionist policies re-emerged. First, while the crisis emphasised some policies to protect workers, they were in fact non-distorting policies and were not meant to benefit SMEs. Also, while credit policies for SMEs continue to attract attention in the Philippines and elsewhere, no large subsidised credit operation for SMEs started during the crisis.

First, as part of the government efforts to protect workers during the crisis the Department of Labour and Employment (DOLE) worked out an agreement dubbed the 'Social Accord for Industrial Harmony and Stability'. Under the accord, employers promised to 'exercise the utmost restraint in lay-offs' and workers pledged to 'exercise utmost restraint in declaring or going on strike'. DOLE has brokered similar accords in various regions of the country and the statistics on labour strikes suggest that the accord is holding. The number of recorded strikes did not rise significantly compared to the years before the crisis. Also, the number of establishments that have resorted to closure, retrenchment and work rotation did increase in 1997 and in the first quarter of 1998, but it is a tiny fraction of all establishments in the country: only about a thousand firms with 100 000 workers in 1997.

Second, other programs focused on credit for displaced workers and SMEs and had an anticipated little impact. For example, the P200 million Emergency Loan Program for displaced workers was approved by the Social Security System in March 1998. By February 1999 the program had approved 25 815 applications with a maximum loan of P12 500 (around US$300). Another program is a guarantee facility for new loans to SMEs which are still 'viable but are under stress' due to the crisis. The program, called the Enterprise Stabilization Guarantee Fund (ESGF), was to be implemented by the Small Business Guarantee and Finance Corporation (SBGFC).

The government has continually been interested in supplying more credit to SMEs in the Philippines. Financial reforms have generally favoured access to credit for all enterprises, including SMEs. In the 1980s, financial liberalisation started to take place, ushering in the dismantling of many restrictions on financial intermediaries as well as the reorienting of credit policies towards the market (for an overview of the financial sector, see Lamberte and Llanto 1995). The expectation was that with market rates prevailing the playing field would be more or less level between borrowers of all sizes such that banks would no longer ration out credit to SMEs.

The ability to charge market interest rates does not resolve all of the problems associated with lending to SMEs, such as imperfect information, risk and uncertainty, especially during a crisis. For example, asymmetric information makes it costly for the lenders to obtain information on the borrowers – especially SMEs with a high propensity to fail, default or run into arrears – so that a natural response from the banks is to ration credit at lower interest rates only to creditworthy clients.

The government of the Philippines recognises the difficulties faced by SMEs in accessing credit in the formal financial sector, and has responded with directed credit programs. By 1995 there were more than 100 different direct lending programs (see OECF 1995), which prompted numerous proposals to rationalise lending programs for SMEs. A Magna Carta for SMEs (1990) was designed to accomplish this objective, and it imposed a mandatory – and largely ineffective – allocation of credit for SMEs.

While the government continues to support an increase in the credit supply for SMEs, the ways and extent to which this credit actually improves SME performance has been widely debated.[11] Most SMEs do not even demand credit at the start of their operations. Most SMEs begin operations without credit from the formal banking sector and some prefer to use exclusively internal sources. Some lack expertise in meeting the loan requirements of a formal banking institution,[12] so they may prefer to use internal funds instead of external sources if they expect to be turned down because of a lack of creditworthiness or collateral. As might be expected it is difficult to separate demand from supply factors in the determination of the financing behaviour of SMEs.

In the New Economy, it is clear that some firms may still require long-term financing to undertake investments as they did in the Old Economy. Some will require venture capital to start up a new business because of the size and risk of the business. Some will still require the availability of short-term loans to continue their daily operations and survive. While recognising that there may be a role for governments to play in the provision of credit to SMEs, it is also true that government policies are not required for all types of credit or for all types of SMEs.

5.5 SUMMARY AND CONCLUSIONS

The Philippines has shown slow growth for decades, despite some recent recovery efforts. The evidence indicates that the SME sector was emerging from the deep economic crisis of the 1980s and experiencing the first positive effects of the economy-wide reforms implemented in the late 1980s and early 1990s.

By the mid-1990s Philippine SMEs appeared to have recovered from a long period of decline, but their performance, by itself, does not seem to have been vigorous enough to boost the Philippine economy after the 1997–98 crisis. In recent years, manufacturing has shown strong signs of growth. A growing information technology sector in manufacturing dominated by multinational companies, but also comprising some small production units, has emerged and shown a persistent growth pattern via exports.

Large firms with foreign ownership have traditionally characterised the Philippine manufacturing sector. During a period of deep market reforms in the 1990s, the country opened up to more FDI. Trade and financial reforms helped to improve the growth scenario without providing a period of high growth. During the recent crisis, modern manufacturing dominated the recovery by exporting high-end products and helped buffer other negative impacts on Philippine manufacturing, while creating a new, but small, breed of SMEs: small or medium foreign-owned enterprises in electronics.

While the policy response to the financial crisis has focused on underfunded programs, government policies to replicate the exporting success of electronics are still to come. Moreover, government policies towards credit for SMEs have focused on the supply side while more focus is needed on the actual demand for credit among the different types of SMEs and the different stages of development of SMEs.

NOTES

1   Rodlauer et al. (2000).
2   Elmeskov, J. (2000).
3   For some of the effects of liberalisation on Philippine SMEs, see Rodriguez and Tecson (1998).
4   The bulk of manufacturing employment in the Philippines has always been located in the informal (household) sector, that is, establishments of fewer than 10 workers.
5   After 1972 the percentage of employment (and value added) for SMEs are slightly inflated because they include the additional group of firms with 10–19 workers. However, one does not observe a major splicing problem between pre- and post-1972 figures because of the relatively small significance of firms with 10–19 employees in terms of employment (and value added).
6   As far as we have been able to ascertain, this was not due to changing composition by sector or some similar phenomenon.
7   Mini and Rodriguez (2000) use the 1994 census of manufacturing establishments to investigate the relationship between size and technical efficiency in the textile sector. They find that efficiency, measured using the stochastic production frontier approach, is on average a little higher in large (100–199 workers) and very large (200 workers and up) establishments compared to small and medium ones. The average gap was 4 per cent and 9 per cent, respectively.
8   Forty-eight per cent of all firms were 1–5 years old, 26 per cent were 6–10 years old, while the rest were in operation for over 10 years (Fajardo, as cited by Tecson et al. 1990).
9   Regardless of their export potential, some industries – such as textiles or non-ferrous metals – will simply have low subcontracting because there are few possibilities for components and subassembly operations in these industries.
10   The 1994 census asked for the first time in a census of establishments a question on exports. However, the same census excludes micro enterprises from answering this question.
11   For example, Lamberte (1990) concluded that the performance of SMEs was improved by access to credit at the start of business. Those firms that had access to credit were found to have become more capital intensive than those that did not, implying that credit-led firms grow in assets faster than in employment generation. On another aspect of performance, a more recent evaluation report

of the World Bank finds no significant difference in TFP between SMEs that borrowed from the World Bank facility and those that did not (World Bank 1998).
12   A typical bank would require financial statements, project feasibility studies, collateral papers, and other official documents from the borrowing enterprise. On the other hand, small enterprises are handicapped by poor accounting procedures and record keeping, weak financial management and a lack of proper cash control techniques.

REFERENCES

Anderson, D. and F. Khambata (1981), 'Small Enterprises and Development Policy in the Philippines: A Case Study', Staff Working Papers No. 468, Washington, DC: World Bank.
Audretsch, D. (1991), 'New-firm Survival and the Technological Regime', *Review of Economics and Statistics*, 73 (3): 441–50.
Baldwin, J., L. Bian, R. Dupuy and G. Gellatly (2000), *Failure Rates for New Canadian Firms: New Perspectives on Entry and Exit. Statistics Canada*, Cat No. 61–526-XPE.
Bernard, A.J. and J.B. Jensen (1999), 'Exporting and Productivity', NBER Working Paper No. W7135, National Bureau of Economic Research, May.
Berry, A. and B. Levy (1999), 'Technical, Financial and Marketing Support for Indonesia's Small and Medium Industrial Exporters', in Brian Levy, Albert Berry and Jeffrey B. Nugent (eds), *Fulfilling the Export Potential of Small and Medium Firms*, Boston, Mass.; London: Kluwer Academic Publishers, pp. 31–72.
Berry, A. and D. Mazumdar (1991), 'Small-scale Industry in the Asian-Pacific Region', *Asian-Pacific Economic Literature*, 5 (2), September: 35–67.
Berry, A. and E. Rodriguez (2001), 'Dynamics of SMEs in a Slow-growth Economy: The Philippines in the 1990s', World Bank Institute Working Paper, Stock No. 37181, World Bank Institute.
Bruch, M. and U. Hiemenz (1983), *Small and Medium-scale Industries in the ASEAN Countries: Agents or Victims of Economic Development?*, Boulder, CO and London: Westview Press.
Canlas, D. (1991), 'Labour Policies and Their Impacts on Cottage, Small and Medium-Scale Enterprises', in Gilberto Llanto, J. Viray and E. Hyman (eds), *Macro Policies Affecting Small Enterprise Development in the Philippines*, Manila: Appropriate Technology International – Philippines and the Congressional Planning and Budget Office, in cooperation with Appropriate Technology International, Washington, DC and International Development Research Centre, Ottawa, Canada, pp. 146–59.

Cortes, M., A. Berry and A. Ishaq (1987), *Success in Small and Medium-scale Enterprises: The Evidence from Colombia*, New York: Oxford University Press.

Csorgo, L.D. (1994), 'Subcontracting in the Philippine Informal Sector', University of Toronto, Department of Economics, unpublished PhD dissertation.

Elmeskov, J. (2000), 'Is there a New Economy? First Report on the OECD Growth Project', ECO/CPE, 9, unpublished.

Esguerra, E. (1995), 'Financial Assistance for Small and Medium Enterprises in the Philippines: An Overview', Quezon City: University of the Philippines School of Economics, mimeo.

Fischer, S. (1999), 'The Asian Crisis: The Return of Growth', Speech at the Asia Society, Hong Kong, 17 June, Washington, DC: International Monetary Fund.

Hill, H. (1985), 'Subcontracting, Technology Diffusion, and the Development of Small Enterprise in Philippine Manufacturing', *Journal of Developing Areas*, **19** (2), January: 245–61.

Hill, H. (1996), 'Industrial Policy and Performance: "Orthodoxy" Vindicated', *Economic Development and Cultural Change*, **45** (1), October: 147–74.

International Labour Office (1997), *Yearbook of Labour Statistics 1997*, Geneva: ILO.

Lamberte, M. (1990), 'Impact of Special Credit and Guarantee Programs for SMIs on Employment and Productivity', ILO-Japan-DOLE, Project on Strategic Approaches Toward Employment Promotion, Manila, August.

Lamberte, M. (1995), 'Small Enterprises' Access to Formal Financial Services: A Review and Assessment', Discussion Paper Series no. 95-23, Manila: Philippine Institute for Development Studies.

Lamberte, M., C. Coronacion, M. Guerrero and A. Orbeta (1999), 'Results of the Survey of Philippine Industry and the Financial Crisis', Philippine Institute for Development Studies, prepared for the World Bank project 'Asian Corporate Recovery', revised March.

Lamberte, M. and G. Llanto (1995), 'A Study of Financial Sector Policies: the Philippine Case', in S. Zahid (ed.), *Financial Sector Development in Asia: Country Studies*, Manila: Asian Development Bank, pp. 235–301.

Lapar, M.L. (1994), 'Credit Constraints among Rural Non-farm Enterprises: Evidence from the Philippines', unpublished PhD dissertation, Ohio State University, mimeo.

Leidholm, C. and D. Mead (1999), *Small Enterprises and Economic Development: The Dynamic Role of Micro and Small Enterprises*, London: Routledge.

Liu, L. and J.R. Tybout (1996), 'Productivity Growth in Chile and Colombia: The Role of Entry, Exit, and Learning', in M.J. Roberts and J.R. Tybout (eds), *Industrial Evolution in Developing Countries*, New York: Oxford University Press for the World Bank, pp. 73–103.

Mini, F. and E. Rodriguez (2000), 'Technical Efficiency Indicators in a Philippine Manufacturing Sector', *International Review of Applied Economics* (UK), **14** (4): 461–73.

National Statistics Office (1995), *1995 Philippine Yearbook*, Manila: NSO.

Ofreneo, R.E. (1983), 'International Subcontracting and Philippine Industrial Relations', *Philippine Journal of Industrial Relations*, 5 (1–2): 31–43.

Overseas Economic Cooperation Fund (OECF) (1995), 'Policy-based Directed Credit Programs in the Philippines', OECF Discussion Papers, Research Institute of Development Assistance, Tokyo, Japan (January).

Organisation for Economic Cooperation and Development (OECD) (2000), *OECD Information Technology Outlook: ICTs, E-commerce, and the Information Economy*, Paris: OECD.

Rodlauer, M., P. Loungani, V. Arora, C. Christofides, E. De La Piedra, P. Kongsamut, K. Kostial, V. Summers and A. Vamvakidis (2000), 'Philippines: Towards Sustainable and Rapid Growth', Occasional Paper No. 187, March, Washington DC: IMF.

Rodriguez, E. and Tecson, G. (1998), 'Liberalisation and Small Industry: Have Manufacturing Philippine SMEs benefited?', *Small Enterprise Development* (UK), 9 (4), December: 14–22.

Tecson, G. (1999a), 'Present Status and Prospects of Supporting Industries in the Philippines', in *Present Status and Prospects of Supporting Industries in ASEAN (I): Philippines – Indonesia*, Institute of Developing Economies, Japan External Trade Organisation, March, pp. 1–50.

Tecson, G. (1999b), *The Hard Disk Drive Industry in the Philippines*, Report 99-01, San Diego: The Information Storage Industry Center, Graduate School of International Relations and Pacific Studies, University of California.

Tecson, G., L. Valcarcel and C. Nuñez (1990), 'The Role of Small and Medium-scale Industries in the Industrial Development of the Philippines', in *The Role of Small and Medium-scale Manufacturing Industries in Industrial Development: The Experience of Selected Asian Countries*, Manila: Asian Development Bank, pp. 313–423.

University of the Philippines Institute for Small Scale Industries (UPISSI) (1998), *Dreamers, Doers, Risktakers: Entrepreneurial Case Stories. Small Enterprises Research and Development Foundation and UP Institute of Small Scale Industries*, Diliman: University of the Philippines.

World Bank (1998/9), *World Development Report 1998/9*, Washington, DC: Oxford University Press.

World Bank (1982), *World Development Report 1982*, Washington, DC: Oxford University Press.

World Bank (1998), 'World Bank Support for Small and Medium Industries in the Philippines: An Impact Evaluation', Operations Evaluation Department, World Bank, Report No. 18041, June, Washington, DC.

6 Old Policy Challenges for a New Administration: SMEs in Indonesia

Hal Hill

6.1 INTRODUCTION

Small and medium enterprises are an important subject of study and policy analysis, both in general and for the new administration of President Abdurrahman Wahid, for a number of reasons.[1] First, SMEs play a pivotal role in economic development. They typically employ 60 per cent or more of a country's industrial workforce and generate up to half of the sector's output. SMEs are therefore an important component of an understanding of the broader industrialisation process. Second, SMEs are a clear and consistently enunciated Indonesian government priority. They feature prominently in key government documents, such as five-year plans (*Repelita*), the Broad Outlines of Government Policy (GBHN), and many official statements. This support has manifested itself in a separate ministry for SMEs (together with cooperatives) since 1993. At Indonesia's instigation, for example, they were introduced into the APEC process following the 1994 Bogor Summit. Offical support for SMEs has been a feature of all post-Independence governments from Sukarno (on which see, for example, Glassburner 1971) to Wahid. Indeed, arguably their emphasis has increased under both the Habibie and Wahid administrations, certainly as compared to Soeharto.

Third, SMEs assume particular importance in Indonesia owing to their link to equity issues. In particular, they are seen as a vehicle for promoting *pribumi* business, and therefore as a means of asset redistribution along ethnic lines. This constant, if unstated, tension between efficiency and distributional/welfare goals has always complicated official thinking and program implementation. While official statements have tended to emphasise the former, for most government officials (and a vocal *pribumi* constituency) the latter have been uppermost in their thinking. It is probably because ethnic relations are more sensitive in Indonesia than in any other East Asian country that the gap between official pronouncements and implementation with regard to SMEs is the widest.

More generally, there is a disjunction between the standard economist's approach to policy intervention, which emphasises market-oriented solutions as the key to rapid economic development, aside from specific justifications for intervention such as public goods, market failure and externalities, and a widespread popular sentiment according to which SMEs 'need' special support on the grounds of social justice, or because (it is alleged) these firms are inherently disadvantaged by the unfettered operation of markets.

Fourth, it cannot be assumed that the same sorts of policies which are drawn up for larger industrial units will necessarily apply to SMEs. SMEs display a pronounced concentration in particular industrial activities. Spatially they generally exhibit a less pronounced concentration around major urban centres as compared to larger units. SMEs are less likely to be foreign (or government) owned, and are believed to be less export oriented (at least as concerns direct exports).

Fifth, international experience suggests that an efficient SME sector is conducive to rapid industrial growth and a flexible industrial structure. Taiwan is often held out as an example of an economy built on the foundations of an efficient SME sector.[2] Moreover, it is one which is regarded as preferable to the 'Korean model' of large industrial conglomerates both on equity grounds and because it is more resilient in times of economic crisis. A particular strand of this argument emphasises the importance of a well-developed SME sector in underpinning the key electronics, machine goods and automotive industries through the establishment of subcontracting networks.

Finally, there is a particular current interest in SMEs in Indonesia since these firms appear to have weathered the economic crisis of 1997–98 better than larger industrial units. This proposition appears to be true both for intra-country comparisons (that is, large and small firms within a given country) and across economies (for example, the Korea–Taiwan comparison again).

This chapter is organised as follows. In Section 6.2 there is a review of the government's policy framework, together with some conceptual and analytical issues as they relate to SMEs. In Section 6.3, the empirical evidence on SMEs is reviewed, referring both to aggregate macro-level evidence and case studies, and including some of the emerging material on the impact of the recent crisis. Section 6.4 asks whether there is any special case for intervention in favour of SMEs, and points to areas where government policy has and has not worked. Finally Section 6.5 highlights gaps in the data base and research material. Following much of the literature the discussion focuses primarily on the industrial sector, although where relevant it casts the net more widely.

6.2   THE EXISTING POLICY FRAMEWORK

Successive Indonesian governments have never enunciated a coherent, clearly defined and prioritised SME policy and strategy. There are a plethora of programs designed to assist SMEs, but they have rarely amounted to much. Meanwhile, various other interventions have tended to cut across these SME programs, and render them still less effective.

Table 6.1 provides a summary of various Indonesian government SME initiatives since the 1970s. Most official statements stress the importance of SMEs as a means of:

- generating employment;

- achieving greater equality through a more diverse ownership structure in business;

- promoting rural and regional development;

- providing a basis for entrepreneurial development; and

- redressing the perceived ethnic imbalance in business ownership.

Policy instruments in pursuit of these goals may be broadly classified into three areas:

- *Financial assistance*: This is now relatively unimportant, but in the past many programs were introduced to assist SME firms. Some involved subsidised credit (whose importance peaked during the oil boom period, 1973–82), others a requirement that banks allocate a certain percentage of their portfolio to these firms.

- *Technical assistance*: These have typically involved training schemes, industrial extension services (for example, BIPIK, LIK), specialised vocational programs, and domestic and international marketing advisory services. The delivery mechanisms and conditions vary greatly. Some are provided free, although more commonly there is some cost-recovery component. Some are provided as part of an integrated package including financial and technical inputs.

- *Regulation and coercion*: The reforms of the 1980s meant that a regulatory approach to SME promotion is now out of favour. But the government has experimented with a variety of programs based on compulsion. These have included enforced subcontracting schemes (mainly in the automotive and electronic industries); so-called 'foster parent' (*bapak angkat*) initiatives, whereby larger firms (particularly state enterprises) are required to sponsor and promote local SMEs; preferential government procurement programs; and reservation schemes in which only firms of a certain size are permitted to produce some goods. In addition, cooperatives have been promoted with varying degrees of vigour.

Table 6.1
SME Policy Initiatives in Indonesia

1) Technology

1969   Establishment of MIDC (Metal Industry Development Centre).
1974   Establishment of BIPIK (Small Industries Development Program).
1979   As part of BIPIK, LIK and PIK (Small Industry Estates) were established, and technical assistance to SMEs was intensified through the UPTs (technical service units), staffed by TPLs (extension field officers).
1994   BIPIK was replaced by PIKIM (Small-scale Enterprises Development Project).

2) Marketing

1979   A reservation scheme was introduced to protect certain markets for SMEs.
1999   The anti-monopoly law included explicit provisions in support of SMEs.

3) Finance

1971   PT ASKRINDO was established as a state-owned credit insurance company.
1973   KIK (Small Investment Credits) and KMKP (Working Capital Credits) were introduced to provide subsidised credit for SMEs.
1973   PT BAHANA, a state-owned venture capital company, was established.
1974   KK (Small Credits), administered by Bank Rakyat Indonesia, was launched; subsequently (1984) it was changed to the KUPEDES (General Rural Saving Program) scheme, aimed at promoting small business.
1989   SME loans from state-owned enterprises were mandated.
1990   The subsidised credit programs (KIK, KMKP) were abolished, and the unsubsidised KUK (Small Business Credits) was introduced.
1999   Directed credit programs were transferred from the Central Bank to PT PNM (a state-owned corporation for SMEs) and Bank Ekspor Indonesia.
2000   All government credit programs for SMEs are to be abolished.

4) General

1978   A Directorate General for Small-scale Industry was established in the Ministry of Industry.
1984   The *bapak angkat* ('foster parent') scheme was introduced to support SMEs. Later (1991) it was extended nationally.
1991   SENTRAs (groups of SMEs) in industrial clusters were organised under the KOPINKRA (Small-scale Handicraft Cooperatives).
1993   The Ministry of Cooperatives was assigned responsibility for small business development.
1995   The Basic Law for Promoting Small-scale Enterprises was enacted.
1997   The *Bapak Angkat* program was changed to become a Partnership (*Kemitraan*) program.
1998   The Ministry of Cooperatives and Small Business added medium-scale business to its responsibilities.
1998   Under Minister Adi Sasono, the promotion of SMEs as part of the People's Economy (*Ekonomi Rakyat*) became a national slogan.

Sources: Based on Thee (1994) and Hayashi (2000).

There has never, to this author's knowledge, been a comprehensive evaluation of these programs and their effectiveness. But almost all pieces of empirical research have concluded that they are largely ineffective: they lack resources; they lack a clear policy rationale; they – particularly the subsidised credit programs – have been beset by problems of corruption; they tend to be supply driven, that is, drawn up by bureaucrats without a clear incentives framework; and they rarely engage large firms and commercial services to support their objectives. We shall return to some of these issues below.

The notion of a technologically progressive, outward-oriented SME sector has somehow 'fallen through the cracks' in Indonesian official thinking. Depkop (Departemen Kooperasi dan Pembinaan Pengusaha Kecil, Department of Cooperatives and Development of Small Entrepreneurs) and other agencies in Indonesia responsible for SMEs frequently have a rationale and world view which was popular in the 1960s. They tend to favour a paternalistic approach which involves 'protecting' SMEs. They are suspicious of markets and economic liberalism. They tend to view the industrial sector in terms of various size compartments, with little firm mobility between these groupings. They tend to have a strong 'welfare' orientation. Consequently, these agencies have generally not adapted easily to the post-1985 policy environment which emphasises efficiency and outward orientation. Former President, and long-time Research and Technology Minister, B.J. Habibie had a well-known scepticism towards SMEs, together with labour-intensive industries such as garments and textiles. Rather his focus was on the major strategic industries, all of which were large in scale. Such a view also finds support in the government's technical departments, such as Industry and Trade, which at the senior echelons have a grand technological vision heavily influenced by their predominant engineering training. Finally, the Finance Ministry is generally uncomfortable with the approach of Depkop and like-minded agencies, with the consequence that the latter have not been centrally involved in major economic policy debates.

While, as noted, such agencies derive some popular political support from a 'welfare approach' which favours the advancement of cooperatives, *ekonomi rakyat* (literally 'people's economy'), and *pribumi* business development, in practice this rationale has complicated the task of efficient SME promotion. It has encouraged these agencies to base their advocacy on populist measures, it has developed a constituency – particularly during the period of Minister Adi Sasono, 1998–99 – which expects subsidies, and it has diverted the government's attention from developing meaningful support programs.

In assessing the government's SME policy framework, it is very important to distinguish between explicit (or 'intended') policies and effects, and those which are 'unintended'. The latter are arguably more important, and they further highlight the difficulty of defining, much less quantifying the effects of, government policy.

For all the government rhetoric concerning the importance of SMEs, paradoxically public policies in Indonesia often actually discriminate against SMEs in a number of ways.[3] First, trade policies have been biased against SMEs. There have always been considerable inter-industry variations in effective rates of protection in Indonesia. These do not have a particular scale objective. But, in practice, the major recipients have been industries dominated by large firms. Casual observation supports such a notion. The highly protected industries – automobiles, steel, aircraft, glass, fertiliser – are all overwhelmingly populated by large-scale enterprises.[4] Conversely, the trade reforms of the past 15 years are progressively reducing such a bias – a point often overlooked by proponents of 'SME first' strategies, who often also oppose trade liberalisation.

A second more general instance where government policies often harm SMEs is the regulatory framework. This occurs both directly and indirectly. Directly, some government programs have a specific size requirement. For example, fiscal incentives may only apply to investments of a certain minimum size, or exemptions to foreign investment restrictions may be waived only for projects larger than a specified threshold amount.

Financial regulations have sometimes worked against the interests of SMEs, although these are now much less common than was previously the case. For example, regulations imposing a ceiling on lending rates often penalised smaller enterprise. The per unit transactions costs in processing and screening loan applications inevitably decline with scale. (Default rates may be higher among SMEs, although this is not necessarily the case.) Banks need to build in these higher costs in their lending rates. If they are unable to because of regulation, they will be reluctant to lend to SME firms. Most of the country studies in Meyanathan (ed.) (1994) cite this as a current problem, or one of the recent past. Innovatory financial reform of the type introduced in Indonesia in the late 1980s also dispel the myth that credit ceilings are necessary to help SMEs. Indeed, the detailed panel data assembled and examined by Goeltom (1995) demonstrates clearly that, following the 1980s financial reforms, smaller industrial enterprises obtained much better access to the formal financial market. Certainly, interest rates in the formal financial sector rose, but firms who were able to access such credit were better off since they were able to shift out of the very high rate informal financial sector. She concluded that: 'For small establishments, the economic reforms have a positive effect on their overall performance ... liberalisation has helped to redistribute credit towards small firms' (Goeltom 1995, pp. 31–2).

Indirectly, there are costs involved in all manner of transactions with government agencies. These are larger the more complex the regulatory regime, and they are often a fixed cost in nature. It is the latter feature which may harm SMEs. For example, in applying for licences and fiscal concessions, and in dealings with labour or taxation offices, the same bureaucratic procedures may be involved regardless of the scale of an investment. Research in Indonesia has indicated that these cost penalties may be sizeable, perhaps of the order of 5–8 per cent of operating costs, or Rp 15–24 billion in total (Thee 1994; see also Sjaifudian 1997). In addition, and more generally, the political economy of regulation is such that personal connections with key government officials are very important, and inevitably the owners of large corporations are generally at an advantage in this respect.

Finally, the regulatory regime has explicitly or implicitly impeded the development of foreign direct investment (FDI)–SME linkages, thereby denying these firms crucially important technological, financial and marketing inputs. Until the mid-1990s, foreign investments which were below US$1 million were either prohibited or denied facilities. Even though this restriction has been reduced, the Investment Coordinating Board (BKPM) implicitly encourages and provides expeditious treatment for larger units. SMEs also routinely experience difficulty with expatriate work permits.

6.3   EMPIRICAL EVIDENCE[5]

6.3.1   The Macro Picture

We begin first with a general profile of SMEs based on secondary data.[6] According to the last complete enumeration of firms, the 1986 Economic Census, SMEs (defined as firms with 5–199 workers) in Indonesia generated 21 per cent of industrial output and employed 52 per cent of the workforce. Using a more restrictive definition – 5 to 49 workers – the shares fall to 10 per cent and 39 per cent, respectively. Perhaps surprisingly the shares of SMEs in Indonesia are lower than that in most of its ASEAN neighbours. There is no obvious explanation for such a difference, but two tentative explanations might be advanced. First, owing to its natural resource endowments, and to government policy, Indonesia has a larger share of capital-intensive (mainly resource-based) industries than would be expected on the basis of its per capita income. For example, the exclusion of petroleum processing (ISIC 353) alone increases the SME share of total manufacturing value added from 21 per cent to 32 per cent. The importance of industries such as cement, fertiliser, and pulp and paper further depresses the aggregate share of SMEs. Second, Indonesia (along with the Philippines) has traditionally been the most regulated and protected economy among the 'ASEAN five'. As noted above, it might be argued that the policy regime has also depressed the share of SMEs, to the extent that it has encouraged the development of scale-intensive activities.

Compared to its ASEAN neighbours (especially Malaysia and Singapore), Indonesian SMEs are also much more labour intensive relative to larger units. This is a less surprising feature, and is to be expected for a low-income economy. Factor markets are less well developed, and there are stronger vestiges of 'dualism' in firm characteristics. Policy distortions, particularly in the capital market, may have contributed, and industry structure is, again, probably relevant.

There has been a clear trend towards industrial agglomeration in Indonesian manufacturing. The average size of large and medium firms (defined as at least 20 employees) rose from 92 to 161 persons from 1974 to 1990. The increase since the mid-1960s would have been much greater still, but over the longer period there are no reliable data available which employ consistent definitions. What of trends in SME shares over time? The only reasonably complete secondary data come from the

1974/75 and 1986 Industrial Censuses. The data suggest that there was very little change in the size distribution of manufacturing, at least as far as employment patterns are concerned. The employment share of large- and medium-sized firms remained unchanged, that of small firms rose marginally, while the cottage sector declined very slightly. Cottage industry employment still accounts for over one-half of total employment. However, these figures need to be treated with great caution, as the cottage industry database is extremely weak. The picture is a good deal clearer for firms with a workforce of at least five employees. The evidence suggests that firms with a workforce of 5–19 employees grew nearly as quickly in terms of both output and employment as those with 20 or more employees during this inter-censal period.

Consistent annual data are available only for firms with at least 20 employees. Shares for three major size groups for such firms are presented in Table 6.2. Here also, and focusing on 'current year' series, the picture is one of little change (see

Table 6.2
Size Distribution of Manufacturing, 1977–91
(% of total value added)

	(a) Current year Size group (employment)			(b) Initial year Size group (employment)		
	20–99	100–499	500+	20–99	100–499	500+
1977	9.0	24.2	66.8	15.9	35.8	48.2
1978	8.8	25.2	66.1	16.7	34.3	49.1
1979	8.1	25.7	66.3	18.9	36.1	45.0
1980	7.3	25.0	67.7	20.3	33.6	46.1
1981	6.6	23.8	69.6	20.9	31.9	47.2
1982	6.9	25.1	68.1	23.1	32.4	44.5
1983	6.4	23.3	70.3	23.7	30.0	46.3
1984	6.4	22.7	70.8	25.4	28.8	45.8
1985	12.0	30.3	57.6	27.3	28.6	44.2
1986	8.4	27.3	64.3	27.5	28.3	44.2
1987	7.4	27.0	65.7	25.7	29.3	45.0
1988	9.1	28.6	62.3	27.3	30.8	42.0
1989	7.6	27.4	65.0	26.0	30.7	42.3
1990	7.0	27.3	65.7	25.4	32.9	41.7
1991				25.4	36.4	38.3

Note: Shares of value added are based on the three size groups. 'Current year' refers to shares for the relevant years. 'Initial year' refers to the shares of firms based on their size distribution at the commencement of the data series (1975) or when the firm commenced operations.
Source: Aswicahyono et al. (1996, Table 5).

Aswicahyono et al. 1996). The share of the smaller firms, those with a workforce of fewer than 100 persons, declined marginally since the late 1970s, but there was no clear trend. Similarly, for the largest group of firms, with a workforce over 500, the shares fluctuate around a broadly constant trend line. A similar conclusion holds for the medium-sized group. None of the changes is significant. It should be noted that these data exclude the oil and gas processing sector. Data on the size distribution of these firms are not available, but they almost certainly belong to the largest group. The inclusion of this declining sector would therefore result in a falling share for the large firms.

One important qualification to these data is that the results are sensitive to the manner in which 'size' is defined. The first three columns ('current year') follow the conventional approach and classify firms by their size in the year of enumeration. This is the simplest approach empirically, but analytically it is rather deficient. Ideally, one needs to know more about the industry dynamics: whether the changing size shares, small as they are, are explained mainly by differential growth rates among firms of different size, or whether they are the result of firms shifting among the size groups. The second set of columns offers insights on this issue. Firms in this case are classified throughout by their size in the base year (1975 – the year the data set commences – or, if later, either the year the firm commenced operations, or entered the data set by reaching the employment level of 20 or more workers). That is, regardless of their size subsequently, for the purposes of measuring shares of the three size groups, firms remain in their initially classified group. The second set of data, *prima facie*, reveal a good deal of dynamism on the part of smaller firms, as shown by the fact that the share of the 20–99 group is consistently higher in the 'initial year' series. For all three series using the 'initial year' data the differences between the two periods are highly significant.

Table 6.3 presents some comparative data on the relative importance of SMEs in major industry groups for Indonesia and two of its ASEAN neighbours. There are considerable inter-industry variations in SME shares in Indonesia, reflecting the interplay of industrial organisation, public policy and historical factors. That is, certain industries are more likely to be 'SME intensive' in virtually all countries (see, for example, Gang 1992), but there are additional country-specific factors at work. As would be expected, in labour-intensive industries, where an ability to adapt to customer requirements is an advantage, and in which scale economies and brand names are not generally significant, SMEs are of above-average importance in Indonesia. Examples include leather products, footwear, furniture, printing, rubber processing, plastic products, structural clay products, metal products and miscellaneous manufactures. Conversely, below-average shares are found in tobacco products, petroleum refining, cement, fertiliser, basic metals and electrical equipment, again to be expected.

Another variation which is often observable is the concentration of SMEs outside major urban and industrial centres. However, in Indonesia, such a pattern is hardly discernible (see Hill 1990). The share of SMEs in Jakarta's industrial output is above the national average, though it is somewhat below in the case of employment. Some

Table 6.3
SME Shares in Major Industries
(% of SMEs in industry value added)

(ISIC)	Industry	Indonesia	Malaysia	Philippines
(311)	Food products	37.3	53.1	19
(312)	Food products	69.5		
(313)	Beverages	26.6	9.9	7
(314)	Tobacco	5.6		1
(321)	Textiles	20.4		14
(322)	Garments	57.3	24.5	12
(323)	Leather	93.3		38
(324)	Footwear	54.4		33
(331)	Wood products	23.6	69.2	25
(332)	Furniture	94.7		35
(341)	Paper products	16.5	51.1	15
(342)	Printing & publishing	71.9		55
(351)	Basic chemicals	20.0	58.8	49
(352)	Other chemicals	61.6		37
(353)	Petroleum products	0	1.1	0
(355)	Rubber products	31.8	48.7	28
(356)	Plastics	78.2		67
(361)	Ceramics	8.2		6
(362)	Glass products	3.0	39.5	41
(363)	Cement	24.0		5
(364)	Bricks, tiles etc	93.7		na
(369)	Other non-metallic minerals	74.8		44
(37)	Basic metals	1.4	32.9	10
(381)	Metal products	38.7	63.3	46
(382)	Non-electric machinery	33.0	69.8	32
(383)	Electrical equipment	18.2	20.5	12
(384)	Transport equipment	35.2	20.0	26
(385)	Professional equipment	95.2	na	29
(39)	Other manufacturing	74.2	28.8	40
Total		20.5	38.7	21

Note: Excluding petroleum products (ISIC 353), the aggregate SME share for Indonesia rises from 20.5 per cent to 36.1 per cent.

Source: Hill (1995, Table 4).

of the provinces which have a strong tradition of small-scale, off-farm rural enterprise – notably Central Java, Yogyakarta and Bali – have higher SME shares, as do some of the more remote provinces such as Nusa Tenggara and parts of Sulawesi. But some distant, lightly industrialised provinces, such as those in Kalimantan, also have very low SME shares.[7]

Related to the regional location of SMEs is the question of clustering, in the past decade an issue of considerable research and policy discussion.[8] Broadly speaking, clusters may be horizontally or vertically integrated collections of firms found in proximate spatial locations. The latter case deals with subcontracting relationships, to be discussed further below. There is no doubt that, as in all economies, firms engaged in the same industry tend to cluster together. There may be common determining factors – for example, proximity to inputs or markets, availability of physical infrastructure (especially road networks) – or there may be spillover (or 'demonstration') effects, whereby a successful firm induces new entrants to the industry. Sometimes government policies may have a direct influence on their establishment.

There are numerous and well-documented instances of industrial clustering in Indonesia, including (to mention just a few) *batik*, textiles, weaving, *kretek* cigarettes, furniture making, bricks and tiles, metal-working, machine goods and automotive suppliers. Whether the existence of such clusters is conducive to efficient SME development is another matter, however. Some researchers (for example, Sandee 1995) have found a link between clustering and various 'external efficiencies', such as an improved capacity to innovate, and access to lower-cost inputs and services. It may also be easier for governments to deliver services to a target group of firms in such cases. Other studies have cast doubt on these findings (for example, Sato 2000), arguing that the pooling of technological and marketing resources is not so common. These results are not necessarily in conflict, of course, since they are based on micro-level studies, and it is quite possible that divergent experiences are to be found. Further research in this area would be helpful, while recognising that there may not be any immediate policy implications. Certainly, the government should not include clustering as a specific regulatory target or policy goal.

It also appears that small firms participated in the growth of manufactured exports which got under way in the mid-1980s. The database here also is rather weak, but estimates prepared by the Department of Industry suggest small industry exports rose from US$137 million to US$2.1 billion over the 1983–92 period. According to these figures, small firms have kept pace with larger units in their export growth, and the share of the former has actually risen for the period as a whole. As with larger firms, textiles, clothing and footwear have been extremely important, and by 1992 constituted almost 60 per cent of the SME total. Plywood, by contrast, has been unimportant, since most of the forest concessionaires have established plants which are larger than the official definition of small industry. Very little is known about small enterprise export activity. The strong export performance does *a priori* question the conventional wisdom that pecuniary economies of scale are important in international markets.[9] It is likely though that a good deal of the garment exports are undertaken through international and domestic subcontracting networks involving larger firms.

6.3.2 Case Studies

Numerous case studies have investigated the dynamics of SMEs by way of firm surveys, finding as would be expected cases of both success and failure. It will be useful here to refer to some success stories, both for the lessons learned and the policy implications. Two sets of studies are of particular interest: Cole's (1998) study of the Bali garment export industry and research on the export-oriented SME furniture manufacturers in the town of Jepara, northern Central Java by Berry and Levy (1999), Sandee and colleagues (2000), and Schiller and Martin-Schiller (1997).

The Bali garment industry, which grew spectacularly in the 1980s and almost exclusively based on small firms, was practically an 'accidental' case of industrialisation. Foreign tourists, mainly surfers wishing to support a recreational life-style, saw commercial opportunities in Balinese garments and its indigenous design capacity. They were able to act as marketing intermediaries, connecting local producers with retail outlets abroad, in the process dispensing important information on designs and production techniques. Later, as the island's fame spread, these links developed quickly, and the industry mushroomed from its seasonal, cottage origins to larger production units and some local design capacity. The Jepara furniture industry had its origins further back, but it too began to grow quickly in the 1980s. The industry lacked the tourism connection but it did have a good local skills base together with access to raw materials, and foreigners quickly saw the opportunities for profitable export as deregulation proceeded.

These studies suggest a model of successful and innovative SME development in which the following ingredients appear to be important:

- some basic industrial competence in a particular field of activity (for example, as in these cases, garment or furniture manufacturing);

- a conducive macroeconomic environment, including especially a competitive exchange rate;

- reasonably good physical infrastructure, extending in these cases (but especially Denpasar) to proximity to import and export facilities which function without too much inconvenience; and

- injections of technical, design and marketing expertise which link small producers to new ideas and major markets.

With the possible exception of the first ingredient, all four elements are directly amenable to public policy. They may also be present in different institutional arrangements, as for example in the emerging subcontracting networks found in the automotive and machine goods industries (Harianto 1993). And the general model developed here is equally applicable in agriculture, and in larger-scale industry where barriers to the development of technology transfer channels are generally lower than in the case of SMEs. It might be argued that these examples are special cases, which are not easily transferred to the bulk of small firms, especially those operating in remote locations and catering to low-income markets. But neither garments nor furniture could be regarded as 'niche markets'; on the contrary they are mass consumption goods. Admittedly Bali has intense exposure to international markets through tourism, but Jepara is some distance from a major port (Semarang) and is not a tourist destination.

These case studies also have important implications for government policy. Neither resulted from any deliberate government promotional measures. The government did play an important role in providing a supportive macroeconomic environment and in the provision of a rapidly improving infrastructure. In Bali, the local government generally adopted a fairly open policy towards the presence of foreign entrepreneurs, and export procedures were not unduly burdensome most of the time. The June 1994 reform of FDI regulations, lowering the minimum capital requirement from US$1 million to US$250 000, made it easier for small foreign investors to operate in the country without harassment. These of course hardly constitute 'contributions' from government, except in the negative sense of avoiding a harshly restrictive regulatory regime.[10] By contrast, reports from Jepara in 1997 reveal that foreign workers, on whom the industry depends, were being harassed and mostly deported.

Cole's study is also important because the dynamics of the process of SME technological adoption do not appear to be of interest to, or understood by, the relevant government agencies. Former President Habibie, for example, frequently dismissed the garments industry as irrelevant for Indonesia's technological future even though, as these and other studies have shown, a good deal of dynamic innovation is evident. Moreover, the intellectual framework of Depkop is almost completely irrelevant to the needs of the Balinese garment producers. Rather than Depkop's focus on partnership schemes (*Kemitraan*), subsidies, regulation and protection from competition, these firms are more interested in efficiently functioning credit markets, good infrastructure, freedom from bureaucratic harassment, and perhaps some carefully targeted industrial extension support.

A second focus of case-study research has been on subcontracting networks. The earlier work on this subject (for example, Thee 1985) found these networks to be rather limited and quite different from Japanese-style intense and durable arrangements, in which 'parent' (or assembler) firms played a key role in fostering the development of SME suppliers. In contrast, Thee and colleagues concluded generally that, notwithstanding some government prodding, the networks were shallow, fluid, sometimes characterised by opportunistic behaviour, and not providing much basis for viable SME growth. It is possible that these results reflected the nature of Indonesian industrialisation through to the early 1980s. The country was still in its industrial infancy then, and modern sector firms were moving rapidly into more sophisticated areas of industrialisation, some beyond the supply capacity of SMEs.

A considerable amount of research has been conducted on this topic since the mid-1990s.[11] Putting aside the immediate impacts of the crisis, how does the picture look after 30 years of rapid industrialisation? It is varied across industries and locations, as would be expected, but in general these linkages appear to be strengthening over time. Sato (2000) examined metal casting in the village of Ceper (Central Java), home to over 300 foundries of varying size. She found (p. 159):

> [a] subcontracting system and a putting-out system coexist in this rural cluster. Subcontracting linkages with the urban modern machinery industry, with large assemblers at its apex, have reached top-layer firms in the cluster. At the same time, many firms have formed linkages with wholesalers outside the cluster.

Assembler firms generally provided little assistance, but private business institutions and wholesalers are important means of channelling marketing, technology and financial assistance to the smaller firms. Among the former the activities of an offshoot of the Astra conglomerate in nurturing potential future suppliers was considered significant, particularly for larger firms within the sample. The government and foreign donors were not major factors. The former in particular was criticised for programs which did not meet SMEs' major needs, and for concentrating more on targets than actual delivery.

Hayashi (2000), in research-in-progress based on 58 firms in the automotive and motorcycle industries, also detected quite well developed subcontracting networks. Perhaps reflecting his choice of industries and firm locations, he found stronger assembler–supplier relationships. About 80 per cent of the suppliers interviewed reported that they had benefited in some form from the ties, most especially in the areas of technology and marketing, but not much in finance. Quality control techniques were an important example (on which see also Sato 1998b), as was practical shop-floor advice. He also found that the strength of the ties varied according to the size of the firm and the ethnicity of the owner, with larger and non-*pribumi* firms better able to utilise opportunities arising from subcontracting relationships. Smaller firms were thought to lack absorptive capacity, and were more reliant on government programs.

6.3.3   Impact of the Economic Crisis

Anecdotal evidence suggests that SMEs weathered the crisis somewhat better than many larger firms. This is to be expected: they are generally less exposed to the modern financial sector; they tend to produce 'necessities' rather than 'luxuries'; and they are generally more nimble and less burdened by expensive overheads. Indeed, some researchers have concluded that SMEs flourished during the crisis, with upbeat assessments suggesting the 'rebirth' of a newly invigorated people's economy. Jellinek and Rustanto (1999, pp. 1–2) provide an example of the latter:

> Indonesia's informal sector has picked up the slack and seems to be

experiencing an economic boom. ... Small enterprises, killed off during 20 years of economic boom of the New Order, are being revived. Old traditions of artisanship and trade are being rediscovered. Rich and middle class consumers who formerly bought from the formal sector are now buying from traditional markets. ... In contrast to the economic crash depicted in the official, national and international media, we are witnessing an unprecedented economic boom in the small-scale sector.

Many SMEs are closely linked to the agricultural sector, in processing and distribution activities, and most of these are presumably doing quite well. A case study of SME furniture producers in the town of Jepara (referred to above) by Sandee et al. (2000) concluded that these firms were actually expanding during the crisis. Van Diermen (ed.) (2000), in a more general survey, also reached a largely positive conclusion. Nevertheless, it may simply be that export orientation is the key to success during the crisis, and that this – more than scale – is the critical variable in the Jepara and other case studies. Moreover, Jepara had a well-established export capacity pre-crisis, and its SME firms were therefore better placed than most to take advantage of the highly competitive exchange rate from late 1997.

More comprehensive data are required to reach firm conclusions. In the absence of such data, a deficiency to which attention is drawn in our conclusion, we are simply making speculative guesses. One additional point should be emphasised in this context: there is nothing inherently desirable in a rising SME share. Indeed, it may be undesirable, to the extent that SMEs are associated with poorly paid work and unsanitary working conditions. That is, rising SME shares could be a sign of 'involution' and declining living standards.

6.4   A CASE FOR INTERVENTION?

6.4.1   Is there a Case for Special SME Assistance?

The fundamental economic rationale for supporting an activity arises when that activity is socially profitable, and where private and social costs and benefits diverge. In the case of enterprise of a particular scale (for example, SMEs), there needs to be evidence that the target group for assistance exhibits higher social efficiency than other groups. As the previous section pointed out, there is no decisive empirical evidence to support SMEs on these grounds. The fact that SMEs appear to be more efficient users of capital is suggestive but not conclusive evidence in this respect. And, on the contrary, some studies show that small firms are less capital efficient than medium or large units (see, for example, the evidence cited in Little et al. 1987). If one were to rely on this criterion alone, therefore, it is not obvious that small firms in particular would receive any special support.

A range of less technical arguments are sometimes advanced in favour of SMEs.

These firms are said to justify support because they are more labour intensive, they are spatially more dispersed, they provide the basis for entrepreneurial development, or on the grounds of equity smaller units are inherently deserving of assistance. None of these arguments is very persuasive.

If labour intensity were the goal the appropriate strategy would be to subsidise labour use in all activities, perhaps employing tax instruments to further this end. But what is important in this context is the adoption of a labour-intensive growth path, which is export oriented in nature so as to enable a country to exploit its comparative advantage as labour-abundant activities. There is a marked contrast in this regard between India, which has a long commitment to SME promotion but a poor record of employment generation, and the East Asian economies, which have not paid great attention to SMEs but have a superior employment record.

Similarly, it is not obvious that SME promotion *per se* is the most effective means of tackling poverty. For the poor the most effective strategy is to provide productive employment opportunities, combined with the increased supply of public goods such as education, health and housing. It needs to be noted, moreover, that employment conditions in SMEs are frequently very poor – low wages, insecure employment and unsanitary working conditions. Frequently, these units are small precisely because their owners wish to avoid surveillance by labour officials and trade unions. Most other arguments for SMEs also confuse means and ends. There may be a case for regional promotion and decentralisation initiatives, but this will almost certainly be achieved more effectively by fiscal equalisation measures or special grants in favour of the target regions and by infrastructure development.

6.4.2   What Works?

The key to promoting an efficient and dynamic SME sector is to create an environment in which these firms may prosper without long-term dependence on government support. Such an approach requires that bottlenecks be removed, and that governments and international development agencies play a catalytic role which does not necessarily imply a permanent institutional commitment. The previous section suggested some generalisable lessons from case studies of successful SMEs. This subsection draws attention to some additional examples of policy creativity leading to improved efficiency and/or equity outcomes.

The most frequently discussed obstacle to SME development is finance. Capital markets are regarded as being imperfect in the sense that there are information bottlenecks or uncompetitive market structures. Recent research and policy innovations in Southeast Asia have cast doubt on both these assertions.

One example concerns the nexus between clear land titles, the credit market, and agricultural productivity. Detailed research in Thailand by Feder et al. (1988) shows that those farmers having clear land titles are able to obtain credit at lower interest rates than those without such access. Programs of land titling and ownership demarcation can play an important role in linking small farmers into formal credit markets. These researchers suggest that the pay-offs through this route will be greater than schemes which simply attempt to impose artificially low credit ceilings. Although the focus here is on agriculture, there is little doubt that it has wider implications for SMEs. The smaller of these firms in rural areas frequently use land as collateral for borrowing. The key point here is that capital markets may indeed pose problems for SMEs, but the approach should be to identify the problems at source rather than simply attempt to regulate them away.[12]

A second example of successful financial innovation comes from Indonesia, and draws on the research of Patten and Rosengard (1991). Indonesia operated a number of subsidised SME credit programs from the early 1970s, all in the context of a heavily regulated and state-dominated financial sector. By the early 1980s, however, there was a rethink of these policies, for at least two reasons. One was simply financial – with the collapse in oil prices, the government was no longer able to sustain the subsidies. But, in addition, there was much abuse in the schemes, and no conclusive evidence that access to subsidised credit was a crucial factor in SME success.[13] The government therefore introduced schemes which placed more emphasis on access and outreach and less on regulation and price. The main schemes were implemented by government banks and their agencies, the Bank Rakyat Indonesia and the Badan Kredit Kecamatan. They permitted the banks to recoup the higher costs of rural small-scale lending, nevertheless at rates well below those prevailing in the informal markets, and to introduce mobile and flexible services. The programs have grown at a spectacular rate, their loss rate is very low, and they involve very little subsidy. Both of the last two features are in marked contrast to the programs they replaced.

A third example where intervention appears to have had some success is in the area of marketing support. In their case study of Indonesia, Berry and Levy (1999) show that private marketing channels work well for many SMEs, especially those which have subcontracting relationships with larger firms and which are non-*pribumi* owned. They found that, consistent with the argument above, most government support schemes have had little beneficial impact. But one form of support apparently valued by smaller firms lacking knowledge of international (and even broader national) markets is participation in international trade fairs and other mechanisms which enable these enterprises to better connect to marketing channels. There appears to be a role for the public sector as a catalyst in assisting smaller firms to cross this threshold into commercial success. The assistance is likely to be short term, perhaps even one-off, in nature, and will be more effective when there are already in existence well functioning markets supplying other inputs such as finance and technology.

6.5   CONCLUSIONS: AN AGENDA FOR POLICY-ORIENTED RESEARCH

SMEs will continue to receive policy emphasis in Indonesia. The policy challenge is to ensure that government interventions focus on genuine market failures, that is, identifying areas where the government can overcome market failures and thereby ensure that a more efficient SME sector can emerge, to facilitate the employment creation objectives and to provide a broad-based industrial sector. In the process, as has been argued above, it will be important to guard against 'overloading' the SME policy program with equity objectives which, commendable though they may be, are best addressed via alternative policy instruments.

Three areas commend themselves for further investigation and support. First, the secondary database. Though better than many other developing countries, it is still weak. Reasonably comprehensive data on very small units (fewer than 20 employees) are generated only on a decennial basis. Inter-censal surveys of these units are not of high quality. The annual *Statistik Industri* (SI), which includes firms with 20 or more employees has substantial under-enumeration, although it is considerably improved on the 1980s. It has not been possible, for example, to obtain a clear picture of the impact of the economic crisis upon firms of different size groups. Admittedly, it is difficult to collect data on very small cottage/household enterprises, but it should be possible to extend the surveys to firms with five or more employees. This could be achieved within given resources by reorganising data collection procedures. First, the Central Board of Statistics (BPS) currently collects much data in its SI series which are not essential on an annual basis. Examples include very detailed data on raw material usage and capital transactions. This could be collected on a five-yearly basis, without any loss of relevance, and the data collection resources redeployed into a wider enumeration of industrial units but with a much simplified list of questions. Second, there is considerable overlap between the BPS and the relevant line ministries. Each collects its own database, and there appears to be little cooperation or sharing of data. This represents a wasteful duplication of effort, and imposes unnecessarily on firms. With greater coordination, more useful data could be collected without any increase in expenditures.

Secondly, industrial extension programs need to be reformed and invigorated, to provide services which are genuinely useful and likely to enhance firm-level productivity. It is doubtful whether this can be achieved within the existing policy framework and bureaucratic institutions, and therefore new structures independent of the government will most likely have to be created. Unlike some of those in agriculture the author is not aware of any major industrial extension scheme in Indonesia having been successful, in the sense of contributing to increased industrial efficiency in a cost-effective manner. It is puzzling that this is so, given all the talk about the need to develop SMEs and *pribumi* enterprise. The issue of efficient industrial promotion will become all the more important as other means of industrial promotion – tariffs, state-owned enterprises – are gradually stripped away.

Past policies have delivered very little, as the case studies referred to above, and other material, have emphasised. Although resource constraints have been a factor, a more significant constraint has been the model adopted. The challenge is to develop a demand-driven, responsive approach which identifies obstacles to growth. These obstacles need to be highlighted on the basis of industry-level research, in which knowledgable respondents are involved in the process. It would draw on international best-practice, such as in Taiwan (see Lin 1998). Cases of successful agricultural extension (for example, the spectacular growth of rubber smallholders in Thailand) may also be relevant. The emphasis should not be on subsidies (although partial subsidies might be present), nor should it aim to guarantee the existence of all SMEs currently operating. Size *per se* should not be a criterion for such a program, although in practice it is likely that the majority of participants would be SMEs. It should certainly not attempt to be a *pribumi* development scheme, since the Chinese business community should be actively engaged in such programs.

Foreign donors might be involved in such schemes, but cautiously, since there is a danger that commercial interests or a priori models of industrialisation might dilute the crucial demand-driven aspects of the programs. As industry associations develop in Indonesia, they could be involved more directly in the schemes. But this will be a medium-term goal, as they are currently very weak in most industries.

Third, more micro-level SME case studies are required, to understand SME dynamics, and the major bottlenecks these units face (marketing, product design and innovation, production technology and so on). There are already a limited number of case studies suggestive of the essential ingredients – a conducive commercial environment, good physical infrastructure, mechanisms which facilitate access to foreign technologies and markets, avoidance of an intrusive government presence. But more case-study work needs to be done to supplement this picture, and to discern whether there are cases of positive intervention. The evidence seems to suggest that these success stories were largely 'accidents', and occurred *in spite of* the government. If bureaucratic reform is not possible, then the best advice might be a 'hands-off' strategy, in which the government does little more than providing an enabling environment.

NOTES

1   For a general survey of the East Asian literature on SMEs, see Berry and Mazumdar (1991). Little et al (1987) summarise the results of a large World Bank study of India and other developing countries. Meyanathan (ed.) (1994) provides case studies of SMEs in four of the ASEAN countries, while Bruch and Hiemenz (1984) is an earlier study with similar country coverage. General surveys of SMEs in Indonesia include Van Diermen (1997), Pangestu (ed.) (1996), Sandee (1995), Tambunan (2000) and Thee (1994).

2   See Chapter 10.

3   Bruch and Hiemenz (1984) documented these 'perverse interventions' in the Southeast Asian context in great detail up to the early 1980s. Although their analysis is now rather dated, many of the conclusions still have some validity.

4   The empirical evidence linking inter-industry variations in effective protection and average firm size in Indonesia is mixed. Basri and Hill (1996), for example,

found a negative relationship, significant at 5 per cent, but it is probable that this variable also reflects related structural variables such as value added per worker and ownership.

5   It should be noted in passing that there is no single official definition of 'SMEs'. The Central Board of Statistics (BPS) defines small firms as 5–19 employees, and medium as 20–99. Bank Indonesia has had definitions based on the value of assets, while technical ministries have their own measures. The issue of where precisely to draw the line is not of great importance, but for illustrative purposes the focus is generally on firms with fewer than 200 employees.

6   Some of the comparative material in this paragraph draws on Hill (1995).

7   Part of the explanation for this unexpected pattern is that a small number of industries in which larger firms predominate – mostly fertiliser and plywood – account for much of the regional industrial value added. If these industries were not included, or if the small number of regional concentrations in which they are found were excluded, a more familiar pattern of SME dominance would emerge.

8   See, for example, Sandee (1995), Klapwijk (1997) and Weijland (1999).

9   Based on a firm-level analysis of the 1986 Industrial Census, however, and lending support to this argument, Hill and Kalirajan (1993) found that export orientation was a significant correlate of firms' technical efficiency. Note in this context that the definitions of 'small industry' employed by the Central Bureau of Statistics and the Department of Industry do differ.

10 As Cole puts it (1998, p. 277), '[b]eyond these points, the role the government played seems more positive in its absence than in its actions'.

11 See, for example, Goeltom (1997), Thee (1997), Sato (1998a, 2000) and Hayashi (2000).

12 A related point here, of more general relevance, is that better physical infrastructure leads to more competitive product and factor markets, often to the substantial benefit of small firms and farmers, especially in remote areas. For an Indonesian case study demonstrating this point, see Hayami and Kawagoe (1993).

13 See Bolnick and Nelson (1990) for a detailed study of the impact of the schemes, and a comparison of recipient and other firms.

REFERENCES

Akiyama, T. and A. Nishio (1997), 'Sulawesi's Cocoa Boom: Lessons of Smallholder Dynamism and Hands-off Policy', *Bulletin of Indonesian Economic Studies*, **33** (2): 97–121.

Aswicahyono, H.H., K. Bird and H. Hill (1996), 'What Happens to Industrial Structure when Countries Liberalise? Indonesia Since the mid 1980s', *Journal of Development Studies*, **32** (3): 340–63.

Basri, M.C. and H. Hill (1996), 'The Political Economy of Manufacturing Protection in LDCs: An Indonesian Case Study', *Oxford Development Studies*, **24** (3): 241–59.

Berry, A. and B. Levy (1999), 'Technical, Marketing and Financial Support for Indonesia's Small and Medium Industrial Exporters', in B. Levy, A. Berry and J.B. Nugent (eds), *Fulfilling the Export Potential of Small and Medium Firms*, Dordrecht: Kluwer Academic Publishers.

Berry, A. and D. Mazumdar (1991), 'Small-scale Industry in the Asia-Pacific Region', *Asian-Pacific Economic Literature*, **5** (2): 35–67.

Berry, A., E. Rodriguez and H. Sandee (1999), 'Firm and Group Dynamics in the Role of the SME Sector in Indonesia and The Philippines', paper presented to a World Bank conference on The Role of Small and Medium Enterprises in Economic Development, Chiang Mai, August.

Bolnick, B. and E.R. Nelson (1990), 'Evaluating the Impact of a Special Credit Programme: KIK/KMKP in Indonesia', *Journal of Development Studies*, **26** (2), pp. 299–312.

Bruch, M. and U. Hiemenz (1984), *Small and Medium Scale Industries in the ASEAN Countries: Agents or Victims of Economic Development?*, Colorado: Westview Press.

Cole, W. (1998), 'Bali's Garment Export Industry', in Hill and Thee (eds), *Indonesia's Technological Challenge*, Singapore: Institute of Southeast Asian Studies, pp. 255–78.

Fane, G. and T. Condon (1996), 'Trade Reform in Indonesia, 1987–1995', *Bulletin of Indonesian Economic Studies*, **32** (3): 33–54.

Feder, G., et al. (1988), *Land Policies and Farm Productivity in Thailand*, Baltimore, MD: Johns Hopkins University Press (for the World Bank).

Gang, I.N. (1992), 'Small Firm 'Presence' in Indian Manufacturing', *World Development*, **20** (9): 1377–89.

Glassburner, B. (1971), 'Economic Policy-making in Indonesia, 1950–1957', in B. Glassburner (ed.), *The Economy of Indonesia*, Ithaca, NJ: Cornell University Press, pp. 70–98.

Goeltom, M.S. (1995), *Indonesia's Financial Liberalisation: An Empirical Analysis of 1981–88 Panel Data*, Singapore: Institute of Southeast Asian Studies.

Goeltom, M.S. (1997), 'Development and Challenges of the Machinery Industry in Indonesia', in Pangestu and Sato (eds), *Waves of Change in Indonesia's Manufacturing Industry*, Tokyo: Institute of Developing Economies, pp. 137–179.

Harianto, F. (1993), 'Study of Subcontracting in Indonesian Domestic Firms', *Indonesian Quarterly*, **21** (3): 331–43.

Hayami, Y. and T. Kawagoe (1993), *The Agrarian Origins of Commerce and Industry: A Study of Peasant Marketing in Indonesia*, New York: St Martin's Press.

Hayashi, M. (2000), 'Support Mechanisms for the Development of SMEs in Indonesia, with Special Reference to Inter-firm Linkages', unpublished paper, Australian National University.

Hill, H. (1990), 'Indonesia's Industrial Transformation', *Bulletin of Indonesian Economic Studies*, part I, **26** (2): 79–120; part II, **26** (3): 75–109.

Hill, H. (1995), 'Small-Medium Enterprise and Rapid Industrialisation: The ASEAN Experience', *Journal of Asian Business*, **11** (1): 1–31.

Hill, H. (1997), 'Indonesia's Microeconomic Policy Challenges: Industry Policy, Competition Policy, and SMEs', *Indonesian Quarterly*, **27** (1): 22–33.

Hill, H. and K.P. Kalirajan (1993), 'Small Enterprise and Firm-level Technical Efficiency in the Indonesian Garment Industry', *Applied Economics*, **25** (9): 1137–44.

Hill, H. and Kian Wie Thee (eds) (1998), *Indonesia's Technological Challenge*, Singapore: Institute of Southeast Asian Studies.

Jellinek, L. and B. Rustanto (1999), 'Survival Strategies of the Javanese during the Economic Crisis', unpublished paper, International Labour Organisation, Jakarta.

Klapwijk, M. (1997), 'Rural Clusters in Central Java, Indonesia: An Empirical Assessment of their Role in Rural Industrialisation', PhD thesis, Vrije Universiteit, Amsterdam.

Lin, O.C.C. (1998), 'Science and Technology Policy and its Influence on Economic Development in Taiwan', in H.S. Rowen (ed.), *Behind East Asian Growth: The Political and Social Foundations of Prosperity*, London: Routledge, pp. 185–208.

Little, I.M.D., D. Mazumdar and J. Page (1987), *Small Manufacturing Enterprises: A Comparative Study of India and Other Economies*, New York: Oxford University Press (for the World Bank).

McLeod, R. (1991), 'Informal and Formal Sector Finance in Indonesia: The Financial Evolution of Small Businesses', *Savings and Development*, **15** (2): 187–209.

Meyanathan, S.D. (ed.) (1994), *Industrial Structures and the Development of Small and Medium Enterprise Linkages: Examples from East Asia*, Washington, DC:EDI Seminar Series, World Bank.

Pangestu, M. (ed.) (1996), *Small-scale Business Development and Competition Policy*, Jakarta: Centre for Strategic and International Studies.

Pangestu, M. and Y. Sato (eds) (1997), *Waves of Change in Indonesia's Manufacturing Industry*, Tokyo: Institute of Developing Economies.

Patten, R.H. and J.K. Rosengard (1991), *Progress with Profits: The Development of Rural Banking in Indonesia*, San Francisco: International Center for Economic Growth.

Sandee, H. (1995), 'Innovation Adoption in Rural Industry: Technological Change in Roof Tile Clusters in Central Java, Indonesia', PhD thesis, Vrije Universiteit, Amsterdam.

Sandee, H., R.K. Andadari and S. Sulandjari (2000), 'Small Firm Development during Good Times and Bad: The Jepara Furniture Industry', in C. Manning and P. van Diermen (eds), *Indonesia in Transition: Social Aspects of Reformasi and Crisis*, Singapore: Institute of Southeast Asian Studies, pp. 184–98.

Sandee, H. and H. Weijland (1989), 'Rural Cottage Industry in Transition: The Roof Tile Industry in Kabupaten Boyolali, Central Java', *Bulletin of Indonesian Economic Studies*, **25** (2): 79–98.

Sandee, H., et al. (1994), 'Promoting Small-scale and Cottage Industry in Indonesia: An Impact Analysis for Central Java', *Bulletin of Indonesian Economic Studies*, **30** (3): 115–42.

Sato, Y. (1998a), 'The Machinery Component Industry in Indonesia: Emerging Subcontracting Networks', in Y. Sato (ed.), *Changing Industrial Structures and Business Strategies in Indonesia*, Tokyo: Institute of Developing Economies, pp. 107–48.

Sato, Y. (1998b), 'The Transfer of Japanese Management Technology to Indonesia', in Hill and Thee (eds), *Indonesia's Technological Challenge*, Singapore: Institute of Southeast Asian Studies, pp. 326–41.

Sato, Y. (2000), 'Linkage Formation by Small Firms: The Case of a Rural Cluster in Indonesia', *Bulletin of Indonesian Economic Studies*, **36** (1): 135–64.

Schiller, J. and B. Martin-Schiller (1997), 'Market, Culture and State in the Emergence of an Indonesian Export Furniture Industry', *Journal of Asian Business*, **13** (1): 1–23.

Sjaifudian, H. (1997), 'Graft and the Small Business', *Far Eastern Economic Review*, 16 October.

Steel, W.F. et al. (1993), *Annotated Bibliography on Small-scale Enterprises in Indonesia and Other Asian Countries*, Jakarta: Bappenas.

Tambunan, T. (2000), *Development of Small-scale Industries during the New Order Government in Indonesia*, Aldershot: Ashgate.

Thee, K.W. (ed.) (1985), 'Kaitan-Kaitan Vertikal Antarperusahaan dan Pengembangan Sistem Subkontraktor di Indonesia: Berberapa Studi Kasus' [Vertical Interfirm Linkages and the Development of the Subcontracting System in Indonesia: Several Case Studies], special issue of *Masyarakat Indonesia*, **12** (3).

Thee, K.W (1994), 'Indonesia', in S.D. Meyanathan (ed.), *Industrial Structures and the Development of Small and Medium Enterprise Linkages: Examples from East Asia*, Washington, DC: EDI Seminar Series, World Bank, pp. 95–122.

Thee, K.W. (1997), 'The Development of the Motor Cycle Industry in Indonesia', in Pangestu and Sato (eds), *Waves of Change in Indonesia's Manufacturing Industry*, Tokyo: Institute of Developing Economies.

Van Diermen, P. (1997), *Small Business in Indonesia*, Aldershot: Ashgate.

Van Diermen, P. (ed.) (2000), *SME Policies in Indonesia: A New Direction*, Manila: Asian Development Bank.

Weijland, H. (1999), 'Microenterprise Clusters in Rural Indonesia: Industrial Seedbed and Policy Target', *World Development*, **27** (9): 1515–30.

7 An Overview of the Macroeconomic Contribution of SMEs in Malaysia

Moha Asri Abdullah

7.1 INTRODUCTION

Small and medium enterprises are the 'backbone' of the economy in most countries. In Malaysia, where they operate in all industries and sectors of the economy, SMEs' contributions to the Malaysian economy are highly crucial. In terms of number, SMEs provide a significant input into various economically diverse activities. Figures provided by the Malaysian Institute of Economic Research (MIER) indicate that SMEs comprise 90 per cent of total manufacturing establishments, 29.7 per cent of total employment, 18.9 per cent of total manufacturing output, and 20.9 per cent of the total value-added services of all manufacturing establishments (MIER 2000).[1] These figures suggest that SMEs are an integral part of the economic development of the country.

SMEs contribute a vital role as they tend to: create more jobs per unit of capital compared to large enterprises; serve as a training background for upgrading and developing the skills of industrial workers, technicians, managers and entrepreneurs; provide the impetus for inter-firm linkages to the domestic economy; play a vital complementary role to large corporations and are a major vehicle for transferring or developing technical know-how; reduce import requirements and consequently save foreign exchange. Despite their important role in the Malaysian economy, SMEs have attracted limited research and study. Although there is a significant number of SMEs, little is known about the sectors that they are involved in, their activities, their business profile trends, and their problems and key issues, in a detailed and systematic manner. Relatively little has been written about small and medium enterprises in Malaysia. Stepanek's (1960) paper on the development of small and medium enterprises in the Federation of Malaya was possibly the first study ever conducted. This study, however, was constrained by severely limited data since no field study was carried out. Another early study is that of Wong and Schippers (1970). However, that study was restricted to an examination of the desirability of the consultative

181

approach rather than on the contribution and development of small and medium enterprises. Chee (1979, 1986) has written on the characteristics and development of SMEs in the country. None the less, his studies cover a sample of only 377 small firms across economic sectors and might be regarded as under-representative, while the detailed development and contribution of SMEs did not receive special attention. The World Bank (1984) and the Asian Development Bank (1990) have also been involved in the study of SMEs in the country. Both studies again focused on the technological development and obstacles faced by SMEs in the manufacturing and services sectors, with some recommendations on the need for changes in the existing policy support programs and institutional involvement with respect to enhancing technology adoption among SMEs. Furthermore, there are also a number of studies which have been carried out on specific topics but with limited scope on SMEs in the country, including Aziz (1981), Salleh (1991), Moha Asri (1997a; 1997d; 1998b; 1999b), and Rahmah (1995).

The importance of SMEs in all sectors in the economy is indicated by the fact that their contribution was worth about RM 4.3 billion or around 20 per cent of the Malaysian gross domestic product (GDP) in 1990; this is projected to increase to around 50 per cent or RM 120 billion by 2020 (*New Straits Times*, 8 June 1994). In the Sixth Malaysia Plan (1991–95), the government expected SMEs to have invested around RM 80 billion increasing to RM 126 billion under the Seventh Malaysia Plan (1996–2000) (see Malaysia 1991 and 1996). The figures presented clearly show that SMEs contribute significantly to Malaysia's manufacturing sector and indeed they are the backbone of the country's economy.

Previous research studies on SMEs in Malaysia have tended to focus on observing, reporting and highlighting demographic characteristics of SMEs, their business problems and weaknesses as well as support programs. Studies on their various contributions in the different industries and sectors in economically diverse activities are limited, especially with regard to their status and contributions in the manufacturing sector. More research is clearly needed on SMEs from a variety of perspectives. This chapter therefore attempts to examine and discuss the role and contribution of SMEs in the Malaysian economy, especially in the manufacturing sector since data on other sectors are not available. It is hoped that this chapter will provide a better understanding of the existing status, and contributions of SMEs to answer the question of why SMEs form a vital component and are an integral part of the Malaysian economy.

The chapter proceeds as follows. Section 7.2 identifies what constitutes an SME in Malaysia. Section 7.3 focuses upon the impact of the financial crisis on Malaysian SMEs. Section 7.4 conducts an overview of the contribution of SMEs to the macroeconomy. Section 7.5 analyses the significance of SMEs to economic and business development in the country, while Section 7.6 identifies their strategic contribution in the manufacturing sector. Finally, Section 7.7 presents a summary of the major conclusions to be derived from this chapter.

7.2   WHAT CONSTITUTES AN SME?

A study by the Georgia Institute of Technology cited by Manuh and Brown (1987) identified more than 55 different definitions for SMEs in 75 countries. This reflects a lack of consensus on what criteria should be applied to define a small–medium enterprise. Most definitions appear to be governed by the interest of the perceivers, purposes to be served and the stage of development of the particular country (ILO 1986). A general tendency in empirical studies is, however, to define an SME by the number of workers employed, or the value of paid-up capital (and/or fixed assets) or a combination of both. Others use less common methods such as shareholders' funds, value and/or volume of output, sales, turnover, legal status, capital/labour intensity and so on. Having acknowledged this it is illustrative at this juncture to explore some existing definitions formulated by different government agencies and researchers in Malaysia before establishing an operational definition. Indeed, as in other countries, a similar difficulty occurs in obtaining a definition of SMEs in the country. So far there has not been a formal legal or clear-cut categorisation of what constitutes an SME in Malaysia. Various government agencies and/or institutes have adopted different definitions. A review of such definitions is now briefly conducted.

The Ministry of International Trade and Industry (MITI), which is responsible for licensing manufacturing establishments in the country, has defined (albeit indirectly) small and medium enterprises differently over time. For instance, under the Industrial Co-ordination Act (ICA), which was introduced in 1975, all new and existing industrial establishments with more than 25 workers and paid-up capital of more than RM 250 000 were required to apply for a new manufacturing licence. In 1985, the ICA was amended to cover establishments with a paid-up capital of up to RM 1 million and a full-time workforce of more than 50 employees. A year later, another amendment was adopted extending its regulation to establishments with paid-up capital of up to RM 2.5 million and engaging more than 75 full-time employees. The purpose of these amendments is understood to allow more small and medium sized enterprises to operate without having to register with the ICA, and hence giving them more responsibility for their own survival and market conditions (see MIDA 1991).

The Co-ordination Council for the Development of Small Industry defined a small firm as one that has fixed assets of less than RM 250 000. Recently, this Council was transferred to the Ministry of International Trade and Industry and was renamed the Small-scale Enterprises Division (SSED) which is responsible for coordinating government policies and programs for promoting the development of small- and medium sized enterprises. It has now classified a small enterprise as having paid-up capital not exceeding RM 500 000 and a medium enterprise as having paid-up capital not exceeding RM 2.5 million (MITI 1990). Meanwhile, under the Credit Guarantee Corporations (CGC), a small and medium enterprise is defined as one with having paid-up capital that does not exceed RM 100 000 for 'non-Bumiputera' enterprises and RM 200 000 for 'Bumiputera' enterprises.

The National Trust of People (MARA) has also used its own definition, classifying all enterprises with paid-up capital less than RM 200,000 as being small and medium enterprises. It is widely acknowledged that the different definitions of a small and medium enterprise serve specific purposes for the respective establishments. In three studies conducted in Malaysia by three international agencies, that is, World Bank (1984, p. 4), United Nations Industrial Development Organisation (1986, pp. 15–16) and Asian Development Bank (1990, p. 9), the following definition was adopted: (i) small-scale enterprises – establishments employing fewer than 50 workers; (ii) medium-scale enterprises – those having between 50 and 199 workers; (iii) large-scale enterprises – enterprises having more than 200 employees.

In addition, MITI's report of January 1998 defines a small-sized firm as 'a firm with less than 50 full-time employees, and with an annual turnover of not more than RM10 million'; and a medium sized firm as 'a firm with between 51 and 150 employees, and with an annual turnover of between RM10 million and RM25 million'. Another agency that plays a significant role in the development of the country is the Small and Medium Industrial Development Corporation (SMIDEC) which was established in 1996. SMIDEC defines an SME as an enterprise which has fixed assets of not more than RM 2.5 million.

Besides agencies and institutions, independent researchers have used several other measures to define small and medium enterprises in the country. Chee (1986, pp. 2–3), in his study of small industry in the manufacturing sector, defined small enterprises and medium enterprises as those employing fewer than 50 and 200 full-time workers, respectively. In a study of a specific small and medium Bumiputera entrepreneur in Johor Bharu, Aziz (1981) also proposed a definition of small and medium enterprises as those having fewer than 200 employees. On the other hand Chapham (1982, pp. 2–5) classifies small and medium enterprises in Malaysia as those having a workforce between 10 and 100 full-time employees. Similar to the definitions adopted by Chee (1986) and Aziz (1981), Salleh (1991, pp. 2–3) has categorised small enterprises and medium enterprises as those having fewer than 50 employees and 200 employees, respectively.

7.3   SMES IN MALAYSIA DURING THE ECONOMIC CRISIS AND BEYOND

The Asian financial crisis had wide-ranging effects on Malaysia. It weakened the financial sector, affected the real economy, weakened the stock and property markets, undermined public and investor confidence and had socio-economic implications for income per capita, affordability and the cost of living. The financial crisis affected regional economies during the fourth quarter of 1997 and particularly in the first and second quarters of 1998. The depreciation of the ringgit increased domestic prices as a result of rising costs of imported intermediate goods; decreased real household income and wages; increased the value of external debt denominated in foreign currencies; and lowered the growth rate of domestic private investment as a result of exchange rate uncertainties; lowered business confidence; and resulted in a credit crunch. The crisis clearly disrupted the achievement of GDP targets (Prime Minister's Department 1999). The basic indicators of the economy were revised and re-estimated showing that the real GDP growth rate in 1998 was –6.7 per cent and 1.0 per cent in 1999. The unemployment rate increased from 2.8 per cent in 1995 to 3.9 per cent in 1998, and 4.5 per cent in 1999. Meanwhile, the inflation rate increased from 3.0 per cent in 1995 to 5.3 per cent in 1998, declining slightly to 4.0 per cent in 1999.

Reports showed that during the economic crisis the most affected businesses were SMEs. The substantial depreciation of the Malaysian ringgit impacted immediately on the cost of key imported goods. Imported consumer goods became more costly and domestically produced consumer products that relied on imported inputs became subject to inflationary pressures. This resulted in an overall reduction in consumer spending power, which in turn manifested itself in increased unemployment as businesses responded to the lowering in levels of demand for their products. The most affected businesses were SMEs since they were largely reliant upon the domestic market. For SMEs that were unable to redirect their efforts to foreign markets survival would become a priority, and cash flow became the immediate issue. Press reports (for example, *Star*, 11 March 1999) suggested that SMEs found it very hard to secure loans from banks and other financial institutions.

SMEs in the manufacturing sector that relied on imported goods faced substantial upward pressures on costs, and were reluctant to quote prices for their products as their costs were constantly increasing and eroding their competitiveness. SMEs that positioned themselves as major suppliers to multinational corporations were substantially affected by resultant low order levels and even order cancellations. Some faced severe cash flow problems as sales levels fell to a record low. Retrenchment of workers was commonplace (see *Star*, 20 March 1999). Based upon a case study conducted on SMEs in the Northern Region of Peninsular Malaysia in late 1999, it was estimated that the profit margin of SMEs fell by more than 89 per cent, with more than 78 per cent having declining orders and 76 per cent of SMEs reducing their purchases of raw materials (Moha Asri 2001).

The National Economic Action Council (NEAC) asserts that the Malaysian economy has a bright outlook in the immediate term and a sustainable recovery in the year 2000. A revised forecast of the Malaysian economy indicates that GDP growth will reach 8.5 per cent. However, Table 7.1 shows that estimated GDP growth in selected Asian countries indicates that better prospects are in sight. The ADB (2000) report indicates that the best performer in 2000 is likely to be South Korea with 7.5 per cent growth. Malaysia could be the second fastest growing economy, expanding by an estimated 6.0 per cent.

A continuing momentum in the recovery is apparent from Malaysia's Economic Report 1999/2000, which noted the turn around in the real GDP growth rate from an average annual rate of 7.2 per cent during the second half of 1999, against a 1.4 per cent real GDP growth rate in the first half (Ministry of Finance 1999). Improvements

Table 7.1
GDP Growth in Selected Asian Countries

Country	1997	1998	1999	2000e	2001e
Rep. of Korea	5.0	−6.7	−6.7	7.5	6.0
Malaysia	7.3	−7.4	5.6	6.0	6.1
Thailand	−1.8	−10.4	4.1	4.5	4.6
Indonesia	4.7	−13.2	−13.2	4.0	5.0
Philippines	5.2	-0.5	3.2	3.8	4.3

Note: e = estimate.

Source: Asian Development Bank (2000), *Asian Development Outlook* (April), ADB: Manila.

in other economic indicators are also noted. These include strengthening of the balance of payments position as well as a lower rate of inflation. The external trade position recorded a surplus of RM 46.2 billion in the first eight months of 1999 to RM 30.7 billion in the first six months of 2000. The annual rate of inflation decelerated to average 3 per cent in 1999 and 4.4 per cent in 2000 from 5.3 per cent in 1998 (Ministry of Finance 1999). Underpinned by the recovery in external and domestic demand, value added in the manufacturing and the services sectors showed a turnaround to record positive growth in 1999 and 2000. The average output growth of the manufacturing sector during the first eight months of 1999 was 6.4 per cent and is expected to reach a double-digit rate of growth in year 2000. Export-oriented manufacturing industries are expected to step up their output in 1999 by 6.7 per cent and in 2000 by 23.4 per cent against −6.3 per cent in 1998 (see Table 7.2). This occurred in response to an improvement in global demand for electronic equipment and components, in addition to a significant increase in the production of transport equipment following a surge in demand for passenger cars in the domestic market.

SMEs have great potential for further growth in view of these encouraging economic figures and a continued strengthening of national economic fundamentals. This would give SMEs excellent opportunities for more efficient capital utilisation, greater productive employment, entrepreneurship and training development, better regional distribution of industry, better linkages with large firms and a complementary role to multinational corporations (MNCs) and greater room and scope for technology transfer. With a strong economic recovery it is anticipated that SMEs have a bright and promising future in Malaysia. Their role and contributions will be critical for the economic future of the country.

Table 7.2
Main Economic Indicators, 1999 and 2000

Item	1999	2000e
Rate of GDP (per cent)	4.2%	8.5%
Inflation (CPI) rate	3.0%	4.4%
External trade surplus (RM)	RM 46.2 billion	RM 30.7 billion
External reserves	RM 125.5 billion	na
Per capita GNP	RM 12,369	RM 28,006
	(US$3,255)	–
Growth of manufacturing output (rate)	6.4%	23.4%
Export-oriented manufacturing		
output (rate)	6.7%	8.3%
Total employment (number)	8.741 million	8.981 million
Rate of increase in the total employment	1.7%	2.8%
Unemployment rate	3.0%	2.9%

Note: e = estimate.

Sources: Ministry of Finance, *Economic Report 1999/2000*, Pusat Percetakan Nasional Bhd.; Kuala
Lumpur; Malaysian Institute of Economic Research (MIER), *MIER Monthly Monitor*, Kuala
Lumpur: MIER; *ASIAWEEK*, 9 June 2000.

7.4   THE CONTRIBUTION OF SMES TO THE MALAYSIAN MACROECONOMY: AN OVERVIEW

SMEs in Malaysia account for a large proportion of the total establishments in the
various sectors, and this has been consistently the case for the last few decades. SMEs
can be broadly categorised into four major sectors. First, SMEs in the agricultural
sector are largely concentrated in the production of agricultural and natural products
such as rubber, paddy, oil palm, coconuts, cocoa, pepper, tobacco, timber, livestock,
fish and chicken. Second, SMEs in the construction sector comprise small constructors
in all types of construction industries. Third, SMEs in the services sector comprise
those which are involved in wholesale, retail trade, restaurant, chalet and hotel, tourist
agents, transport and storage, and business services and activities. Lastly, SMEs
involved in the manufacturing sector comprise those which operate in the processing
and production of raw materials such as food, beverages, textiles, wood, chemicals,
petroleum, rubber, plastic, metallic and non-metallic materials, transport equipment,
as well as assembling and manufacturing electrical and electronics appliances and
information technology components.

Of the four sectors, SMEs appear to be relatively more important to the
manufacturing sector (Salleh 1991; Moha Asri 1997a). SMEs also contributed about

97.7 per cent of the total establishments and 41.2 per cent of the total employment in the manufacturing sector in 1981 (Chee 1986). Table 7.3 indicates that 28.2 per cent of SMEs in the manufacturing sector are in the electrical and electronics subsector, while non-metallic products and wood-based products are also quite important. However, based upon this listing, SMEs are quite diverse in terms of their distribution. Meanwhile, Table 7.4 shows that a substantial proportion of SMEs operate in the state of Selangor, followed by the states of Johor, Penang and Perak.

Based upon definitions given by a number of agencies and scholars (see World Bank 1984; UNIDO 1986; Chee 1986; ADB 1990; Salleh 1991; and Moha Asri 1997a, 1998b and 1999b),[2] a much clearer picture of the contribution of SMEs in the manufacturing sector can be seen in Table 7.5. It shows that SMEs accounted for 93.8 per cent of the total number of establishments (21 071), almost 36.2 per cent of the total employment (502 645 workers), 29.6 per cent of the value of gross output (RM 73 281 587) and 36.3 per cent of total fixed assets (RM 26 739 383) in the sector in 1995. It is noteworthy that between 1975 and 1995 the contribution of SMEs to

Table 7.3

Distribution of SMEs (registered with SMIDEC) by Types of Products in the Manufacturing Sector, as at June 1999

Type of product	Number	%
Food products	82	3.6
Textiles and garments	30	1.3
Wood and wood-based products	147	6.5
Paper and printing products	34	1.5
Petroleum products	51	2.3
Chemical products	7	0.3
Rubber and rubber-based products	48	2.1
Non-metallic products	203	9.0
Base-metal products	103	4.5
Fabricated metal	129	5.7
Machinery	120	5.3
Electric and electrical products	639	28.2
Transport equipment	87	3.8
Poultry farming	3	0.1
Other products	264	11.7
No information	318	14.0
Total	2 265	100.0*

Note: * Rounded.

Source: SMIDEC (1999).

Malaysia's manufacturing sector declined in terms of their share of total employment generated as well as in terms of the total value of gross output, while SMEs' share of the total number of establishments and total value of fixed assets was somewhat stagnant. Compared to 1995 the percentage of fixed assets of SMEs fell in 2000, which could be attributed to a fall in inventories. A number of implications are associated with the reduction in inventories. First, it may indicate that because of the country's earlier economic crisis, SMEs were less optimistic about the future of the economy and, therefore, reduced their inventories. Second, bank loans on average accounted for about 38 per cent of SMEs' current liabilities. The financial and economic crisis that started in late 1997 caused the percentage of pre-paid income to fall, that is, normal sources of short-term borrowing were not sufficient to cover current liabilities. Therefore, SMEs had no alternative sources of meeting short-term financial needs. Consequently, SMEs had to close down their businesses as a result of withdrawal of credit by banks during the financial crisis. The number of closures could have reached as high as 20 per cent of SMEs.

Table 7.4
Distribution of SMEs (registered with SMIDEC) in Malaysia
in the Manufacturing Sector, as at June 1999

State	Number	%
Johor	268	11.8
Kedah	112	4.9
Kelantan	19	0.8
Malacca	67	3.0
Negeri Sembilan	64	2.8
Pahang	89	3.9
Perak	133	5.9
Perlis	4	0.2
Penang	263	11.6
Selangor	806	35.6
Terengganu	43	1.9
Kuala Lumpur	54	2.4
Sabah	31	1.4
Sarawak	3	0.1
No information	309	13.6
Total	2 265	100.0*

Note: * Rounded.

Source: SMIDEC (1999).

Table 7.5
Contribution of SMEs to the Manufacturing Sector
by Size of Establishment in Malaysia (%)

Contribution of SMEs	1975	1985	1995	2000*
Percentage share of SMEs in the total number of establishments:				
0–49 workers (SSEs)	69.1	64.0	79.3	76.8
50–199 workers (MSEs)	23.4	28.1	14.5	19.8
0–199 workers (SMEs)	92.4	92.1	93.8	96.6
Percentage share of SMEs in the total number of employment:				
0–49 workers (SSEs)	18.5	16.5	13.1	14.9
50–199 workers (MSEs)	29.5	32.9	23.1	26.5
0–199 workers (SMEs)	48.0	49.4	36.2	41.4
Percentage share of SMEs in the total value of gross output:				
0–49 workers (SSEs)	15.4	9.1	6.9	8.7
50–199 workers (MSEs)	32.3	37.6	22.7	31.6
0–199 workers (SMEs)	47.7	46.7	29.6	40.3
Percentage share of SMEs in the total value of fixed assets:				
0–49 workers (SSEs)	10.6	7.8	9.2	8.7
50–199 workers (MSEs)	28.9	23.6	27.1	26.7
0–199 workers (SMEs)	39.5	31.4	36.3	35.4

Notes: * Estimated figure.
            SSEs (small-scale enterprises); MSEs (medium-scale enterprises); SMEs (small and medium enterprises).

Sources: Department of Statistics, *Annual Survey of Manufacturing Industries* (1976, 1986 and 1996), Kuala Lumpur.

7.5   SIGNIFICANCE OF SMES TO ECONOMIC/BUSINESS DEVELOPMENT

The most popular argument in favour of SMEs is that they create substantial employment opportunities. This is argued on the basis that SMEs, by their nature, use relatively labour-intensive production techniques. Thus, they may employ more labour than otherwise would be the case. Salleh (1991), for example, has found that fixed assets per worker rises significantly with employment size, that is, fixed assets per worker in establishments employing 100 full-time workers and above are more than 40 times higher than in establishments with fewer than 100 full-time workers. This reflects the fact that SMEs tend to use less capital per worker compared to large-scale counterparts. This suggests that, since SMEs use less capital, a given amount of capital will create more jobs if it is spread over a large number of SMEs than if it is focused on a few large ones.

In addition, the evidence indicates that the smallest group size operates at the lowest level of mechanisation and vice versa, and that the capital–labour ratio gives a rough indication of the level of mechanisation of production. Chee (1986, p. 5) found that the total capital per worker increased for all small establishments but was about 12 per cent lower than that for large establishments. SMEs also contribute to total saving in the national economy. The main sources of finance and credit for SMEs are the owners' own family, friends, relatives as well as traders who extend them credit. This is especially so during their early period of operations. Chee (1986) reported that 77.5 per cent of the initial capital for small establishments came from the owners/promoters. For large establishments the proportion was only 55.8 per cent. Thus, SMEs tend to provide a larger proportion of their own capital than large firms. It is arguable that at least some of the capital mobilised for investment in SMEs would have otherwise been devoted to consumption expenditure. This propensity to save and invest, induced by the development of SMEs, can, therefore, directly contribute to the overall savings ratio in Malaysia.

SMEs serve as a 'training ground' for upgrading and developing the skills of industrial workers and entrepreneurs. The lower cost of setting up small and medium-scale units enable enterprising workers not only to provide themselves with a livelihood but also to offer employment to others. Many employees in SMEs do not have a high level of education (Chee 1986). These employees would have found it difficult to secure well-paid jobs in the labour market. Out of 882 full-time workers in SMEs in Kuala Lumpur, studied by the author in 1991, 59.1 per cent had attained the Lower Certificate of Education (LCE) or equivalent, while 29.5 per cent of them had only attended primary school (Moha Asri 1993, p. 144). None of them had obtained a tertiary certificate. Moreover, the training and experience that they acquired in the operation of their enterprises enabled their SMEs to expand and grow. Similarly, Chee (1986) found that 74.8 per cent of SME owners did not have upper secondary education. Therefore, it is imperative to emphasise that SMEs can play an active role in upgrading the country's efforts towards achieving the knowledge-based economy through training for their workers. It is time that a shift in the mode of production from production-based workers to knowledge-based workers, through the provision of training and upgrading of worker skills, among export-oriented SMEs in the country should occur. It is highly important that globalisation and competitive global markets require SMEs to play an active role in promoting knowledge-based workers, mastering technical, engineering and design skills, rather than solely assembling products.

Meanwhile, the role of promoting entrepreneurship is very much related to SMEs. However, large enterprises also have a complementary role to play. There have been entrepreneurs who received their initiation in a large enterprise. In this regard, large enterprises normally provide them with the skills, knowledge and opportunities to acquire the necessary capital to start their own venture. Thus, the establishment of a small enterprise enables the newly initiated entrepreneurs to apply their skill and knowledge to daily practice. Through SMEs, entrepreneurs are able to acquire further experience and to improve their abilities gradually with the growth of the business. Moreover, SMEs provide a platform from which indigenous entrepreneurs can progressively upgrade their investment and management skills. SMEs play many vital roles in providing avenues for local investors to diversify into manufacturing outputs, and at the same time develop the skills and knowledge of local entrepreneurs.

In addition, SMEs, which are mostly indigenously-owned enterprises, through their linkages with large multinational corporations in Malaysia can be seen as a means of enhancing the development of local SMEs *vis-à-vis* indirectly encouraging large firms to foster the growth and expansion of SMEs. It has indeed to be realised that as the Malaysian economy moves into a more complex phase of industrialisation and becomes much more globalised, backward and forward integration of an efficient network of supplier industries is essential for export-oriented activities. Furthermore, many SME assembler firms in Malaysia are either joint ventures with foreign companies or at least licensees of foreign firms. In this view, technological transfer and other spin-offs to domestic supplier firms are relevant with respect to the issue of inter-firm linkages. Most of all, as feeder industries to larger firms, SMEs could provide ready business networks and distribution channels through which further industrial deepening and diversification could be enhanced. This is highly important since more and more SMEs in the country act as specialist suppliers to large companies. This can be seen through the increasing number of SMEs becoming vendors through the Vendor Development Programs, such as those SMEs in food, furniture and automobile subindustries. A study conducted by Salleh (1991) indicated that the linkages between MNCs and local SMEs provide more business for local SMEs through MNCs' local sourcing of their component parts, tools, equipment and sub-contract jobs of general services, in addition to helping upgrade the technical capabilities of the local SMEs (Salleh 1991, p. 18).

In many cases, as Meredith and Suresh (1986) noted, large firms often rely on SMEs (wholesalers and retailers) for the distribution of their products to consumers. Further evidence provided by Sironopolis (1994) reflects that SMEs readily provide large enterprises with many services, supplies and raw materials, such as that of General Motors which buys from 37 000 suppliers, most of whom are small. In 1999, the Malaysian national car-maker, PROTON, had about 91 vendors who are SMEs. Although there is no accurate information on SMEs as a source of innovation in Malaysia, their involvement in economically diverse activities appears to suggest that SMEs contribute to this aspect of innovation at all levels. This is simply due to the fact that they are more flexible, dynamic, and more sensitive to shifts in demand than larger firms (Wyer et al. 2000). This contribution can be also correlated to the fact that SMEs are the seed-bed from which large enterprises can grow. This is indeed the case in the developed countries such as the United Kingdom, the US and importantly Japan. In the US, for instance, many of the Fortune 500 companies started as small enterprises. These include Ford Motors, Chrysler, Sears Roebuck, and McDonnell Douglas, which were started by entrepreneurs with very limited capital. The evidence in Malaysia suggests some of the large publicly listed companies grew from being smaller enterprises. As such there are quite a number of small private enterprises that managed to grow big and become listed on the Kuala Lumpur Stock Exchange (KLSE) as public companies. Table 7.6 shows examples of 10 publicly listed companies that started as small enterprises, some owned by only one person, but managed to survive and grow big.

SMEs, through their growth, expansion and development, enhance regional development and create a more equitable income distribution. Large and giant firms normally tend to produce a small number of high-wage incomes and this results in a relatively small number of families with high incomes. SMEs produce a significant number of relatively low-wage payments. The income distribution characteristics of different establishment sizes can be deduced by observing the wages rates, the wages share and, to the extent possible, the distribution of labour and capital income. Chee (1986) found that small establishments paid their workers, on the average, 40 per cent less than large establishments.[3] Therefore, the development of SMEs would increase income for a relatively large number of people and one may conclude that the income distribution impact of SMEs is more favourable than that of large-scale

Table 7.6
SMEs That Became Publicly Listed Companies

No.	Name of company	Year of start-up	Type of product
1	Thong Guan Industries Bhd.	1942	Plastic products
2	Audrey International (M) Bhd.	1950	Garments
3	Yung Kong Galvanising Bhd.	1960	Iron and steel
4	Pensonic Bhd.	1965	Electrical products
5	Woodlander Holdings Bhd.	1967	Wood products
6	Elba Holding Bhd.	1969	Garments
7	Komarcorp Bhd.	1975	Labels
8	Rhytim Consolidated Bhd.	1976	Paper products
9	Zaitun Bhd.	1978	Consumer products
10	Caelygirl Bhd.	1986	Garments/textiles

Source: Khairuddin et al. (1999).

enterprises. SMEs also offer a better regional distribution of industry and more variety and diversity in term of products and services, choices and preferences to the local consumers.

This is especially so when the ability of individual enterprises to develop external markets is one of the most important factors determining the long-term growth prospects of any economy (Wyer et al. 2000). Although SMEs that market their products or services outside regional and international markets vary considerably between sectors and locations, they contribute significantly to regional income generation through external sales and import substitution. Although there are no accurate figures on income generation through external sales for manufacturing SMEs, the share of the manufacturing sector in total exports has been consistently increasing since 1990. The data suggest that the manufacturing sector contributed significantly to the total exports of the country, increasing from 69 per cent in 1992 to 80.7 per cent in 1999 (see Table 7.7). Since there has been an increase in the external sales of SMEs in the manufacturing sector, the increased share of the manufacturing exports to total national exports is partly contributed by SMEs either by directly exporting their products or supplying parts and components that are used by large firms for export. A study conducted on SMEs in the states of Perak, Penang, Kedah and Perlis in 1997 found that 75 per cent out of 100 SMEs in the manufacturing sector generated their revenues through external sales (Khairuddin et al. 1999).

Table 7.7
Contribution of the Manufacturing Sector to Total Exports

Year	Contribution of manufacturing to total exports (%)
1992	69.0
1993	74.3
1994	75.2
1995	75.4
1997	79.8
1999	80.7

Source: Ministry of Finance, Annual Economic Report (various issues), Percetakan Nasional Malaysia Bhd., Kuala Lumpur.

7.6   THE STRATEGIC CONTRIBUTION OF SMES IN THE MANUFACTURING SECTOR

Malaysia's economic and industrial development has been closely linked to developments in the international economy, mainly due to the 'openness' of the economy and the dominance of the trade sector. Over the past three decades the growth of the industrial sector has been strong, involving significant changes in the structure of output, exports and employment. Until the late 1960s the expansion of domestic demand, supported by earnings from primary commodity exports, provided the main impetus to industrial growth. Resource-based industries (both agricultural and mineral) had contributed about 60 per cent to overall industrial sector growth. Their contribution, however, fell in the 1970s with the rise in importance of non-resource-based industries, most particularly electronics and textiles. Malaysia entered the 1980s and 1990s with an export-oriented industrial structure, but narrowly concentrated in the electronics and electrical subsector, and relying heavily on competitive wages, and still vulnerable to adverse external developments. Malaysia's manufacturing sector generally is still at a stage at which it imports most of its technologies from abroad. The processes involved in introducing the imported technologies locally have required a minimum of design, development and engineering capabilities. In the absence of the stimulus and support normally expected from large-scale enterprises, technical, engineering and design skills remain scarce and relatively underdeveloped throughout the manufacturing sector. The development of ancillary industries as a mechanism for the transfer of technology and thereby for a more internally integrated industrial structure has remained at a minimal level.

These central features in Malaysia's pattern of industrialisation embody a number of structural problems and weaknesses. The greater tendency towards capital and import intensity inherent in the changes which occurred in Malaysia's industrial structure, hindered the development of a more diversified and balanced industrial base. The free trade zones-based, footloose, primarily assembly-type operations which are predominantly foreign owned, transferred few skills, introduced limited technology, contributed little to local technological development and to the deepening and widening of Malaysia's domestic industrial structure. Linkages with the rest of the economy have remained weak. In view of this phenomenon, Malaysia needs to achieve an optimum configuration between the large, mainly foreign-owned enterprises, and the small and medium-scale, mainly locally owned enterprises, in order to enhance inter-sector and inter-industry linkages and the development of SMEs. It is within this framework that the focus on the strategic role and growth potential of SMEs in general, and on technology-based export-oriented SMEs in particular, should be fully realised, to further foster the impetus in Malaysia's industrialisation drive in the new millennium.

Government support programs for SMEs play a potentially important role, because the development of SMEs will provide room for a counterbalancing force which could reduce an existing imbalanced industrial base and hence lead to a widening of the pattern of domestic manufacturing activity. It is, therefore, accepted that in order to achieve a more balanced industrial structure the promotion of SMEs should be effectively integrated into the mainstream of industrial development. In particular, SMEs would have the potential to reduce the dependence on large foreign-owned investments, which predominantly control many industrial subsectors in the country. In this respect, SMEs are seen as being essential in contributing towards developing a much wider structure of the manufacturing-based activity in the Malaysian economy.

The government has now fully realised the development potential of SMEs as compared to decades ago, and has made a commitment and effort towards developing SMEs. Presently there are as many as 13 ministries and 30 government agencies with varying responsibilities, offering a wide variety of programs to promote SME development. The Small and Medium Industrial Development Corporation (SMIDEC) was established in the early 1990s to coordinate support programs along with the existence of 30 other agencies. Overall, the support programs offered to SMEs in the country fall into six main categories: financial and credit assistance; entrepreneurial development, business management and human resource management; consultancy and marketing services; technical and vocational programs; locational and infrastructural facilities; and fiscal incentives. Direct policy intervention through various programs in order to enhance the development and growth of viable, resilient and forward-looking SMEs, indeed comprise part of the country's integral-development plan to prepare for the challenges of global market competition.

7.7   CONCLUSION

SMEs are considered to be the backbone of support industries in most economies, and SMEs also form a vital part of the Malaysian economy. With the change of the environment for world trade and industrialisation, Malaysian SMEs need to adapt and amend their mode of operations and management. It is evident that in an increasingly borderless and frictionless world economy, which offers both opportunities and risks, only SMEs that are capable of meeting the new challenges can survive. Creating and nurturing viable, resilient and forward-looking SMEs is the challenge for Malaysia.

Domestically, SMEs seem to have great potential for further growth over the next few years and beyond. This is especially so in line with the continued strengthening of national economic fundamentals. SMEs also offer excellent opportunities for more efficient capital utilisation, greater productive employment, entrepreneurship and training development, better regional distribution of industry, better linkages with large enterprises and a complementary role in the economy, greater room and scope for technology transfer, and in promoting changes for widening and strengthening the industrial base and structure of the country. In view of this, it is believed that SMEs have a bright future in Malaysia. As the country's industrialisation develops further SMEs will become even more strategically important, and they will be accorded even greater priority than that presently assigned to them by the government. The experience of developed countries supports this view. In countries such as the United States, Japan and Canada, there is a strong tendency to associate SMEs with large enterprises. Yet, SMEs remain a vital force in industrial activities and their importance has increased rather than diminished. Moreover, the governments in these countries recognise the strategic role of SMEs, and they have continued to extend various forms of assistance to their respective SMEs. In Canada, there is a Minister of State for Small Business, whose department is responsible for providing unequivocal support to SMEs. In the United States there is the Small Business Administration, which was created in 1976 to protect, strengthen and effectively represent SMEs within the Federal government. The important role of SMEs in the Japanese economy resulted in the establishment of several agencies to promote and assist SMEs, in addition to legislation pertaining to the development of SMEs. The best-known agency is the Small and Medium Enterprise Agency which not only performs functions similar to those of its US counterpart, but also has branches in many other countries where Japanese SMEs conduct their business.

Currently, many SMEs are quite inefficient and still rely on traditional organisation and techniques of production (see Moha Asri 1997b; 1997c; 1999c). Thus, there is a clear need for SMEs to modernise, change or modify their product lines, and update their production technology. Although the vast majority of SME owners have demonstrated their ability to go into business and survive without government support, it is plausible to argue that survival is not sufficient for the country without a clear vision of future industrial development. Indeed, to become an industrialised country, adequate attention must be paid to the development of SMEs, and a widening and strengthening of the Malaysian domestic-industrial structure. On the whole SMEs in Malaysia have plenty of scope and there is ample evidence that they can substantially increase their productivity and rate of growth in the wake of the Malaysian economic recovery, which in turn provides further impetus for SMEs' activities in the overall industrial development of the country. Faced with the current global business environment and a high level of business competition, SMEs will need to be more adaptable, especially towards the use of information technology, to maintain their present contribution to the Malaysian economy. While SMEs will need new strategic direction and planning and outward-looking managers and entrepreneurs with knowledge and skills, the continued efforts and support of the government in enhancing the development of SMEs remains crucial. This will require more commitment and hard work from both the public and private sectors to utilise and maximise the available resources and opportunities to ensure that SMEs are capable of meeting the challenges of globalisation.

NOTES

1   Elsewhere, SMEs account for a large proportion of the total number of establishments: 99 per cent in Canada; 99.3 per cent in South Korea; 98.3 per cent in Thailand; 98 per cent in Taiwan; 99 per cent in New Zealand; and 99.4 per cent in Japan (see Moha Asri and Baker 2000).
2   Following the convention used by the World Bank as well as the Industrial Master Plan (I), relevant agencies noted and other scholars, the study indicated uses the following definitions: that small-scale enterprises (SSEs) are enterprises employing fewer than 50 workers; medium-scale enterprises (MSEs) are those employing 50–199 workers.
3   See Chee (1986, Tables 1.7, 1.8, 1.9 and 1.10).

BIBLIOGRAPHY

Anderson, T. (1987), *Profit in Small Firms*, Aldershot: Avebury.
Asian Development Bank (ADB) (1990), 'Malaysia: Study on Small and Medium Enterprises with Special Reference to Technology Development', Staff Working Paper, April, Kuala Lumpur.
Asian Development Bank (ADB) (2000), *Asian Development Outlook*, April, Manila: ADB.
Aziz, A. (1981), *Malay Entrepreneurship: Problems in Development*, Kuala Lumpur: Heng Lee Press.
Bromley, R. (1985), *Planning for Small Enterprises in Third World Cities*, Oxford: Pergamon Press.
Chapham, R. (1982), *Small and Medium Enterprises in South East Asia*, Singapore: Institute of South Asian Studies, NUS.
Chee, P.L. (1979), 'A Study of Small Entrepreneurs and Entrepreneurial Development Programs in Malaysia', PhD thesis (unpublished), University of Malaya, Kuala Lumpur.
Chee, P.L. (1986), *Small industry in Malaysia*, Kuala Lumpur: Berita Publishing.
Cortes, M., A. Berry and A. Ishaq (1987), *Success in Small and Medium-scale Enterprises – the Evidence from Colombia*, World Bank Research Publication, London: Oxford University Press.
Department of Statistics (1976), *Annual Survey of Manufacturing Industries*, Kuala Lumpur.
Department of Statistics (1986), *Annual Survey of Manufacturing Industries*, Kuala Lumpur.
Department of Statistics (1996), *Annual Survey of Manufacturing Industries*, Kuala Lumpur.
Federation of Malaysian Manufacturers (1996), *Small and Medium Size Industries: Business Guide*, Kuala Lumpur: FMM.

International Labour Organization (ILO) (1986), *The Promotion of Small and Medium-sized Enterprises*, Geneva: ILO.

Khairuddin, H., M. Sulaiman and S.W. Azizi (1999), 'Entrepreneurial Characteristics, Strategy Types and Performances of Small and Medium-sized Enterprises in the Malaysian Manufacturing Sector', International Conference on Small and Medium Enterprises at New Crossroads, 28–30 September, University Science Malaysia, Penang.

Malaysia (1976), *Third Malaysia Plan (1976–1980)*, Kuala Lumpur: Government Printer.

Malaysia (1981), *Fourth Malaysia Plan (1981–1985)*, Kuala Lumpur: Government Printer.

Malaysia (1986), *Fifth Malaysia Plan (1986–1990)*, Kuala Lumpur: Government Printer.

Malaysia (1991), *Sixth Malaysia Plan (1991–1995)*, Kuala Lumpur: Government Printer.

Malaysia (1996), *Seventh Malaysia Plan (1996–2000)*, Kuala Lumpur: Government Printer.

Malaysian Institute of Economic Research (MIER) (2000), *MIER Monthly Monitor*, July, Kuala Lumpur: MIER.

Manuh, G. and R. Brown (1987), *Resources for the Development of Entrepreneurs: A Guided Reading List and Annotated Bibliography*, London: Commonwealth Secretariat.

Meredith, J.R. and N.C. Suresh (1986), 'Justification Techniques for Advanced Manufacturing Technologies', *International Journal of Production Research*, **24** (5), 1043–57.

Malaysian Industrial Development Corporation (MIDA) (1991), *Malaysia: Investment in the Manufacturing Sector: Policies, Incentives and Procedures*, Kuala Lumpur: Percetakan Mega.

Ministry of Finance (1999), *Economic Report 1999/2000*, Kuala Lumpur: Percetakan Nasional Malaysia Bhd.

Ministry of International Trade and Industry (MITI) (1990), *Annual Report*, Kuala Lumpur: MITI.

Moha Asri Abdullah (1993), 'Government Support Programmes, Inter-firm Linkages and the Performance of Small Firms: A Case Study of Textile and Apparel Industry in Malaysia', PhD thesis, Development Planning Unit, University of London, London.

Moha Asri Abdullah (1997a), *Industri Kecil di Malaysia* [*Small Industry in Malaysia*] (in Malays), Kuala Lumpur: Dewan Bahasa dan Pustaka.

Moha Asri Abdullah (1997b), *Pembangunan Perindustrian di Malaysia* [*Industrial Development in Malaysia*] (in Malays), Kuala Lumpur: Fajar Bakti.

Moha Asri Abdullah (1997c), 'Interfirm Linkages and the Performance of Urban Small Firms in Malaysia', *Malaysian Management Review*, **32** (1), March, 49–60.

Moha Asri Abdullah (1997d), *Industri Kecil dan Sederhana* [*Small and Medium Industry*] (in Malays), Kuala Lumpur: Fajar Bakti.

Moha Asri Abdullah (1998a), 'Perception of Entrepreneurs of Small–Medium Enterprises Towards Training in Malaysia', *International Journal of Industry and Higher Education*, **12** (2): 115–21.

Moha Asri Abdullah (1998b), 'The Impact of Entrepreneurial Characteristics on Financial Performance of SMEs in Malaysia', *Journal of International Business and Entrepreneurship*, **6** (1&2), December: 1–28.

Moha Asri Abdullah (1999a), *Pembangunan Industri Kecil dan Sederhana* [*The Development of Small and Medium Industry*] (in Malays), Kuala Lumpur: Fajar Bakti.

Moha Asri Abdullah (1999b), 'The Accessibility of the Government Sponsored Support Programmes for Small and Medium-sized Enterprises in Penang', *International Journal of Urban Policy and Planning (Cities)*, **16** (2), April: 83–92.

Moha Asri Abdullah (1999c), *Small and Medium Enterprises in Malaysia*, Aldershot: Ashgate.

Moha Asri Abdullah (ed.) (2001), *Asian Small and Medium Enterprises: Challenges in the 21st Century*, Leeds, UK: Wisdom House.

Moha Asri Abdullah and Mohd Isa Baker (2000), *Small and Medium Enterprises in Asia Pacific: Prospects in the New Millennium*, New York: Nova Science Publishers.

New Straits Times (1994), 'SMIs are the Backbone of the Economy', 8 June, p. 9.

Prime Minister's Department (1999), *The Malaysian Economy in Figures*, Economic Planning Unit, Kuala Lumpur: Percetakan National Malaysia Bhd.

Rahmah, I. (1995), *Malaysian Small Industries: Funding, Technology and Marketing Issues* (in Malay), Bangi, Selangor, Malaysia: National University of Malaysia's Publisher.

Salleh, Mohd Ismail (1991), *Promotion of Small-scale Industries and Strategies for Rural Industrialisation: The Malaysian Experience*, Kuala Lumpur: Sun U Book.

Sironopolis, N. (1994), *Small Business Management: A Guide to Entrepreneurship*, 5th Edition, Boston, MA: Houghton Mifflin.

Small and Medium Industrial Development Corporation (SMIDEC) (1999), 'The Listing of SMIs in the Manufacturing Sector' (unpublished data), Kuala Lumpur: SMIDEC.

Star (1999a), 'New Challenges for our SMIs', 11 March, p. 25.

Star (1999b), 'SMIs Should Be for Global Economy', 20 March, p. 6.

Stepanek, J. (1960), 'Measures for the Development of Small-scale Industries in the Federation of Malaya', Economic Planning Unit (mimeo), Kuala Lumpur.

United Nations Industrial Development Organisation (UNIDO) (1986), *Policies and Strategies for Small-scale Industry Development in Asia and the Pacific Region*, Kuala Lumpur: UNIDO.

Wong, L. and F. Schippers (1970), 'Small-scale Industries – Joint Report on Mission to Malaysia, Economic Planning Unit' (mimeo), Kuala Lumpur.

World Bank (1984), 'Malaysia: Development Issues and Prospects of Small Enterprises', Working Paper, Washington, DC.

Wyer, P., D. Smallbone and D. Johl (2000), 'The Implications of the Economic Crisis on SMEs: A Micro Perspective', in Moha Asri Abdullah (ed.), *Small and Medium Enterprises in Asian Pacific Countries*, New York: Nova Science Publishers, pp. 17–38.

8   Policies for SME Recovery in Thailand

Peter Brimble, David Oldfield and Manusavee Monsakul

8.1   INTRODUCTION

Since the emergence of the financial and economic crisis in mid-1997, the Thai government has shifted its industrial policy priority towards the promotion and development of the SME sector. It recognised the positive contribution that the sector can make to overcoming the impact of the crisis affecting Thailand and to enhance and sustain the economic growth of the country. The Thai economy suffered severely from the collapse of its financial sector, which subsequently caused production, investment and domestic demand to collapse and unemployment to increase. A great number of government policies and assistance measures were initiated to rescue SMEs from their bankruptcy, and the emphasis of industrial policy was shifted towards industrial upgrading and improving the competitiveness of local companies.

The chapter presents a review of SME developments in Thailand in the wake of the crisis, emphasising the SME policies that were altered and created to manage the crisis. Emphasis is also placed on identifying the critical issues currently facing SMEs and the effectiveness of current policies, in order to provide some implications for future policy in order to improve the growth and competitiveness of this sector in an increasingly globalised economy.

This chapter proceeds as follows. Section 8.2 deals with the definitions of SMEs used in Thailand. Section 8.3 covers the contribution of SMEs to the economy and the country's overall economic development. Section 8.4 analyses the impact of the financial and economic crisis on Thailand's SMEs and their responses to it. Section 8.5 conducts a review of the evolution of SME policies in Thailand. Section 8.6 evaluates the major challenges facing Thailand's SME sector and related policy makers. Finally Section 8.7 presents a summary of the major conclusions from this chapter.

8.2   DEFINITION OF SMES IN THAILAND

There is continual debate in Thailand about the correct definition of what constitutes an SME and how to classify them. Different Thai government agencies apply different definitions of SMEs typically based on the size of net fixed assets, number of employees, sales per annum, registered capital, and at times their type of economic activity. For the latter classification, whether or not farm-related activities constitute SMEs is subject to debate. However, in general, definitions of SMEs are based on two key measures: the number of employees and the level of fixed assets.

Thailand's Ministry of Industry (MOI) adopted the size of employment and fixed assets as criteria in defining SMEs. Presently, the MOI defines a small-scale industry as having fewer than 50 workers and invested capital (equity) not exceeding 10 million baht. A medium-scale industry is defined as having employment ranging from 50 to 200 workers and invested capital of more than 10 million baht but not exceeding 100 million baht. Large-scale enterprises are categorised as employing more than 200 workers and having invested capital of over 100 million baht.[1]

Thailand's Office of the Board of Investment (BOI) defines SMEs slightly differently from the MOI. According to the BOI small enterprises hold fixed assets of less than 10 million baht while medium-scale enterprises hold fixed assets between 10 million and 100 million baht. To add to the confusion the Industrial Finance Corporation of Thailand (IFCT), the Small Industrial Finance Corporation of Thailand (SIFCT), and the Bank of Thailand, define small industries as those with fixed assets of less than 20 million baht.

The general definition of SMEs in Thailand is further confused by the differing classification standards for the kinds of business activities such as manufacturing, services, and trading. These three categories of SMEs encompass the following activities (Allal 1999b, p. 7):

1. *Manufacturing sector*: including enterprises involved in processing activities and the assembly of components.

2. *Services sector*: including hotels and restaurants; real estate and business activities; recreational and cultural services; and personal and household services.

3. *Trading sector*: including wholesale and retail trade.

The Institute for Small and Medium Enterprise Development (ISMED) defines SMEs in each broad sector according to the level of fixed assets as identified in Table 8.1.

The Department of Industrial Promotion (DIP) takes a similar definition in terms of the type of economic activity, but it also adds 'number of employees' as an additional component (see Table 8.2).

Table 8.1
Institute for Small and Medium Enterprise Development (ISMED)
Definition of SMEs

Sector	Medium enterprises	Small enterprises
Production sector (including manufacturing, agriculture and mining)	200 million baht	50 million baht
Service sector	200 million baht	50 million baht
Trade sector (wholesale)	100 million baht	50 million baht
Trade sector (retail)	60 million baht	30 million baht

Note: Levels of fixed assets.

Source: ISMED.

Table 8.2
DIP Definition of SMEs According to Sector

	Fixed assets (million baht)		Number of employees (workers)	
	Medium	Small	Medium	Small
Production sector	200	50	200	50
Service sector	200	50	200	50
Trade sector (wholesale)	100	50	50	25
Trade sector (retail)	60	30	30	30

Source: Department of Industrial Promotion.

8.3   STATUS AND CONTRIBUTION OF SMES IN THAILAND

For decades, attention in Thailand's economy focused on the agricultural sector and the large industrial conglomerates which dominated the domestic scene. Only recently have SMEs been recognised for their substantial contributions to, and composition of, the national economy. SMEs are now seen as the backbone of Thailand's future industrial development and have thus been accorded greater attention from the government.[2] However, the severe neglect of SMEs throughout Thailand's rapid industrialisation has put them at a distinct disadvantage both domestically, when compared to the conglomerates, and abroad in relation to other countries' SMEs. This neglect by both the government and financial institutions has led to Thai SMEs being: inefficient; lacking innovation; inadequately financed; and poorly integrated into domestic and international supply chains. Development of SMEs has been given relatively little attention during the past several decades of industrial development. Experts have said that SMEs need special assistance from the government due to the lack of resources available as compared to larger companies. Due to shortcomings in promoting the development of Thai SMEs, they have not been able to fully achieve one of the strengths of being SMEs, which is their flexibility to adapt to fast-changing economic and market conditions.[3]

The exact number of SMEs and their percentage of all firms in Thailand are unknown, as multiple government departments handle their registration and use different classification methods for SMEs. Data from various departments within the Ministry of Industry and the Ministry of Commerce indicate that SMEs comprised between 90 and 98 per cent of all firms in the early 1990s, with the low value in the range referring to 'informal enterprises' and the higher value referring to the percentage of firms in the manufacturing sector (see Sevilla 2000; and Deyo 1999). Bangkok Bank, the country's largest bank, reported that there were 311 518 SMEs in 1998, totalling 92 per cent of all enterprises.

SMEs in the trading sector comprise the largest category of SMEs in Thailand, with 43.1 per cent of all SMEs engaged in trading (approximately 134 171 enterprises). SMEs in manufacturing account for 28.9 per cent of all SMEs (around 90 122 firms) while the remaining 28 per cent (87 225 firms) are in the services sector.[4] However, despite the significantly higher number of SMEs in the trading sector the Ministry of Industry has focused more of its attention on the manufacturing SMEs, which is a natural consequence of the ministry's orientation towards the manufacturing sector (Sevilla 2000). The result has been that most SME support programs, financing and laws are often oriented towards manufacturing firms, and thus service and trading SMEs are still struggling to receive law, regulations and programs tailored more specifically towards their needs.

As in other countries Thai SMEs have played an understated role in the economy. The output from SMEs makes up a substantial proportion of Thailand's exports and GDP. SMEs contribute 50–60 per cent of the country's GDP and account for approximately half of its exports (Sevilla 2000; Deyo 1999). SMEs also constitute a large proportion of the labour force, with 60–70 per cent of industrial workers employed by SMEs (Deyo 1999).

Thailand's industrialisation has been centred in and around Bangkok, with the result that SMEs are concentrated in the capital and its five surrounding provinces. Around 45 per cent of all manufacturing SMEs are situated in the Bangkok Metropolitan Area (Sevilla 2000) despite the fact that it comprises slightly over 10 per cent of Thailand's population. One consequence of this metropole growth has been the migration of villagers and farmers migrating from the outer provinces to seek employment in Bangkok. Thailand's SMEs are flexible: they can accommodate seasonal agricultural workers and new graduates, they provide linkages to large enterprises as supporting industries and they also help industrial distribution to rural areas.[5]

8.4 THE IMPACT OF THE ECONOMIC CRISIS ON SMES AND THEIR RESPONSES

Signs of an economic slowdown appeared in 1996 when Thailand's exports declined 1.9 per cent, its current account deficit rose to 8 per cent of GDP, and the country's foreign debt amounted to US$90.5 billion. Of this US$90.5 billion, nearly US$74 billion was private sector debt. By 1997 the economy began to unravel. The stock market continued its plunge from over 1 200 points in mid-1996 to 370 at the end of 1997 and as low as 253 by the third quarter of 1998. The Thai baht faced increasing pressure as speculators began to attack what had become a vulnerable and overvalued currency, forcing the Bank of Thailand (BOT) to expend billions of dollars in foreign reserves defending its pegged value of 25 baht to a basket of currencies dominated by the US dollar.

With foreign reserves nearly depleted at US$800 million, the Thai government decided on 2 July 1997 to float the value of the baht. Thailand's currency immediately depreciated which in turn opened up a Pandora's Box of other problems, including triggering a regional currency crisis. The baht began a downward spiral, made worse by the eventual depreciation of other currencies in the region, and hit an all-time low of 56.2 to the US dollar in January 1998. As a result of this development the heavily indebted private sector could no longer afford to repay short-term debt to foreign institutions and domestic lending institutions, thereby setting off a financial and banking crisis in Thailand. The early stages of the crisis exposed the irregular practices of Thailand's financial and banking institutions and the inadequate regulatory framework and supervision by the government. The end result was the closure of 56 finance firms by the end of 1997 and the nationalisation of six commercial banks in 1998.

The economic crisis that erupted in mid-1997 had numerous devastating effects on Thai SMEs. The first, and perhaps most substantial, impact was the severe credit crunch for small and large firms alike. Thailand's financial sector nearly collapsed in 1997 with dozens of finance companies and banks shut down because of staggering levels of non-performing loans (NPLs). The finance companies and banks that remained open were also saddled with bad debts, in some cases as high as 70 per cent of all loans, and responded by terminating lending for fear of increasing their NPLs (Paetkau 1999, p. 6). With SMEs accounting for up to 90 per cent of NPLs, they were designated as high-risk loans and banks and finance companies became reluctant to extend additional credit lines.[6] Moreover, the rise in interest rates made borrowing prohibitively costly for most SMEs. In addition, the subsequent tightening of lending regulations made accessing credit even more difficult for SMEs. Before the reforms in the banking and finance sector began in 1997–98, questionable lending practices allowed firms to acquire loans without submitting audited financial statements.[7] However, with the new regulations lenders introduced more cautious screening of applicants, and the traditionally poor bookkeeping habits of SMEs meant that many SMEs were unable to finance their business operations or repay their old debt. Compounding matters was the fact that large firms that utilised SMEs as suppliers of components were unwilling and often unable to assist their suppliers with finance, technology, and training (Deyo 1999).

A second major effect of the crisis on Thai SMEs was their vulnerability to foreign acquisitions. Being unable to finance their debt due to the dramatic depreciation of the baht, and lacking access to new credit, meant that SMEs were ripe for outright foreign takeovers, or forced to accept significant equity holdings by foreign firms in the form of joint ventures or debt–equity swaps (Deyo 1999). Hence, many SMEs either went bankrupt or were consolidated by foreign firms.

The third impact of the crisis on SMEs was increased foreign competition stemming from the liberalisation measures required under the International Monetary Fund (IMF) and World Bank loan packages. Parliament amended laws that previously denied foreign participation in certain sectors of the Thai economy, forcing local SMEs to compete with 100 per cent foreign-owned firms even at the small supplier level. Deyo (1999) notes that many of the larger foreign-owned firms in Thailand developed linkages with their fellow countrymen who had taken advantage of the amended laws to establish small supplier firms. New foreign firms entering the market with modern technology and large amounts of capital quickly displaced the increasingly uncompetitive Thai SMEs.

The fourth major effect of the economic crisis on Thai SMEs was cost-cutting pressure imposed by large firms. The large firms in Thailand suffered as well during the crisis, especially in terms of debt financing, and responded by focusing on short-term, cost-related strategies. According to Deyo (1999), large companies pressured their small supplier firms to reduce costs rather than assist them in technology transfers and human resource development. Such strategies became more viable and cost-effective for large companies because of the increasing competition for Thai SMEs from new foreign suppliers.

A fifth effect of the crisis on SMEs relates to the new developments in corporate governance in Thailand, which will be discussed in greater detail in Section 8.6. The economic crisis revealed the dire need for strengthened corporate governance to avoid a repeat of some of the contributing factors to the near collapse of Thailand's economy. Higher standards of corporate governance include improved government regulation in sectors such as banking and finance, but also greater self-regulation and higher ethical conduct by the firms themselves. Higher standards in corporate governance affect SMEs in two critical ways. First, with the stricter lending practices of banks and finance companies, SMEs will have to improve their record-keeping and disclosure practices in order to acquire credit. Second, with the arrival of more foreign firms in the Thai economy and increased opportunities for (or in some cases the necessity of) joint ventures or equity deals, Thai SMEs must operate in a much more transparent manner than they have been accustomed to in the past.

The challenge, then, is for Thai SMEs to quickly reorient themselves and adjust to the new, often harsher, realities of the post-crisis trends, such as greater foreign competition in the domestic market, stricter disclosure requirements and standards for financing, and the need to upgrade the utilisation of technology and human resources. Rising to the challenge is necessary both for the individual firms' survival but also for the sake of the overall economy because of the prominent role that SMEs play.

An article in the *Bangkok Post* in April 1998 captured the essence of SMEs' responsibility in moving the Thai economy forward, but it also noted their failure at the time of shouldering the burden:

> The realisation of industrial reform to achieve greater productivity and improved competitiveness rests with the participation of small and medium industrialists. But the lack of enthusiasm among small and medium enterprises remains the main obstacle to achieving the goal, former deputy industry minister Sompop Amatayakul said yesterday. 'If the SMEs are ready, the whole industry sector will be able to reform,' said Mr. Sompop, also chairman of the Industrial Restructuring Program. (*Bangkok Post*, 29 April 1998)

8.5   THE EVOLUTION OF SME POLICIES

The evolution of Thailand's policies on SMEs encompasses two basic stages: (i) the pre-crisis era when SMEs were a low priority in the minds of national leaders; and (ii) the post-crisis period when SMEs have become bombarded with new policies, programs and assistance to the point where coordination and duplication have become the new problems.

8.5.1   Developments Before the Crisis

Prior to the economic crisis in 1997, the SME sector received scant attention from the government. Economic policies essentially aimed at the development of large businesses and the agricultural sector. The Ministry of Industry realised the importance of the supporting industries which consisted to a large extent of small and medium-scale enterprises (JICA 1995, 2-1-6), but its recognition did not necessarily translate into effective promotional policies for SMEs. Many of the policies for SMEs merely entailed industrial decentralisation to promote the location of small and medium sized manufacturers, particularly the cottage industries, away from the congested urban area of Bangkok and its surroundings to the outer provinces (JICA 1995, 2-1-10).

The relative neglect of the SME sector during Thailand's industrialisation process is seen in the repeatedly failed attempts at promulgating an SME law. The former director-general of the Department of Industrial Promotion – DIP (currently permanent secretary), Manu Leopairote, who has overseen SMEs for the past ten years – has mentioned in public seminars that the department had drafted bills to promote the SME sector a decade ago but the proposed legislation failed to gain the support of the parliament at the time. Presumably it was because of personal connections between big businesses and key political parties in the coalition governments. That is, many firms and individuals, wanting to gain access to particular state services, financed the political parties. Political parties relied on financial support from these businesses and represented the demands of that group. Certain sectoral interests tended to ally with particular political parties due to the latter's access to relevant cabinet positions. For example, the Chart Thai Party once exerted strong control over the Ministry of Industry, the agency responsible for regulating the party's industrial supporters, such as textiles, glass and sugar milling (Doner and Ramsay 1997, p. 267).

SME support programs: BUILD and NSDP supplier programs

Two programs initiated to promote industrial subcontracting before the crisis struck were the BOI Unit for Industrial Linkage Development (BUILD) program and the National Supplier Development Program (NSDP). The BUILD program is under the authority of the Board of Investment and, like the NSDP, aims at promoting the growth of supporting industries, which are mostly small and medium-scale industries. The BUILD scheme is a subcontracting development program begun in 1992 and is aimed at boosting the development of supporting industries in Thailand by strengthening linkages and fostering cooperation between large enterprises and supplier companies. The information on local suppliers is provided to the buyer firms, which mostly are multinational corporations (MNCs). BUILD helps the MNCs seek sourcing networks of suppliers in Thailand, while small and medium-scale Thai parts manufacturers benefit by achieving the standards required to enter into productive subcontracting arrangements. Therefore, the BUILD program boils down to providing matching and information services for large enterprises and SMEs alike (JICA 1995, 2-1-10).

During its initial years BUILD implemented a rather passive strategy, that is it waited for customers to stop by and ask for information. However, the BOI eventually realised that this strategy did not work. In July 1997, at the outbreak of the economic recession and the devaluation of the Thai baht, several assemblers called upon BUILD to search for local parts suppliers capable of producing the parts they required. Accordingly, the Unit decided to modify its strategy to be more proactive, which led to the complementary 'Vendors Meet Customers' (VMC) program. The VMC program brings together parts suppliers (many of which are SMEs) with mainly multinational assemblers. The program was designed to bring suppliers to the assembly plants to foster arrangements for the parts and components desired and the quality expected by the assemblers (Office of the Board of Investment 1999).

NSDP is a joint program between the BOI and the Ministry of Industry that emphasises training and upgrading the capacity of SMEs. Like BUILD, NSDP aims to promote the growth of supporting industries. The program aims at the development of small- and medium-sized parts manufacturers by cooperating with private business groups and relevant government offices (JICA 1995, 2-1-12).

Training and technology support institutions
As noted earlier little of the government's attention focused on SMEs before the economic crisis erupted in 1997. Industry initiatives undertaken by the MOI prior to 1997 typically applied to industry as a whole rather than explicitly addressing the needs and circumstances of SMEs. This indirect approach to assisting SMEs is clearly manifest in the types of support institutions created by or placed under the authority of the MOI. At present, nine specialised institutions for the promotion and development of Thailand's industrial sector fall under the jurisdiction of the MOI. Four of these institutions were established before the crisis in 1997 (see Box 1), with the remainder formed during the peak of the crisis (see Box 2). What is worth noting is that the only institution devoted exclusively to SMEs did not exist until 1998, which demonstrates how far off the 'radar screen' SMEs were in the minds of policy makers.

8.5.2   Policy Developments During the Crisis and Beyond

Thailand had clearly not invested sufficiently in upgrading its export industries to stay ahead of regional and global competition, as the country gradually lost its comparative advantages in low-technology industries to newly emerging countries that were able to offer cheaper products and lower labour costs. Protection in the domestic market also hindered the upgrading of industries as local firms received special export incentives and tariff protection to incubate them from foreign competitors. The result was a stagnant industrial sector mired in outdated technology, rising wages for labour-intensive activities, and little innovation due to weaknesses in management and the lack of research and development.

The MOI perceived that industrial development in an environment of increasingly intense competition in international trade and rapidly changing globalisation conditions is beyond the resource of government mechanisms alone. The crisis served as a wake-up call to both the government and the private sector and gave a strong impetus for a new model of industrial development. This new model encompasses a stronger partnership between the public and private sectors and places SMEs at the forefront of economic development.

The Institute for SME Development
One priority of the MOI has been to establish more specialised institutions for the key industrial sectors, including one explicitly for SMEs (see Box 2). In 1998 the MOI created the Institute for Small and Medium Enterprise Development jointly with Thammasat University and in cooperation with several other educational

institutions in Thailand. ISMED reflects the government's new priority for SME development and promotion. The MOI envisages ISMED playing the leading role in the development of SMEs through entrepreneurship training, advisory services, and research activities.

Box 1: Pre-crisis specialised institutions under the MOI

Thailand Productivity Institute (TPI)
Established: January 1994
Summary: The Thailand Productivity Institute seeks to increase Thailand's industrial productivity and the country's overall competitiveness by providing advisory services and training related to ISO 9000, ISO 14000, and general human resource development (HRD); formulating recommendations for productivity to the government; and disseminating information to the public.

Thai-German Institute (TGI)
Established: January 1995
Summary: The Thai-German Institute seeks to facilitate the transfer of state-of-the-art manufacturing technology to Thailand's industrial sector in order to increase the country's efficiency and competitiveness. Its major tasks entail providing training to industrial personnel on the latest manufacturing technology; providing advisory services on production and automation technology; conducting product testing and quality control; providing information services on manufacturing technology and HRD; and conducting research and development (R&D) in production and automation technology.

National Food Institute (NFI)
Established: October 1996
Summary: The National Food Institute falls under the realm of the Industrial Development Foundation, although it acts as an autonomous organisation comprising public and private sector board members. Its overall objective is to support the development of the food industry in order to increase the country's food exports. NFI's main duties include promoting the usage of improved technology in the food industry; providing information on global trading and R&D, providing laboratory services to the public and private sectors; providing assistance for value-added product development and increased exports; promoting product quality and safety through improved packing technology; and supporting environmental protection through responsible food processing.

Thailand Textile Institute
Established: October 1996
Summary: The Thailand Textile Institute intends to enhance the textile industry by improving the quality of goods and promoting higher-value-added products. Its key functions include compiling and disseminating R&D related to production, quality and standards; providing training and seminars for improved human resources; providing inspection, analysis, testing, and standards certification services; and engaging in marketing promotional activities for domestic and foreign markets.

Box 2: Specialised institutions under the MOI, crisis years (1997–98)

Management System Certification Institute (MASCI)
Established: October 1997
Summary: MASCI seeks to upgrade Thailand's industries to international standards and to increase the country's competitiveness. Among its main duties are providing certification, inspection and monitoring related to ISO 9000, ISO 14000, and TISI 18000; developing personnel involved in certification and standards; and serving as a coordinator between industry and government regarding technical issues and policy issues.

Cane and Sugar Research Institute
Established: March 1998
Summary: The Cane and Sugar Research Institute undertakes research and development (R&D) for the cane and sugar industry. The objective is to utilise applied research to increase Thailand's competitiveness in the global sugar market. The institute's key functions are conducting R&D related to cane, sugar and machinery; disseminating the results of research; providing training and seminars to develop human resources; providing inspection, testing and analysis services, along with issuing quality certificates; and providing other consulting services and information to cultivators and manufacturers.

Electrical and Electronics Institute
Established: July 1998
Summary: The Electrical and Electronics Institute intends to increase the competitiveness of Thailand's electronics industry. Its main tasks entail formulating policy recommendations; issuing Thai and international electrical and electronics standards certificates; providing information services related to the industry; engaging in transaction services such as trading or exchange of parts domestically and internationally and conducting training and seminars based on the latest R&D.

Thailand Automotive Institute
Established: July 1998
Summary: The Thailand Automotive Institute is a joint effort between the public and private sectors to develop a centre for increased competitiveness of the automotive industry, including parts and assembly. Its major functions entail policy proposals and coordination; testing services and issuing industrial standards certificates; improving industrial technology and overall quality; and developing human resources.

The Institute for Small and Medium Enterprise Development (ISMED)
Established: April 1999
Summary: ISMED is a joint endeavour conducted by the Department of Industrial Promotion and several Thai universities and other educational institutions. Its main activities include the development and creation of SME entrepreneurs; devising training methodologies and tools for the development of services for entrepreneurs; facilitating a network for services, training, and consultation between Thai SMEs and international industrialists; and providing various certification services. ISMED also provides numerous training courses for SMEs. A brief listing of some of the courses include the following: Creating SMEs Business, Managing SMEs Business, Enhancing Management Skills of SMEs, Small Business Management, New Business Creation, E-Commerce, and Technology Management.

ISMED set forth an ambitious five-year goal for its training activities, targeting five broadly defined groups (see Table 8.3). More specifically the training will be aimed at existing SME entrepreneurs, new entrepreneurs or interested persons, recent graduates, unemployed people with management or other appropriate background, and people in SME-related activities such as business, financial, accounting and production consulting. However, as seen in Table 8.3 the emphasis will be on developing new entrepreneurs.

Since ISMED commenced in 1999, the institute has focused on short-term and medium-term training and financial support for business expansion and capacity enhancement. The institute will also coordinate with financial institutions to provide credit to SMEs. ISMED's medium-term and long-term activities involve developing long-term training courses, conducting research relating to SMEs, devising business capability indicators, establishing an SME database and SME network, and training SME consultants.

Table 8.3
ISMED's Training Goals for 1999–2003

Result	Unit	Fiscal year				
		1999–2000	2001	2002	2003	5-year total
1. Existing entrepreneurs	Person	8 400	8 000	8 000	8 000	32 400
2. New entrepreneurs	Person	24 000	20 000	20 000	20 000	84 000
3. SMEs receiving advice	Enterprises	400	400	400	400	1 600
4. Developed SMEs lecturers and consultants	Person	320	480	480	480	1 760
5. Trained, certified and registered evaluators	Person	–	200	200	200	600

Source: Ministry of Industry.

The Miyazawa Fund

In 1999 Japan extended a 53 billion baht loan package known as the Miyazawa Fund. The Fund covered several of the hardest hit economies in the East Asian economic crisis and was intended to stimulate their domestic economies.[8] Of the 3.7 billion baht directed to the Ministry of Industry approximately one-third of it was channelled into promoting SMEs. One billion baht was allocated to the establishment of ISMED, and another 100 million baht for an SME fair. However, according to one MOI official, a great deal of criticism centred on how the money was spent in terms of merely promoting the idea of SMEs rather than working towards solving their problems in a sustainable way.[9] Much of the MOI's Miyazawa Fund money went into training programs run by the specialised institutions under its authority.

8.5.3   Financial Support Institutions and Programs – Public and Private

Even before the onset of the economic crisis the Thai government established various financial institutions aimed at SMEs. Other state-run financial institutions that have a broader scope, such as the Government Savings Bank (GSB), responded to the current problems of SMEs by setting aside a certain quota for lending to SMEs. The key government financial institutions explicitly dealing with SMEs are the following.

The Government Savings Bank (GSB)
Established in 1913, GSB extends loans to the public and private sectors for working capital and fixed asset acquisitions. Private sector borrowers can receive a maximum loan amount of 10 million baht, but until recently its lending activities focused on the public sector. In mid-1999 GSB was far behind its stated goal of lending 1 billion baht to SMEs for the whole year, as the bank extended only 50 million baht by June 1999 (Paetkau 1999, p. 20).

The Industrial Finance Corporation of Thailand (IFCT)
IFCT is a 30-per-cent government-owned finance corporation concentrating on private sector industrial and capital markets. Among its activities are extending term and working capital loans (essentially project based), equity investment, loan syndications, guarantees, and various advisory services (Paetkau 1999, p. 21). IFCT has increased its emphasis on SMEs during the past few years, as in 1998 when 87 per cent of new project approvals were for small and medium industries (SMIs) (Paetkau 1999, p. 23). IFCT also announced in 1999 that it would offer greater financial assistance to SMIs, especially for manufacturing firms with an export orientation (Paetkau 1999, p. 23). Of IFCT's 2000 clients, 1 600 are SMEs, yet they account for only 30 per cent of the total loans distributed by IFCT.[10] The Bank of Thailand injected 9 billion baht worth of soft loans into IFCT explicitly for use in assisting SME financing.

Small Industry Credit Guarantee Corporation (SICGC)
SICGC, created in 1991 and owned by several government institutions, aims to facilitate and expand credit extension from financial institutions to SMEs and to create a more reassuring lending environment between creditors and small borrowers (Paetkau 1999, p. 24). SICGC provides credit guarantees of between 200 000 baht and 10 million baht for institutions that lend to SMEs. Most of SICGC's guarantees (63 per cent in 1998) are for the manufacturing sector, but all sectors are eligible. Despite its name implying guarantees for small firms, SICGC's guarantee habits appear to be aimed at medium sized firms, with an average guarantee equalling around US$40 000 (Paetkau 1999, p. 26).

Small Industry Finance Corporation (SIFC)
Established in 1991, SIFC is another government lender for SMEs seeking capital expenditures, working capital, and debt repayment. Loans range from a minimum of 500 000 baht to a maximum of 25 million baht. Between 1993 and 1998 SIFC extended 3.5 billion baht worth of loans with an average loan amounting to 3.8 million baht (Paetkau 1999, p. 28). In May 2000 the SIFC president explained that the corporation allocated only 700 million baht to SMEs in 1999 because of poor sales recorded by SMEs and low profit margins, which made it difficult to service debt. However, he claimed SIFC would extend 6 billion baht in credit to SMEs during 2000 contingent on their improved performance.[11]

Export–Import Bank of Thailand (EXIM)
Created in 1993 and commencing with banking activities the following year, EXIM offers services in long-term lending, term loan investment, advisory services, and guarantees and financing working capital for Thai firms operating domestically and abroad. In order to compete with the larger banks, EXIM has sought to fill a niche by catering to SMEs.

In response to the many debt-ridden and cash-strapped SMEs since 1997, the government devised several financial programs for industry as a whole and for SMEs in particular. Most of the funding for these financial programs derived from Japanese assistance, the World Bank, and the Asian Development Bank. Under the Japanese loan program, Japan's Export–Import Bank (JEXIM) injected US$1.35 billion to help Thai businesses restructure their debts, particularly SMEs in supporting industries that were caught in the liquidity squeeze. JEXIM's contribution includes a US$600 million co-financing deal with the World Bank and US$750 million in loans to the Industrial Finance Corporation of Thailand and the government-owned Krung Thai Bank to support manufacturing firms.[12]

In May 2000 the Department of Industrial Promotion set aside a 95 billion baht fund to support SMEs and boost the overall economy. The fund is a combination of state and private financial institutions along with two state-run venture capital funds. The venture capital funds comprise a one billion baht fund for small firms and a US$100 million fund supported by the Asian Development Bank for medium-sized enterprises.[13] The government approved a 50.3 billion baht fund for SMEs to be issued through state financial institutions and another 10 billion baht from three of the leading private commercial banks and the state-run Krung Thai Bank.

The allocation of 95 billion baht represented a significant increase over 1999 when only 40 billion baht was made available for SMEs. The new funds were aimed at upgrading machinery, relocating firms to industrial estates, energy saving programs, working and investment capital, and for research and development.[14]

To provide equity investment to support new investments as well as to assist the restructuring efforts of Thailand's business sector, including SMEs, the government announced its intention in 1999 to establish three funds: the Thailand Equity Fund, the Thailand Recovery Fund, and the Fund for Venture Capital Investment in SMEs.

Investments by these funds will help to lower the debt-to-equity ratios of Thai businesses as well as to lower financial costs and reduce business risks. The Thailand Equity Fund is expected to receive an initial investment of US$500 million, and will be financed by the Thai government, Thai private investors, the World Bank's International Finance Corporation, and foreign investors. The Thailand Recovery Fund will be a privately managed fund with 3.7 billion baht in initial capital.

8.5.4   Other Support Programs

The Thai government recognised that financing is only part of the problem (and solution) for SMEs. In order to ensure their long-term viability a comprehensive set of support programs and activities became equally important for SMEs and for the recovery of Thailand's economy. One program involves the creation of financial advisory centres for SMEs. Twenty five of these centres are now operating at provincial branches of the Federation of Thai Industries, and provide consulting services on marketing, product design and on business plans for loan applications. According to a report in *The Nation* (26 May 2000), over 12 000 companies have utilised the services of the financial advisory centres.

A potentially significant contribution to SMEs could come from the establishment in 1999 of the Market for Alternative Investment (MAI). The need to raise additional capital is a must for most SMEs, yet the tight credit and high interest rates in the banking and financial sector often put loans out of their reach. For instance, in 1999 SMEs incurred interest rates of 10.5 per cent compared to the minimum lending rate (MLR) of 9 per cent that most large corporations received.[15] The MAI offers an alternative to loans from financial institutions by allowing SMEs to raise venture capital. The MAI is specifically designed for SMEs because of its easier listing requirements as compared to the Stock Exchange of Thailand (SET), and theoretically could serve as a springboard to listing on the SET.

New support programs for SMEs are springing up in the information technology realm as well. In April 2000, Advance Datanetwork Communications launched a new private communication network service called 'Datanet'. The service, which is the first network service provider for SMEs, offers low-cost networking for firms within Thailand, and allows SMEs to contact their branches and customers all across Thailand.[16] Another information technology service will soon be offered by the Department of Industrial Promotion. In August 2000, DIP commenced with a free online 'storefronts' project for SMEs. The project is designed to encourage SMEs to engage in e-commerce by assuming the initial start-up costs that presumably deter some firms from conducting e-commerce activities. The project arises out of DIP's disappointment in the number of SMEs undertaking e-commerce despite their participation in the multitude of e-commerce courses offered throughout Thailand. Sensing that Thailand could once again fall behind, DIP's service will promote the companies themselves and their products. However, the initial service will not offer online transactions.[17]

8.5.5 The SME Master Plan

Having seen the ill effects of an incoherent and fractional set of SMEs policies and regulations on industrial development, the MOI set out in 1998 to prepare the country's first comprehensive master plan for SMEs. The SME Master Plan contains seven principal strategies for strengthening Thailand's SMEs and enhancing their global competitiveness, as seen in Box 3.

8.5.6 The Small and Medium Sized Enterprises Promotion Act

Two explanations sometimes offered for the underdevelopment of Thai SMEs are: the absence of a specific law for the promotion of SMEs; and a lack of governmental

---

Box 3: The seven strategies of the SME master plan

Strategy 1: Upgrade Technological and Management Capabilities of SMEs
Measures:
- Establish an enterprise diagnosis system as a tool for promoting and supporting potential SMEs
- Develop a consultancy system for business improvement and problem solving
- Support the modernisation of facilities and international standard management systems
- Improve product quality to international standards
- Develop networking and improve the efficiency of R&D institutes

Strategy 2: Develop Entrepreneurs and the Human Resources of SMEs
Measures:
- Create and incubate new entrepreneurs and develop existing entrepreneurs
- Enhance the efficiency and flexibility of training services
- Improve the efficiency and coverage of industrial skill standards certification systems
- Improve curriculum and methods in educational establishments to meet industry's needs

Strategy 3: Enhance SMEs' Access to Markets
Measures:
- Improve SMEs' access to government procurement
- Promote subcontracting and linkages with large enterprises, both domestically and internationally
- Expand and strengthen export promotion activities for SMEs
- Promote cross-border trade and linkages with trading companies

Strategy 4: Strengthen Financial Support System for SMEs
Measures:
- Expand and develop credit guarantee systems for SMEs
- Establish a Venture Capital Fund for SMEs
- Establish an SME Promotion Fund
- Strengthen financial advisory services for SMEs

Strategy 5: Provide a Conducive Business Environment
Measures:
- Establish and strengthen local information centres for SMEs
- Develop mechanisms for reviewing and revising laws, regulations, and administrative procedures to redress disadvantages of SMEs
- Support SMEs' preparations for the information technology age
- Improve the efficiency of distribution channels
- Strengthen the services and planning capabilities of regional and local authorities and organisations
- Promote establishment of SME parks

Strategy 6: Develop Micro Enterprises and Community Enterprises
Measures:
- Incubate 'strategic' micro enterprises and community enterprises
- Promote the commercialisation of indigenous know-how
- Upgrade management and encourage SMEs to enter the formal sector
- Promote business associations and cooperation among SMEs

Strategy 7: Develop Networking of SMEs and Clusters
Measures
- Conduct studies of various cluster models which enhance overall efficiency
- Support pilot projects to develop clusters in each region
- Promote associations and business relations as a stepping-stone towards cluster relationships
- Provide infrastructural support, incentives, and financing

institutions directly responsible for overall SME policies. Throughout the industrialisation process no clearly identifiable governmental institution held responsibility for overseeing SMEs. Policy decisions were made by each sector with little coordination between ministries and institutions. Compounding matters was the absence of a comprehensive law for SMEs or a strategic plan for their development and inclusion in the economic growth of the country. The result is that the few disjointed policies that did exist were not implemented properly, nor did the government foresee the critical role that SMEs play in driving an economy forward.

Finally, in 1998, with the economy in ruins, the idea for an SME promotion law resurfaced after failed attempts in the past at promulgating such legislation. The Department of Industrial Promotion had years ago prepared a draft bill but, because of indifference or outright opposition to an SME law by key government officials, the draft never reached parliament.

In September 1998 the cabinet decided to establish a special committee to oversee the development of SMEs. The committee was entrusted with devising a clear policy framework and recommendations for promoting SMEs. Soon afterwards the Ministry of Industry began preparing a draft bill for the promotion and protection of SMEs.

The objective was to increase their efficiency and competitiveness so that SMEs could make a greater contribution in supporting the industrial and export sectors. In order to accomplish these goals the drafting committee focused on upgrading financial and operations management, technology and the marketing of SMEs.

By November 1998 the MOI hosted a public hearing for interested parties to express their opinions on the proposed bill. Among the participants of the hearing and brainstorming session were the Federation of Thai Industries, the Board of Trade, banking representatives, and academics. However, soon after the public hearing the MOI called for a meeting to discuss the definition of SMEs, which was naturally a source of some contention among government and private sector representatives. Once again government officials from several ministries and agencies assembled with private sector representatives to agree upon a classification scheme for SMEs. In the end the MOI accepted a definition of SMEs based on the value of fixed assets (Sevilla 2000, p. 2).

In December 1998 the cabinet approved the SME Promotion Bill along with the revised definition of SMEs. The House of Representatives gave its consent in September 1999, but it took an entire year for the Senate to finally approve the bill, but with amendments, which meant that it had to go back to the House of Representatives. After a few weeks of deliberation the House of Representatives agreed with the Senate changes in January 2000, and the law came into effect upon the king's signature in February.

The SME Promotion Act contains three main features: new government agencies explicitly for SMEs, an SME Promotion Fund, and an SME Action Plan. The law calls for the creation of two new governmental institutions: the SME Promotion Committee and the SME Promotion Office. The Promotion Committee will consist of 25 members, including: the prime minister as chairman; the ministers of industry, commerce, agriculture and finance; permanent secretaries from the Ministry of Labour and Social Welfare, Ministry of Science, Technology and Environment, and the Ministry of Industry; the secretary-general of the National Economic and Social Development Board; the secretary-general of the Board of Investment; representatives from the Board of Trade and the Federation of Thai Industries; and 12 others, with at least six of these from private organisations.

The SME Promotion Committee will have several responsibilities, including the following:

- recommend to the cabinet policies and plans to promote SMEs;

- submit a status report on SMEs to the cabinet and public at least once a year;

- consider and approve action plans to promote SMEs;

- make recommendations to government agencies, state-owned enterprises, and private organisations related to the action plans;

- propose additional laws or amendments to laws related to SMEs;

- suggest measures to reinforce cooperation and coordination among government agencies, state-owned enterprises and private organisations.

The SME Promotion Office will be established as a special executive agency with a certain degree of autonomy and chaired by the MOI's permanent secretary. Among the Office's functions will be:

- recommend the types and sizes of SMEs and policies and plans for promoting SMEs;

- coordinate and prepare action plans for promoting SMEs;

- prepare the SME status reports;

- recommend to the SME Promotion Committee new laws, amendments and revisions to laws related to SMEs;

- manage the SME Promotion Fund;

- subsidise or assist in the promotion of SMEs in various ways, including lending and shareholding.

The SME Promotion Fund will acquire its financing from numerous sources, such as an initial fund from the government, subsidies from annual budgets, and supplementary fund contributions, but details are not specified. Who, in particular, will contribute and how much financing will likely become available is certainly open to question.

The Promotion Fund will be utilised in several ways. The law states that individual SMEs or groups of SMEs can borrow from the fund to establish new activities and improvements to existing ones to make the enterprises more efficient and capable. Government agencies, state-owned enterprises and private organisations can also receive assistance from the fund to carry out the action plans to promote SMEs. A third use is for financial assistance to subsidise investment related activities to the establishment, expansion of activities, and R&D for SMEs.

The SME Promotion Action Plan intends to cover a wide range of support measures for SMEs, including: measures for financial and other forms of assistance to SMEs; development or establishment of a capital market or money market for SMEs; human resource development; marketing support; product development; information and technology dissemination; strengthening private sector organisations; recommendations for legislative and regulatory amendments and more. The challenge will be for the SME Promotion Committee and the executing agencies to devise a systematic and integrated SME Promotion Action Plan that can cover the 18 areas as listed in the SME Promotion Act.

8.5.7   Future Policy Developments

The economic crisis highlighted the importance of SMEs to the economy, and how much effort will be required to restructure Thai SMEs in order to put them on the path to global competitiveness. The once ignored small and medium sized enterprises have suddenly come under the spotlight from politicians looking to new bases for support. Not surprisingly, the major political parties are exploiting the crisis in order to gain political popularity within the SME sector. Key political parties such as the Democrats, Chart Pattana, and Thai Rak Thai have espoused various policies designed to assist SMEs. At the elections for the House of Representatives held in early 2001, the major political parties proclaimed their empathy for the farmers, one of the traditional bastions of support, and also for SMEs now that they have become a focal point for the economic recovery. The extent to which this newly found concern for SMEs among politicians translates into effective policy making and implementation remains tenuous at best because of the big business connections and personal interests of the leading politicians. Many of them likely sang a new tune to the SMEs throughout the crisis all the while knowing that elections were soon imminent as the new constitution took effect. The new administration has expressed strong commitment to continuing the focus on SME development.

8.6   CRITICAL ISSUES FACING SMES IN THAILAND

A World Bank study identified six target areas for the Thai government to assist SMEs. The six areas are: managerial and technological upgrading; manpower development; expanding market exposure; strengthening financial capabilities; improving the business environment; and cultivating micro enterprises.[18] While in general agreement with the World Bank's priority issue areas, the authors offer a slightly modified classification structure for analysing the critical issues facing Thailand's SMEs.

8.6.1   Managerial and Staff Human Resource Development

Thai SMEs are generally seen as lacking many of the vital skills required for modern management. According to the SME Development Master Plan, managers of SMEs are deficient in, among other skills, understanding market competition and utilising strategic planning. Standards and quality management system seminars and training courses abound in Thailand, yet few SMEs actually adopt these systems. Part of this can be explained by the high service costs for systems such as the International Standards Organisation (ISO) and total quality management (TQM). Moreover, many Thai SME managers are deficient in basic skills such as those relating to computers, finance, marketing and accounting, not to mention the increasingly important 'sophisticated' skills such as market analysis and strategic planning. It is paramount for Thai SME managers to enhance their own personal skills along with implementing international standard management systems and quality control to meet the stricter standards demanded by many foreign firms, and an increasingly rising number of large domestic firms. Unless Thai SMEs can raise their management and quality standards and develop more sophisticated business strategies, they will be left out of the global supply-chains that are quickly integrating the world's businesses.

In addition to management weaknesses, another serious shortcoming in Thailand is the level of skilled labour. Thailand's workforce, especially in its SMEs, is notorious for its chronic shortage of trained personnel in engineering, computer science, and research and development. Due to a lack of skilled workers in science and technology and R&D, virtually all technology is imported with only slight modifications made as necessary for the local circumstances. Part of the blame for this lies with the Thai educational system, which is currently undergoing extensive reform. Science and technology have received scant attention in the Thai educational system, and thus there are critical shortages of engineers, technicians and other skilled personnel for SMEs. Compounding the problem is the general lack of research skills instilled in Thai students during their basic education and even in higher education. More directly related to the SMEs, however, are the costs of training, especially for computer and information technology skills, which are typically beyond the budgets of many SMEs.

Moreover, managers of SMEs are concerned that, after receiving additional training and new skills, many employees will seek new opportunities for employment, particularly with the larger more sought-after multinationals and local conglomerates. Therefore, SME owners are reluctant to pay for training programs for their staff.

8.6.2   Technology and Information

The overall lack of technology utilised by Thai SMEs translates into an inability to meet customers' demands. Without adequate production technology or quality control, goods produced by SMEs are often below export quality standards or fail to meet the assemblers' requirements. Also, as noted above, many managers of SMEs are unaware of the prevailing international standards. Thai SMEs are falling further behind on the technology curve because of a lack of foresight of managers and a dearth of domestic R&D activities.

Some government offices and independent agencies offer testing and certification services for goods, but the fees are often prohibitively expensive for SMEs and some services are not up to accepted standards. In a related matter, the exigency of gathering, processing and analysis of information has stormed onto the business scene with the advent of the Internet and other forms of communication and information. Thai SMEs must rise to the challenge to keep up with the rapid changes occurring in the domestic and global markets, but once again are falling behind regional competitors. The absence of appropriate technology and the lack of information technology (IT) skills among managers of SMEs are critical issues that need to be addressed. A World Bank (World Bank 1999) study noted that even with issues directly related to them, many Thai SMEs are unaware of the regulatory and promotional policies of the Thai government for SMEs (as cited in the SME Development Master Plan). The Thai government recognises the deficiencies in the flow of information to SMEs, and therefore included measures for promoting the use of information technology in the SME Promotion Action Plan. However, much of the burden falls upon the SMEs themselves to procure not only the necessary technology components but also the individual skills and motivation to utilise them.

8.6.3 The Need for Sustained Links to Finance

Clearly, Thailand's financial institutions are currently unable to satisfy the demand and need for financing SMEs' business activities. The level of non-performing loans is still extremely high, 36.5 per cent of all outstanding credit as of June 2000, although declining, but it will be some time before normal lending resumes as banks and finance companies fear taking on more non-performing loans. Even before the economic crisis in Thailand, however, banks extended very little credit to SMEs, instead preferring to lend to the large companies and especially the dominant conglomerates. The credit squeeze for SMEs was exacerbated by the economic crisis, when credit as a whole essentially dried up because of the near collapse of the banking and financial sector.

Interest rates have also presented major obstacles to Thai SMEs. Unlike firms in the export sector that typically receive interest rates at 3 per cent above the minimum lending rate, during the crisis Thai SMEs were usually required to pay a 16–17 per cent interest rate – a level which was far above their counterparts in Japan, for example, where the interest rate was 0.5 per cent.[19] Thus, not only was credit unavailable for most SMEs, it was prohibitively costly for the ones that could receive a credit line.

A multitude of changes are required in the lending behaviour of banks, the accounting practices of SMEs, and the relevant regulations and laws, before the SME financing issue can be adequately resolved. First, SMEs need to overcome the glaring weaknesses that make them high-risk borrowers: poor information and reporting practices; and a lack of financial management skills. SMEs will have to demonstrate individually and collectively that they have viable business plans and straightforward and transparent bookkeeping in order to attract long-term credit. Until managers of SMEs adopt transparent and accurate accounting systems they will continue to be denied access to adequate levels of credit. Second, banks and finance companies can also play an instrumental role in assisting SMEs in their credit applications. More trained officers are needed to work with SMEs in the preparation of documentation required for a loan request and also in evaluating SMEs' accounts and record keeping.[20] Improved financial access for SMEs requires more than just direct lending by state financial institutions and commercial banks. A third element for reform is that legislative changes must also occur to allow state financial institutions such as IFCT to lend to more types of SMEs. Under its current legislative mandate IFCT can only lend to small and medium industries (that is, manufacturing firms), which obviously excludes SMEs in services and other sectors. Other legislative changes may also be required to assist SMEs in accessing finance. The Federation of Thai Industries (FTI) recommended to the Ministry of Finance a new accounting system for SMEs in order for them to acquire loans more easily. In 1999, TFI urged lawmakers to consider a new accounting law for SMEs.[21]

An important strategy to compensate for the inadequate flows of financing from banks and financial institutions to SMEs, but one that is not being utilised effectively, is to channel more investment into SMEs. Thus a fourth critical area for financing SMEs is to explore measures that facilitate the flow of investment, both domestically and foreign, into Thai SMEs. Not only would this solve the problem of capital shortage but it would also promote the transfer of technology to Thai SMEs from larger firms that seek subcontracting agreements for components.

8.6.4 Moves to Better Corporate Governance

The World Bank study broadly identified the need for an improved business environment to foster the development of SMEs. One critical component of this is the issue of stronger corporate governance in Thailand. Corporate governance typically involves management control, transparency, appropriate regulatory systems, and relationships between shareholders and stakeholders (Levinson 1999, p. 84) – in essence, a mix of statutory regulation and self-regulation (World Bank 1999). The current principles of corporate governance entail transparency, accountability, fairness and responsibility, and these are quickly spreading worldwide as the level of transnational production and foreign investment grow seemingly exponentially.

In Thailand, especially before the onset of the economic crisis, there were severe shortcomings in corporate governance, particularly related to transparency and inadequate legal and regulatory frameworks. The weak system of corporate governance and the infamous corruption found in Thai government circles were instrumental in the collapse of the economy in 1997. According to the World Bank report on corporate governance:

> The economic crises in East Asia and other regions have demonstrated how macroeconomic difficulties can be exacerbated by a systemic failure of corporate governance stemming from weak legal and regulatory systems, inconsistent accounting and auditing standards, poor banking practices, thin and unregulated capital markets, ineffective oversight by corporate boards of directors, and little regard for the rights of minority shareholders. (World Bank 1999, p. 2)

Several reforms of the Thai economy and government are under way as a result of the near consensus in the country that higher ethical standards and better regulatory mechanisms are needed to avoid another disaster like that in 1997. New oversight institutions came out of the 1997 constitution, particularly for the political realm in the form of a counter corruption committee, the Election Commission, and others. The urgency of the economic crisis also led to a flurry of new regulatory agencies and a tightening of existing ones, especially in the financial sector.

Thai SMEs are not immune from the prevailing mood of reform. Like the governmental agencies overseeing them, SMEs will have to face the challenge of meeting standards which are becoming global and determine, for instance, whether or not investors choose to invest in particular enterprises. Thai SMEs fail to recognise that responsible and transparent companies see their reputations and value increase, and therefore they either reluctantly accept or outright resist voluntary corporate governance practices.

Nowhere is this need for better corporate governance among firms more apparent than in the financial realm. The slow pace of debt restructuring for SMEs is partially due to the fact that many of them did not want to disclose information, as they did not understand the process of restructuring. Thai SMEs must recognise that investors, banks and finance companies will increasingly base their financing and investment decisions on a company's governance record as well as its potential for growth. Sloppy bookkeeping and a failure to disclose financial information will have to give way to independently audited records if SMEs expect to acquire working capital. In the past, Thai financial institutions based their decision to loan on the applicant's collateral. Since the crisis, however, financial institutions are placing greater emphasis on documentation and transparency when considering lending. Additionally, with the establishment of the Market for Alternative Investment, which is designed for small companies to raise venture capital, transparency and high accounting standards will be demanded by potential shareholders.

Since the crisis, listed companies are required to establish audit committees comprising independent directors. However, a major constraint to the effectiveness of this requirement is the lack of experienced people to serve in this capacity. Another issue related to corporate governance is the disclosure of information to boards of directors, namely in terms of general availability, timeliness, and reliability of the company data. Many Thai firms are still not dealing effectively with this process, partly because a large proportion of board members lack the sophistication in knowing what kind of information to request from the management.[22] Once again the importance of human resource development and improved managerial expertise is shown for the future development of Thailand's new economy.

The burden of self-regulation will only get heavier as the Thai government gradually scales back its active role in the economy through privatisation and decentralisation. The Thai government endeavours to become a facilitator for the development of the private sector by providing a competitive and fair business environment, but this means many current regulatory and monitoring activities will have to be played by the private sector. However, in order to make the system sustainable and ensure that competition and fairness prevail, the private sector will have to adopt much higher standards of corporate governance than are currently found in Thailand. Fortunately this move towards a facilitating role as opposed to a direct participating role opens up greater opportunities for public and private sector partnerships, whereby joint planning, decision making, and implementing can more accurately reflect the needs of SMEs.

8.6.5   New Roles for Industry Associations

SMEs in Thailand, like elsewhere, face several challenges that, when handled individually, are quite daunting, if not impossible, to overcome. Many of these challenges, however, can be effectively managed through collective action within and across business associations. Well-developed business associations can play critical roles in the development of the industry and provide members, particularly SMEs, numerous benefits that otherwise would not be attainable for individual small firms.

Address industry-wide challenges: Business associations can help strengthen the domestic business sector by addressing challenges which most firms in that industry face. The issues and challenges can be identified more readily by the industry, while a wider variety of solutions and policy recommendations can be compiled.

Articulating obstacles and recommendations to policy makers: Through a business association, firms in a particular sector are more effective at articulating and channelling their problems and recommended policies to the government decision makers. SMEs are unlikely to make contributions to policy making as compared to the collective actions of the industry. Business associations at local, regional, and national levels can therefore serve as a mechanism for dialogue with policy makers.

Reduce transaction costs: Business associations can effectively reduce a variety of transaction costs for firms. Among the transaction costs that associations can reduce are searching for new markets, suppliers, services, technology and expertise. Often the costs involved in these vital activities are exorbitantly high for individual small firms, whereas the business association can help pool the resources and disseminate the information to its members (Doner et al. 4/2000).

Coordinate the value chain: Similarly, business associations can foster linkages within an industry between the various producers and suppliers in the value chain.

Communication channel within the industry and with others: Related to coordinating the value chain, business associations can serve as effective and efficient channels of communication within the industry and among other sectors. Business associations can be repositories of information, dispense relevant information to members, and coordinate with related industry associations.

Training: Human resource development can be a core function of business associations. SMEs often cannot afford to train workers, and if they do support formal training then they risk losing that employee to higher paying, typically larger, firms (Doner et al. 4/2000). Business associations could help provide such training, with the advantage that more people could receive training and without the risk of employers losing their financial 'investment' in human resource development.

Setting and maintaining industry standards: Business associations can play an instrumental role in setting standards in an industry and ensuring that members maintain them. The setting and maintaining of standards are increasingly important in international markets, because low-quality products from just a few firms reflect poorly on the industry as a whole (Doner et al. 2000). Raising standards will be critical for Thai SMEs as the requirements of the ASEAN Free Trade Area (AFTA) and the World Trade Organisation (WTO) are gradually implemented.

Strengthening interface between foreign and local firms: When foreign firms seek to enter a new market or explore partnerships, often one of the first stopping points would be a business association. Hence, business associations can facilitate the interface between foreign and local firms, which expands the opportunity for joint ventures, new distribution channels, technology and expertise transfers, and other benefits.

Organise special promotional events: Another important role often played by business associations is organising special promotional events for an industry. These can be seminars, exhibitions and trade fairs, both at home and abroad. Conducting such events for an industry helps reduce the costs that individual firms would incur in advertising or promotional campaigns.

Business associations in Thailand will likely play a much more prominent role with the advent of the SME Promotion Law coupled with the decentralisation and streamlining of government offices and activities. Private sector associations will be expected to carry more of the load in meeting the needs of SMEs in areas such as training, research, information dissemination, marketing, and consultancy. While many SMEs might fear losing direct government assistance and support the private sector is much better placed to serve most of its own needs, particularly through business associations. Of course, such a trend would require the development of existing business associations and likely the formation of new ones to cover important SME sectors. One notable problem is that large conglomerates dominate the major business associations, leaving SMEs with little influence in the direction of the influential associations.

8.6.6 The Challenge of Restructuring – The Third Wave

With the onset of the economic crisis in 1997 the need for many firms to restructure became evident for both SMEs and large conglomerates. However, the poor fundamentals of many firms led to a great deal of consolidation in several sectors through mergers and acquisitions (M&As). Essentially three phases, or 'waves', of M&As have occurred since 1997 in Thailand, with each one having distinct characteristics in terms of the predominant pattern of M&As.

The first wave, the 'recapitalisation wave', began in 1997 and peaked the following year, and was characterised by horizontal M&As particularly in the banking and finance sector and tailed off by mid-1999. The second wave, the 'restructuring wave', emerged in 1998 and peaked in early 1999. The restructuring wave consisted mainly of large and listed firms that were targeted for take-overs or partnerships from foreign companies, and it has gradually wound down since early 2000. The last wave is the 'consolidation wave', and this one involves small and non-listed firms to a great extent. New or existing strategic investors who are seeking to expand their production capacity target small firms that are typically inefficient and have relatively low accounting standards for takeover. With M&As seemingly reaching the saturation point for the larger listed firms, SMEs, with their vulnerability to take over because of cash-flow problems and the credit crunch, have become rather easy prey. Many Thai SMEs that have not undergone restructuring, whether because they are unable or simply because they resist the process, are being consolidated or are at least at risk.

The near future does not bode well for these weak, inefficient SMEs. As liberalisation measures under regional and global economic schemes are gradually implemented, such as AFTA and the WTO, Thai SMEs will be increasingly vulnerable to competition, mandating that they restructure and upgrade. For instance in January 2000, under AFTA, local content regulations for the automotive industry were lifted, and thus auto manufacturers in Thailand and elsewhere are able to procure parts more easily throughout the region. SMEs that supply to the auto manufacturers must ensure that they can offer high-quality parts at a competitive price or else risk losing their major clients. Unfortunately many of the Thai suppliers remain inefficient and offer substandard quality, as many of them concentrate on finding short-term financial solutions to stay afloat instead of fundamental upgrading and restructuring.[23] One automotive parts supplier summed up the situation by saying, 'The only real option is to find foreign partners with the capital and the technology if the industry is to survive. Otherwise within two years we will lose all our market share to regional competitors'.[24]

The challenge, then, for many Thai SMEs that want to avoid being consolidated is to find ways to solve their immediate credit and cash-flow problems, while at the same time commencing with restructuring and upgrading in order to become competitive regionally, let alone solvent, in the very near future. The former seems more viable with the plethora of new financing programs being made available to SMEs and if banks resume normal lending to smaller firms. However, the greater challenge may well be adjusting their business strategies and acquiring the necessary technology, and the corresponding labour skill to utilise it, to become more efficient and offer higher-quality products. Achieving these requirements will not be easy without caving in to larger firms and foreign firms in particular.

8.6.7   Competitiveness

Thai SMEs, like others in many areas around the world, are facing intense pressures to meet the challenges confronting them from globalisation. As markets continue to liberalise through the mandates of global and regional economic arrangements such as the WTO and AFTA, Thai SMEs will come under increasing pressure from foreign competitors. Thai SMEs languish in labour-intensive, low-technology activities, while neighbours such as Singapore and Malaysia have demonstrated greater innovation and sophistication by moving into higher-value-added and higher-technology industries. Moreover, Thai SMEs have been reliant on imported factors of production, even for export-oriented manufacturing.

Thailand's labour costs have risen sharply since the 1980s and its labour supply is no longer competitive in the region with the likes of Indonesia, Pakistan, Vietnam, Bangladesh and many others. Thai firms in general fail to employ greater use of technology, and when combined with rising wages the country quickly became less competitive in the region. One of the key challenges, then, is for SMEs to shift towards competitive advantage as opposed to comparative advantage through applying higher technology, reducing imported inputs to production, and moving into higher-value-added products.

An added pressure to Thai SMEs is the need to meet higher international standards, not only in product quality and safety but also with regard to the production process. Environmental issues have become worldwide concerns, and firms will be expected to comply with universal environmental standards that are perceived by many firms as increasing production costs. While it has been shown that improved environmental protection measures can actually lead to less waste and more efficient production processes, the initial costs of restructuring a firm's production process can appear overwhelming. Thailand's environmental standards are comparable to many international standards, but the problem has been enforcement. In due course environmental protection laws will be enforced more consistently and thus require many firms to adjust their production processes.

However, the gradually converging international standards and markets open as many opportunities for Thai SMEs as they present challenges. For instance, under AFTA Thai goods will be able to circulate more readily throughout the other nine ASEAN countries as tariffs and other barriers are gradually reduced – for some goods down to a 0 per cent tariff. Thai SMEs will need to develop a more regional strategy like their counterparts in Singapore and Malaysia if they are to take advantage of what AFTA and other ASEAN economic cooperation schemes can offer. Thai goods easily found their way into neighbouring markets such as Laos and Cambodia, but that was more or less by default from a lack of competition in border areas. Thai goods are produced in greater quantities, have higher quality, and in many cases are of lower prices than domestically made goods in Cambodia and Laos, but they will not be the only viable choice when AFTA is fully implemented.

SMEs will need to develop more appropriate regional and global strategies, particularly by filling market niches and moving into international subcontracting, but at the same time they will need to defend their domestic market share through more efficient operations.[25]

8.6.8   Linkages with Larger Firms, Clusters and Networking

Since the economic crisis the Thai government has been obligated to liberalise certain aspects of its economy as a requirement for the multilateral loan packages, not to mention the country's additional obligations under the WTO and AFTA. These liberalisation measures are having an impact on Thai SMEs in that they must become more competitive as foreign firms enter economic sectors that were previously insulated from foreign competition. Despite the seemingly disadvantaged situation that SMEs find themselves in, in relation to the powerful multinational corporations, small firms are discovering ways to compete in the global marketplace. One such strategy is the concept of 'clusters'. Porter (1998) defines clusters as:

> geographic concentrations of interconnected companies and institutions in a particular field. Clusters encompass an array of linked industries and other entities important to competition. They include, for example, suppliers of specialised inputs such as components, machinery, and services, and providers of specialised infrastructure. Clusters also often extend downstream to channels and customers and laterally to manufacturers of complementary products and to companies in industries related by skills, technologies, or common inputs. Finally, many clusters include governmental and other institutions – such as universities, standard-setting agencies, think tanks, vocational training providers, and trade associations – that provide specialised training, education, information, research, and technical support.

Clusters provide numerous advantages to private enterprises, especially for small firms. A brief listing of some of the foremost benefits includes the following. First, clusters often bring *cost reductions*. Second, *technological spillovers and other means of upgrading* can spread among the firms in a cluster when one or a few firms have a higher level of technology. Likewise, *information spillovers* can occur. Third, clusters often promote the *sharing of scarce resources*. Fourth, *achieving and enforcing international standards* often arise from greater local cooperation among firms in a cluster. A related benefit is also an *increase in the quality of products* as a result of cooperation within a cluster. Access to the major export markets such as the US, the European Union, and Japan depends on meeting quality standards. Improvements in quality can be the outcome of raised standards in an industry but also from the technological or other spillovers that occur within a cluster. Fifth, firms in a cluster appear to *respond more quickly to challenges* from other competitors, particularly international competitors, and *to change in an industry*. Once again, collective action promotes greater efficiency and sharing of information, which in turn leads to an enhanced ability to respond to changing circumstances. Thus, firms in a cluster become more flexible. Sixth, *learning* can be an important benefit of clusters, especially for first-time exporters. Rather than learning individually what works and does not work, clusters promote shared learning. Seventh, research suggests that clusters help small firms *overcome growth constraints* in the early stages of development and enables them to compete in distant markets. In summary, clusters can promote collective efficiency by means of cooperation among firms in close proximity, and thereby improve the performance of firms individually and as a whole.

Clusters and their accompanying linkages and networks are emerging in several sectors in Thailand, most notably in the automotive industry. An opportunity presents itself for Thai SMEs to improve and expand their role in the production subcontracting system through clusters and networks, but this is an area that Thai SMEs have traditionally not fulfilled very well. During the Seventh Five-Year Plan the government attempted to promote the greater application of production subcontracting. Achievements during that five-year span fell far short of expectations, and thus the promotion of subcontracting has continued during the current Eighth Five-Year Plan.[26]

Having recognised the failings among Thai SMEs in developing industrial networks, the DIP is promoting linkages at several layers: rural and urban firms; between large firms and SMEs; and between Thai SMEs and foreign enterprises. To this end a draft law on subcontracting promotion intends to provide explicit measures for subcontracting arrangements between SMEs and large firms, including international firms.[27]

Thai SMEs are at risk of being displaced or obstructed from entering the supplier–assembler networks that are quickly taking shape in Thailand, because of the quick response of several foreign firms in establishing local subsidiaries and affiliates to supply components to their larger parent companies or fellow national firms. The Japanese promptly responded to the opening of certain sectors to greater foreign participation by setting up smaller affiliates to serve as suppliers to the MNCs. Naturally these smaller foreign firms retain significant advantages over their Thai competitors because of greater access to state-of-the-art technology and strong connections with their national firms. The MNCs are more than willing to utilise these smaller foreign firms in their respective clusters and networks because of the aforementioned reasons, but also because Thai SMEs often cannot produce the quality of goods demanded by the large assemblers. This problem derives from the use of inadequate technology, outmoded production processes, and low management capabilities.

8.6.9   Legislative Issues

Thailand's legislative process appears to be responding to the needs of SMEs, as discussed in an earlier section. In the past, laws related to SME activities centred on controlling and regulating the conduct of SMEs rather than promoting their development. The SME Development Master Plan has proposed altering the focus of legislation to promote and encourage SMEs, and the new SME Promotion Law appears to be an important step in the right direction. The SME Promotion Law is also significant in that it is the first piece of comprehensive legislation directly related to SMEs.

The effectiveness of this new law will rely on its successful implementation, which is often not the case in Thailand as seen in the environmental field and others. Enforcement and implementation are far from assured in a country plagued by frequently changing policies, regulations and governments. A recurring pattern in Thai politics is that whenever a new government comes into office, its predecessor's policies and contracts are scrapped in favour of new ones to suit the interests of the new leaders. In their favour, however, SMEs have become a prominent political issue in the wake of the crisis, and one that seemingly can no longer be ignored. Hence, the Parliament, cabinet, and relevant ministries will likely be under pressure to produce some tangible benefits for SMEs and ensure their long-term viability with supportive policies and programs.

8.6.10   Policy Effectiveness and Reach

It might be too early and too difficult to assess the policy effectiveness and predict policy outcomes of the above-mentioned SME policies created and altered during the crisis. However, the impediments raised to the policy implementation can to some extent give us a clue to the possible policy effectiveness. First, respecting the funding for the financial programs obtained from Japanese government assistance, the World Bank and the Asian Development Bank, it seems that the government was unable to spend the loan package effectively to stimulate the economy in general, and to rescue and support the existing SMEs in particular as targeted. In 2000 the targeted loans for SMEs of the state financial institutions amounted to 46 billion baht. However, loans already approved to the SMEs during the first six months of 2000 amounted to only 13 billion baht, accounting for only 28 per cent of total targeted loans (see Table 8.4). It is a critical question for Finance and Industry Ministries to find the way as to how to manage excessive credits remaining in both public and private financial institutions to help SMEs address their cash-flow problem.

In addition, it can be noted that the policies designed to assist SMEs partly derived from party policies. As stated above political parties in the previous coalition government attempted to promote themselves through policies assisting the harshly hit private sector, and particularly the SME sector. One critical question arises here: whether SMEs are the agents of economic development or the instruments of politicians to gain political popularity within the SME sector. It seems that SMEs were exploited by political parties to gain their votes during the past general election. As noted earlier, a number of policies on SMEs were initiated by major political parties such as the Democrats, Chart Pattana and Thai Rak Thai. It will be interesting to follow up whether these SMEs policies will be seriously implemented under the new Thai Rak Thai-led government, and whether such key government agencies as MOI, ISMED and BUILD will be earnestly supported by the key economics ministers of the new government.

Table 8.4
Summary of Assistance Loans for SMEs, January to June 2000

		Targeted amount of loans (million baht)	Loans approved (million baht)	%
1.	State financial institutions			
	• IFCT	15 000	4 423	29
	• Bank of Thailand	13 000	4 082	31
	• EXIM	7 000	1 496	21
	• SIFCT	6 000	632	10
	• Bank for Agriculture and Agricultural Cooperative	4 000	2 258	56
	• GSB	1 300	459	35
	Total	46 300	13 350	28
2.	Commercial banks			
	• Bangkok Bank	10 000	11	0.12
	• Thai Farmers Bank	20 000	na	na
	• Thai Commercial Bank	10 000	na	na
	• Thai Military Bank	10 000	na	na
	• Krung Thai Bank	5 500	593	10

Source: Than Settakit, 27–29 July 2000.

8.7   SUMMARY AND CONCLUSIONS

The growth and development of the Thai SME sector will be a critical element of Thailand's future growth process. In recent years policy makers appear to have realised this and have considerably improved the business environment for SMEs, both in terms of the legislative environment and support programs and institutions. However, significant scope still remains for improved policy coordination and better integration of the various support initiatives for SMEs in Thailand.

One major constraining factor is the lack of accurate and up-to-date information on SMEs. Considerable efforts need to be made to improve the SME databases and develop better understanding of the characteristics, constraints, needs and potential of the SME sector. It is worth noting that a number of studies under way for the Department of Industrial Promotion are expected to rectify the dearth of information to some extent. These studies are expected to be completed by mid-2001.

In conclusion, in order for SMEs to play a greater role in maintaining Thailand's competitiveness, several key factors need to be stressed or addressed in the Thai context:

- SMEs critically require long-term access to finance and to financial institutions, and the provision of this access must be an integral part of the reforms in the finance and banking sector since the financial crisis;

- SMEs need to break through the low-technology threshold and begin to undertake much greater efforts to improve their capacities for technological development. Government support programs and institutions can play a major role in supporting the human resource development, technological upgrading, and behavioural changes that are necessary, especially through providing better access to technical and managerial know-how;

- SMEs need to know where they stand. Most government programs to date have not succeeded in providing SME clients with a clear 'benchmark' of where they are strong and where they are weak. The effective provision of such benchmarks (in technology, marketing, management, governance and so on) will be a critical success factor in the future implementation of programs to support SMEs as they work to enhance productivity and competitiveness;

- SMEs do not exist in a vacuum. They must be integrated more effectively into the various industry value chains or clusters, with special emphasis placed on developing innovative mechanisms to strengthen linkages with large domestic and foreign firms. This really calls for a new paradigm of industrial development that focuses more on clusters and value chains and the measures that strengthen these;

- SMEs need more supportive networks. Institutional developments that create stronger networks among SMEs, academic institutions, government agencies, and other firms must be nurtured. In particular, the role of business associations in creating flows of information and knowledge to SMEs need to be encouraged and enhanced.

NOTES

1   See, for example, the following website <www.dip. go.th/policy/epolicy4/htm>.
2   *The Nation*, 6 November 1998.
3   *The Nation*, 16 October 1998.
4   See the Department of Industrial Promotion website <www.dip. go.th>.
5   See the Department of Industrial Promotion website <www.dip. go.th>.
6   *Bangkok Post,* 26 January 1999.
7   *Bangkok Post*, 6 May 1999.

8   See for example Chapter 4 for a discussion of the Miyazawa Fund in the context of Vietnam.
9   *The Nation*, 22 March 1999.
10 *Bangkok Post*, 3 April 2000.
11 *Bangkok Post*, 26 May 2000.
12 *Bangkok Post*, 1 March 2000.
13 *Bangkok Post*, 26 May 2000.
14 *The Nation*, 27 April 2000 and *Bangkok Post*, 26 May 1999.
15 *The Nation*, 20 April 1999.
16 *The Nation*, 27 April 2000.
17 *The Nation*, 17 May 2000.
18 *The Nation*, 25 August 1999.
19 *The Nation*, 20 November 1998.
20 *The Nation*, 15 March 1999.
21 *The Nation*, 25 August 1999.
22 Richard Moore, *Bangkok Post*, 10 May 2000.
23 *Bangkok Post*, 2 May 2000.
24 Quoted from *Bangkok Post*, 2 May 2000.
25 See the Department of Industrial Promotion website <www.dip. go.th>.
26 See the Department of Industrial Promotion website <www.dip. go.th>.
27 See the Department of Industrial Promotion website <www.dip. go.th>.

BIBLIOGRAPHY

Allal, M. (1999a), *Business Development Services for Micro and Small Enterprises in Thailand*, Working Paper 1, Micro and Small Enterprise Development and Poverty Alleviation in Thailand Project ILO/UNDP:THA/99/003, July.

Allal, M. (1999b), *Micro and Small Enterprises (MSEs) in Thailand: Definitions and Contributions*, Working Paper 6, Micro and Small Enterprise Development and Poverty Alleviation in Thailand Project, ILO/UNDP:THA/99/003, July.

Department of Industrial Promotion, Ministry of Industry, <www.dip. go.th>.

Deyo, F.C. (1999), 'The Politics of Crisis Management: Thailand's SME Sector', paper prepared for the conference 'Toward APEC's Second Decade: Challenges, Opportunities, and Priorities', organised by the APEC Study Centre Consortium in Auckland, New Zealand, 31 May – 2 June.

Doner, R.F. and A. Ramsay (1997), 'Competitive Clientlism and Economic Governance: The Case of Thailand', in S. Maxfield and B.R.Schneider (eds), *Business and the State in Developing Countries*, Ithaca, NY: Cornell University Press, pp. 237–76.

Doner, R.F., F. Recanatini and B.R. Schneider (2000), 'Business Associations and Development', unpublished monograph, Industrial Finance Corporation of Thailand, April, <www.ifct.co.th/backgr_sme.htm>.

Japan International Cooperation Agency (JICA) (1995), *The Study on Industrial Sector Development Supporting Industries in the Kingdom of Thailand*, Tokyo: Japan International Cooperation Agency.

Levinson, M. (1999), 'Competitiveness and Globality', *The Global Competitiveness Report 1999*, Geneva: World Economic Forum.

Maitree, W. (1999), *The Needs and Characteristics of a Sample of Micro and Small Enterprises (MSEs) in Thailand*, Working Paper 5, Micro and Small Enterprise Development and Poverty Alleviation in Thailand Project, ILO/UNDP:THA/99/003, July.

Ministry of Industry (1999), *Ministry of Industry: Looking beyond 2000*, Bangkok: Ministry of Industry.

Office of the Board of Investment (1999), *Annual Report*, [in Thai], Bangkok: Office of the Board of Investment.

Paetkau, M. (1999), *Financial Support for Micro and Small Enterprises in Thailand*, Working Paper 4, Micro and Small Enterprise Development and Poverty Alleviation in Thailand Project, ILO/UNDP:THA/99/003, July.

Pasuk, P. and C. Baker (1998), *Thailand's Boom and Bust*, Chiang Mai: Silkworm Books.

Porter, M. (1998), 'Clusters and the Economics of Competition', *Harvard Business Review*, **76** (6): 77–90.

Sevilla, R.C. (2000), 'SMEs in Thailand: Vision and Reality', unpublished monograph, January.

White, S. (1999), *Creating an Enabling Environment for Micro and Small Enterprises in Thailand*, Working Paper 3, Micro and Small Enterprise Development and Poverty Alleviation in Thailand Project, ILO/UNDP:THA/99/003, July.

World Bank (1999), *Thailand Economic Monitor*, October.

References from Newspapers

'All Systems Go for SME Master Plan', *The Nation*, 25 August 1999.

'Ex-MITI Expert Helps Boost Status of SMEs', *The Nation*, 15 March 1999.

'SME Clients Account for up to 90% of Bad Loans', *Bangkok Post*, 26 January 1999.

'Tighter Reins on Executives', *Bangkok Post*, 6 May 1999.

'Wider Participation Key to Successful Industrial Reform', *Bangkok Post*, 29 April 1998.

Busaba Sivasomboon, 'Long-ignored SMEs Suddenly Find They Are in the Political Spotlight', *Bangkok Post*, 11 December 1998.

Busrin Treerapongpichit, 'Parts Makers Under Pressure', *Bangkok Post*, 2 May 2000.

Chiratas Nivatpumin, 'Export–Import Bank Links Loans to Restructuring', *Bangkok Post*, 1 March 1999.

Cholada Ingsrisawang, 'IFCT May Turn into SME Bank', *Bangkok Post*, 3 April 2000.

Moore, Richard, 'Good Governance Needs New Approach', *Bangkok Post*, 10 May 2000.

Nophakhun Limsamarnphun, 'Government to Set Up Mechanism for Funding SMEs', *The Nation*, 6 November 1998.

Pichaya Changsorn, 'Survey Finds Little Changes Among SMEs', *The Nation*, 18 August 1997.

Watcharapong Thongrung, '400 SMEs Complete Debt Revamp', *The Nation*, 20 November 1998.

Watcharapong Thongrung, 'Bill Proposed to Protect SMEs', *The Nation*, 16 October 1998.

Watcharapong Thongrung, 'Industry Ministry Rushes Business Plans', *The Nation*, 22 March 1999.

Yuthana Priwan, 'B95bn Funds Boost SMEs and Recovery', *Bangkok Post*, 26 May 2000.

The Nation, 20 April 1999, 'What Do SMEs Want from the Government?'.

The Nation, 27 April 2000, 'Joint Loans for SMEs Leap to Bt100bn'.

The Nation, 27 April 2000, 'New Network Service Targeting SMEs'.

The Nation, 17 May 2000, 'SMEs Get Entry to E-commerce World'.

9 Promoting SMEs in Korea: Government Response to the Asian Financial Crisis

Gary D. Gregory

9.1 INTRODUCTION

The global market is currently undergoing a process of rapid integration, spurred by the removal of trade and investment barriers. In order to sustain healthy growth and a balanced economic structure the promotion of small and medium sized enterprises (SMEs) is becoming increasingly important to many industrialising nations. Constituting the majority of the corporate sector in Korea (99.7 per cent of all manufacturing companies and 72.1 per cent of all manufacturing employees) SMEs are obviously the mainstay of the national economy and the driving force behind sustained economic growth and balanced economic structure in the 21st century.

However, there are a number of critical issues facing SMEs in Korea. First, many SMEs are facing financial and manpower shortages and decreasing sales. The 1997 financial crisis, accompanied by a serious credit crunch, failed payments and a rapid drop in factory operation ratio due to the contraction of demand and increased prices, precipitated a chain of bankruptcies among SMEs (Choi 1999). One of the major government initiatives to spark economic recovery in Korea is the policy program to revitalise SMEs and venture business. The government is attempting to create a business environment that will help SMEs exploit competitive advantages such as flexibility and rapid adaptability. Second, one of the principal constraints faced by a majority of the country's SMEs has long been the lack of access to financial resources. The chronic shortfall of financial resources for SMEs is largely attributable to a financial strategy focused on larger firms with lower risk based on the belief that such firms were 'too big to fail'. The credit allocation system set a fixed interest rate that led to an insufficient supply of financing for SMEs (Kwack 1999). Recently, however, the government's SME policy has shifted focus to guaranteeing SMEs greater access to loans from financial institutions with sufficiently liberalised interest rates. Additional plans are geared towards reducing the number of bankruptcies among SMEs.

Besides limited financial availability, manpower shortages have also plagued SMEs, largely due to a high turnover rate (Park 2000). The key role of government must be to develop an educational system that corresponds to the long-term manpower needs of both industries and businesses. Along with financing and labour shortages, there are difficulties in the sales of SMEs. The government plans to rework the procurement system to provide SMEs with more opportunities to provide their goods and services to a global marketplace by assisting SMEs in finding overseas markets, promoting exports and supporting their international marketing and advertising capabilities. To remain competitive in the technology age the use of electronic commerce must be a part of every sales strategy. The government has plans to enlarge the number of export companies listed on the Internet and increase World Wide Web sites to advertise the products of prominent SMEs. Cooperation between large and small companies in Korea is another influential means of promoting competitiveness. Particularly in today's global economy, cooperation between large firms and SMEs is necessary to ensure the competitiveness of Korean industries. To encourage such partnerships the government has improved the subcontracting practice between large firms and SMEs, and encouraged and fostered collaborative partnerships in trade, investment, production and training.

This chapter covers the role of small and medium sized enterprises in (South) Korea and the impact of the financial crisis of 1997 on the SME sector in Sections 9.2 and 9.3. Section 9.4 discusses the restructuring of the Korean economy and the role of government in developing SME policy since the financial crisis. Particular attention focuses on the Korean government's role in developing SME policy with respect to access to finance, development of human resources, use of technological/scientific achievements, globalisation through the use of electronic commerce, and building relationships by networking with other businesses. Section 9.5 evaluates the government's promotion of *venture enterprises*, or technology-intensive SMEs, and the significance placed upon them to increase exporting, foster cooperation with foreign companies, and ensure the long-term success of Korean SMEs into the 21st century. Finally, Section 9.6 presents a summary of the major conclusions from this chapter.

9.2   THE ROLE OF SMES IN THE KOREAN ECONOMY

Korean SMEs are defined as firms that employ fewer than 300 persons and whose capital amounts to less than US$66 million. Small-scale business is classified based on industry type, with 50 employees or less for manufacturing, 30 employees or less for construction, and 10 or fewer employees for commerce and services. Medium-scale business is also classified on industry type, with 50–300 employees in manufacturing, 30–200 employees for construction, and 11–20 employees for commerce/services (see Table 9.1 for the classification of SMEs in Korea). While medium-scale business is common, small-scale businesses still represent over 99 per cent of all SMEs in Korea. The number of SMEs in Korea totals 2.67 million, representing over 99.5 per cent of all Korean businesses. These businesses account for 99.1 per cent of all manufacturing companies, and 69.2 per cent of all manufacturing sector employees (Government of the Republic of Korea 1998e). The importance of SMEs cannot be disputed – they play a vital role in economic growth in the Asia–Pacific economies. This is especially true in the Korean economy, where SMEs contribute towards employment creation, innovation, export value, and flexibility to adapt to changes in the local and regional economy.

Currently, SMEs employ 9.1 million persons, representing nearly 80 per cent of the total national workforce. The value of production by these businesses amounts to 187.92 trillion won, or 46.8 per cent of the nation's total (Government of the Republic of Korea 1998e). The value of their value-added activities is 82.28 trillion won, or 47.2 per cent of the nation's total. Although the labour–capital ratio varies from industry to industry, SMEs still tend to be more labour intensive than large firms. The lack of workers with technical skills is one of the most significant barriers to the growth of SMEs in industry and services. The Korean government realises the importance of human resource development, and since the financial crisis has invested in training and development of basic skills of workers by providing sector-specific technical, management, entrepreneurship and financial training for SMEs. With the rising unemployment rate across all sectors of the economy the government will need to initiate projects aimed at creating jobs and encouraging foreign investment across a broader range of industrial sectors. Since a majority of the workforce relies on SMEs for employment, human resource development will need to be aimed at training a technical workforce and expanding employment in the small and medium business sector.

Table 9.1
Classification of SMEs in Korea

Industry	Small-scale business	Medium-scale business
Mining, manufacturing, transportation	50 or fewer employees	51 to 300 employees
Construction	30 or fewer employees	31 to 200 employees
Commerce, other service	10 or fewer employees	11 to 20 employees

Source: Small and Medium-sized Business Administration, Government of the Republic of Korea, 1998, <www.smba.go.kr>.

SMEs not only contribute to the country's wealth and employment, but also serve as the primary vehicles by which new entrepreneurs provide the economy with a continuous supply of ideas, skills and innovation (Government of the Republic of Korea 1998b). With research and development (R&D) and innovation becoming a critical source of comparative advantage, many SMEs are looking at new strategies to optimise their existing technological strengths through which to create new opportunities for wealth generation. Alliances and partnerships are becoming an essential way of accessing key resources, personnel, know-how and markets. In order for Korea to have a comparative advantage over others in certain areas of technology it needs to reinforce the implementation of the national R&D programs for the development of the emerging technologies for SMEs. To achieve this goal the Korean government is making every effort to foster venture enterprises and start-up SMEs with advanced technology. Since the beginning of 1997, over 4 500 SMEs have been designated as venture firms. Furthermore, 200–300 companies are newly designated as venture firms each month (Government of the Republic of Korea 1998c). Compared with traditional small and medium firms, venture enterprises demonstrate higher technological capabilities and managerial performance, while showing much higher growth potential. Table 9.2 compares growth rates in sales, profits and R&D for venture enterprises, traditional SMEs and large conglomerates over the 1997–98 period. Venture enterprises not only realise greater growth rates in sales and profits, but also create more jobs in total when compared to big companies or traditional small firms (Government of the Republic of Korea 1998c). In this context the Korean government clearly recognises the importance of venture enterprises to the development of the regional and national economy, and will need to continue to formulate policy measures that promote technology-driven venture enterprises.

In terms of exporting, SMEs contribute anywhere from 15 per cent to 50 per cent of exports within the Asia–Pacific region, with between 20 per cent and 80 per cent of SMEs actively engaged in exporting activities (Government of Australia 1996). In

Table 9.2
Venture Enterprises Compared with Traditional Small and Medium Firms

Classification	Venture enterprises (1998)	Traditional firms (1997)	Conglom- erates (1997)
Sales increase rate (%)	21.9	7.02	12.92
Rate of profit from sales (%)	19.4	4.98	9.72
R&D ratio (%)	24.1	0.74	1.50

Source: Small and Medium-sized Business Administration, Government of the Republic of Korea, 1998, <www.smba.go.kr>.

Korea SMEs play a large role as exporters and were responsible for nearly 50 per cent of total exports in 1998, up from 27 per cent of total exports in 1994 (Government of the Republic of Korea 1998e). In 1998 the exports of SMEs decreased due to the slowdown of the world economy and the financial crisis in the Asian region. Their proportion in the nation's total exports, however, has been maintained at a higher level than the period prior to the crisis in 1997. Naturally, the exporting performance of SMEs varies across sectors. Figure 9.1 shows SME exports by sector in 1998.

While larger firms provide relatively standardised products in larger volumes to national markets, SMEs tend to supply niche or specialised products in small volumes to specific markets. One of the main obstacles to SMEs going abroad lies in the high costs associated with collecting and analysing information on foreign markets. Export and import financing has also been identified as major barriers to exporting for SMEs. Given the importance of SMEs in becoming active in the international marketplace, it seems desirable for the Korean government to reduce transaction and financial costs for SMEs when operating in export markets. Currently there are 11 regional

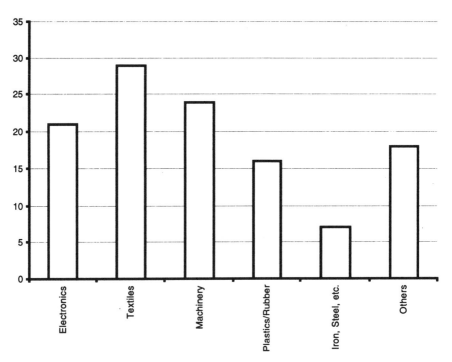

Source: Small and Medium-sized Business Administration, Government of the Republic of Korea, 1998, <www.smba.go.kr>.

Figure 9.1   SME Exports by Sector (%) in 1998

SME export support centres across the country to support exporting activities for 4 000 firms. Additionally, 25 trade missions are dispatched overseas to help Korean SMEs develop export markets (Government of the Republic of Korea 1998c). However, to truly assist SMEs in the globalisation process it may be necessary for government to further strengthen international cooperative relations, foster international cooperative projects, facilitate managerial and technological exchanges both at home and abroad, and provide additional local and regional centres for SMEs to gain access to information on foreign markets (Buckley and Mirza (eds) 1997; Choi and Chung 1997).

Because SMEs are often more flexible than large firms, they are better able to adapt to new customer requirements, make workforce changes, adopt new technologies, and expand operations to overseas markets. While not all SMEs are growth oriented, approximately 25 per cent rapidly adapt new technologies and strategies in order to remain internationally competitive (Fujita 1997). This is especially true in industries where SMEs play a major role, such as new industries or niche markets. However, not all SMEs are able to adapt quickly to changes in the regional economies. A large number of SMEs are either not oriented to growth or do not engage in international activity (Choi and Chung 1997; Fujita 1997). Although they employ a significant proportion of the labour force, they have a relatively short life expectancy. These firms depend on the local economy and are insulated by protectionist policies. Most of these SMEs are in the highest risk category for bankruptcy. Governmental policy needs to focus on assisting these firms so that they can become more competitive and have greater access to information and markets. On the other hand, approximately 25 per cent of SMEs are considered growth oriented and entrepreneurial (Government of the Republic of Korea 1998c). These SMEs play an important role in restructuring existing industries and generating new ideas. Table 9.3 summarises the role of SMEs in the Korean economy. Many of these 'fast-growth' SMEs are internationalised, leading to greater flexibility during turbulent times (Government of the Republic of Korea 1998c). Policies for these firms need to continue

Table 9.3
Role of SMEs in Korean Economy

- Driving force for sustaining economic growth
- Promotion of social stability by the creation of employment
- Enhancement of industrial restructuring
- Promotion of ability to meet changing market situations
- Promotion of international trade and cooperation
- Satisfaction of diversified tastes on the part of consumers
- Stimulation of local economies on a balanced basis

Source: Small and Medium-sized Business Administration, Government of the Republic of Korea, 1998, <www.smba.go.kr>.

to foster growth by providing greater access to markets, acquiring suitable managerial skills, and allowing greater access to finance for overseas expansion.

9.3   THE IMPACT OF THE FINANCIAL CRISIS ON THE SME SECTOR

Nearly three decades ago Korea's GDP per capita was comparable with levels in the poorer countries of Africa and Asia. Today its GDP is seven times India's, 13 times North Korea's, and approaching that of the lesser economies of the European Union. During the 1980s, Korea's economy prospered due to a system of close government business ties, including directed credit, import restrictions, sponsorship of specific industries, and a strong labour effort. The government promoted the importation of raw materials and high technology, while at the same time encouraging savings and investment rather than consumption. However, when the Asian financial crisis of 1997–98 occurred it exposed certain longstanding weaknesses in Korea's economic policy, evidenced by high debt-to-equity ratios, massive foreign borrowing, and an undisciplined financial sector (Park 1999).

The Korean economy has suffered immensely from the Asian financial crisis. Table 9.4 highlights the dynamics of Korea's industrial production during the financial crisis of 1996–99. First, Korea's total industrial production went from a growth rate of 8.7 per cent in 1996, dropping to a 7.3 per cent decrease in 1998, and eventual increase to 4 per cent by 1999. Second, the SME manufacturing sector appears to have been hurt most, going from an industrial production growth rate of 3.1 per cent in 1996, to a record low 29 per cent decrease in production by 1998, then ending with a 27.5 per cent decrease in 1999. Third, SME light industries, traditionally one of the

Table 9.4
Percentage (%) Change in Industrial Production
of Korean SMEs, 1996–99

Industry	1996	1997	1998	Feb. 1999
All industries	8.7	5.3	–7.3	4.0
SMEs in manufacturing	3.1	–1.4	–29.0	–27.5
• Heavy and chemical industries	3.7	–1.1	–28.7	–21.1
• Light industries	2.8	–1.7	–29.3	–34.1

Source: Small and Medium-sized Business Administration, *Monthly Bulletin of Small and Medium Business*, Government of the Republic of Korea, March 1999.

stronger and dominant SME sectors, seem to have been more adversely affected than heavy industries. In 1996 light industries experienced an increase of 2.8 per cent, yet by 1999 they had realised a 34.1 per cent decrease in production. The SME heavy industries were also significantly affected, going from a 3.7 per cent increase in production growth in 1996 to a 21.1 decrease in overall production in 1999.

In addition to a poor production performance the SME sector has also been plagued by increased bankruptcy as a direct result of the financial crisis (Park 1999). Table 9.5 illustrates the significant increase in number of bankruptcies of SMEs during the 1996–99 period. From a bankruptcy rate of 14 per cent in 1996, SME failure (bankruptcy) increased to approximately 40 per cent in 1997 and 1998. In terms of SME failures this translates into an almost 100 per cent increase in bankruptcies over a three-year period (1996–98), from 11 589 in 1996 to 22 828 SME bankruptcies in 1998. In comparison to SMEs big firms (including *chaebols*) also had a significant increase in bankruptcies during the same period. From a low of only seven bankruptcies in 1996 the number of big firm bankruptcies increased to 58 and 39, in 1997 and 1998, respectively.

Table 9.5
Production Performance and Bankruptcy of Korean SMEs, 1996–99

Indicators	1996	1997	1998	1999
Production growth rate (%)	3.1	–1.4	–29.0	–27.5
Rate of bankruptcy (%)	14	40	38	10
Number of bankrupt SMEs	11 589	17 168	22 828	6 718
• Monthly average	966	1 431	1 902	560
Number of bankrupt large firms	7	58	39	na

Source: Small and Medium-sized Business Administration, *Monthly Bulletin of Small and Medium Business*, Government of the Republic of Korea, March 1999.

At the beginning of the crisis in December 1997 the Korean government's top priority was to secure a sufficient supply of foreign liquidity to establish a solid foundation for overall restructuring. In order to secure foreign exchange liquidity and strengthen the nation's credit ratings, the government felt that it needed to replenish its foreign currency reserves by attracting foreign capital, issuing government bonds, and extending the maturity of short-term foreign loans (Park 1999). To create a more supportive and convenient system of foreign direct investment (FDI) the government began formulating a new foreign investment promotion program. The Foreign Investment Promotion Act passed on 2 September 1998 was developed to create a more transparent and liberalised system, abolish the cumbersome regulations and augment incentives, and to provide a one-stop service through the Korea Investment

Service Centre (KISC) by incorporating the following seven major objectives (Government of the Republic of Korea 1998f):

1. liberalisation and protection of FDI;

2. augmentation of tax incentives;

3. enhancement of property incentives and subsidies;

4. simplification of procedures;

5. provision of a one-stop service;

6. establishment of foreign investment zones (FIZs);

7. establishment of the Commission on Foreign Direct Investment Policy.

Additionally, Korea's monetary policy is aimed at stabilising the foreign exchange market following the devaluation of the Korean won. By maintaining high interest rates and preventing an inflationary spiral the government began its long road to institute a flexible fiscal policy for the nation's foreign exchange market. However, there were still a number of uncontrollable regional factors affecting the Korean economy. To reduce the chance of external factors affecting Korea's stability during the crisis the government found it necessary to engage in negotiations with the International Monetary Fund (IMF), the World Bank (International Bank for Reconstruction and Development: IBRD), and the Asian Development Bank (ADB) (Government of the Republic of Korea 1997).

The IMF recommended that the Korean government formulate a tight macroeconomic policy to prevent capital flight and stabilise local financial markets. This resulted in the elimination of the daily exchange rate fluctuation band and the cap on interest rates (Government of the Republic of Korea 1997). As a result exchange and interest rate volatility significantly increased. The result of this policy sparked a chain reaction of bankruptcies in thousands of financial institutions, especially those that engaged in reckless lending practices contributing to the crisis (Government of the Republic of Korea 1997). A series of bankruptcies of big conglomerates during the crisis led to the deterioration of international investors' confidence in the Korean economy as a whole. Because the Korean government did not manage these bankruptcies in an appropriate manner, and together with the fact that the major Korean banks and financial institutions were linked with financially exposed *chaebols*, a chain reaction occurred in which international investors lost confidence in the Korean economy (Government of the Republic of Korea 1997). As a result, the corporate and financial sectors underwent structural changes. For example, five commercial banks have been closed and merged by others, and the government sold two other major commercial banks to foreign investors. Merchant banks have been reduced by as much as 60 per cent through the shutdown of non-viable institutions. Additionally, securities, insurance and leasing companies had strong restructuring requirements imposed upon them. As a result by the end of 1999 Standard & Poors, Moodys, and IBCA Fitch upgraded the creditworthiness of some of the major Korean banks, leading to an overall improvement of foreign investors' confidence in the economy (Government of the Republic of Korea 2000c).

By the beginning of 1998 the Korean government realised that SME policies were needed to eliminate the threats to the stabilised management of SMEs, including major funding shortages and lack of credit opportunities necessary to operate within the Korean economy (Government of the Republic of Korea 1998d). Additionally, the financial crisis forced policy makers to focus on the creation of new jobs and the easing of unemployment (8.6 per cent of the labour force in February 1999), together considered one of the most urgent challenges for the nation's economy during the crisis. Along with the stabilisation of the economy the government prioritised the need to build up infrastructure such as technology, human resources development and operation of start-up assistance centres to help SMEs grow steadily. At the same time policies were being considered to assist SMEs locally and to enhance their international competitiveness.

While SMEs experienced significant decreases in industrial production during the crisis the declining growth was not nearly as severe in export markets. As shown in Table 9.6, exports continued to grow in 1997 by 5 per cent across all sectors, including SMEs and big firms. By 1998 the total exports for all firms declined by 2.8 per cent; big firms declined by 4.2 per cent, while SMEs realised only a 1 per cent decline in exports. This gap widened even further by February 1999, with total industry exports declining by 16 per cent. Big firms suffered the greatest decline at 25 per cent, while SMEs had only a moderate decline in exports by 3.1 per cent. Overall, the share of SMEs in Korea's total trade balance changed from 41.8 per cent of all Korean exports in 1996 to nearly 46 per cent of total exports by 1999.

In mid-1998 the Korean government began to appreciate the role of SMEs as a

Table 9.6
Export Performance of Korean SMEs and Big Firms, 1996–99

Export sectors	1996 Amount	1997 Amount	1997 Change (%)	1998 Amount	1998 Change (%)	Feb. 1999 Amount	Feb. 1999 Change
Total exports	129 715	136 164	5.0	132 313	−2.8	9 422	−16.0
SMEs	54 205	56 910	5.0	56 349	−1.0	4 309	−3.1
Big firms	75 510	79 254	5.0	75 777	−4.2	5 071	−25.0
Share of SMEs (%)	41.8	41.8		42.6		45.7	

Source: Small and Medium-sized Business Administration, *Monthly Bulletin of Small and Medium Business*, Government of the Republic of Korea, March 1999.

major driving force for sustaining economic growth. A number of key issues affecting SME success were identified, such as: technology transfer; human resource development; access to finance; access to markets; access to information; identification of suitable network partners and joint venturers; barriers to entry into foreign markets; and an overall ability to remain internationally competitive (Government of the Republic of Korea 1998d). To help SMEs overcome some of these barriers it was necessary for the Korean government to first focus SME policies on the elimination of the threats to their stabilised management, and access to financial resources. As a start, a general management stabilisation fund of US$567.3 million has been provided for attaining policy goals such as export promotion, commercialisation of new technologies, quality and management innovation and so on, with an additional US$50 million being used as emergency funds to respond to rapid changes in management conditions (Government of the Republic of Korea 1998d). Next, the Korean government needed to continue to promote long-term international competitiveness by supporting structural reforms and technology development. Programs that foster technology-based development, such as venture enterprises, are aimed specifically at SME development and are intended to promote the restructuring of the nation's industry as a whole. To complement this program an additional US$26.6 million was used to establish the Technology Innovation and Development Fund in 1998 to facilitate SME research and development efforts (Government of the Republic of Korea 1998d). Together these policies, along with numerous others, represent a proactive approach to dealing with the financial crisis that occurred in 1997.

In sum, since the financial crisis in 1997, Korea's big enterprises and financial institutions have undergone extensive restructuring. As a result the nation's economy has experienced drastic changes in the industrial and financial sectors, which traditionally were dominated by big businesses. No longer able to depend on big business groups (for example, *chaebols*) to lead the nation's economic growth, the Korean government is placing greater emphasis on SMEs for future growth. Accordingly, SMEs that embrace technological knowledge and skills are expected to replace big business groups in leading the nation out of the financial crisis. SMEs not only have the flexibility to adopt knowledge and information, but also to adapt themselves to the rapidly changing technological environment while proceeding with continuous innovation. Thus, the Korean government has placed the highest priority on SMEs, not big conglomerates, as the key driving force for the industrial development during the 21st century (Government of the Republic of Korea 1998d).

9.4   INVOLVEMENT OF SMES IN THE GLOBAL ECONOMY: RESTRUCTURING OF KOREAN SME POLICY

In 1998 the Korean government began to take major steps to assist SMEs to enhance their international competitiveness. In response to the financial crisis of 1997 a number of policies were developed to eliminate the threats to the stabilised management of SMEs; to promote the restructuring of the nation's industry as a whole; and to promote the development of SMEs. The following sections focus on the 1998 policy responses to the crisis relative to access to finance, development of human resources, use of technology and scientific achievements, globalisation through electronic commerce, and the building of relationships through networking.

9.4.1   Access to Finance

One of the first priorities for the Korean government after the financial crisis was to develop policies focusing on the serious funding shortages and credit crunch threatening many SMEs. To alleviate the fund shortages, the Bank of Korea raised the total loan ceiling to US$6.3 billion in September 1998 from US$3 billion one-year prior (Government of the Republic of Korea 1998e). Additionally, the maturity of US$33.7 billion lent to SMEs had been extended. To prevent a chain of bankruptcies of SMEs an 'exceptional resurrection fund' of US$10.4 billion was provided. Meanwhile, the total government contribution to the credit guarantee fund more than doubled from nearly US$500 million in 1997 to just over US$1 billion in 1998, enhancing the credit guarantee capacity for SMEs. In 1999 the government provided an additional US$1 billion to the credit guarantee fund for SMEs, securing a total amount of US$24.8 billion. To ensure the success of the credit guarantee system the roles and functions of the credit guarantee institutions were specialised and the linkage of the SME assistance funds and credit guarantees were strengthened (Government of the Republic of Korea 1998e).

In an attempt to minimise bankruptcies of SMEs and stabilise their management, the Korean government developed a bill insurance system whereby they insured SMEs' notes receivable and began paying insured money in the case of a bankruptcy. However, there are still a number of SMEs that remain idle and/or are in a position to be taken over by other firms. To deal with these SMEs a total of US$1.17 billion has been used for accelerating the restructuring of SMEs that will contribute to the enhancement of their competitiveness (Government of the Republic of Korea 1998e). The idle facilities information centres have been established in 11 locations throughout the country to promote the transaction of the idle facilities of SMEs. Additionally, the establishment of the SME merger and acquisition (M&A) Centres have been set up within the Small and Medium Industry Promotion Corporation (SMIPC) to support the acquisition of bankrupt SMEs and facilitate the settlement procedures (Government of the Republic of Korea 1998e).

To help ease the funding shortages of SMEs an SME Management Stabilisation Fund was created. This fund consists of the General Management Stabilisation Fund of US$567.3 million to be provided for attaining policy goals, including export promotion, commercialisation of new technologies, quality and management innovations and so on. An additional US$50 million was set aside for the Extraordinary Management Stabilisation Fund, to be used as emergency funds in response to rapid changes in management conditions (Government of the Republic of Korea 1998e). In response to tight monetary policies in the wake of the restructuring of financial institutions, the SMIPC is now allowed to make loans directly to SMEs for their structural improvements. This direct loan system will continue to be operated by the SMIPC for an effective and timely supply of funds to SMEs in the wake of the financial crisis. The Korean government's commitment to providing additional loans through the SMIPC can be seen in the increase from US$441.5 million in 1998 to US$1 billion in 1999. Furthermore, the operational system of providing SME assistance funds has been improved in a more efficient way by simplifying assistance procedures, implementing measures to prevent overlapping assistance, and establishing an evaluation system for fund allocation (Government of the Republic of Korea 1998e).

Measures have also been taken to diversify the fund procurement systems for SMEs. To help alleviate fund shortages faced by SMEs, a number of restrictions on the regional banks have been eased. Specifically, the Enterprise Improvement Fund of US$25 million was established in 1999 by the SMIPC to purchase stocks and bonds of SMEs to help improve their financial structures (Government of the Republic of Korea 1998c). Additionally, a total of US$475 million was provided in the form of direct lending to help improve management and production of SMEs, especially service businesses and knowledge-based manufacturing firms (Government of the Republic of Korea 1998c). At the regional level the Provincial SME Fostering Fund has been expanded to US$710 million in 1998, enhancing further managerial stability to a wider scope of businesses. Together with the 16 provincial SME support centres the operation of existing provincial credit guarantee associations have been strengthened for the local SMEs.

Finally, the government has increased the supply of business foundation funds towards the development of small and medium venture enterprises. Enterprise foundation funds in excess of US$330 million have been provided to venture enterprises. To assist in the development of SME ventures, in 1998 the Korean government established 30 business foundation and fostering centres. Furthermore, the government and private investors have jointly provided funds to establish a Venture Investment Association, entrusted to professional fund managers to generate investments into venture enterprises (Government of the Republic of Korea 1998c).

In sum, the Korean government has given top priority to fostering SMEs and continues to provide financial support in the wake of the financial crisis. The government has made major steps in providing SMEs greater access to finance through the restructuring of financial institutions. They have made sufficient provisions for SMEs that have been adversely affected by the financial crisis, while at the same time providing emergency relief funding so that SMEs can avoid bankruptcy. As a result of the policies implemented since the crisis the credit crunch facing SMEs has been eased to a considerable extent, bringing the bankruptcy rate back to the level prior to the IMF bailout. Owing to the downward stabilisation of market interest rates and the efforts of the financial institutions to support SMEs, the loans to SMEs have recently been gradually increased. Numerous additional funding opportunities now exist for SMEs to receive financial assistance at the local, regional and national levels. With the inauguration in June 1999 of the Venture Net, venture enterprises are now able to exchange information with prospective investors, receive information on business foundation fund application procedures, and gain greater access to venture capital to remain internationally competitive well into the 21st century.

9.4.2 Development of Human Resources

Since the financial crisis in late 1997 the number of unemployed has increased as the business environment deteriorated due to the declining value of the won, rising interest rates and sagging domestic demand. From the last quarter of 1997 rates of unemployment continued to rise, not only in the manufacturing sector but also in other sectors such as construction, social infrastructure and services. In an effort to reduce the unemployment rate the government brought down interest rates by stabilising the foreign exchange market, lowering exchange rates, improving business conditions by relaxing credit regulations, promoting restructuring of economic and financial sectors, and expanding credit guarantees for SMEs (Government of the Republic of Korea 1998d).

The Korean government's desire to create jobs resulted in a number of important human resource policy changes. First, a number of public works projects were created to assist with unemployment, such as cleaning rivers and coastal seas and re-afforestation projects. Second, the government created jobs by extending support for export industries and fostering growth in high technology-oriented (venture) enterprises. Third, there was a generation of jobs through the liberalising of foreign direct investment policy, directly resulting in increased employment across a number of employment sectors. Additional jobs were saved by allowing hostile mergers and acquisitions of Korean companies by foreign investors; while at the same time jobs were created by revising the laws to allow foreign entities to purchase real estate. Fourth, a large number of government-funded 'human resource banks' now operate across the country to help the unemployed find jobs through online systems that link employers with those seeking jobs. Fifth, the involvement of the Korea International Cooperation Agency (KOICA) in finding overseas jobs for those unemployed has generated employment opportunities. Finally, job training for those changing careers has been provided by the Industrial Manpower Management Corporation, the Chamber of Commerce and Industry, and the vast number of universities, vocational colleges and on-the-job training sites around Korea. Considering that the overall unemployment rate was only 2 per cent in 1996, after reaching as high as 8.6 per cent in January 1999, the effects of these policies were being felt as unemployment dropped to 5.3 per cent in February 2000 (Government of the Republic of Korea 2000c). By 2003 the Korean government predicts that an additional 2 million new jobs will be created and full employment will be achieved. These jobs are expected to come in high-value-added industries such as SME/venture enterprises, tourism, culture and telecommunications (Government of the Republic of Korea 2000b).

Small and medium enterprises play an important role in human resource development by contributing significantly to national wealth and employment, as intermediate and final producers, and as consumers of goods and services. However, one of the most significant barriers to growth for SMEs is the lack of workers with technical 'value-added' skills. The Korean government realises how important human resource development is for businesses, especially SMEs, and has established a number of programs designed to help SMEs build their knowledge base. To help ease skilled human resource shortages facing SMEs, a total of 42 850 industrial technicians have been assigned to a total of nearly 10 000 SMEs in 1998 (Government of the Republic of Korea 1998e). Current technical on-the-job training programs for SMEs have over 30 000 industrial trainees at over 6 500 SME manufacturers, greatly contributing to the alleviation of skilled worker shortages.

To reinforce education and training the SME Training Institute under SMIPC has provided various educational opportunities to workers of small and medium businesses. Consignment training programs and the focus on skilled workers are being considered as a possible remedy to manpower shortages faced by SMEs. To start, access to managerial consulting through the small merchants and industrialists support centres has been established in 14 locations across the nation to support business foundation skills for SMEs (Government of the Republic of Korea 1998e). The government-funded SME management and technology service teams have also provided consulting services for over 10 000 SMEs across Korea in 1998 (Government of the Republic of Korea 1998e). To improve research skills, preferential treatment is given by the government to small firms, export-oriented SMEs and venture enterprises in the form of allocation of professional research personnel (that is, military service personnel). By providing support through research personnel the government is contributing towards the training and transfer of important technical skills, especially for high-tech venture enterprises. Finally, realising the importance of fostering women entrepreneurs the government established the Act on Support of Women-owned Enterprises and set up counselling centres around the country to provide managerial training courses for women interested in managing SMEs.

As Korea enters the 21st century the government continues to place even greater emphasis on the underlying forces affecting SMEs. This is especially true for human resource development. The foundation for human resource policy since the financial crisis has been to focus on employment creation and training programs aimed at the transfer of technology-based skills. By fostering technologically advanced skills through training assistance the government is directly contributing to the development of 'value-added' human resources for SMEs. As a first step reforms have been implemented to reduce unemployment. Second, a public sector incentive system will be consistently reformed to nurture a more creative and competitive atmosphere for the transfer of skills and knowledge. Third, the government plans to set up an information-sharing system to help its officials identify value-added work. Last, state-run companies will be continuously reformed so as to reduce unemployment and provide on-the-job training to update skills (Government of the Republic of Korea

1998d). To this end the government will continue to reorganise the labour market by encouraging new systems and investing in high-technology skills. The support for venture enterprises is just one example of the government's commitment to facilitate technology sharing among SMEs, creating a greater number of new jobs and contributing directly to the fundamental solution to the unemployment problem.

9.4.3 Use of Scientific and Technological Achievements

Science and technology (S&T) development was initiated by the Korean government as early as the 1960s, and since then the government has continued to be the driving force behind innovation activities. Not only has the government been involved in strengthening and expanding the domestic technological base, but they are also responsible for setting direction for international cooperation in S&T partnerships. While the general policies by the Korean government in S&T have been positive prior to the financial crisis, simply maintaining existing S&T policies was not going to enable Korean firms to continue their growth performance. When the financial crisis occurred in late 1997, it became clear that many Korean firms were not going to be able to compete internationally unless the government shifted policy towards market orientation of economic activities. Additionally, the government needed to totally liberalise foreign direct investment if they were to attract important R&D funds from abroad. Along with the liberalisation of foreign investment the government needed to continue to launch new policy programs to promote the globalisation of R&D activities in both the private and public sectors.

As Korea enters the 21st century, growth will depend largely upon the new innovations coming from public and private laboratories, universities, and small and medium 'venture enterprises' (Government of the Republic of Korea 1998c). Global sourcing and international strategic alliances will become major modes of international technology cooperation for many Korean SMEs. The thrust of Korean S&T policy will need to adjust to changes in the international environment – including the globalisation of markets, the emergence of new knowledge-based venture enterprises, competitive cooperative partnerships, and the economic interdependence among the nations in the Asia–Pacific region. For SMEs there are numerous benefits to consider in the globalisation of R&D activities (Buckley and Mirza 1997). Table 9.7 presents some common motives for globalising R&D.

Table 9.7
Common Motives for Globalisation of R&D Activities

- Acquire new technology
- Reduce costs of technological innovation
- Maximise use of global resources
- Support needs of foreign operations

Globalisation of S&T activities can only be accomplished when a system that facilitates competition and cooperation in R&D among individual scientists, academia and international research organisations is promoted (Gemunden and Heydebreck 1995). Hence, one of the top priorities for the Korean government to strengthen technological and quality competitiveness of SMEs is to provide the necessary infrastructure for SMEs to develop S&T achievements both locally and abroad. In doing so the Korean government is focusing on four major areas of S&T policy formation for SMEs (Choi and Chung 1997):

1. provide a foundation for technology improvement;

2. strengthen technological competitiveness;

3. strengthen technical cooperation and exchanges;

4. support and reinforce information capabilities.

To provide a foundation for technology improvement the first step by the government was to offer SMEs 'knowledge-based' skills. In response, educational programs are currently being offered to improve 'knowledge management' skills in Korea. Additionally, over 5 000 management and technology consultants provide guidance in R&D activities for SMEs (Government of the Republic of Korea 1998e). A database of consultants, industrial professionals, academics and researchers is also available to access information on technology improvement. As an additional incentive to participate in educational programs the government offers consulting personnel educational opportunities through training and re-education courses. Technology innovation programs such as these have provided opportunities to over 700 SMEs to participate in consortiums composed of industry, academia and research centres (Government of the Republic of Korea 1998e). Also, an SME Support Council of Research Institutes will be operating with the cooperation and participation of 15 government-run research institutes around the country. The goal of this support council is to provide a database of new technologies developed by universities and research institutes for SMEs to utilise when commercialising S&T achievements. Increased funding since the financial crisis has resulted in 85 new regional consortiums for joint technology development and 360 cooperative groups on joint research, up nearly 20 per cent from the previous year (Government of the Republic of Korea 1998e). Together, these efforts provide an important foundation for technological improvement for SMEs by linking the industrial, academic and research sectors.

Strengthening the technological competitiveness of SMEs is essential if SMEs hope to become internationally competitive. In 1998, the Technology Innovation and Development Fund increased to US$26.6 million to facilitate SMEs in conducting R&D projects (Government of the Republic of Korea 1998e). Technology innovation support has now been extended to over 700 SMEs through R&D consortiums composed of industry, academia and research centres. The government plans to increase the number of consortiums to 100 by 2000, in addition to easing the conditions required for consortium formation. These efforts are aimed at reinforcing technology development of SMEs. One of the major barriers to S&T development for SMEs, occurs in the design and prototype development stages. The Small and Medium Industry Promotion Corporation's (SMIPC) recently developed Automation Centre will play a central role in helping SMEs resolve technological difficulties in design, pilot product manufacturing, prototype development and engineering. Furthermore, a number of public research institutes will be further encouraged to transfer their technologies to SMEs. In 1999 alone the government selected 250 SMEs for a program to transfer technology. These enterprises received strong support from the government so that they can grow into leading enterprises equipped with world-class advanced technologies. In an effort to assist SMEs facing managerial and technological difficulties the government is providing 80 per cent funding for comprehensive consulting services to an additional 1000 SMEs (Government of the Republic of Korea 1998e). To upgrade the capabilities of technical personnel and ensure technological innovation, specialised educational programs are being offered to SMEs. To further enhance competitive advantage for SMEs the government promotes a quality competitiveness campaign, resulting in the issuance of quality certificates to a total of 523 SMEs in 1998 (Government of the Republic of Korea 1998d). Together these programs are aimed at transforming SMEs into firms that are competitive technologically and equipped with flexibility and mobility. In this context the Korean government hopes that technology- and knowledge-based SMEs, with their excellent organisational flexibility, will be the sources of state-of-the-art technology development and future economic growth.

At the same time, it is very important for Korea to invest in a global network of R&D programs to conduct research abroad in cooperation with local scientists so as to strengthen technical cooperation and facilitate the exchange of S&T achievements among SMEs (Lee and Chung 1997). To expand exchanges between businesses of different types the government has created nearly 400 different-type businesses exchange groups by the end of 1999. The group advisers and leaders of these groups have been provided with additional training to facilitate the exchanges among these enterprises. Technological cooperation with other nations and research centres has also been promoted through the establishment of an Overseas Technology Training Association (OTTA). The primary goal of OTTA is to facilitate the introduction of advanced technologies by SMEs into foreign markets (Government of the Republic of Korea 1998d). SMEs are also encouraged to participate in international technology fairs held locally and abroad. Additionally, the Korea Trade Promotion Corporation (KOTRA), a non-profit governmental organisation, further promotes technological cooperation among SMEs by gathering and disseminating industrial technology information and holding various technology transfer meetings, seminars and exhibitions (Government of the Republic of Korea 1998i). International strategic alliances and joint ventures between SMEs have emerged as a business and technology strategy of first choice, leading to the wide geographic dispersal of activities, not only for production but also for R&D, design, sourcing inputs and marketing

(Government of the Republic of Korea 1998i). To this end the Korean government has made great strides in helping SMEs globalise their R&D efforts and strengthen international cooperative relations.

A number of facilities have been provided to support and reinforce information capabilities of SMEs. To ensure that SMEs had a smooth transition to the 21st century the government invested US$25 million to conduct over 15 000 site examinations and provide assistance to help solve potential Y2K problems. Additional 'information' education programs are currently being offered to inform SMEs as to the base of knowledge available from government, industrial, and academic sources (Government of the Republic of Korea 1998f). For SMEs that have outdated computer systems, or do not have access to information technology, the Small and Medium Business Administration (SMBA) has developed the Enterprise Information Incubator Project. This project serves as an invaluable source of information linkages for SMEs. Some of the SMBA information services include development of Internet homepages, access to Internet sites on trade (KOTRA) and investment (KISC), and procurement information networks at home and abroad (Government of the Republic of Korea 1998i). As a central government agency designed to assist SMEs in their information needs the SMBA has 11 regional offices throughout the country which work for the growth and information support of SMEs in close cooperation with related organisations. Finally, to help promote the dissemination of information to SMEs, eight database networks including Venture Net and Techno Net are providing information about SME support policies.

Since the financial crisis in 1997 the Korean government has sought to strengthen the competitive advantage of SMEs by providing the technological infrastructure to develop S&T achievements and improve their technological capabilities. Various technology development programs have been implemented in the last few years that have allowed SMEs to have greater access to technology from other organisations, academia, and research centres locally and abroad (Lee and Chung 1997). The government has paid particular attention to fostering venture enterprises to strengthen the competitiveness of industry and serve as future potential growth into the 21st century. Additionally, tripartite cooperation among SMEs, institutions of higher education and research organisations have been promoted along with technology guidance programs. It is expected that international cooperation programs with overseas companies and related organisations and institutions will continue to be expanded to assist SMEs sustain their competitive advantage in an increasingly competitive global marketplace. SMEs will continue to be given the fullest attention in developing technologies, exploring international strategic alliances, and in fostering international cooperative relations with partners abroad for joint investment in R&D.

9.4.4   Globalisation Through Electronic Commerce

The Korean government has tried to enhance the competitiveness of firms as a strategy to foster economic growth. By investing in globalisation and technology-driven venture enterprises the government is counting on SMEs to pull them out of the Asian financial crisis of 1997. Electronic commerce (e-commerce) is one way to facilitate the globalisation of SMEs. E-commerce involves research and exchange of information, use of e-mailing, promotion and online selling, and allocation of resources for products (for example, consumer goods) and services (for example, information, financial, legal) (Fariselli et al. 1999). For many SMEs it may encompass such diverse activities as information gathering, e-mail, purchasing, advertising and marketing, and online sales. Table 9.8 lists 'Common E-commerce Activities for SMEs'.

E-commerce not only increases the efficiency of resource allocation it also improves a firm's competitiveness, enhances their economic effectiveness in entering global markets, and promotes overall growth in the global economy. The implications for SMEs utilising e-commerce technologies are numerous. Electronic business can create instantaneous access to new markets, new products and services, and new relationships with other businesses. Firms can engage in collaborative design, engineering, and value-added processes in production. Because they do not have to rely on economies of scale in mass production, SMEs can more easily overcome traditional barriers to foreign markets that only large companies could afford. Distance becomes less relevant in allocation, and digitisation of information generation provides for ease in transfers and transactions of products and services. E-commerce also allows firms to reduce costs by reducing the number of distributors and channel members (Fariselli et al. 1999). Thus, by engaging in e-commerce activities SMEs are better able to mass customise their offerings at a lower per unit cost, thereby creating opportunities to become global niche marketers.

Although there are a number of positive impacts from using e-commerce there are also barriers and obstacles in using advanced technologies, especially for SMEs. The barriers and obstacles most significant to SMEs include: lack of awareness of e-commerce capabilities; uncertainty about its benefits; concerns about lack of human resources and skills; complexity in use; set-up costs; and concerns about security. SMEs' ability to adopt e-commerce activities depends on various factors, most of which lead to the value placed upon the benefits versus the costs of investing capital

Table 9.8
Common E-commerce Activities for SMEs

Trading of goods and services	Online sourcing
Online delivery of digital content	Procurement of goods
Electronic fund transfers	Advertising and consumer marketing
Electronic share trading	Collaborative advertising
Electronic bills or lading	Servicing of products
Commercial auctions	After-sales service
Collaborative design and engineering	

and resources into the necessary infrastructure (such as equipment, human resources, and set-up and access costs). However, with the advent of the Internet most governments have come to the realisation that they need to develop policies to promote the use of e-commerce by SMEs. The challenge for governments is first to create awareness of e-commerce activities, then to translate awareness into adoption, investment, and use of advanced technologies to globalise operations. This suggests that government policies that encourage e-commerce activities will not only allow SMEs to have immediate access to highly dynamic and competitive markets, but will also enhance their competitiveness and lead to future economic growth.

In Korea the Ministry of Commerce, Industry and Energy (MOCIE) initiated building institutional policies related to e-commerce. Policies revolved around three main areas of e-commerce: business-to-consumer; business-to-business; and government-to-business/consumer. While Internet-based business in Korea is expected to generate nearly US$2 billion of revenues by 2005, nearly 80 per cent of Internet-based business is comprised of business-to-consumer activities. According to the National Computerisation Agency (NCA), business-to-consumer electronic commerce in Korea is expected to increase by 25 per cent, from US$85 million in 1999 to nearly US$350 million in 2000 (Government of the Republic of Korea 1998g). One of the main contributing factors to this growth is the opening of cyber malls. In 1996 the first cyber mall, the Lotte Internet Department Store, was opened and afterwards numerous cyber malls were established. Currently, approximately 400 malls are in operation. While this number is relatively small when compared to the 500 000 plus cyber malls in the US, many consider the cyber mall still to be in the embryonic stage in Korea (Government of the Republic of Korea 1998h). This is especially true given that 58.3 per cent of total malls began their business as recently as 1998. Korea's business-to-business e-commerce activities began as early as 1987. It was then that the Pohang Steel Company introduced their Electronic Data Interchange (EDI) system linking ordering and inventory systems among their suppliers and customers, respectively. Although the EDI system is typically a proprietary one the efficiencies from electronic exchanges among businesses led to the immediate adoption of Internet and web-based systems in the early 1990s. To increase the interconnections among Korean firms and enhance international business operations the Korean private sector has joined together to launch a project named ELECTROPIA (e-commerce and utopia) (Government of the Republic of Korea 1998g). The goal of this project is to establish an Internet-based system through which Korean firms may develop industrial parts for common use, procure necessary resources together, and establish a common logistics and distribution system. It is believed that ELECTROPIA may increase the effectiveness of internal business practices by changing business processes, as well as enhancing Korean firms' competitiveness through the exposure to new customers and markets (Government of the Republic of Korea 1998h). Finally, government-to-business/consumer e-commerce in Korea primarily involves an EDI or a CALS system, and was introduced to handle customs clearance, procurement and construction projects. Since its inception in the late 1980s the Korean government has expanded activities using the Internet to systems in defence and for the private sector to access the government more conveniently when engaging in procurement transactions (Government of the Republic of Korea 1998h).

Recent efforts by the Korean government to encourage SMEs in maximising the benefits of electronic commerce include policy initiatives in the following areas: changes to laws and regulations; policies to persuade collaboration between SMEs and large businesses; establishing an infrastructure for e-commerce; and strengthening international cooperation in e-commerce (Government of the Republic of Korea 1998g). In July 1999 the Korean government passed the Electronic Transaction Act, whose main purpose was to give legal validity to electronic documentation as well as electronic signature. This law was designed to increase protection of consumers' information and enhance security of e-commerce activities. At this same time the Digital Signature Act was passed to provide the process through which a digital signature system can be implemented. The primary goal of these two laws was to ensure consumers that it was safe to engage in transactions over the Internet. To persuade collaboration between SMEs and large businesses in e-commerce the government has introduced CALS/EC systems across the nation's largest industries, including electronics, automobile, ship-building, steel and textiles (Government of the Republic of Korea 1998g). These systems will enable SMEs to easily forge relationships with large businesses in joint procurement, joint distribution and overall product standardisation. Efforts by the Korean government to build an infrastructure for e-commerce involved promoting the development of e-commerce technology, expansion of standardised protocols and procedures, and upgrading of communication lines to facilitate rapid Internet access. Currently 50 000 product catalogues by over 10 000 SMEs are being displayed over the Internet through the 'Small and Medium Enterprises of Korea' showcase (Government of the Republic of Korea 1998h). Additionally, a number of 'electronic commerce resource centres' were established around the country to support SMEs with training, technological advice and consulting services in e-commerce technologies (Government of the Republic of Korea 1998g). To further increase the utilisation of e-commerce by SMEs the government has held and will continue to hold nationwide conferences explaining the benefits of e-commerce. Lastly, to promote international cooperation the government plans on continuing its efforts to initiate multilateral talks regarding e-commerce policy, including talks with the Organisation for Economic Cooperation and Development, the World Trade Organisation and the Asia–Pacific Economic Cooperation (APEC) forum.

The growth of e-commerce has the potential to offer SMEs an important means of access to global markets. E-commerce has opened up new possibilities for the creation of networks among SMEs, thus allowing these firms to compete with larger companies on more equal terms. E-commerce in Korea is expected to skyrocket to 3.78 trillion won in 2002 from 150 billion won in 1999 (Government of the Republic of Korea 1998g). However, there is a need for public policies to promote the creation and deployment of new technologies such as e-commerce, especially for small and medium businesses. The Korean government recognises the importance of facilitating e-commerce activities for SMEs, but has only recently begun to make changes in e-commerce policy to encourage and reward both businesses and consumers to continue using this important communication medium. While core technology for e-commerce is in high demand, many SMEs find it difficult to develop this technology on their own due to the high risks involved. Developed technology will first be applied in the public sector and then at a later stage commercialisation will be granted to SMEs in the information technology (IT) industry. It is expected that by 2001 a total of 43 different types of technology, including digital payment systems, will be transferred to private businesses (Government of the Republic of Korea 1998g). As e-commerce continues to grow, governments and policy makers alike will need to focus on the challenges facing SMEs, and develop policies that facilitate the transfer of technologies and utilisation of e-commerce activities.

In addition to government efforts to facilitate e-commerce, in October 2000 a small venture company named Bizsens.com launched Korea's first and only business-to-business (B2B) services marketplace for SMEs (Government of the Republic of Korea 2000a). This 'request for quote' system allows SMEs to quickly and inexpensively research, locate and retain top quality service providers using the company's website (www.bizsens.com). Additionally, Bizsens provides SMEs with consulting services on Web strategy and implementation. By helping firms leverage the power of the Internet this company allows SMEs to become more competitive. SMEs can request and receive competitive bids from pre-screened service providers in a number of different service areas, including web designs, Web hosting, recruitment, translation, IT equipment rental and patent, trademark and incorporation legal assistance (Government of the Republic of Korea 2000a). Leveraging a number of foreign contacts and experience, Bizsens.com provides valuable support in helping export-oriented SMEs extend their foreign sales online.

With the advent of e-commerce in Asia, many SMEs will be forced to engage in online business following their bigger competitors/customers in the region. Given that the Asian SME segment will likely become increasingly competitive and difficult to penetrate, e-marketplaces serve as a viable, if not necessary, option for SMEs to target consumer and business markets with greater pricing power and sustainable networks. Even though there are a number of technological barriers in e-commerce, SMEs in Korea are increasingly turning to the Internet to achieve competitive advantages in the Asian region. By the end of 1999 only 14 per cent of Korea's 2.7 million SMEs were online, yet by 2004 the percentage is expected to jump to 55 per cent representing an online market of over 1.7 million companies (Government of the Republic of Korea 2000a). In order for SMEs to survive and thrive within the competitive Asian region, they will have to begin developing products and services that meet the unique needs of the increasingly demanding consumer and business markets. To do this, Korean SMEs must learn to sell, save and solve business issues online.

9.4.5 Building Relationships Through Networking

Developing relationships is an important part of everyday business for many small and medium enterprises. With an increase in globalisation of markets many SMEs are finding it necessary to forge relations with other businesses. Collaboration with other firms, or networking, provides an important source of new ideas when developing a competitive advantage. Networking involves the mix of formal and informal contacts between business, professional, social and personal counterparts. Networks allow SMEs to exchange information, gain greater access to resources, integrate operations with other firms, reduce R&D costs, minimise risk, and provide greater access to new markets (Fariselli et al. 1999). The outcomes of networking are numerous, including increased sales and profits, improved innovations through cooperative technological achievements, ease of entry into foreign markets, and overall enhanced competitiveness of the firm (Gemunden and Heydebreck 1995).

In an effort to promote networking and trade cooperation among Korean businesses (including SMEs), the Korean government established in 1962 the Korea Trade Promotion Corporation (KOTRA). The primary objectives of KOTRA are to encourage trade promotion activities, exchange trade information, and provide market research services and business matchmaking. In 1995 KOTRA assumed the responsibilities for cross-border investment promotion and support for technological and industrial cooperation projects. Immediately following the financial crisis in 1998, the Korea Investment Service Centre (KISC) was established within KOTRA as the country's sole authorised investment promotion organisation. The primary function of KISC is to provide foreign investors with one-stop service, covering everything from investment plan consultation to settlement support. After the financial crisis of 1997 the focus of investment strategy in Korea has been to encourage exports and induce foreign investment. In sum, the Korean government is hoping to return the country to prosperity and sustainable growth by promoting international cooperation between Korean firms and foreign investors. In doing so, the government has implemented the following 5-step approach (Government of the Republic of Korea 1998i):

1. exploring markets globally;

2. promoting international investment;

3. collecting information to serve business better;

4. facilitating mutual understanding;

5. creating virtual access to the Korean market.

To assist SMEs in *exploring markets globally*, KOTRA has created a business matchmaking program that links Korean firms with foreign partners. A Business Service Centre has been established in this regard to assist buyers visiting Korea in arranging business meetings with Korean firms, as well as to facilitate the collection of information on Korean products and suppliers. Additionally, KOTRA organises trade missions to enable Korean SMEs to penetrate world markets. The trade mission program helps SMEs to enter foreign markets by providing valuable information on market conditions and potential distributors in overseas markets. International exhibitions are also held each year, where thousands of Korean firms participate by displaying their products and services. The newly built Seoul Trade Exhibition Centre (SETEC) allows both domestic and foreign exhibitors to showcase their state-of-the-art products and services (Government of the Republic of Korea 1998i).

When foreign firms have decided to invest in Korea the government's investment agency, KISC, provides a comprehensive service to promote international investment. The services provided in KISC's one-stop service include support for handling of administrative procedures, consultation on mergers and acquisitions, advice on legal, accounting and tax matters, and settlement assistance with respect to accommodation, schooling and health care. KOTRA also plays an important role in disseminating investment information through their online database to more than 100 countries around the world. KISC currently maintains 36 Korea trade centres specialising in investment services, and publishes the *Korean Trade & Investment*, *Korea Biweekly* and *Strategic Investment Guide* to aid Korean investment in such markets (Government of the Republic of Korea 1998i). Along these lines KOTRA plays a crucial role in collecting information to serve business better. By generating and publishing reports on a variety of topics, KOTRA is providing a valuable service to both foreign and domestic clients. Reports include investment opportunities, environmental analysis, legal regulations and trade conditions for Korea as well as a number of foreign markets. KOTRA also operates departments that specialise in specific geographic regions. These departments specialise in conducting marketing research by tracking current market issues, trade regulations, and other related topics pertinent to the countries it covers (Government of the Republic of Korea 1998i). If SMEs want further information on entering foreign markets or linking up with foreign partners, they can visit the Trade Library at KOTRA's head office. This library provides a state-of-the-art computerised system with information on economics, business conditions and trade investment. The extensive range of resources at the Trade Library also includes business directories, tariff schedules and periodicals in overseas markets.

Since the costs for SMEs to enter markets and establish cooperative relationships often serve as a major barrier to internationalising operations, KOTRA provides a number of services to help *facilitate mutual understanding* between SMEs and foreign partners. One such service involves the promotion of technology transfer. By gathering and disseminating industrial technology information KOTRA promotes technological cooperation between SMEs and potential overseas partners. KOTRA also holds various technology transfer meetings, seminars and exhibitions in an attempt to foster cooperative relations (Government of the Republic of Korea 1998i). Furthermore, workshops are organised to better promote communications and sharing of information among related organisations, and publications are distributed dealing with information on both Korean and foreign markets and products. In 1999, KOTRA organised the

APEC Investment Mark to promote cooperative relations within the APEC region economies. KOTRA also invests in training as an important means to foster mutual cooperation among developing countries through networking and the sharing of experiences (Government of the Republic of Korea 1998i). Finally, with the advent of the Internet and electronic communications, KOTRA has invested in a program to create virtual access to the Korean market for overseas investors. Through their homepage the government has created 'Virtual KOTRA'. Digital KOTRA provides access to a vast range of information on the Korean economy, investment environment, products, companies and exhibitions. They also collect trade inquiries from buyers worldwide and pass them on to Korean firms via the Internet. For Korean firms that want to disseminate export inquiries, Virtual KOTRA communicates automatically to nearly 10 million companies connected to the Global Trade Point Network (GTPNet). Lastly, the government has created Cyber KISC, an interactive database system designed to communicate investment opportunities in Korean industries to potential overseas investors (Government of the Republic of Korea 1998i).

9.5   PROSPECTS FOR KOREA'S SMES IN THE 21ST CENTURY

As a result of the financial crisis in 1997 the Korean government focused restructuring efforts on the two areas of the economy most in need: financial institutions and big enterprises (that is, *chaebols*). During this time the nation's economy has experienced drastic changes in its industrial structure, which in the past was centred around big businesses. It was at this time that the government began to realise that they can no longer depend on large multinational firms to fuel the economy, leading them to shift emphasis from big business to small and medium enterprises. It was anticipated that SMEs, especially those equipped with technological capabilities, will replace big business conglomerates as the main thrust in economic growth. Not only are SMEs regarded as a major source of job creation during the last few years, they are also expected to reshape the overall Korean industry and enable the Korean economy to recover its competitiveness (Government of the Republic of Korea 1998d). Moreover, SMEs that can easily adapt themselves to the rapidly changing technological environment, while proceeding with continuous innovation, are those expected to experience continued growth well into the 21st century. It is these particular SMEs, or 'venture enterprises', that the Korean government is putting a top policy priority on to help them regain their competitive advantage (Government of the Republic of Korea 1998c).

A venture enterprise is defined as a 'technology-intensive enterprise' or an 'enterprise based on a highly advanced technology'. To be classified as a venture enterprise an SME must satisfy any of the following four conditions (Government of the Republic of Korea 1998c):

1. have at least 10 per cent of the total capital generated from venture capital;

2. invest at least 5 per cent or more of total sales revenue into R&D;

3. have at least 50 per cent or more of its total sales generated from sales of patents and new technology products;

4. be recognised by the government as having excellent technology.

Since 1997, when the government introduced measures to foster venture enterprises, 4 200 small and medium companies have been designated as venture firms. It is estimated that between 200 and 300 companies are newly designated as venture firms each month (Government of the Republic of Korea 1998c). Venture enterprises demonstrate higher technological capabilities and managerial performance, and realise greater growth rates than other SMEs and big conglomerates. They also create more jobs than big companies or traditional small firms, and make greater contributions to development of regional and national economies. Realising the importance and growth potential of venture enterprises, the Korean government in 1997 passed the Law on Special Measures for Fostering Venture Enterprises. This law focuses on three main areas to foster the development of venture enterprises. These areas include improving the atmosphere to form venture enterprises, improvement of funding opportunities, and encouraging globalisation of venture enterprises (Government of the Republic of Korea 1998c).

To create an atmosphere to form venture enterprises the government has focused its start-up campaign around universities and research institutes. They are hoping to tap into the young and ambitious university student and research personnel market with various supports to make start-up of venture firms easier. By providing students with initial expenses for starting businesses, they are also hoping that they will quickly advance into promising venture firms. The government will exempt university students from obligatory military service, allow professors and research fellows to temporarily retire, and even provide initial expenses for starting businesses all in the hope of encouraging the formation of venture enterprises. Once a venture enterprise has been formed, measures to improve funding opportunities are necessary. To encourage investment in venture enterprises tax benefits have been expanded to include venture capital invested in venture enterprises (Government of the Republic of Korea 1998c). Furthermore, the Korean government is creating a source of public capital aimed at supporting preliminary business starters and newly inaugurated businesses in which private venture investors are reluctant to make investments. With the formation of the Korea Venture Fund in 1999 an additional US$83 million has been set aside for direct investment in venture firms (Government of the Republic of Korea 1998c). Finally, to ensure long-term success of venture enterprises it is necessary that these firms compete effectively with their counterparts in the world market. In an effort to encourage globalisation of venture enterprises the Korean government provides assistance in exporting, foreign direct investment in overseas firms, formation of collaborative partnerships with foreign companies, and funding to establish overseas factories and offices.

Although the government has focused on lifting various administrative restrictions and on encouraging the growth of venture enterprises immediately following the financial crisis, more work is needed to improve the infrastructure for fostering such venture businesses. Specifically, many venture businesses are still undergoing financial difficulties owing to the lack of venture capital and angel funds available. Recently, in response to these difficulties, more than 40 business incubators across the country have been established to assist the start-up of new venture enterprises. By the year 2002 it is expected that more than 100 incubators will be in existence to help nearly 2000 new venture enterprises get started (Government of the Republic of Korea 1998c). Additional infrastructure development includes the establishment of six 'techno-parks' in the major cities in Korea, along with a 'venture town' in the city of Taejon and a 'high-tech complex' in Seoul. As mentioned previously the launch of the Venture Net has greatly facilitated the sharing of information on business, technology and investment opportunities with government agencies, private organisations and other venture businesses. Finally, the government has created the KOSDAQ, a Korean version of NASDAQ, as a virtually exclusive stock exchange for small business and venture enterprises. This represents a vital source of venture capital with hundreds of venture companies currently trading on the KOSDAQ. By the end of 1999 over US$2 billion changed hands per day on KOSDAQ. With a market valuation reaching US$100 billion, trading on KOSDAQ represented nearly one-third of the Korea Stock Exchange in 1999 (Government of the Republic of Korea 1998c).

Despite the challenges that lie ahead the new generation of small- and medium-sized venture enterprise entrepreneurs are better educated, have developed a business plan based on technological innovation and niche market specialisation, and have anticipated the need to raise capital through venture capital and/or the stock market. By the beginning of 2000 venture companies numbered over 5 000, of which many are considered competitive and capable of flexibly responding to changing markets and customer needs and demands (Government of the Republic of Korea 2000c). By June 2000 Korea had 8 768 certified technology ventures, placing it as the third largest market worldwide for venture business (Government of the Republic of Korea 2000d). The government plans on continuing to expand its investment into venture companies, and by the end of 2000 raised venture funds in cooperation with the private sector in excess of US$1 billion. These funds will be used to nurture approximately 10 000 venture companies, creating an additional 100 000 new jobs. Additionally, the government has provided a special guarantee through the Technology Trust Guarantee Fund of over US$2 billion to be provided through 23 financial institutions throughout Korea (Government of the Republic of Korea 2000d). The information-oriented Enterprises Promotion Fund has been established to provide nearly US$100 million for software venture enterprises.

9.6   SUMMARY AND CONCLUSIONS

Over the past few years Korea has been developing a foundation for its knowledge-based or 'new' economy, focusing on developing an information infrastructure that promotes information and communications-related technologies, e-commerce activities, and the formation of venture enterprises (Government of the Republic of Korea 2000b). From 1991 to 1999 Korea's knowledge-based industries realised an average annual real growth rate of 13.7 per cent. In 1999 knowledge-based industries accounted for 45.6 per cent of the nation's annual GDP growth rate of 10.7 per cent (Government of the Republic of Korea 2000c). Korean SMEs and venture enterprises are an important part of Korea's new economy. The government needs to continue to support venture enterprises by streamlining laws and expanding the support of both management stablisation and structural improvement funds, especially for those firms involved in knowledge-intensive industries (Government of the Republic of Korea 1998a). However, to meet the competitive demands of the 21st century, SMEs will also need to make efforts to respond to the changes in economic conditions at home and abroad. This includes securing core technologies and competencies necessary to adapt to changing competitive conditions. Even though the Korean economy grew strongly in 1999, concerns still remain about the sustainability of its recovery through 2000 and beyond. Employment in industry, agriculture and services sectors has remained weak with much of the recent increase in jobs coming from self-employment and the public sector. While considerable restructuring has occurred among smaller *chaebols* and SME sectors the question for Korea is whether the slow restructuring of larger *chaebols* will impede SME growth.

Globalising operations, developing and sustaining up-to-date information systems, and transforming themselves into highly competitive technology-based firms equipped to deal with flexibility and mobility are necessary first steps for SMEs in the 21st century. Fortunately for Korean SMEs and venture enterprises, the Kim Dae-jung government has proclaimed the 21st century to be the 'Age of SMEs' (Choo 1999). This is evident through the outstanding support provided to SMEs in a number of key areas, including access to finance, human resources management, scientific and technological achievements, promotion of e-commerce, and promotion of collaborative relationships through networking. Although the Korean government still has room to improve upon SME policies, since the financial crisis they have provided a solid foundation for economic stabilisation by: reforming financial institutions and big businesses; transforming its economic system into a knowledge-based economy; liberalising its markets to foreign investment; strengthening its efforts to cooperate with foreign countries; and focusing on SMEs and venture enterprises as a 'key' driving force in establishing Korea as a global economy, ready to embrace the challenges that the 21st century has to offer.

REFERENCES

Buckley, P.J. and H. Mirza (eds) (1997), *International Technology Transfer by Small and Medium-sized Enterprises*, Basingstoke, UK: Macmillan.

Choi, J. and S.C. Chung (1997), 'The Role of Government in S&T Co-operation: The Case of Korea', OECD Working Paper DSTI/STP/TIP(97)14/FINAL.

Choi, Y.B. (1999), 'On the Causes of Financial Crisis in Korea', *Multinational Business Review* (Fall): 45–53.

Choo, June-Suk [Administrator, Small and Medium Business Administration] (1999), 'Regional Economic Problems' (1999), Keynote Speech at Christchurch, New Zealand, 27 April..

Fariselli, P., C. Oughton, C. Picory and R. Sugden (1999), 'Electronic Commerce and the Future for SMEs in a Global Market-place: Networking and Public Policies', *Small Business Economics*, **12**: 261–75.

Fujita, M. (1997), 'Small and Medium-sized Enterprises in Foreign Direct Investment', in P. Buckley and H. Mirza (eds), *International Technology Transfer by Small and Medium-sized Enterprises*, Basingstoke, UK: Macmillan, pp. 9–70.

Gemunden, H.G. and P. Heydebreck (1995), 'The External Links and Networks of Small Firms – Their Role and Nature', in D.P. O'Doherty (ed.), *Globalisation, Networking and Small Firm Innovation*, London: Graham & Trotman, pp. 87–100.

Government of Australia (1996), *APEC Project on Business Matching and Facilitation Services and Electronic Databases Available to SMEs to Facilitate Trade and Investment, Department of Industry, Science and Tourism*, Canberra: Australian Government Publishing.

Government of the Republic of Korea (1997), 'Moody's Report on the Korean Economy', Korea Investment Service Centre, <www.kisc.org.kr>.

Government of the Republic of Korea (1998a), 'Investment Environment and Prospects for Venture Business in Korea', Small and Medium-sized Business Administration, <www.smba.go.kr>.

Government of the Republic of Korea (1998b), 'Korea's SMEs Preparing for the 21st Century', Small and Medium-sized Business Administration, http://www.smba.go.kr>.

Government of the Republic of Korea (1998c), 'Korea's Venture Enterprises and Policy Directions for Fostering Them', Small and Medium-sized Business Administration, <www.smba.go.kr>.

Government of the Republic of Korea (1998d), 'Policy Direction for Small and Medium Enterprises', Small and Medium-sized Business Administration, <www.smba.go.kr>.

Government of the Republic of Korea (1998e), 'Status of Small and Medium Enterprises', Small and Medium-sized Business Administration, <www.smba.go.kr>.

Government of the Republic of Korea (1998f), 'The New Foreign Direct Investment Regime', Small and Medium-sized Business Administration, <www.smba.go.kr>.

Government of the Republic of Korea (1998g), *Maximizing the Benefits of Electronic Commerce: Korea's Initiatives*, OECD Working paper DSTI/ICCP(98)15/PAR2/REV1.

Government of the Republic of Korea (1998h), *SMEs and Electronic Commerce* (1998), OECD Working Paper DSTI/IND/PME(98)18/REV1.

Government of the Republic of Korea (1998i), 'What Is KOTRA?', Korea Trade Promotion Corporation, <www.kotra.or.kr>.

Government of the Republic of Korea (2000a), 'Bizsens.com, Inc. has launched Korea's first and only B2B Business Services Marketplace for SMEs', Ministry of Finance and Economy, 16 October, <www.mofe.go.kr>.

Government of the Republic of Korea (2000b), 'Korea Economic Update', Special Edition: Economic Policy Directives for 2000, Ministry of Finance and Economy, 24 January, <www.mofe.go.kr>.

Government of the Republic of Korea (2000c), 'Korea Economic Update', Ministry of Finance and Economy, 20 April, <www.mofe.go.kr>.

Government of the Republic of Korea (2000d), 'Korea Economic Update', Special Issue: First-Half Economic Achievements of 'the Kim Dae-jung Administration', Ministry of Finance and Economy, 19 September, <www.mofe.go.kr>.

Kwack, S.Y. (1999), 'Korea's Financial Crisis: Causes and Restructuring Tasks', *Multinational Business Review* (Fall): 55–9.

Lee, M.J. and S.C. Chung (1997), 'Globalisation of Industrial Research and Development: The Korean Experience', OECD Working Paper DSTI/STP/TIP(97)14/FINAL.

Park, H.J. (2000), 'Modernization, Competitiveness, and the Politics of Small Business in Korea', unpublished manuscript.

Park, S.H. (1999), 'The Impact of the Korean Financial Crisis on SMEs: A Case Study of Korea', working paper.

10   Government Policies and Programs for SMEs in Taiwan

Matt Ngui

10.1   INTRODUCTION

Taiwan, the 'Silicon Island' as it is promoting itself to be, has a population of 21.7 million ethnic Chinese. It has been admired for its stable economic development and the resilience of its SMEs in the 1980s and 1990s, and their ability to withstand the financial crisis of 1997–98. In 1998 Taiwan recorded a 4.8 per cent economic growth rate compared to Japan with –2.9 per cent, South Korea, –5.8 per cent, Malaysia, –7.5 per cent and Singapore, 1.5 per cent. In 1999 most of the East Asian and Southeast Asian economies, with the exception of Indonesia, managed to record positive economic growth rates. In 2000 Taiwan posted a 6.7 per cent growth rate, second only to the People's Republic of China (PRC) which recorded a 6.9 per cent growth rate (APEC 1999). This stable economic performance is the result of a combination of economic, cultural, entrepreneurial and government intervention to sustain economic growth, and especially that of SMEs. The steady growth of SMEs has been one of the distinctive characteristics of Taiwan's economy. However, in 2001 the new Premier of the Republic of China, Taiwan admitted that 'the global economy is encountering a slowdown; as an export-oriented economy, Taiwan is therefore affected'.[1] The government of Taiwan then proceeded to announce an Eight Point Program to regenerate the economy,[2] with the role of SMEs remaining critical for economic sustainability.

There are a number of intriguing questions in relation to Taiwan's SMEs. How did they weather the 1997 financial crisis? What policies and programs were in place to cushion the SMEs against the adverse impact of the crisis? Will Taiwan continue its dynamic growth, led by SMEs, into the next decade?

In an attempt to partially understand Taiwan's economic success this chapter aims to explore the public policy background behind the country's robust and resilient SME sector, and proceeds as follows. Section 10.2 clarifies the definition of an SME in the Taiwan context, while Section 10.3 identifies the size of the sector, its distribution across industries, its contribution to employment, sales and export values, its primary organisational form and geographical location. Section 10.4 provides a historical overview of the major long- and short-term policies and programs to support the sustained growth of SMEs. The reliance on government documents means that the overview of SMEs in Taiwan has certain limitations, particularly in painting a rosy picture of public policies and programs for business. Section 10.5 discusses the impact of and response to the financial crisis. Section 10.6 discusses new policy initiatives of the Taiwan government to attain full recovery from the crisis. Section 10.7 discusses some of the key features of Taiwan's SMEs. Section 10.8 looks at initiatives in the area of information technology and electronic commerce to maintain the efficiency and the competitive edge of the country's SMEs. Section 10.9 discusses how Taiwan manages its human resource shortages to maintain its relatively high economic growth rate. Finally, Section 10.10 presents a summary of the major conclusions from this chapter.

10.2 SME DEFINITION IN TAIWAN

What is an SME? A large variety of definitions exist where the country in which an SME operates establishes the relevant criterion. It may have a lot to do with what benefits were intended for SMEs such as in the form of grants, subsidies and loans made available by government. Typically, an SME is defined according to three major criteria, assets, persons employed and volume of sales. Regardless of definitions or country of origin, SMEs constitute, in terms of absolute numbers, the most significant form of business in any economy. For instance, Hall (1995) estimated that 40 million or so SMEs exist in the 21 economies of the Asia–Pacific Economic Cooperation (APEC) Forum region. No universal or definitive data exists for comparing SMEs across economies. SMEs can only be explained within the economic and cultural contexts in which they survive and grow.

In Taiwan, the current definition of an SME in the mining, quarrying, manufacturing, and construction industries is an enterprise with fewer than 200 employees and less than NT\$60 million of invested capital. In the service and other industries, an SME is a business with fewer than 50 employees and less than NT\$80 million of sales volume (MOEA 2000, p. 276).

In spite of the differing definitions of SMEs across countries it is still possible, with qualifications, to compare features of the small business sector in selected countries such as Japan, the USA, the UK and South Korea, as shown in Table 10.1.

Table 10.1 shows that Taiwan's SMEs are performing well in comparison to those of Japan and South Korea using these broad indicators. The USA remains the most robust economy in terms of the growth of SMEs, but beyond general statements it is difficult to make definitive statements about the comparative performance of SME 'well-being'. However, the significance and role of SMEs in the Taiwanese economy continues to represent a model of economic development for its regional neighbours.

Table 10.1
A Comparison of SMEs in Taiwan, Japan, USA, UK and South Korea

Features	Taiwan ('99)	Japan ('99)	USA ('98)	UK ('99)	South Korea ('97)
No. of non-agricultural SMEs (million)	1.048	5.089	24.8	3.49	2.67
% of non-agricultural enterprises	97.7	99.7 (1996)	99.7	99.8	99.1
% of total non-agricultural employees (all sectors)	76.39	72.7	53	54.4	77.4
SMEs % of total sales	28.95	42.5	47	51	46.3 (manuf.)
SMEs % of total value added	47.58 (1996)	56.6	51		46.5 (manuf.)
SMEs % of total exports	21.11	7.3 (ind. 1996)	29.5 (1992)	·	42 (manuf.)
% of new SMEs	7.34 (1999)	3.7 (1994–96)	14 (1994)	13 (1988–94)	na
% SMEs ceasing operations	5.03 (1999)	3.8 (1994–96)	11.8 (1994)	13 (1988–94)	na
Long-term trend	No. of new SMEs consistently higher than those ceasing business	From 1989 no. of new SMEs are lower than those ceasing business	No. of new SMEs consistently higher than those ceasing business	1988–94 no. of new SMEs very close to those ceasing business	na

Notes:
1. The definition of an SME in the USA is any firm employing 500 or fewer people.
2. The definition of an SME in Japan is any firm employing 300 or fewer people.
3. In Taiwan the definition is based on capitalisation of under NT$60 million or employing fewer than 200 people for manufacturing, construction and mining.
4. For the UK an SME is a firm employing not more than 250 people.
5. In South Korea an SME is a firm employing fewer than 300 people and with less than US$60 million in assets.
6. na = not available.

Source: MOEA (2000, p. 51).

Taiwan's SMEs can be argued to possess the following characteristics: they have a high orientation towards exports; they have a high degree of adaptability, they possess strong teamwork spirit; and they have the ability to reduce risks effectively and rapidly. The Taiwanese government argues that these characteristics have provided the platform for a business culture on which stable economic growth can be developed to withstand volatile changes in the international or regional economy (MOEA 2000). One such dramatic development was the financial crisis of 1997–98 that impacted on SMEs in the Asia–Pacific region.

10.3   SIZE, SCOPE AND POLICY BACKGROUND OF SMES IN TAIWAN – AN OVERVIEW

To fully appreciate the magnitude and depth of SMEs in Taiwan, it is necessary to describe and analyse this sector qualitatively and quantitatively.

10.3.1   Size of the SME Sector

Table 10.2 shows that the total number of enterprises and total number of SMEs increased steadily over the 1995–99 period, with the share of SMEs remaining fairly constant at above 97 per cent of all enterprises. In 1999 Taiwan had a total of 1 085 430 enterprises of which 1 060 738 were SMEs, or 97.73 per cent of the total number of enterprises.

Table 10.2
Number and Share of SMEs, 1995–99

Year	All enterprises ('000)	Larger enterprises ('000)	SMEs ('000)	SME share % of all enterprises
1995	1 012	21	992	97.96
1996	1 020	17	1 003	97.94
1997	1 043	23	1 020	97.81
1998	1 069	24	1 045	97.76
1999	1 085	25	1 061	97.73

Source: Adapted from MOEA (2000, p. 28).

10.3.2   Distribution of SMEs by Industry

Table 10.3 shows the distribution of SMEs in Taiwan over the 1995 to 1999 period. The number of enterprises increased annually in the commercial, social and personal services and construction industries. Manufacturing SMEs, however, experienced a decrease in the absolute number of enterprises from 154 400 in 1995 to 142 700 in 1999. The largest component of SMEs are those in the commercial sector. In 1999 SMEs in the commercial industry numbered 642 200, followed by manufacturing industry with 142 700, then the social and personal services industry with 88 300, and finally the construction industry which had 74 300 SMEs.

Table 10.3
Distribution of SMEs by Industry in Taiwan

Year	Commercial ('000)	Manufacturing ('000)	Social and personal services ('000)	Construction ('000)
1995	585.4	154.4	84.0	62.9
1996	598.3	150.8	83.8	64.9
1997	615.5	147.5	83.1	66.6
1998	632.4	145.3	85.4	71.0
1999	642.2	142.7	88.3	74.3

Source: Adapted from MOEA (2000, p. 29).

10.3.3   Employment

In 1995 Taiwanese SMEs employed a total of 7.2 million persons rising marginally to 7.3 million in 1999. As Table 10.4 indicates, there was a steady increase in the number of people employed in all businesses in Taiwan. SMEs and large firms both recorded increased numbers of people employed. Interestingly, although the total number of employees in SMEs increased from 1995 to 1999 the percentage of total employed in all enterprises decreased marginally from 79.74 per cent in 1995 to 78.25 per cent in 1999. The total number of persons employed by all firms being less than the sum of persons employed by SMEs and large firms could be explained by the small percentage of micro firms, or subsistence or home-based enterprises, which employ the single owner who is also the worker and manager.

Table 10.4
Persons Employed by SMEs, 1995–99

Year	All firms ('000)	SMEs ('000)	SME share of all firm employment	Large firms ('000)
1995	9 045	7 213	79.7	829
1996	9 068	7 131	78.6	910
1997	9 176	7 197	78.4	956
1998	9 289	7 265	78.2	1 049
1999	9 385	7 344	78.3	1 080

Source: MOEA (2000, p. 38).

10.3.4   Sales

Table 10.5 shows that SMEs generated a total of NT$6.84 trillion or 35.97 per cent of total sales revenue generated by all enterprises in 1995. While total sales revenue increased further to NT$6.91 trillion by 1999, this represented a decline in the SMEs' share of total sales to 28.95 per cent. This decreasing trend in SME sales share of total sales has prompted both the business sector and the government to consider means whereby the SME sector can be restructured to improve its performance. The total values of sales by all enterprises, both large and SMEs, in Taiwan continued to increase from 1995 to 1999. It is worthy of note that this occurred despite the dramatic slowdown in regional economic growth during the period of the financial and economic crisis of 1997–98.

Table 10.5
Total Sales of SMEs, 1995–99 (trillion NT$)

Year	All enterprises	Large enterprises	SMEs	SME share of total sales (%)
1995	19.02	12.18	6.84	36.0
1996	19.60	12.88	6.72	34.3
1997	21.38	14.52	6.86	32.1
1998	22.75	15.85	6.91	30.4
1999	23.85	16.95	6.91	29.0

Source: Adapted from MOEA (2000, p. 43).

10.3.5 Exports

Table 10.6 shows that the total value of SME exports decreased from NT$1.25 trillion in 1997 to NT$1.20 trillion in 1999, and the percentage of total enterprise exports accounted for by SMEs similarly decreased from 26.4 per cent in 1995 to 21.1 per cent in 1999.

Between 1995 and 1999 the performance of Taiwan's business enterprises as indicated by the number of persons employed, volume of sales and value of exports is impressive, although these indicators suggest a deterioration in the relative performance of SMEs. Over the period of the financial and economic crisis the deterioration has been most noticeable in terms of share of sales revenue and, in particular, exports. A number of international, regional and local reasons have contributed to the downward trend in export value share by SMEs in Taiwan. The financial crisis of 1997–98 is clearly one of the major factors suggesting that SMEs were relatively more adversely affected, and this may have been exacerbated by increased competition in computing manufacturing and peripherals.

Table 10.6
Value of Exports by SMEs, 1995–99 (trillion NT$)

Year	All enterprises	Large enterprises	SMEs	SME share of total sales (%)
1997	4.74	3.49	1.25	26.4
1998	5.18	3.95	1.23	23.7
1999	5.68	4.48	1.20	21.1

Source: Adapted from MOEA (2000, p. 46).

10.3.6 The Organisational Forms of SMEs

As shown in Table 10.7, in Taiwan, the predominant business organisational form of SMEs is the sole proprietorship. This is particularly the case for commercial and manufacturing SMEs. In 1999, 63.8 per cent of total SMEs, or 409 827 enterprises, were sole proprietorships, followed by 28.0 per cent, or 179 507 enterprises, of limited corporation or limited company and finally, 6.4 per cent, or 40 985 enterprises, were share limited corporations or publicly listed companies. The predominance of the sole proprietorship form of ownership implies that owners of SMEs in Taiwan possess tremendous financial and production flexibility in response to changing market conditions and demands. But it also puts intense pressure on such owners in terms of the failure or otherwise of the enterprise, and could restrict the ability of the enterprise to expand due to limitations in access to credit by the sole owner.

Table 10.7
Organisational Forms of SMEs in Taiwan (%)

Year	Sole proprietorship	Limited corporation	Share limited corporation
1997	62.8	29.1	6.6
1998	63.1	28.7	6.5
1999	63.8	6.5	6.4

Source: MOEA (2000, p. 35).

10.3.7   Geographical Location and Sectors of SMEs

The geographical location of SMEs follows the major concentrations of population in Taiwan. These are in Taipei City, Taipei County, Taichung County, Kaohsiung City, Taoyuan County and so on. Table 10.8 shows that in 1999 Taipei City had 190 000 SMEs compared to 189 600 in 1998 and 188 100 in 1997 (MOEA 2000). In addition, in Taiwan, the three major SME sectors are commercial (69.6 per cent), business services, (8 per cent) and social and personal services (6.6 per cent). In Kaohsiung City, South of Taiwan, the commercial sector constituted 62.7 per cent, social and personal services, 8.5 per cent and construction, 8.2 per cent. The same proportion of sectors in Taiwanese SMEs is reflected in Taoyuan, Taichung and Taipei counties. While the same pattern of SMEs is found across Taiwan there is a degree of specialisation in each location. For instance, Taipei City is where the computing industry predominates and in the South, Kaoshiung City is predominantly heavy industry and construction (MOEA 2000). While the majority of SMEs in Taiwan are in the commercial sector, followed by business services, social and personal services and construction, there is, therefore, diversity in local specialisation.

Table 10.8
Geographical Location of SMEs in Taiwan, 1997–98 ('000 enterprises)

Year	Taipei City	Taipei County	Kaoshiung City	Taichung City	Taoyuan County	Taichung City
1999	190.0	156.6	79.9	72.7	68.5	60.3
1998	189.6	154.9	78.3	71.6	65.6	58.4
1997	188.1	151.5	66.7	69.2	62.2	58.4

Source: Adapted from the MOEA (2000, p. 30).

This brief overview of the contribution of SMEs to the Taiwanese economy indicates their significance in terms of employment, sales, and exports. However, to fully appreciate the impressive development of SMEs in Taiwan, it is essential to trace, from a historical perspective, the context in which certain policies were implemented in response to internal and external economic conditions.

10.4   POLICY CONTEXT

In 1945 Taiwan's economy was based substantially on agricultural production, and characterised by having low wages, abundant cheap labour and a handful of SMEs. In the space of 50 years, Taiwan has developed its industrial and commercial sectors to the extent that its people now enjoy a high standard of living, education, health and prosperity. Taiwan is now a global manufacturer of computer motherboards, sewing machines, bicycles, surveillance equipment, scanners, machinery, computers and circuit boards, to name but a few products.

The sustainable development of Taiwan's economy and the SME sector was the result of a combination of government policy, programs and financial support. Taiwan 'kick-started' its economy with a series of infrastructure reforms such as 'Land to the Tiller', the 'Four Year Economic Reconstruction Plan' in 1953, 'Compulsory Education' in 1968 and 'Ten Major Infrastructure Projects' in 1973. These initiatives cumulatively generated a favourable environment for the growth of the economy and SMEs, assisted by a stable political and economic environment. Unemployment remained relatively low, as did wages and business establishment costs in the 1960s, 1970s and 1980s (MOEA 1999a, p. 5).

Political stability in Taiwan was accompanied by industrial development built on a family-business culture. Initially, in the 1950s, SMEs in Taiwan focused upon the food, clothing and shelter industries. In the 1970s and 1980s, the direct and substantial intervention strategy of government with the objective of expanding the export of Taiwanese products, resulted in a rapid growth of SMEs. This trend matured into an SME production network characterised by flexibility, rapid response to changed market conditions and efficiency. In addition, one of the most unique features of SME development in Taiwan is an SME network built on family ties, friendship and cooperatives, which combined to meet the social and financial gaps critical to SME growth. This business diaspora is not a uniquely Taiwanese phenomenon but a natural development in many Chinese, Italian, Greek, Arab, English, Canadian and American cultures. However, the Chinese and Taiwanese (who are ethnically Chinese) and many other cultures, possess the enduring value that owning one's own business is an important measure of independence and wealth. This, coupled with a tendency to be thrifty and to have a 'love' of working long hours and to possess considerable financial acumen, all contributed to a spectacular growth of SMEs in Taiwan.

Taiwan's Ministry of Economic Affairs, SME Administration, identified eight distinctive periods of SME development, as shown in Table 10.9.

- *1945–48* After the occupation of the island of Formosa, small private family enterprises dominated the economy with most firms employing an average of 4.4 persons.

- *1949–52* The government invested a large volume of human resources into the construction of power and transportation industries, with factories employing an average of 13.3 persons.

- *1953–60* An import substitution policy was implemented aimed at developing labour-intensive light-manufactured industries. Priority was also given towards increasing exports, coupled with agricultural reforms, the encouragement of investment and expanded loans to SMEs.

- *1961–70* Emphasis on export expansion in plastics, textiles, glass, cement, plywood and heavy industries, steel, machinery and shipbuilding. The manufacturing sector grew by 17 per cent and SMEs grew phenomenally during this period.

- *1971–80* Development of capital intensive industries, raw material import substitution, the global oil crisis in 1973 and 1979 had a severe impact on export-oriented SME; the focus of SMEs changed to computers and peripherals.

- *1981–87* A trade deficit with the USA, Taiwan's major export market, led to a relaxation of foreign exchange controls in 1987.

Table 10.9
Development of Taiwan's Economic Policies Towards SMEs

Period	SME development
1945–48	Small private family firms
1949–52	Government human resource investment, heavy industries
1953–60	Import substitution, focus on light industries
1961–70	Export expansion – SME take-off
1971–80	Capital intensive, SME refocused on computers
1981–87	Foreign exchange control introduced
1988–96	Cost escalation, SMEs restructure and upgrade
1997–present	SMEs restructure to meet new challenges, e-commerce

Source: Data abstracted from MOEA (1999a).

• *1988–96* Although the total number of SMEs grew, increased land costs, wages and labour shortages, the environmental impact of industrial growth as well as international competition forced the restructure and upgrade of SMEs.

• *1997 to present* Growth and further development of SMEs with new challenges emerging (MOEA 1999a, p. 8).

The eight periods of growth of SMEs paralleled the development of the Taiwanese government's establishment of its administrative and management arm. The government of Taiwan had the vision to provide loans and working capital for SMEs as far back as 1966. The International Economic Cooperation Commission of the Taiwanese government, Executive Yuan (Cabinet), created an 'SME Working Group' to develop these ideas further (MOEA 1999a, p. 2). Two years later an 'SME Guidance Office', with a strong small business advisory focus, was established to conduct, among other services, surveys and investigations of domestic and international strategies of developing sustainable SMEs and the promotion of technology, management, financing and cooperative organisations.

By 1970 the Ministry of Economic Affairs' Industrial Development Bureau refined its strategy for SMEs by establishing a 'Joint Service Centre' performing all the functions of the 'Guidance Office' but with the added strength of an SME Bank and Credit Guarantee Fund. The banking and credit service is critical to the survival and growth of micro businesses. This early support of SMEs in the 1970s continued during the next decade with the establishment of an ' SME Administration' whose functions were stipulated by an Act of Parliament proclaimed on 28 November 1984 (MOEA 1999a).

The statutory support of the functions of the SME Administration continued with a new statute of SME Development proclaimed in February 1994, spelling out the 'standards', utilisation and safe-keeping of its funds and continuing its 'guidance and methods' system in Taiwan's SMEs. Here, one notes the language and principles of 'quality' management introduced into the statutes. Further government development of SMEs continued with the creation of an SME Policy Committee in 1995. In the same year, for manufacturing sector SMEs, the government raised its capital from NT$40 million to NT$60 million. Similarly, in the commerce and service sectors, the capital available for assistance was doubled to NT$80.

To enshrine the functions and assistance to SMEs in Taiwan, the Small and Medium Enterprises Administration (SMEA) was included in an amendment to the Constitution in 1997. It charged the SMEA to provide 'guidance' and evaluation, surveys, training, finance and management improvement of SMEs in Taiwan (MOEA 1999a, p. 3).

10.5   IMPACT OF, AND RESPONSE TO, THE FINANCIAL AND ECONOMIC CRISIS, 1997–98

10.5.1   Financial Crisis

In an insightful analysis of the 1997 financial crisis, Delhaise (1998) encapsulated the implosion in the following words:

> The economic, financial and political turmoil that struck Asia in mid 1997 represents both a crisis and panic. The crisis was one of fundamentals. It is a growth crisis. At its core were antiquated financial systems that relied exclusively on commercial banks to provide capital for economic expansion. These institutions were very highly leveraged and poorly regulated for the most part, could no longer support the high growth that most of the region had sustained for nearly two decades. Everything else was panic: the currency crisis, the debt crisis, the social crisis and even the political crisis are but a string of consequences following from the main source. (Delhaise 1998, p. 21)

Delhaise was not referring to Taiwan specifically when he wrote these words. Rather, the 1997 financial crisis highlighted structural weaknesses such as under-regulation of the financial sector and weak corporate governance among a number of regional economies. These were major issues for the economies of Thailand, Indonesia, the Philippines and South Korea, which were most adversely affected by the crisis. For those less affected by the crisis, such as Taiwan, it nevertheless stimulated a critical examination of existing domestic business and financial strategies.

The financial crisis in East Asia commenced with the collapse of the Thai baht in July 1997 followed by an unprecedented collapse of currencies for a number of regional economies including that of Indonesia, Malaysia, the Philippines and eventually South Korea. Indonesia continues to struggle in its recovery from the regional crisis and its currency remains relatively weak. Some commentators predicted the end of the 'Asian miracle'. Others, like APEC, have claimed that from the second half of 1999 recovery has been in sight, although the financial shortcomings highlighted by the crisis remain to be remedied in many countries (APEC 1999).

10.5.2   General Economic Impact on Taiwan

Since 1998 most of the economies of East and Southeast Asia, and indeed the rest of the developing nations, have registered a lower rate of economic growth. All the major East and Southeast Asian economies registered negative growth rates as shown in Table 10.10, with the exception of China, Singapore and Taiwan. Taiwan's growth rate fell from 6.8 per cent in 1997 to a still respectable 4.8 per cent in 1998. This is a respectable rate of growth when compared to Indonesia, which experienced a decline in its economic growth rate from 4.9 per cent in 1997, to –13.7 per cent in 1998 and Thailand, from –1.3 per cent to – 9.4 per cent. Malaysia recorded a negative growth rate of –7.5 per cent in 1998, and South Korea's growth rate fell from 5 per cent to –5.8 per cent during the 1997–1998 period. Indonesia was the only country that recorded a negative growth rate in 1999. By 2000, all the East Asian economies included in Table 10.10 recorded positive economic growth rates once again.

Extensive academic and public discussions, analysis and comments followed the 1997 crisis (see, for example, Corsetti et al. 1998; Dornbusch 1998; Fischer 1998; Krugman 1998a, 1998b; and Radelet and Sachs 1998a, 1998b). Some responses consisted of reactions, while others were more serious in attempting to understand the underlying causes of the foreign currency crisis. While each contribution recognised weaknesses in economic fundamentals in these countries as being an important contributory factor behind the crises, a key issue, however, was whether these problems added up to the magnitude of the crisis to afflict the regional economies in late 1997 and 1998. Radelet and Sachs (1998a, 1998b, 1999) argued that these problems were not severe enough to warrant a complete collapse of the currencies in the region, a total breakdown of the banking system, and the depth and severity of the economic contraction. Instead they argued that the crisis was mainly the result of a self-fulfilling panic by investors. These economies experienced a surge in capital inflows to finance non-productive investments in the early to mid-1990s that made them vulnerable to a financial panic and a rapid withdrawal of capital. The panic and inadequate policy responses triggered a region-wide withdrawal of capital and financial crisis and subsequent economic disruption.

Table 10.10
Economic Growth Rates for Selected Asian Economies, 1998–2000 (%)

Country	1998	1999	2000
Taiwan ROC	4.8	5.3	6.7
PRC	7.8	7.3	6.9
Japan	–2.9	0.6	1.9
South Korea	–5.8	9.0	5.9
Singapore	1.5	4.9	5.9
Thailand	–9.4	3.7	4.2
Malaysia	–7.5	4.9	5.8
Philippines	-0.5	3.2	4.7
Indonesia	–13.7	–1.1	3.2

Source: MOEA (2000, p. 3: Table 1–1–1, quoting WEFA Group, *Asia Executive Summary*, First Quarter, 2000).

Others argued that a build-up of pressure from country-specific problems, in particular a serious weakness in financial systems, corporate governance, and poor economic policies in the region, led to the crisis (Corsetti et al. 1998; Dornbusch 1998; Krugman 1998a, 1998b),[3] as well as the International Monetary Fund (IMF). Financial weaknesses were generated largely by the lack of incentives for effective risk management (Moreno et al. 1998). The weaknesses of the financial sector were blanketed by rapid growth and accentuated by large capital inflows, partly encouraged by pegged exchange rates.

While these two views are not mutually exclusive, they suggest a quite different policy emphasis specifically in the wake of such a crisis. While both viewpoints would see a need to improve economic fundamentals over the medium to long run, policy emphasis during the period of the financial and economic crisis would be different. The panic viewpoint would emphasise the need to restore investor confidence such as by agreeing to a rollover of international short-term debt. Reforms in the economic structure or in financial sector policy could take place later. If, however, weaknesses in the financial and corporate sector were important contributors to the crisis, reforms needed to be conducted as quickly as possible.

A key ingredient for the recovery of many of the East Asian economies has been a restructuring of their corporate sectors, including that of promoting the growth and development of SMEs. The sustained growth and robust structure of the Taiwanese economy during the period of the crisis, and particularly that of its SMEs, has been nourished and stimulated by the business policies and programs of the government of the day. What then are the business policies and strategies of the Taiwan government in regard to its SMEs?

10.6   TAIWAN'S STRATEGIC POLICIES FOR SMES

10.6.1   Current Situation

Taiwan has an impressive set of policies, programs and funding available to assist in the growth and development of its SMEs. Almost 35 years of sustained support and assistance, aided by the business culture of the Taiwanese, has built strong networks and relationships both internally and externally, to the extent that collectively the SME sector could withstand the vicissitudes of both domestic and international markets.

The current development and growth of SMEs in Taiwan continues to be supported by an integrated set of SME policies, programs, structures and capital. SME policy in Taiwan, according to the Ministry of Economic Affairs, is based on the principles of maintaining fair and reasonable competition, assisting with obtaining relevant information, training, finance, access to government tenders and human resource management. In addition, these programs encourage mutual cooperation between firms through collaborative projects and 'fostering' independence and encouraging the growth of small- and medium-sized firms (MOEA 1999a, p. 16).

Specific current programs to support, encourage and assist SMEs in Taiwan include:

- development funds to provide guarantees and project financing for potential SMEs;

- establishment of an SME policy Deliberation Committee to integrate the diversity of the guidance systems and networks for SMEs;

- ten guidance (advisory) systems (finance and credit systems, management guidance systems, production technology, research and development, information management system, industrial safety, pollution control, marketing, mutual support, quality enhancement); and

- establishment of service network centres for guidance and service across the Island of Taiwan.

Another major element in the strength of the Taiwanese economy and its SMEs is trade with the People's Republic of China. The comparative advantage for Taiwanese SMEs in this regard relates to their geographical proximity, cultural and linguistic similarity, particularly with the Province of Fujian, and general ability to gain access to abundant raw materials and labour in China itself. The Taiwan Mainland Council estimated that in 1990 exports from Taiwan to China grew by 2.26 per cent, representing 4.2 per cent of Taiwan's foreign trade. Eight years on in 1998, Taiwan's exports to China grew by 14.87 per cent. This represented 11.2 per cent of Taiwan's foreign trade.

However, there is an interesting relationship in the trade between China and Taiwan. In a 1998 survey by the Statistics Department of Economic Affairs (MOEA 1999a, p. 9), out of a sample of 1264 companies 63 per cent had invested in China. But in 1997, Taiwanese-owned firms in China purchased 37 per cent of raw materials from Taiwan and 34.5 per cent locally in China. Of the 34.5 per cent, 17.3 per cent were purchased from Taiwanese firms in China and 17.2 per cent from non-Taiwanese firms in China. However, the percentage of raw materials bought from non-Taiwanese owned firms in China has increased. The trend towards Taiwanese firms in China buying more raw materials locally is continuing. In addition, China's reliance on exports by Taiwanese firms has also been decreasing. To what extent this is deliberate policy by both governments is an issue that requires further investigation.

The steady development of Taiwan's economic relationship with China represented a major anchor upon which the country was able to withstand the Asian financial and economic crisis. The impact of the crisis on China's domestic economy was comparatively small, although its foreign trade and exports, particularly to Asia, were severely affected.[4]

10.6.2   Economic Impact of the Crisis

The worst period of the crisis occurred during 1998. During this year, in June, Taiwan's currency was devalued by some 19 per cent relative to the US dollar, bringing it to NT$34 to US$1. Taiwan's foreign trade was also adversely affected – shown by a significant decrease of US$20 billion or approximately 20 per cent of total exports and imports for the whole year. Financial indicators, including fluctuations in the money supply (M1b), in bank deposits and in bank clearings and in the movement of the stock market price index indicated an economic downturn. The value and percentage of bad loans held by banks gradually increased and impacted upon the bankruptcy rate. Statistics from the Ministry of Finance's Taxation Data Centre indicate that a total of 25 763 businesses, 8.2 per cent of the total, ceased operations in 1998. However, in the commercial sector, the total number of new businesses increased as well as the volume of sales increased by 5.4 per cent (excluding restaurant and foreign trade industries). Arising from the increase in the number of business failures the total number of registered unemployed reached 269 000, an increase of 15 per cent over the same figure for 1997.

10.6.3   Short- to Medium-term Strategies

In response to the regional and domestic economic slowdown a number of initiatives by the government were implemented. The government actively promoted public construction projects with the objective of simultaneously stimulating private sector investment, particularly in the construction industry, and therefore domestic demand. The government also implemented measures with the objective of encouraging exports. Under the Global Export Promotion Plan an Export Sales Promotion Service Team, and a Service Team for Assisting Manufacturers to Implement Technology Upgrading was established. A Stock Market Stabilisation Team was established to review the operation of the stock market and to initiate reform and increase efficiency. The government established a team to assist companies with their financial needs in the short term. On the social front the government also implemented a program for Labour Insurance Unemployment Payments, which is equivalent to the unemployment benefits system operated in countries such as the USA, Canada or Australia.

10.6.4   Long-term Strategies

In terms of putting in place strategies to promote sustainable economic growth, two measures essential to the creation of a climate of growth and stability were focused upon. These were:

- strengthening the legal framework; and

- improving government efficiency as well as the implementation of measures to ensure that the economy remains competitive, by lowering costs and increasing productivity, in the face of further globalisation of the economy.

In relation to SMEs, specifically, some of the major initiatives taken by the government included the following:

- *Application of risk avoidance tools* Previous experience of economic crises demonstrated that interest rates and exchange rates both substantially influence the production, sales, cash flow and profits of SMEs. The effective use of risk avoidance strategies and methods were recommended for SMEs in order to reduce the impact of the financial crisis in 1997 and 1998.

- *Government's role in building strategic alliances* The Taiwanese government's realisation of the limitations faced by SMEs in terms of engaging in research and development and marketing, gave it an impetus to actively intervene in assisting firms to construct strategic alliances with international partners. Apart from pricing and cost advantages, technical and research edge increase the ability of SMEs to compete in the international market. This intervention by government has improved business opportunities for many internationally oriented SMEs.

- *New opportunities for government procurement* In May 1999 the government of Taiwan introduced legislation to allow government agencies to assist SMEs to tender for contracts. To encourage greater competition the government made a decision to announce all government contracts in excess of NT$10 million on the Internet.

10.6.5   Other International Developments Impacting on Taiwan's Business Strategies

Three major developments in the international trade arena are likely to influence the long-term strategic position of SMEs in Taiwan. These include:

- *Adjustment prior to membership of the World Trade Organisation* When China joins the World Trade Organisation (WTO) Taiwan expects to follow suit. However, it remains unclear whether it will do so as an independent member or as a Province of China. Irrespective of the status of Taiwan in the WTO its economy will be linked more closely to the international market. With this imminent development, SMEs in Taiwan have been encouraged to become more competitive by: reducing their production costs; increasing their product quality; upgrading their technology; and upgrading the quality of its human resources including restructuring their management to cope with the new global circumstances. While competition from international businesses in the domestic market will develop, cultural issues will need to be overcome by new entrants into Taiwan's market if they are to be successful.

- *Active participation in the Asia–Pacific Economic Cooperation (APEC) forum* Taiwan has taken an active part in the development of a wide range of policy forums in APEC, particularly in such working groups as the Economic

Committee, SME Policy, Human Resource Development, Industry, Science and Technology and Education to name a few. Through its active support of the APEC forum and its working groups, Taiwan has the ability to raise its profile in the international community, exchange ideas, policy and programs with fellow member economies.

- *Establishment of economic and monetary union in Europe* Western Europe, specifically the European Union (EU), is Taiwan's third largest trading partner. With the introduction of the euro, Taiwan expected an initial reduction in the value of its exchange rate relative to the new European currency that would increase business opportunities for Taiwanese SMEs in the EU and the rest of Europe. However, competition in the EU for some Taiwanese products from Eastern Europe where production costs are lower than Taiwan can be anticipated in the long run. To maintain their competitiveness Taiwanese firms selling in Europe need to improve their understanding, and fluency, with regard to the euro.

- *Potential devaluation of the renminbi* China remains one of the major countries in the region that has avoided a devaluation of its currency since the 1997 financial crisis. Consequently, at the current rate of exchange of the renminbi, China's exports are more costly in relation to those of other countries in the region. The growth of China's exports subsequently decreased substantially in spite of government measures to stimulate exports, although the country experienced a marked improvement in export growth in 2000 despite the overvalued currency as China switched towards markets in North America and Europe and away from Asia. If China was to devalue its currency at some point in the future this would have a beneficial impact upon Taiwanese-owned firms that are located in China. This would represent a further incentive for Taiwan's SMEs to establish production facilities on the mainland.

In addition to these strategic economic initiatives and international developments the Taiwanese economy, according to a recent APEC report on SMEs in Taiwan, has developed a number of strong features (APEC 1998). These include high specialisation in production processes, minimum efficiency size (MES) and agency and transaction costs structure that combined to cushion the adverse impact of the 1997 crisis.

However, it is necessary to note that these strategies to strengthen business development and growth in Taiwan were developed after decades of prudent and timely government commitment and public funding to sustain the continued growth of SMEs. A brief history of the context of SME policies and programs is useful in appreciating the development of government strategies for this important sector of business in Taiwan.

10.7   FEATURES OF SMES IN TAIWAN

10.7.1   Network-based Industrial System

Some of the successful Taiwanese SMEs adopted a production system where each firm specialises in a specific stage of production (APEC 1999, p. 29). This system has generated success in the face of competition from other countries such as Korea, China and India. For instance, in a comparative study of the footwear industry in Korea and Taiwan, Levy (Levy 1991, p. 154) observed that:

> The footwear industry in Chinese Taipei is organised via the subdivision among independent firms of the various processes of production. Some specialise in lasting (the assembly of uppers and soles); some in manufacturing of soles; some in the cutting of materials for footwear uppers; and some in stitching of uppers. It is rare for a footwear firm in Chinese Taipei to perform in-house more than at most two of the various sub-processes.

An APEC report compared this network-based industrial system method of production with the same development in the 1970s in California's Silicon Valley and the Boston Route 128, which attracted international acclaim as leading centres of innovation and in electronics (APEC 1999, p. 29). Saxenian (1994) attributed the success of the Silicon Valley development, particularly in electronics, autos and machine tools, to the extensive network of SME suppliers to which they are linked through ties of trust and partial ownership.

10.7.2   Minimum Efficiency Size (MES) and Entry Barriers

The size at which a firm no longer enjoys cost saving as it enlarges is said to be at its minimum efficiency size (MES). This is a point that is critical in determining the size distribution of firms within an industry. In a vertically integrated industry, as the APEC (1999, p. 30) report indicated, a newcomer would need to probably produce most of the intermediate goods as most other firms in the same industry would be reluctant in supplying these to the newcomer. In such a vertically integrated industry entry barriers and MES are relatively high. However, in a networked-based production system, such as in Taiwan, the MES and entry barriers for SMEs are low.

In addition, Hu (1999) applied Stigler's survival test (Boulding and Stigler 1970, pp. 527–61) to measure the MES and discovered that manufacturing SMEs in Taiwan since the 1970s passed the survival test. Other SMEs in the mining, quarrying and construction industries also achieved the same result (Schive 1999). According to Hu, this implied a low MES and entry barriers for SMEs in Taiwan.

10.7.3   Low Agency and Transaction Costs

In large or medium size firms the relationship between the principal, agent and manager are critical to the success of the business venture. However, as in any relationship, its content and shape are germane to the firm. Failure in the fragile relationships between the major roles and functions may generate a high agency cost. The advantage in a small firm, where the principal, agent and manager are often the same person, is the ability to overcome any relationship difficulties between the different roles. There is no cost in the liaison or coordination between the different roles, but the skills required by each may be different. There are also limitations in developing a long-term vision for the small firm if the same person has to attend to the daily grind of generating income. In addition, other costs such as searching for a suitable partner, training and orientation costs will be incurred as new relationships are developed in large or medium-sized firms.

In the case of Taiwan in the networked-based production system where agency costs and entry barriers are relatively low, the large size of its export industries helps to keep strategic transaction costs at relatively low levels through large volumes.

10.8   INFORMATION TECHNOLOGY AND ELECTRONIC COMMERCE

Taiwan is the second largest computer peripheral producer in the world. To maintain this position the government of Taiwan continues to nurture the growth of SMEs in the information technology (IT) sector. While it is impossible to ascertain the precise impact of the financial crisis on SMEs in this sector, it can be argued that the financial crisis of 1997–98 has heightened the awareness of government to upgrade and move SMEs into a higher level of productive capacity (MOEA 2000). This is a positive impact of the 1997/98 financial crisis on the development and growth of SMEs in Taiwan.

Government support for this sector was demonstrated by the introduction of a new program in 1999 entitled Industry Associations' E-Commerce Construction and Applications for SMEs. The aims of this program are designed to: assist 2 000 SMEs to establish data bases; expand this assistance to 100 000 SMEs in three years; introduce enterprise planning software; and encourage effective use of e-commerce by SMEs (MOEA 2000). In addition, the government is collaborating with an APEC forum project to promote transnational transactions entitled Global Information Network (GIN). This APEC network and Taiwan's participation in ECOTECH (economic and technical) committees are avenues to access multilateral collaboration and research and development experience from advanced economies to improve domestic levels of technology (MOEA 2000, p. 22).

But, what are the likely obstacles in introducing and encouraging the use of e-commerce or IT among SMEs in Taiwan? The Institute for Information Industry's Market Research Centre in Taiwan (MOEA 2000, p. 157) estimated that the size of the business-to-business (B2B) commercial information and service market in Taiwan in 1999 was approximately NT$1 billion. This figure is forecast to reach NT$8.66 billion by 2002 (MOEA 2000, p. 158).

The government believes that achieving enterprise competitiveness will be enhanced by the speed facilitated by e-commerce, which will allow better management information systems and perhaps control over finances, materials, transportation, inventory and human resource management. In the IT and electronics sector, Taiwan's main export industry, the introduction of e-commerce is perceived as essential to meeting the changing demands of production in the global market place. The trend towards a 'built-to-order' (BTO) model of production requires very close collaboration between manufacturers (local and international), consumers and component suppliers. The competition from China, Southeast Asia, and soon India, in lower cost production of computer parts has motivated the government to encourage SMEs to be combined manufacturing and service companies as a competitive advantage strategy. In addition, e-commerce will enhance the integration of suppliers with upstream and downstream plants and resources to meet the demand for SME products and services.

In the SME service sector the impact of e-commerce on distribution depends on four categories of firms:

1. those engaged in infrastructure for e-commerce, for example, telecommunications service firms, computer and computer-related service firms;

2. those firms which utilise electronic means of transmitting information, legal services, accounting, financial, marketing, travel and educational services;

3. those service firms such as postal services, express parcel delivery and transportation services; and

4. those firms which benefited from electronic data such as construction, environmental and other services.

The government has stated in official documents that it encourages SMEs to take care in assessing the viability of a product, in particular, to note the nature and reliability of the relationship between suppliers and distributors for online stores (MOEA 2000).

In spite of the encouragement by government to embrace e-commerce, a 1999 survey conducted by the Commerce Department of the Ministry of Economic Affairs of SMEs in fifteen industries revealed disappointing results as shown in Tables 10.11 and 10.12. Of the 416 responses, the survey revealed that medium-sized firms (39 per cent) were significantly more enthusiastic in introducing B2B e-commerce than small firms (24 per cent). However, 28 per cent of medium-sized firms indicated no plans to introduce B2B e-commerce and 33 per cent may do so in the next two years. In addition, 62 per cent of small firms indicated no plans to introduce B2B e-commerce and 14 per cent of small firms are planning to implement B2B e-commerce.

Table 10.11
Medium-sized SMEs' E-commerce Plans

Medium-sized SMEs	E-commerce plans
39%	Already introduced
28%	No plan or desire to introduce
17%	Plan to introduce in 1 year
16%	Plan to introduce in 1 or 2 years

Source: MOEA (2000, p. 169).

Table 10.12
Small SMEs' E-commerce Plans

Small SMEs	E -commerce plans
24%	Already introduced
62%	No plan or desire to introduce
8%	Plan to introduce in 1 year
6%	Plan to introduce in 1–2 years

Source: MOEA (2000, p. 169).

The obstacles to introducing e-commerce in Taiwan's SMEs are shown in Table 10.13. They are predominantly related to a lack of technical support, insufficient market information, transaction security and performance evaluation, and inadequate bandwidth and legal restrictions.

In addition to these factors affecting the introduction of e-commerce in SMEs in Taiwan, there were other concerns expressed by firms in the 1999 survey (see Table 10.14). These concerns include a lack of technical support, e-commerce resulted in a marginal increase in expected sales, and, for SMEs, e-commerce was an inappropriate mode of operation. While the intention of the government to introduce e-commerce may be admirable, SMEs remain sceptical about the benefits of this mode of operation that also requires a level of expenditure far beyond its initial benefits.

Although the 1997 financial crisis has had a positive impact on SMEs in the IT sector in Taiwan, the implementation of e-commerce remains a gradual process as owners and managers remain unconvinced of, particularly for small enterprises, the expected benefits of this mode of operation. At the margins it seems that e-commerce will enhance certain transactions and enable access to information, but the 'real' outcomes in terms of profits continue to be based on sound business strategy in the market be it local or international.

Table 10.13
Factors Inhibiting the Introduction of B2B E-commerce in SMEs (%)

Medium-sized firms	Small firms	Factors
24.4	18.8	Transaction security
14.9	12.5	Insufficient market information
15.6	16.7	Lack of technical support
11.8	18.8	Uncertain technical mechanism
7.5	6.3	Inadequate bandwidth
2.4	2.1	Legal restriction

Source: MOEA (2000), quoting data from the Industry for Information Industry, June 1999.

Table 10.14
Specific Issues Inhibiting the Introduction of B2B E-commerce by SMEs (%)

Medium enterprises	Small enterprises	Factors
1.7	0	Internal resistance to change
4.4	0	Difficult system integration
6.1	10.4	Small cost savings
6.1	6.3	Data leakage
10.5	14.6	Small sale increase
10.2	8.3	Low application need
12.5	11.5	No introduction strategy
12.2	14.6	Lack of technical support
12.5	6.3	Low up/downstream cooperation
15.9	14.6	Unsuitable operation mode

Source: MOEA (2000, p. 175), quoting data from the Institute for Information Industry, June 1999.

10.9   HUMAN RESOURCE DEVELOPMENT ISSUES AND NEEDS

Another major issue for the SME sector, highlighted and accentuated by the financial crisis of 1997, concerns future strategies for training and developing managers and operators of SMEs, particularly in the manufacturing sector where many business owners are facing intense competitive pressures and adverse developments. Hence the financial crisis, particularly in the SME sector, has re-emphasised the critical role of, and need for, human resource development.

According to the Manpower Statistics of Taiwan for 1999, SMEs experienced an increase in the numbers employed by 78 000 in comparison to 1998, and employed 7 344 000 persons representing 78.2 per cent of the total workforce. This workforce was concentrated in the 25–55 age group. The majority of SME owners were educated to senior vocational school, junior high school, or primary school levels, but higher qualified employees tended to be found in medium and large enterprises. The majority of employed persons in SMEs obtained their current positions through recommendations. Labour shortages were more pronounced in the large enterprises than in SMEs; 44.6 per cent of larger manufacturing enterprises experienced labour shortages in 1999, while only 41.8 per cent of manufacturing SMEs did so. SME labour shortages were mainly in assembly-line workers and machine operators, then research and development personnel, indicating that many SMEs are transforming their firms. Table 10.15 shows the occupational categories where skill shortages were reported in 1998 and 1999 for both large enterprises and SMEs. In addition to labour shortages other emerging problems developing for SMEs include: an ageing workforce; high employee turnover; increased pension contributions; rising wages and compensation; and rising health insurance cover costs (see Table 10.16).

Similar to many other countries with skill and occupational shortages in key industries, Taiwan has met this demand for skilled labour, in part, through the importation of skilled overseas workers from the Philippines, Pakistan, India and other Asian and Latin American countries (MOEA 1999b). The meeting of skill shortages in Taiwan from imported labour can be observed from Table 10.17.

Table 10.17 shows that just over 50 per cent of foreign workers in Taiwan are employed by SMEs, predominantly in the manufacturing and construction sectors. This is a massive importation of labour by international standards. The importation of foreign workers may present an issue for the government if unemployment of the domestic labour force rises, unless it trains local Taiwanese to take over the jobs performed by foreigners. However, the 'factory fodder' and low-status occupations presently occupied by foreigners are unattractive to young Taiwanese. The importation of skilled workers and professional people remains a political and policy issue for the government of Taiwan, but it is a situation not uncommon among countries with a high immigrant workforce to meet industrial demand for skilled labour and professional people.

Table 10.15
Percentage of Firms Experiencing Occupational Shortages
in 1998 and 1999, Taiwan

Firms	R&D personnel	Assembly line, machine operators	Production technology	Marketing	Computer software and hardware design
1998					
Total	38.16	44.49	31.63	22.09	22.60
Large firms	45.98	48.47	25.54	20.88	26.69
SMEs	34.23	42.50	33.17	22.69	19.04
1999					
Total	41.90	41.50	30.49	22.35	21.55
Large firms	54.18	41.01	28.10	22.03	28.86
SMEs	36.25	41.72	31.59	22.49	18.18

Source: Modified from the Bureau of Statistics, MOEA, Taiwan, *Survey of the Operational Status of Manufacturing Industry, 1998 and 1999*, p. 72, provided by the Department of Employment, Vocational Education and Training Administration, Council of Labor Affairs (EVTA), Republic of China, Taiwan 1999.

Table 10.16
Percentage of Firms Experiencing Human Resource Management Problems,
1998 and 1999, Taiwan

	Ageing workforce	High employee turnover	Increase in pension fund contribution	Rising wages	Heavy labour insurance and health insurance contribution
1998					
Total	22.84	22.63	21.69	35.42	27.70
Large firms	28.24	27.24	28.13	37.87	27.69
SMEs	20.74	20.82	19.18	34.46	27.71
1999					
Total	28.24	17.28	23.04	27.74	25.53
Large firms	30.70	22.13	26.61	30.43	23.06
SMEs	27.33	15.49	21.72	26.74	26.45

Source: Modified from the Bureau of Statistics, MOEA, Taiwan, *Survey of the Operational Status of Manufacturing Industry, 1998 and 1999*, p. 72, provided by the Department of Employment, Vocational Education and Training Administration, Council of Labor Affairs (EVTA), Republic of China, Taiwan 1999.

Table 10.17
Employment of Foreign Workers by Enterprises

Scale of firms	No. of foreign workers approved	Actual no. of foreign workers
1995		
SMEs	136 654 (53.94%)	100 704 (55.92%)
Large	116 671	79 373
1996		
SMEs	126 576 (51.22%)	115 605 (53.18%)
Large	120 561	101 787
1997		
SMEs	136 499 (50.76%)	108 989 (51.25%)
Large	132 425	103 674
1998		
SMEs	120 772 (45.69%)	118 561 (54.09%)
Large	142 547	113 444
1999		
SMEs	137 972 (53.51%)	118 561 (54.09%)
Large	119 893	100 620

Notes:
1. Includes only foreign labourers imported by manufacturing and construction firms.
2. SMEs are defined as firms with fewer than 200 employees.
3. Figures in parentheses are percentages of the total number of foreign employees.

Source: Modified from the Bureau of Statistics, MOEA, Taiwan, *Survey of the Operational Status of Manufacturing Industry, 1998 and 1999*, p. 72, provided by the Department of Employment, Vocational Education and Training Administration, Council of Labour Affairs (EVTA), Republic of China, Taiwan 1999.

10.10 SUMMARY AND CONCLUSIONS

This chapter has explored the history, scope and depth of support for the development and sustained growth of SMEs in Taiwan. It further demonstrated that the policies and programs initiated by the Taiwanese government have contributed to creating a robust SME sector, one which withstood the adverse impact of the 1997 financial crisis well. The long- and short-term strategies implemented by the government have meant that the crisis had a minimum negative impact on Taiwan's SMEs in 1997 and 1998. A slightly lower rate of growth of SMEs in relation to the total number of enterprises was recorded during 1997 and 1998 and 1999. But the number of SMEs continued to grow slightly during this period. Taiwan had 1 020 000 SMEs in 1997, 1 045 000 in 1998 and 1 061 000 in 1999. In addition, during 1997 and 1998, Taiwan recorded continued SME growth in the number of persons employed and total value of sales but a marginally lower value of exports, from NT$1.23 trillion to NT$1.20 trillion. However, on the other side of the equation the experience of SME owners and managers in Taiwan during the 1997–98 financial crisis has yet to be investigated.

Apart from the performance of SMEs in Taiwan during the financial crisis, other factors demonstrated the strength of the SME sector. More specifically the crisis highlighted the Taiwanese technique of a networked industrial production system, its integration into the economy of China, one of the largest markets in the world, and its business culture of low entry costs, low cost production, thrift and relatively low cost labour. Together, these factors and characteristics place Taiwanese SMEs in a commanding position to withstand any changes in the domestic and international economy.

The 1997–98 financial crisis also generated positive responses by the government towards the SME sector. In particular, the gradual reduction of output in the manufacturing sector, largely in computers, pushed the government to embark on a program to promote the use of e-commerce in all its enterprises, particularly SMEs, as a strategy to further improve the performance and competitiveness of its small-business sector. As the results of a recent survey show, however, SME owners and managers in Taiwan have yet to be convinced of the benefits of e-commerce in small enterprises.

In relation to the human resource development needs of Taiwan, in general terms, it continues to import labour from other South and Southeast Asian countries to meet its manufacturing sector shortages for semi-skilled and skilled workers. Over 50 per cent of Taiwan's human resource development requirements in selected manufacturing occupations are imported. To continue to meet the changing demand for labour at the lower end of skilled and semi-skilled workers, and at the higher end in terms of research and development professionals, Taiwan will continue to import foreigners. The sensitive political issue for the government is the reluctance of indigenous Taiwanese to take up semi-skilled or unskilled work in manufacturing, but the continued importation of workers will create resentment locally, particularly should the local unemployment rate increase. The issue of training and developing Taiwanese workers and graduates is a long-term proposition, one that may not meet the immediate demands of manufacturing industries for workers.

The prospects for SME growth in Taiwan are generally better than those in many economies in APEC, but it is still dependent to a large extent on the health of international trade and the economy. However, Taiwan's growing substantial business and manufacturing links with China will continue to expand in spite of the political sensitivities across the Straits of Taiwan. While political conditions and relationships with China are likely to remain volatile, the increasing economic relationship is likely to develop unabated. Increasing numbers of business persons in Taiwan look towards China as the way ahead for the country's sustained economic growth.[5]

The election of a new government in Taiwan in May 2000 may generate new policies for SMEs, but commentators consider the Chen government is unlikely to implement dramatic changes to business policies in the near future. Some commentators argued that when the new Chen government took over power in May 2000 it would more likely make changes in emphasis rather than in substantial business policy. However, as indicated at the outset, in February 2001 with signs of a global recession occurring that would affect Taiwan, the government announced minor adjustments to economic policy.

NOTES

1   *Taiwan News*, 20 February 2001, p. 1.
2   *The China Post*, 20 February 2001, p. 1.
3   Krugman later changed his point of view on the causes of the crisis. A more recent analysis (Krugman 1999) argues that such weaknesses within the Asian economies, such as corruption and moral hazard, cannot explain the depth and severity of the crisis. It should, instead, be blamed on financial panic and overly liberalised international and domestic financial systems.
4   See Chapter 1, p. 31.
5   See, for example, *The China Post*, 20 February 2001, p. 4.

REFERENCES

Asia–Pacific Economic Cooperation (APEC) (1998), Centre for Technology Exchange and Training for SMEs, <www.actetsme.org/taip/taip98.html>.
Asia–Pacific Economic Cooperation (APEC) (1999), *APEC Economies Beyond the Asian Crisis: A Progress Report by the APEC Economic Committee*, Singapore: APEC Secretariat.
Boulding, K.E. and G.J. Stigler (1970), *Readings in Price Theory*, London: American Economic Association Services, George Allen & Unwin.
Corsetti, G., P. Pesenti and N. Roubini (1998), 'What Caused the Asian Currency and Financial Crisis?', unpublished manuscript, available at <www.stern.nyu.edu/globalmacro/>.
Delhaise, P.F. (1998), *Asia in Crisis: The Implosion of the Banking and Financial Systems*, New York: J. Wiley.
Dornbusch, R. (1998), 'Asian Crisis Themes', mimeo, Massachusetts Institute of Technology (MIT), Cambridge, MA.

Fischer, S. (1998), 'The Asian Crisis: A View from the IMF', <www.imf.org/external/np/apd/asia/FISCHER.html>.

Hall, C. (1995), 'Investing in Intangibles: Improving the Effectiveness of Government SME Advisory Services in the APEC Region', paper delivered at an APEC Symposium on Human Resource Development for SMEs, 8–10 November, Chinese Taipei.

Hu, Ming-Wen (1999), 'The Evolution and Adaptability of SMEs: The Case of Taiwan', 1999 Industry Economics Conference, 12–13 July, Monash University, Melbourne, Australia.

Krugman, P. (1998a), 'Bubble, Boom, Crash: Theoretical Notes on Asia's Crisis', mimeo.

Krugman, P. (1998b), 'What Happened to Asia?', mimeo, MIT.

Krugman, P. (1998c), 'Fire Sale FDI', mimeo, MIT.

Krugman, P. (1999), 'The Return of Depression Economics', *Foreign Affairs*, **78** (1), January/February: 56–74.

Levy, B. (1991), 'Transaction Costs, the Size of Firms and Industrial Policy: Lessons from a Comparative Case Study of the Footwear Industry in Korea and Taiwan', *Journal of Development Economics*, **34**: 151–78.

Ministry of Economic Affairs (MOEA), 'Small and Medium Enterprises Administration', <www.moeasmea.gov.tw>.

Ministry of Economic Affairs (MOEA) (1999a), *White Paper on Small and Medium Enterprises in Taiwan 1999*, Taiwan: Small and Medium Enterprises Administration.

Ministry of Economic Affairs (MOEA) (1999b), *ROC's SMEs Ready for the Next Millennium*, Taiwan: Small and Medium Enterprises Administration.

Ministry of Economic Affairs (MOEA) (2000), *White Paper on Small and Medium Enterprises in Taiwan*, Taiwan: Small and Medium Enterprises Administration.

Moreno, R., G. Pasadella and E. Remolona (1998), *Asia's Financial Crisis: Lessons and Policy Responses, in Asia Responding to Crisis*, Tokyo: Asia Development Bank Institute. Also: Working Paper: PB 98:02, Centre for Pacific Basin Monetary and Economic Studies, Federal Reserve Bank of San Francisco.

Radelet, S. and J. Sachs (1998a), 'The East Asian Financial Crisis: Diagnosis, Remedies, Prospects', *Brookings Papers on Economic Activity*, (1): 1–74.

Radelet, S. and J. Sachs (1998b), 'The Onset of the East Asian Financial Crisis', mimeo, Harvard Institute for International Development, March.

Radelet, S. and J. Sachs (1999), 'What Have We Learned So Far, From the Asian Financial Crisis?', unpublished manuscript, <www.stern.nyu.edu/globalmacro>.

Saxenian, A. (1994), *Regional Advantage*, Cambridge, MA and London: Harvard University Press.

Schive, Chi (1999), *How Did SMEs in Taiwan Survive the Crisis*. 1999 Industry Economics Conference, Monash University, Melbourne Australia, 12–13 July.

11 Small and Medium Sized Enterprises in Australia

James Nguyen, Gary D. Gregory, Charles Harvie, Boon-Chye Lee and Matt Ngui

11.1 INTRODUCTION

During the period of the 1990s, SMEs have represented a dynamic force in national and international economies. As indicated in other chapters in this book, this is especially true for many of the East Asian countries, where they have played a vital role in economic development. Their importance as a means for achieving and sustaining economic growth remains unequivocal. SMEs contribute significantly to employment creation, gross domestic product (GDP), international trade, and commerce within the Asia–Pacific region. They contribute positively to economic development by promoting growth at both the micro and macro levels, and especially through their exporting activities. In the context of Australia, SMEs have played a similarly crucial role in the development of economic output and employment growth. Due to the sheer number of enterprises classified as small or medium, there is an increasing recognition by the Australian government that the nation's sustained economic growth will not only be dependent upon large business conglomerates but also upon SMEs. Therefore, the contribution of SMEs is critical in determining the future health of the Australian economy.

In particular, a key ingredient for the future success of the Australian economy, both at the national, regional and also local levels, will increasingly depend, because of the limited size of the domestic market, upon the ability of its domestic businesses to greatly expand their export capabilities. The sector with the greatest potential in this regard is the SME sector. Rapid advances in information technology have made access to established and emerging domestic and global markets a reality, providing enormous opportunities for small businesses in particular. Those SMEs that have the ability to innovatively: use the products and services made possible by the new technologies; develop new and more sophisticated products; and identify and adapt to changing global market opportunities, are likely to be the most successful in export markets. Australian SMEs have the potential to take advantage of niche markets for high-quality, high-tech products in particular.

This chapter will cover the contribution of SMEs towards the Australian economy, highlight the issues crucial to their development in the wake of the regional crisis, and identify their prospects within the new globalised economy. In doing so the chapter proceeds as follows. Section 11.2 clarifies the definition of an SME as utilised in Australia. Section 11.3 conducts an extensive overview of the macroeconomic contribution of the SME sector to the Australian economy. Section 11.4 analyses the impact of the Asian financial and economic crisis on Australian SMEs. Key issues affecting the current and future development of this sector are discussed in Section 11.5. Section 11.6 focuses upon key policy issues facing the government in its attempts to encourage the future development of SMEs. This section is of particular significance because, although the growth of SMEs is primarily shaped by their own operational decisions, the role of the government will remain important given that many SMEs are faced with resource constraints. Finally, Section 11.7 presents a summary of the major conclusions from this chapter as well as briefly discussing the future prospects of Australian SMEs.

11.2   DEFINITION OF AUSTRALIAN SMES

As discussed in Chapters 1 and 2 there is no international consensus on the definition of what constitutes an SME. SME definitions vary widely and depend on the phase of economic development as well as the prevailing social conditions within a nation. Various indexes are used to define SMEs, including the number of employees, the total amount of invested capital, assets, sales volume and production capability. The most commonly used index is the number of employees.

In 1999, the Australian Bureau of Statistics (ABS) conducted a review of the definition of an SME. It was recommended from the review that, for statistical purposes, firm-size classifications be based on full time equivalent (FTE) employment. The review also recommended that public companies, businesses that are in a parent or subsidiary relationship, and cooperatives and associations, should be excluded from the category of a small enterprise. The boundaries for enterprise classification, in accordance with the review by the ABS, are defined in Table 11.1.

Due to the fact that agricultural businesses often have large-scale operations that employ a large number of seasonal workers, but few permanent employees, the ABS developed a definition of agricultural small businesses that is not based on employment numbers. For statistical purposes, the ABS records a measure of the estimated value added of operations (EVAO) based on:

- the area of crops sown;

- the number of livestock; and

- crops produced and livestock turn-off (mainly sales) during the year.

A small agricultural business is defined as having an EVAO of between AU$20 000 and AU$399 000.[1] Businesses with an EVAO of less than AU$20 000 are excluded from ABS statistics because their contribution to commodity aggregates are generally insignificant.

For the purposes of this chapter an SME is defined in accordance with the definition used by the ABS. Most studies within Australia have employed this definition of an SME and the adoption of this definition will allow for greater comparative analysis of studies conducted on Australian SMEs.

Table 11.1
Enterprise Classification in Australia

Business classification	Definition
Non-employing business	Sole proprietorships and partnerships without employees
Micro business	Businesses employing fewer than five people, including non-employing businesses
Other small business	Businesses employing 5 or more people, but fewer than 20 people
Small business	Businesses employing fewer than 20 people
Medium business	Businesses employing 20 or more people, but fewer than 200 people
Large business	Businesses employing 200 or more people

Source: ABS 1999, 1321.0

11.3   OVERVIEW OF THE MACROECONOMIC CONTRIBUTION OF SMES

11.3.1   Profile of SMEs in Australia

There were an estimated 1 112 200 businesses and public sector organisations in operation in Australia during 1998–99. Private sector businesses totalled just over 1 107 000 and accounted for approximately 99.5 per cent of the total number of businesses. In 1998–99, there were approximately 989 900 non-agricultural private sector businesses operating in Australia, representing 89 per cent of total private sector businesses. From the 989 900 non-agricultural private sector businesses, just over 987 300, or 99.7 per cent of these businesses, were classified as either small or medium in 1998–99 (ABS 1999, 1321.0).

Distribution of small- and medium-sized enterprises by industry

In 1998–99 the services producing industries accounted for 75 per cent (743 100) of small- and medium-sized non-agricultural private sector businesses. Property and business services and retail trade accounted for the largest number of SMEs (199 900 and 155 100, respectively) in the services producing industry. During this period the goods producing industries accounted for 244 200 SMEs, or 25 per cent of small- and medium-sized non-agricultural private sector enterprises. Construction easily accounted for the largest number of small businesses in the goods producing industries (162 800).

As can be observed from Table 11.2 the highest proportion of SMEs within industries in Australia for the year 1998–99 was recorded in the construction and personal and other services industries, with 99.9 per cent of businesses in these two

Table 11.2
Number of SMEs by Industry, 1998–99

Industry type	Number of SMEs in the industry ('000)	SMEs as a % of the total number of enterprises in the industry
Mining	2.7	96.4
Manufacturing	79.2	99.1
Construction	162.8	99.9
Wholesale trade	62.1	99.7
Retail trade	155.1	99.7
Accommodation, cafes and restaurants	35.3	99.7
Transport and storage	57.6	99.8
Finance and insurance	19.4	99.0
Property and business services	199.9	99.8
Education	21.1	99.5
Health and community services	71.8	99.7
Cultural and recreational services	33.3	99.7
Personal and other services	75.0	99.9
Total	987.3	99.7

Source: ABS (1999, 1321.0). Figures are correct subject to rounding errors at source.

industries being classified as an SME. However, SME density within all industries was very significant, with the mining industry having the lowest proportion of SMEs at 96.4 per cent.

Recent trends

Between 1983–84 and 1998–99 the growth of all forms of SMEs outstripped the growth of large enterprises (see Figure 11.1). Growth was most pronounced at the micro-enterprise level (fewer than five employees), increasing by an average 4.8 per cent per annum. Between 1983–84 and 1998–99 the number of SMEs increased by 71.1 per cent, which is equivalent to an average increase of 3.7 per cent per annum. Over the same period the number of large businesses increased at an average annual rate of 2.7 per cent. This highlights the fact that SMEs are the main source of growth of enterprises, in terms of number, in Australia.

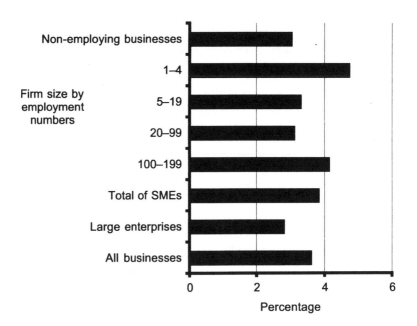

Source: ABS (1999, 1321.0).

Figure 11.1   Average Annual Growth of Businesses by Employment Size Group, 1983–84 to 1998–99 (%)

11.3.2 Employment

The estimated 1 112 200 businesses and public sector organisations in operation in Australia during 1998–99 employed 8 450 700 people. Private sector businesses employed an estimated 7 million people or 83 per cent of the total workforce. In 1998–99 the non-agricultural private sector businesses operating in Australia employed more than 6.7 million people or about 95 per cent of the total private sector workforce. From this the SMEs employed just over 4.9 million people or 73.8 per cent of the total non-agricultural private sector workforce. Just over 80 per cent of persons employed in a small or medium-size business were employees while the remaining 20 per cent were persons working in their own business, either as employers or as own account workers (ABS 1999, 1321.0).

Employment by industry

In 1998–99 the services-producing industries accounted for 77 per cent (or 3 774 300 persons) of SME employment in the non-agricultural private sector workforce. From Table 11.3 it can be observed that property and business services and retail trade accounted for the largest number of SME employment in the services-producing industry (809 600 persons employed in the property and business services industry and 807 700 persons employed in the retail trade industry). In the goods-producing industry the construction and manufacturing industries accounted for the largest number of SME employment (431 800 and 606 600 persons employed respectively).

Across industries the distribution of SME employment showed marked differences. For the goods producing industries the construction industry had 93.1 per cent of its employment through SMEs, while in the mining industry the proportion was only 34.9 per cent. For the services-producing industries, SME employment density was greatest for the property and business services, accommodation cafes and restaurants, and the personal and other services industries. With 81.6 per cent, 85.5 per cent and 91.6 per cent of persons employed in these industries, respectively, employed by SMEs. The finance and insurance industry had the lowest density of SME employment at 38.4 per cent.

Recent trends

Over the three-year period 1995–96 to 1997–98, net employment generation in Australia as a whole showed a steady increase, rising from 205 000 to 361 000. Net employment generation can be mainly attributed to the small- and large-sized business categories. In 1997–98, 50 per cent of net employment generation in Australia came from small-size enterprises, 23 per cent came from medium-size enterprises while 33 per cent came from large-size enterprises. Hence, SMEs contributed 263 530, or 73 per cent, of the net employment generation in Australia in 1997–98 (ABS 1999, 1321.0).

Over a longer time horizon, total small business employment increased between 1983–84 and 1998–99 by 58.9 per cent, or an average 3.7 per cent per annum. During

Table 11.3
Industry Breakdown of Employment in Australia, 1998–99

Industry type	Number of employed persons by SMEs ('000)	Persons employed by SMEs as a % of the industry total (%)
Mining	25.7	34.9
Manufacturing	606.6	61.6
Construction	514.0	93.1
Wholesale trade	478.0	86.2
Retail trade	807.7	66.2
Accommodation, cafes and restaurants	369.8	85.5
Transport and storage	222.9	73.5
Finance and insurance	115.4	38.4
Property and business services	809.6	81.6
Education	155.6	75.6
Health and community services	395.4	73.9
Cultural and recreational services	145.8	74.9
Personal and other services	236.9	91.6
Total	4 883.4	73.8

Source: ABS (1999, 1321.0).

the same period total medium-sized business employment grew by 59.3 per cent, an average annual rate of around 3.7 per cent. This compares with an expansion of total employment for large businesses that increased by 39.2 per cent, an annual average rate of 2.5 per cent. Consequently, the contribution of the small- and medium-size business sector to total non-agricultural private sector employment has increased slightly over the period, rising from 71 per cent to 73.8 per cent. This indicates the importance of SMEs as an engine for employment generation in Australia.

11.3.3   Output

It should be noted that data for sales, operating profit and industry gross product is collected for employing small businesses only. Since own account workers are neglected the data understates the true contribution of the SME sector. This is because, by definition, SMEs include own account workers as well as all businesses employing under 200 employees. As can be observed from Table 11.4, in 1997–98, Australian SMEs contributed approximately 54.5 per cent of the total sales of goods and services in Australia, about 39.6 per cent of operating profit before tax, and about 52.3 per cent of industry gross product.

Table 11.4
Sales, Operating Profit and Industry Gross Product, 1997–98

Item	All enterprises (AU$ million)	SME (AU$ million)	Total of SME contribution (%)
Sales of goods and services	1 055 385	574 712	54.5
Operating profit before tax	107 797	42 642	39.6
Industry gross product	317 699	166 296	52.3

Source: ABS (1999, 8140.0.40.002).

Recent trends

In 1992–93 Australian SMEs contributed approximately 55.6 per cent of the total sales of goods and services in Australia, about 41.1 per cent of operating profit before tax and about 51.9 per cent of industry gross product. Hence, the contribution of the SME sector in these areas has remained relatively constant during the period of the 1990s.

11.3.4   Exports

As shown in Table 11.5, during 1997–98 there were an estimated 21 788 exporting businesses in Australia, which represented 4 per cent of all businesses. These exporting businesses generated over AU$61 billion in export revenue. Of the 21 788 exporting businesses, 76.2 per cent of all exporters (16 601) were small businesses, while 20.6 per cent of all exporters (4 485) were medium businesses. Hence, 96.8 per cent of all exporters were SMEs. While small businesses made up the majority of exporting businesses, they only accounted for 12.6 per cent of total export revenue (AU$7.6 billion). Medium-size businesses accounted for 38.4 per cent of total export revenue (AU$23.1 billion). Hence, the SME sector contributed 51 per cent of total export revenue (AU$30.7 billion). The 700 exporting large businesses accounted for the remaining 49 per cent of export revenue.

Recent trends

Over the three-year period between 1994–95 and 1997–98 the number of exporting businesses increased 26.1 per cent from 17 282 to 21 787, which represented an annual average growth rate of 8 per cent per annum. Over the same period export revenue increased from AU$54.6 billion to AU$60.2 billion, which represented an average growth rate of 3.3 per cent per annum (see Table 11.6). Over the three years growth was strongest for small enterprises, and especially micro enterprises. The number of micro enterprises increased from 5 503 in 1994–95 to 7 532 in 1997–98, representing

Table 11.5
Australian Exporters and Export Revenue, 1997–98

Firm size	Number of enterprises	As a proportion of the total number (%)	Export revenue (AU$ mill.)	As proportion of total revenue (%)
Small business	16 601	76.2	7 579	12.6
Medium business	4 485	20.6	23 108	38.4
Large business	702	3.2	29 486	49.0
Total	21 788	100.0	60 173	100.0

Source: ABS (2000, 8154.0).

Table 11.6
Growth of Exporting Businesses and Export Revenue, 1994–95 to 1997–98

Employment size group (persons)	Average annual rate of change (%)	
	Exporting enterprises	Export revenue
Micro enterprises	11.0	20.4
Other small enterprises	8.7	11.4
Total small enterprises	9.7	14.7
Medium enterprises	4.4	5.1
Large enterprises	–3.3	–0.3
Total	8.0	3.3

Source: ABS (2000, 8154.0).

an average increase of 11 per cent per annum. Other small enterprises also recorded strong growth rates with numbers of exporting other small enterprises increasing at an average of 8.7 per cent per annum over the three years.

In terms of export revenue the total for small enterprises increased from just over AU$5 billion in 1994–95 to AU$7.6 billion in 1997–98, representing an average growth rate of 14.7 per cent per annum. Growth rates for medium enterprises were less pronounced with the number of exporters increasing at an average of 4.4 per cent per annum to 4 485 businesses, and export revenue for the sector increasing at an average of 5.1 per cent per annum to AU$23.1 billion in 1997–98. In contrast, large business enterprises suffered a slight decline in the number of exporters over the three years, dropping from 775 in 1994–95 to 700 in 1997–98 (an average annual decline of –3.3 per cent). Over the same period revenue also dropped marginally from AU$29.7 billion to AU$29.5 billion. This fall in exporting activity by large enterprises was during a period when the total income of large enterprises increased by 7 per cent per annum. Large enterprises' share of total export revenue also dropped over the period from 54 per cent in 1994–95 to 49 per cent in 1997–98. This is indicative that large enterprises in Australia were more adversely affected by the regional crisis than were SMEs.

This data provides evidence to suggest that SMEs are becoming increasingly competitive on the international market, and, hence, are of increasing significance to Australia's export performance. It also suggests that they may be more resilient to fluctuations in overseas markets.

11.3.5 R&D Expenditure

The ABS measures R&D investment by the amount of tax concessions claimed back by firms each financial year through the Australian Taxation Office (ATO). In Australia, firms investing in R&D may claim a 125 per cent tax concession for their R&D outlay.[2] However, this tax concession is only available if the firm invested over AU$20 000 within the financial year. Investments under the AU$20 000 threshold are not eligible for the tax concession, and so are not recorded by the ABS. Therefore, it would be expected that the SME contribution to R&D investment would be understated because the size of some SMEs restrict their ability to invest over AU$20 000 in R&D, and so their investment would not be recorded. Table 11.7 outlines R&D expenditure by firm size in 1998–99.

It can be seen from Table 11.7 that in 1998–99 Australian small enterprises contributed just over 9 per cent of the total R&D investment in Australia. In comparison, medium enterprises contributed over 28 per cent of the total R&D investment in Australia. Combined, SMEs accounted for 37.7 per cent of expenditure on R&D investment in Australia.

Table 11.7
Expenditure on Research and Development, by Employment Size, 1998–99

	Small business (AU$ '000)	Medium business (AU$ '000)	All business (AU$ '000)	Total of SME (%)
Expenditure on R&D	370 529	1 134 943	3 991 735	37.7

Source: ABS (2000, 8104.0).

Recent trends

In comparison to 1996–97 the value of SME R&D investment in 1998–99 slightly decreased.[3] In 1996–97, SME R&D investment totalled AU$1 514 million. By 1998–99, SME R&D investment had decreased to $1 505 million. The fall in the value of SME R&D investment has primarily been the result of the Federal government's 1996 budget, which cut the tax concession rate from 150 per cent to 125 per cent. Prior to the 1996 budget, total R&D investment had experienced a decade of growth.

A surprising finding, however, is that the 1996 budget affected large enterprise R&D investment more than SMEs. Hence, in 1998–99 the contribution of SME investment in R&D, as a proportion of total R&D investment, increased by 1 per cent in comparison to 1996–97. The SME contribution towards R&D investment totalled 37.7 per cent of total R&D investment in 1998–99, an increase from 36.7 per cent of total R&D investment in 1996–97. This indicates that, while large enterprises still dominate R&D investment, SMEs are now playing a larger role. This is of particular importance to SMEs because R&D is the major source of firm innovation.

11.3.6 Taxation

There are no available statistics recording the taxation contribution of Australian enterprises by employment size. Hence, this section will look at the costs that Australia's tax regime places upon SMEs. Generally, taxation imposes three broad types of costs: efficiency (deadweight loss arising from the distortion of prices); administrative (costs to the government collecting the tax); and compliance costs (resources expended by the taxpayer in meeting their obligation). Of particular significance to Australian SMEs are the compliance costs associated with the introduction of the goods and services tax (GST) on 1 July 2000.

The introduction of the GST, and especially the burden it has placed upon small businesses, has been roundly criticised (Hayes 2000; and Surry 2000). The GST had originally forced businesses to provide a business activities statement (BAS) every three months. The complexity of the BAS is evident from the fact that the two-page BAS form requires a 148-page explanation booklet. Given this complexity, it has been estimated that small businesses would incur an average of AU$5 000 and 30 working hours in order to comply with the regulations (Surry 2000). In New Zealand, for example, for every NZ$1 000 of firm revenue, GST compliance costs amounted to NZ$26 for businesses with less than NZ$30 000 in turnover, NZ$16 for firms with a NZ$30 000–$100 000 turnover, and only 5 cents for companies turning over more than NZ$50 million (Gouwland 1998). In light of this the Australian government has proposed a compensation package of AU$500 million for GST compliance, which equates to AU$750 per business (*Australian CPA* 1999). However, even with the compensation package it has been estimated that 'up to 10 per cent of SMEs are in the "at risk" category' of failure due to the GST (Hayes 2000, p. 38). The expected failure of many small businesses is due to the fact that businesses are required to pay GST quarterly, even if they are entitled to a rebate. Given that small businesses are constrained by resource limitations, many of these businesses are expected to experience major cash-flow problems. SMEs are therefore bearing a disproportionate burden of GST compliance costs, and hence placing them at a relative disadvantage. Given the previously identified contribution of SMEs to employment, output and exports, this gives major cause for concern.

A positive note for SMEs with regard to the new taxation system is the fact that company tax rates will fall from 36 per cent to 30 per cent by 2001–2002. However, since large enterprises are more likely to pay company tax than their smaller counterparts, they have a greater potential to gain from this tax change.

11.3.7 Globalisation

High tariff barriers were a feature of Australia's economic policy in the 1960s and 1970s. In 1985, Australia's average tariff on imports was 9.8 per cent.[4] In comparison to other OECD nations, for which data are available, Australia could be seen as taking a more protectionist stance.[5] During this time, Canada had the second highest level of average tariffs on imports at a relatively low level of 3.8 per cent. As well, Australia was the only OECD country where the average tariff on imports had increased. Australia's average tariff on imports increased from 9.6 per cent in 1965 to 9.8 per cent in 1985. While this increase was minimal, all other OECD nations had decreased their average tariff on imports (OECD 1985).

However, from the mid-1980s Australia embraced globalisation, endorsing freer trade and capital mobility.[6] This is readily evident by Australia's active participation in international organisations and trade agreements such as GATT (General Agreement on Tariffs and Trade), WTO (World Trade Organisation), APEC and ASEAN. Hence, Australia's tariff experience since the mid-1980s has been one where its average tariff on imports converged with that in the rest of the OECD. Australia's average tariff on imports fell from 9.8 per cent in 1985 to 6 per cent in 1992. Further reductions in protection were aimed at seeing the average tariff fall to under 3 per cent in 2000 (Economic Planning and Advisory Committee 1996).

As a result of Australia's globalised outlook, its levels of exports and imports of goods and services have increased dramatically. Exports of goods and services for the year 1999–2000 were AU$125 862 million, up 12.5 per cent from the previous year. Imports of goods and services for the year 1999–2000 were AU$140 658 million, up 11.2 per cent from the previous year (ABS 2000, 5368.0). While import volume is greater than export volume, the growth of exports is outstripping the growth of imports. This may indicate that the deregulation of trade has forced Australian firms to be more competitive, a challenge that they have risen too. As well, capital flows in to and out of Australia have also increased. Australian investment abroad for 1999–2000 was AU$318 189 million, up 18 per cent from the previous year. Foreign investment in Australia in 1999–2000 was AU$713 660 million, up 14.6 per cent from the previous year (ABS 2000, 5302.0), indicating that Australia is a major net recipient of foreign investment.

The large flow of goods, services, and capital into and out of Australia indicate that Australia has moved away from a protectionist policy towards one of freer trade. Given Australia's relatively small population of around 19 million people, the embracing of free trade is the only logical option. This is positive news for SMEs which can provide internationally competitive products or services. The limited size of the domestic market places pressure upon many SMEs to find alternative markets. Australia's embracement of free trade and participation in trade agreements such as GATT, WTO, APEC and ASEAN provides SMEs an excellent opportunity to expand their market. However, the extent of the success associated with this will depend on ensuring that Australian SMEs are globally competitive and have the necessary support structures.

11.4 IMPACT OF THE ASIAN FINANCIAL CRISIS ON AUSTRALIAN SMES

Whatever the underlying factors causing the Asian financial crisis, the impact of the crisis for Australia have been upon: exporters; domestic enterprises that invested in the crisis-afflicted economies with the objective of selling their products within those countries; foreign invested enterprises in Australia whose primary source of funding was from East Asia; over-leveraged domestic enterprises that may be subject to higher interest rates; the falling share prices of enterprises with a dependence on markets in East Asia, resulting in more difficulty in raising finance for investment. With the rapid and extreme devaluation of many Asian currencies, exports to many of these nations became economically unfeasible due to the collapse of their domestic demand and a loss of competitiveness for Australian SMEs. Hence, unless exporters could divert their exports to alternative markets, it could reasonably be expected that the volume of exports by Australian SMEs after 1997 would fall. Unfortunately, data is not collected for exports on a country basis by firm size. Therefore a broad picture of exports by country for all firms will be provided, and it is assumed that SMEs followed the same general trend of trade.

Growth in export revenue from 1993–94 to 1990–2000 has been steady at 7.1 per cent per annum. Only in 1998–99 was there negative growth of 2.1 per cent (ABS 2000, 5422.0). However, given that the Asian financial crisis reached its peak in 1997–98, it is unlikely that the downturn in exports in 1998–99 would have primarily arisen because of the crisis. Therefore, it appears that Australia has been relatively well sheltered from its impact. To determine why Australia emerged relatively unscathed, a breakdown of the destination of exports during the period of the crisis is required.

For three years prior to 1996–97, Australian exports to ASEAN nations grew at 11 per cent per annum. Since 1996–97, the growth of exports to this region slumped to 1.5 per cent per annum. Between 1993–94 and 1996–97, Australian exports to the

Republic of Korea grew at a rate of 14.5 per cent per annum. Since the crisis, growth of exports to the Republic of Korea slumped to 2.7 per cent per annum. Out of the Asian nations who experienced financial difficulties, Japan was the only nation where Australian exporters recorded greater post-1996–97 export growth than pre-1996–97 export growth (export growth between 1993–94 and 1996–97 was –1.1 per cent while export growth between 1996–97 and 1999–00 was 7.0 per cent) (ABS 2000, 5422.0). Since Japan was the first Asian nation to experience financial difficulties starting from the early 1990s, it might be expected that the impact and recovery of trade with Japan would occur first.

In the light of the general decline in export growth towards nations from Asia, and the fact that Australian export growth has remained relatively stable at around 7 per cent per annum for the last decade, it is evident that Australian exporters diverted their trade towards other markets. Since 1996–97, export growth to European Union (EU) nations has increased by 13.7 per cent per annum. This is in contrast to the 2.5 per cent per annum growth for the three years prior to 1996–97. Even more pronounced has been the shift of trade towards the US, with export growth to that country increasing by 20.3 per cent per annum since 1996–97 compared to the pre-1996–97 growth of 2.9 per cent per annum (ABS 2000, 5422.0). Given this trend in export growth the US is now Australia's number two export destination behind Japan, whereas it was ranked number four only three years ago in 1996–97. As well, trade to EU nations is now on a par with trade towards ASEAN nations, whereas only three years ago exports to the EU amounted to only 66 per cent of exports towards ASEAN nations. These figures indicate that Australian firms have demonstrated remarkable adaptability in seeking out new export markets in the wake of the Asian financial crisis, helping to considerably cushion the impact of the crisis on the Australian business sector. While it cannot be stated with certainty that Australian SMEs followed the general trend of exports from Asian nations towards the EU nations and the US, the data is suggestive that this is likely to have been the case given that more than 50 per cent of Australian exports are by SMEs (see Table 11.5).

11.5 KEY ISSUES AFFECTING THE DEVELOPMENT OF AUSTRALIAN SMES

This section focuses upon the key issues affecting the current and future performance of Australia's SMEs. Specifically, attention is given to: access to finance; the importance of culture/networking in the conduct of business; access to technology and the adoption of information technology; and progress made in regard to human resource development (HRD).

11.5.1 Access to Finance

SMEs are generally at a disadvantage, relative to their larger counterparts, in accessing finance. With regard to accessing bank loans, Holmes et al. (1994) found that there was a difference in the average interest rate charged by banks for loans made to different-sized firms. On average, Australian small-sized firms were charged 18.34 per cent per annum for their loans, compared to 16.70 per cent per annum charged for loans made to medium-sized firms, and 15.65 per cent per annum charged for loans made to large-sized firms.[7] Hence, the interest rate differential on loans made to small-sized and large-sized firms was 2.69 per cent per annum. The fact that SMEs, on average, face higher interest rate charges than large enterprises is not just confined to Australian SMEs. A study conducted by the European Commission (2000)[8] found that SMEs typically pay an interest rate differential of between 2 and 5 per cent higher than large enterprises. This interest rate differential places an additional burden on SME resources, and has a negative impact on the potential of SMEs for growth and job creation (European Commission 2000, p. 5).

Due to the interest rate differential on loans from banks, many SMEs are forced to turn to alternative sources of finance. An alternative source the Australian government has identified as pertinent to the growth of SMEs, and especially innovative SMEs, is venture capital. This is evident through the legislative changes introduced in 1999 regarding the taxation of venture capital and the introduction of the Innovation Investment Fund Program in 1997. The Innovation Investment Fund Program, launched by the Federal government in 1997, established a AU$200 million pool of capital specifically to encourage small new-technology companies (Chapman 1999). The government has identified these small new-technology companies as the future source for economic growth. Ultimately, it is hoped that the success of these firms will filter throughout the Australian economy.

In addition, the ability of SMEs to attract venture capital is dependent upon Australia's tax regime with regard to venture capital. Prior to December 1999, pension funds from the US, the UK, Japan, Germany, France and Canada were liable to a 36 per cent venture capital gains tax. However, this rate has now dropped to zero if the investment is below AU$50 million, if the investment is held by the investor for at least 12 months, and if the investment is not in real estate or other passive investments. 'Australia is [now on] a level playing field and there should be no tax impediments to attracting venture capital' (*Global Investor* 1999, p. 6). Given this environment it could have been reasonably expected that Australian SMEs would have had little trouble attracting venture capital. However, this has not been the case.

It has been suggested that SMEs in Australia are unable to attract funding because they are not 'investment ready' (Raby 2000). A 1998 survey[9] of venture capital by Arthur Andersen covered 22 Australian-based professional venture capital managers with over AU$1.4 billion under their management. It was found that for the second year in a row the group had over AU$700 million of capital available, but had not committed to business opportunities. From the findings it has been suggested that 'we need to change the mind-set that venture capital is not available in Australia and focus instead on how to help businesses become "investment ready"' (Chapman 1999, p. 33). Assisting SMEs to become 'investment ready' involves setting a business plan so that potential investors can assess the merits of investing in the firm. A typical business plan outlines the firm's long-term vision of the business, information regarding the firm's products, markets, management structure and financial projections (Chapman 1999, p. 34). While the reforms by the Australian government have made the economic environment more attractive for international venture capitalists, it is strictly within the scope of the SMEs' business operations to make themselves 'investment ready'. Unfortunately, Australian SMEs have not realised the full potential of venture capital as a source of finance and may lag behind the world if they do not carry out internal reform to attract international venture capital.

11.5.2 Significance of Culture/Networking in the Conduct of Business

Australia's multicultural society has given Australia a unique advantage with regard to culture and networking in the international conduct of business. With more than 4.2 million people born overseas in 1996 (representing 23 per cent of the total population), Australia has one of the largest immigrant populations in the world (ABS 1997, 3412.0). When compared with other major host nations in the OECD in 1993, only the US, Germany and Canada had larger migrant populations. However, when measured as a proportion of the total population, Australia had the largest migrant population of all OECD nations except Luxembourg, whose relatively small migrant population of 125 000 represented 31 per cent of the total population (OECD 1994). This racial diversity gives domestic firms an insight into the culture and understanding of other nations, thus reducing the cultural barrier as an impediment to trade. As well, it may be easier to form and maintain networks between immigrants living in Australia and firms from their original countries.

On the domestic front, networking is seen as vital for SMEs to overcome their resource constraints. Networking provides the SME a means of sharing information and costs. The Australian government has recognised the importance of networking for SMEs. Between 1994 to 1998 the Australian Business Network Program, sponsored by AusIndustry, created 400 separate networks. During these networking conferences, firms were encouraged to collaborate where appropriate. This involved sharing information, integrating production processes where appropriate so that firms could depend upon each other in the supply process, and sharing marketing costs. The impact of the Australian Business Network Program has been such that commercial relations between members as subcontractors and even partnerships have resulted. The success of the Australian Business Network Program has even led to network formations outside the program (OECD 2000b, p. 29).

In conjunction with the Australian Business Network Program, the Federal government implemented a four-year pilot program in 1998 called the Family and Community Networks Initiative. The initiative, with funding of AU$8.6 million over four years, is aimed at improving access to information and services relevant to families and community organisations, and to enhance the capacity of communities and services to work together more effectively to address the needs of the community. The initiative provides funding of community network projects, funding of one-off projects, and the development of a national website offering links to a comprehensive range of information relevant to family and community networks. Thus it is evident that the Australian government and SMEs view business networks as vital for the success of SME growth and development.

11.5.3   Access to Technology and Use of Information Technology

In the private sector, over half of Australian households have personal computers, and almost 35 per cent have Internet access. Five per cent of Australian adults shopped via the Internet in the 12 months to February 2000. In the business sector, 76 per cent of all businesses used personal computers. Over 56 per cent of all businesses have Internet access, while 16 per cent of all businesses have a website. As well, the estimated total value of sales/orders received by businesses online for the year ending 30 June 2000 was AU\$5.1 billion. This represented approximately 0.4 per cent of total sales/orders received for goods and services for that period (ABS 2000, 8129.0). This means that Australia is consistently rated in the top ten nations globally for its e-commerce environment (NOIE 2000, p. 1).

Table 11.8 provides a breakdown of business use of information technology by employment size for the 1999–2000 period. The table indicates that the proportion of Australian businesses using computers, accessing the Internet and using web sites continued to be higher for larger businesses. However, growth in the use of these technologies was higher for small businesses. For instance, growth in computer use was greatest in micro businesses, increasing from 55 per cent of these businesses at the end of June 1998 to 69 per cent at the end of June 2000. Growth in Internet access was also greatest in micro businesses, increasing from 24 per cent of businesses at

Table 11.8
Business Use of Information Technology, 1999–2000

Employment size	No. of businesses ('000)	Computer use (%)	Internet access (%)	Website (%)
1–4	415	69	50	9
5–19	184	85	65	24
20–99	36	97	83	46
100+	6	100	95	68

Source: ABS (2000, 8129.0).

the end of June 1998 to 50 per cent at the end of June 2000. Growth in the use of a web site was greatest in businesses with employment between 5 and 19 persons, increasing from 8 per cent at the end of June 1998 to 24 per cent at the end of June 2000 (ABS 2000, 8129.0).

The Australian government has recognised the importance of information technology for SMEs, as evidenced by the assistance programs available. The Information Technology On-line Program provides maximum grants of AU$150 000 to assist SMEs to implement projects that are targeted at delivering online business benefits. The program has assisted over 50 projects totalling AU$4.3 million (DEWRSB 2000).

The government has also implemented the Building on Information Technology Strengths Program, running from the year 2000 to 2004. With funding of AU$156 million over the four-year period the program aims to build the strength and competitiveness of the Australian information sector, including fostering much stronger commercialisation linkages with R&D organisations and the creation of innovative and information technology businesses (DEWRSB 2000).

The growth rates of business use of information technology and the assistance provided by the government, indicate that Australian SMEs and the public sector view information technology as both a tool to achieve greater efficiency and a tool to assist market expansion. Australian SMEs have openly embraced the use of information technology, which is a positive sign for their prospects in the computer age.

11.5.4 Human Resource Development

HRD may be seen on two levels: the managerial or entrepreneurial level; and the employee or worker level. On the managerial level a broad set of skills is required, ranging from production technicalities through to financial planning, marketing, distribution and quality controls. Given the resource constraints placed upon owners of SMEs, many find it difficult or even impossible to balance these competing demands associated with operating an SME. Hence, studies have found that the primary causes of SME failures are due to factors within the control of the business (Albert 1981; Report of the House of Representatives Standing Committee on Industry Science and Technology 1990). According to Albert (1981), the main causes of SME failures were incompetence (42.3 per cent), unbalanced experience (23 per cent), lack of experience in the market (13.8 per cent), and lack of managerial experience (13 per cent). According to the Report of the House of Representatives (1990), 75 per cent of failed SME owners lacked managerial and market experience, while in 80 per cent of insolvency cases management accounting records were unavailable or inadequate. Due to the fact that managerial and entrepreneurial ability is of paramount importance to the survival and growth of SMEs, HRD for SME owners is a major issue.

The Australian government provides assistance to train persons on small business management, business skills and business plan developments under the New Enterprise Incentive Scheme (NEIS) (1997–2002).[10] The NEIS also provides an allowance (of around AU$250 per week) as well as business advice and mentor support for up to a year following the training period. The aim of the program is to assist unemployed people to establish commercially viable new businesses (DEWRSB 2000). While such a scheme would protect Australia's human capital stock, little is done to assist SMEs already in business. Many managers of these SMEs also require assistance to maintain their competitiveness. Enhancing the entrepreneurial skills of the unemployed should be done in conjunction with enhancing the entrepreneurial skills of current SME owners. As stated, lack of managerial ability is the key determinant of SME failure in Australia. Hence, training should be aimed at assisting SME owners before, and not just after, the failure of their businesses.

On the employee or worker level, HRD may be recognised as both a public and private issue. Of particular significance with regard to the public issue of HRD at the employee level involves the impact of government regulations on the tertiary sector. Given that the future competitive advantage for Australian firms lies in knowledge-based commodities and services (since Australia's wage rates make competition in unskilled labour-intensive commodities unfeasible against that of many Asian and African nations), the quality of the tertiary sector is vital for Australia's future growth (OECD 2000b). While the present government proclaims the importance of knowledge-based industries, its 1996 budget indicates a contrary policy. By doubling the Higher Education Contribution Scheme (HECS) fees for university students (currently around AU$600 per subject) and lowering the income threshold as to when HECS must be repaid (from average income to AU$22 000 a year), the government has effectively increased the cost of attending university. Hence, for the younger generation of future employees this could act as a deterrent in gaining a tertiary education. Nationwide statistics pre-1996 show that university enrolments had grown by 5 per cent during the previous five years. Since 1996, growth of university enrolments has fallen to 2.7 per cent. Given that overseas students made up 7.6 per cent of total university enrolments in 1995, 6.8 per cent in 1996, and 12.1 per cent in 1999, it is evident that there has been declining growth for university enrolments by domestic students (DETYA 2000). This places Australia in a precarious position with regard to capitalising upon the increasing need to develop, and provide the necessary skilled workforce for, knowledge-based industries.

With regard to HRD at the private level, positive signs are emerging for Australian enterprises. After a steady decline in training expenditures over a number of years, Australian enterprises, more recently, are spending much more on human resources (HR). The HR Benchmarking Annual Report, by the Australian-based HRM Consulting, found that for 190 surveyed organisations, training investment increased to AU$705 million in 1998. This was up from AU$454 million the previous year, which had been the lowest level of expenditure on training since HRM Consulting began the study in 1993. HR training and investment per employee equated to about $1 024 in 1998 (*HR Focus* 1999).

The movement away from low-skilled industries towards knowledge-based industries requires larger expenditure on HRD. As stressed before this trend towards knowledge-based industries is undeniable for Australia, and essential for its future economic growth. If these industries can obtain a competitive advantage on the international market, then high-skilled, highly productive and highly paid workers will dominate the Australian labour market. Clearly, this is beneficial for the economy as a whole. However, for this to eventuate the government must not merely talk up the importance of knowledge-based industries but implement the necessary policies that nurture HRD, which is the key to the development of knowledge-based industries.

11.6   KEY POLICY ISSUES FOR SMES, THEIR PROSPECTS, AND THE ROLE OF THE GOVERNMENT

This chapter has outlined a number of government policies that are aimed at supporting the development of SMEs. This section focuses upon SME participation in these and other related policies. Table 11.9 provides no enlightenment as to the use of specific government programs by firm size.[11] However, the table does suggest that the larger the firm the greater the likelihood that it will be found participating in one or more government programs. This would indicate that governmental programs are primarily aimed at assisting larger firms, since it is these firms that are utilising the programs

Table 11.9
Participation in Government Programs by Firm Size, 1995–96

| Employment size | Firms participating in: | | | | | |
| | No programs | | 1 program | | 2+ programs | |
	No. of firms	%	No. of firms	%	No. of firms	%
1–4	302 760	93.2	17 192	5.3	4 799	1.5
5–9	82 988	83.3	15 454	15.5	1 207	1.2
10–19	35 322	73.7	10 539	22.0	2 039	4.3
20–49	13 266	60.3	7 325	33.3	1 407	6.4
50–99	3 594	60.2	1 760	29.5	615	10.3
100–199	1 053	50.1	613	29.2	436	20.7
200–499	645	48.7	415	31.3	265	20.0
500+	275	38.9	206	29.1	227	32.0
Total	439 904	87.2	53 504	10.6	10 995	2.2

Source: DEWRSB (1996). Figures are correct subject to rounding errors at source.

relatively more. Or indicate a reluctance, or an inability, to take advantage of these programs by SMEs.

Given that SMEs generally lack resources relative to their larger counterparts, this data is not encouraging for Australian SMEs. With 99.7 per cent of businesses classified as an SME, 73.8 per cent of persons being employed by SMEs in the private non agricultural sector, and 52.3 per cent of industry gross product produced by SMEs, the future growth of the Australian economy is dependent upon the success of these enterprises (ABS 1999, 1321.0). Therefore, governmental programs need to increase their focus on assisting SMEs to develop and grow, and be more tailored to their specific requirements.

The OECD Best Practice Policies Report for SMEs (1997) identified three areas of assistance that the government should provide for SMEs so that they can fulfil their potential for growth and development. These areas are in finance, the business environment and access to markets.

With regard to finance the Australian government has implemented the Innovation Investment Fund Program, launched in 1997. However, given that the program is specifically aimed at assisting small innovative companies, and that only 15 to 20 per cent of SMEs in OECD countries may be classified as technology leaders, access to the program is limited to a minority of SMEs (OECD 2000a). Hence further assistance needs to be given to the majority of SMEs.

The Australian government's capital gains tax reform in 1999 is a positive step forward in assisting the general SME population to gain better access to finance. However, as stated, many SMEs are not investment ready, resulting in about AU$700 million of venture capital being left untouched. Australian SMEs must realise the potential of venture capital as a source of finance and make themselves investment ready. Otherwise, Australian SMEs will run the risk of failure. Hence, the prospect for SMEs with regard to finance is bleak unless they recognise that the onus of attracting finance is partly within their domain, and directly address such problems by implementing accounting and management practices that will enable them to attract finance.

With regard to the business environment, two issues are of prominence. The first relates to the implications of the GST. Given that SMEs bear a disproportionate burden of the compliance costs, and the fact that the GST imposes a cash-flow problem for SMEs, the government needs to review two things. First, the government should recognise that its AU$500 million package to assist small businesses with the transition to a GST structure is not enough. Seven hundred and fifty dollars per firm is hardly sufficient for many small businesses that have incurred, on average, AU$5 000 and 30 working hours in regard to GST compliance costs (*Australian CPA* 1999). The second problem of the GST with regard to the cash-flow problem is a much more difficult and controversial issue. The current practice of paying all GST payments quarterly then applying for rebates in the future is the cause of cash-flow problems experienced by many SMEs. A possible solution is that the government should not force firms to pay quarterly GST payments for goods where they will receive a rebate, and hence reduce unnecessary cash flow problems. Whatever the possible solution, a review of the GST implications is required. Clearly, the government did not envisage that the costs associated with the GST could force up to 10 per cent of SMEs to fail (Hayes 2000). At present, the prospects for Australian SMEs with regard to the GST and its impact on the business environment more generally is of concern.

The second issue for the business environment relates to the state of the Australian economy, and indeed the global economy. Clearly, the performance of SMEs, and the performance of all firms for that matter, is dependent upon the state of the domestic and global economies. Over the last decade, with unprecedented levels of economic growth at around 4 per cent and unemployment levels reaching a decade low of 6 per cent in 1999, the health of the Australian economy has remained relatively strong (*The Commonwealth Budget 2000–2001*). However, such is the nature of the economy that, as at 2001, debate in Australia is now centred around the growing concerns of a recession. The December quarter of 2000 saw negative growth for the first time in a decade. Such was the unexpectedness of the data that the Australian government had just made the announcement in its 2000–2001 Commonwealth Budget that it was revising its expected GDP growth for the year 1999–2000 to 4 per cent, up 1 per cent from previous estimates (*The Commonwealth Budget 2000–2001*). Currently, the government has backtracked and there appears to be open disagreement with the Reserve Bank of Australia over whether the GST or poor monetary policy management had contributed to this negative growth. Another contributory factor would be the slowdown of the US economy, now Australia's second largest export market, as well as the global economy more generally. Whatever the underlying factors behind the slowdown in economic activity one thing is certain, a further slowdown of the economy would not be good news for SMEs. Hence, the prospects for Australian SMEs, and indeed the Australian business community, are currently very unclear. Time will tell whether the negative growth was merely a blip, or the result of greater underlying problems such as: poor fiscal management; poor monetary management; poor structural management; other structural deficiencies; or a more general loss of international competitiveness. Either way, there are worrying signs for Australian SMEs.

The third major area that the OECD (1997) identifies as being integral to the prospects of SMEs is their ability to access international markets. This is of greater importance for Australian SMEs given the relatively small domestic market opportunities. The Australian government provides assistance to SMEs wishing to expand their products internationally via the Export Market Development Grants (EMDG) scheme. The EMDG scheme reimburses up to 50 per cent of the eligible SME's expenditure on export promotion.[12] The grant is available to firms that have export sales under AU$25 million per annum and income under AU$50 million per annum. The grant's aim is to assist SMEs to expand their product market by reimbursing expenditure on overseas marketing cost, information gathering cost (including the costs of attending conferences and trade fairs), and with transaction costs arising from different cultural backgrounds where interpreters and professional assistance is required. In 1997–98, 3 307 applicants for the grant were approved, accumulating to AU$147.3 million granted (Australian Trade Commission 1998). Hence, Australian SMEs are generally well placed with regard to assistance in penetrating new markets.[13] Although the EMDG scheme is of vital importance in assisting Australian SMEs to expand their markets, of equal importance to the prospects of such ventures is the economic condition of the world market. As previously indicated, as at 2001, there are considerable concerns about the prospects of a global recession.

11.7   SUMMARY

In conjunction with outlining the macroeconomic contribution of Australian SMEs, this chapter has highlighted the major issues relevant to their growth and development. The contribution of SMEs to the Australian economy is significant. Some 99.7 per cent of non-agricultural businesses are classified as SMEs, they employ 73.8 per cent of the total non-agricultural private sector workforce, and they contribute 52.3 per cent of industry gross product and some 51 per cent of total export revenue. The future growth of the Australian economy is, more than ever, dependent upon the success of these enterprises (ABS 1999, 1321.0). Given the limited size of the domestic market Australian businesses, to be successful, must expand their export capabilities, and with advances in information technology SMEs are well placed to play a crucial role in this regard. The recent impressive redirection of exports away from the markets of East Asia towards the US and the EU is indicative of the degree of adaptability of Australian exporters in general, a strength that should not be underestimated given the volatility of international markets, as well as the commodities they produce. While no definitive data exists it can at least be surmised that SMEs contributed significantly to this development. This adaptability resulted in a relatively limited impact of the regional crisis on the Australian economy. Therefore, governmental programs need to increase their focus on assisting SMEs to develop and grow, and to meet their specific needs. They should not, therefore, be looked upon solely as small, large enterprises. They face their own specific constraints and requirements.

A number of important issues were identified in regard to the immediate- and long-term prospects of the sector. The first relates to the implications of the GST. It was found that the compliance costs of the GST are regressive in nature since such costs are negatively correlated with firm size. This places an additional burden upon the smaller-sized enterprises and hinders their prospects for development. The second issue concerns the role of R&D expenditure. Although there was a reduction in R&D concession rates in 1996, the data indicates that SMEs are now playing a greater role in R&D expenditure. This is an extremely positive indicator for Australian SMEs given the fact that R&D expenditure is positively correlated to innovation which, in turn, is seen as the key to facilitating SME growth (Bloodgood et al. 1996; Jones 1999; and OECD 2000a). However, to effectively enhance the international competitiveness of Australian SMEs a review of the tax concession rate may be required. The third issue highlighted relates to the trend towards globalisation. With the decrease in trade barriers and increased capital mobility that is associated with globalisation, Australian SMEs have an unprecedented potential to enter and expand into new and existing international markets. This is of particular importance for Australian SMEs, given the limited domestic market.

It was further found that SMEs faced considerable impediments to finance, reflected by the fact that they face higher interest rate charges than their larger counterparts (Holmes et al. 1994). This, coupled with the fact that the use of information technology is positively correlated with firm size, highlights the resource constraints faced by SMEs. There is little doubt that resource constraints limit the ability of SMEs to play a more dominant role in the economy. However, a worrying sign for Australian SMEs is the fact that the problem of limited resources has not been effectively addressed by the government, reflected by the fact that government programs are utilised relatively more often by large enterprises. While the onus is still within the operation of the firm to improve its competitive advantage, it is imperative that public policies realise the potential that Australian SMEs possess and assist them in reaching this. This requires policies to be more SME specific, by recognising the fact that SMEs are not merely scaled-down versions of large enterprises. SMEs are unique in that their primary competitive advantage stems not from economies of scale, but rather from their flexibility advantages (Foster 1987; Acs and Audretsch 1990; Dodgson 1990; and Pratten 1991) and ability to satisfy niche markets. The latter is becoming of increasing significance with rising affluence both domestically and globally. Hence, policies attempting to assist Australian SMEs need to be geared towards fostering this competitive advantage via promoting R&D and innovative practices, and assisting the implementation of information technology. This can only be achieved if policies are specifically focused upon assisting SMEs to overcome their resource constraints.

NOTES

1   AU$ represents Australian dollars.
2   AusIndustry works in conjunction with the ATO to provide this tax concession.
3   In addition to R&D tax concessions there are grants for R&D relating to the R&D Start Program, administered by AusIndustry, which was implemented in the 1996–97 Budget, with funding of AU$520 million over four years provided. The grant promotes industry-based R&D projects to achieve internationally competitive products, and graduate-based R&D projects to achieve linkages between industry and tertiary/research institutions (AusIndustry 1998).
4   The average tariff on imports is the ratio of receipts from customs and import duties to the value of imports (OECD 1985).

5   The other OECD nations referred to here include Belgium, Canada, Denmark, Finland, France, Great Britain, Germany, Italy, Japan, Netherlands, Norway, Sweden and the United States (OECD 1985).

6   Signalled by the floating of the Australian dollar in December 1983.

7   It should be noted that the findings were not statistically significant.

8   The European Union defines an SME as all non-agricultural enterprises employing 499 or fewer persons; having net fixed assets of less than ECU 75 million; and having not more than one-third of its capital held by a large firm.

9   The study was after the implementation of the Innovation Investment Fund Program and before the changes regarding capital gains tax.

10   The NEIS was established in 1997 to provide training, monetary allowances, business advice and mentoring support for unemployed persons to establish commercially viable new small businesses.

11   The government programs comprise: AusIndustry/NIES; R&D tax concessions; grants for R&D; New Enterprise Incentive Scheme; Export Access; Export Finance and Insurance Corporation facilities; Austrade grants and services; Commonwealth, State or local government employment programs; and other Commonwealth and State government industry programs (DEWRSB 1996, p. 156).

12   This scheme is operated through Austrade.

13   Other schemes available to assist SME exports include Export Access and the Export Finance and Insurance Corporation (EFIC). Export Access, established in 1991 and having assisted over 3 200 SMEs, assists SMEs to become sustainable exporters by providing assistance with regard to identifying export markets, preparing for overseas market visits, and post market visit evaluations (Australian Trade Commission 2000). The EFIC is Australia's government owned export credit agency. EFIC's credit insurance services provide payment protection to exporters selling goods and services on payment terms less than 180 days. EFIC's export finance services include long-term loans, guarantees and political risk insurance (Export Finance and Insurance Corporation 2000).

REFERENCES

Acs, Z.J. and D.B. Audretsch (1990), 'Small Firms in the 1990s', in Z.J. Acs and D.B. Audretsch (eds), *The Economics of Small Business: A European Challenge*, (1990), Dordrecht: Kluwer Academic Publishers, pp. 1–24.

Albert, K.J. (1981), *Straight Talk about Small Business,* New York: McGraw-Hill Book Company.

AusIndustry (1998), *DIST Annual Report 1996/97*, available at <www.isr.gov.au>, Canberra: Commonwealth of Australia.

Australian Bureau of Statistics (1997), *Migration, Australia*, Catalogue no. 3412.0.

Australian Bureau of Statistics (1998), *Research and Experimental Development, Business, 1997–1998*, Catalogue no. 8104.0

Australian Bureau of Statistics (1999), *Small Businesses*, Catalogue no. 1321.0.

Australian Bureau of Statistics (1999), *Summary of Industry Performance*, Catalogue no. 8140.0.40.002.

Australian Bureau of Statistics (2000), *Balance of Payments and International Investment Position*, Catalogue no. 5302.0.

Australian Bureau of Statistics (2000), *International Trade of Goods and Services*, Catalogue no. 5368.0.

Australian Bureau of Statistics (2000), *International Merchandise Trade*, Catalogue no. 5422.0.

Australian Bureau of Statistics (2000), *Research and Experimental Development, Business, 1999–2000*, Catalogue no. 8104.0.

Australian Bureau of Statistics (2000), *Business Use of Information Technology, Australia,* Catalogue no. 8129.0.

Australian Bureau of Statistics (2000), *A Portrait of Australian Exporters: A Report Based on the Business Longitudinal Survey*, Catalogue no. 8154.0.

Australian CPA (1999), 'Compensation for Small Business Insufficient', *Australian CPA*, **69** (7), available at <//global.umi.com>.

Australian Trade Commission (1998), *Annual Report 1997–98*, Canberra: Commonwealth of Australia.

Australian Trade Commission (2000), 'Austrade Information about Export Assistance Programs', available at <www.austrade.gov.au>, Canberra: Commonwealth of Australia.

Bloodgood, J.M., H.J. Sapienza and J.G. Almeida (1996), 'The Internationalisation of New High Potential US Ventures: Antecedents and Outcomes', *Entrepreneurship Theory and Practice*, **20** (4), 61–76.

Chapman, P. (1999), 'Venture Capital: Financing Growth', *Australian CPA, *69** (6), 33–5, available at <//global.umi.com>.

Commonwealth Budget 2000–2001, available at <www.budget.gov.au>, Canberra: Commonwealth of Australia.

Department of Education, Training and Youth Affairs (DETYA) (2000), 'Characteristics and Performance Indicators of Higher Education Institutions Preliminary Report', available at <www.detya.gov.au>, Canberra: Commonwealth of Australia.

Department of Employment, Workplace Relations and Small Business (DEWRSB) (1996), *A Portrait of Australian Business*, Canberra: Commonwealth of Australia.

Department of Employment, Workplace Relations and Small Business (DEWRSB) (2000), 'Commonwealth Initiatives', available at <www.dewrsb.gov.au>, Canberra: Commonwealth of Australia.

Dodgson, M. (1990), 'Technology Strategy in Small and Medium-sized Firms', in Z.J. Acs and D.B. Audretsch (eds), *The Economics of Small Business: A European Challenge*, Dordrecht: Kluwer Academic Publishers, pp. 157–67.

Economic Planning and Advisory Committee, (1996), *Tariff Reform and Economic Growth*, Canberra: Australian Government Publishing Service.

European Commission (2000), 'Small- and Medium-sized Enterprises: A Dynamic Source of Employment, Growth and Competitiveness in the European Union', available at <www.cier.edu.tw>.

Export Finance and Insurance Corporation (2000), 'EFIC News', available at <www.efic.gov.au>, Canberra: Commonwealth of Australia.

Foster, R. (1987), *The Attacker's Advantage*, London: Pan Books.

Global Investor, (1999), 'Australia Opens Doors to Venture Capital Firms', *Global Investor*, **127**, available at <//global.umi.com>.

Gouwland, L. (1998), 'Negotiating the Regulatory Maze', *The Independent Business Weekly*, 30 September, pp. 29–30.

Hayes, G. (2000), 'Wavering or Drowning?', *Australian CPA*, **70** (7), available at <//global.umi.com>

Holmes, S., K. Dunstan and D. Dwyer (1994), 'The Cost of Debt for Small Firms: Evidence in Australia', *Journal of Small Business Management*, **32** (1), 27–31.

HR Focus (1999), 'Training Budgets Fattened in Australia', *HR Focus*, **76** (9), 5, available at <//global.umi.com>.

Jones, M.V. (1999), 'The Internationalisation of Small High-Technology Firms', *Journal of International Marketing*, **7** (4), 15–41.

National Office for the Information Economy (NOIE) (2000), 'E-Commerce Across Australia', available at <www.noie.gov.au>.

Organisation for Economic Cooperation and Development (OECD) (1985), *Costs and Benefits of Protection*, Paris: OECD.

Organisation for Economic Cooperation and Development (OECD) (1994), *Trends in International Migration, Annual Report*, Bologna: OECD.

Organisation for Economic Cooperation and Development (OECD) (1997), 'Best Practice Policies for Small- and Medium-sized Enterprises', available at <www.oecd.org>.

Organisation for Economic Cooperation and Development (OECD) (2000a), *Workshop 1: Enhancing the Competitiveness of SMEs through Innovation*, Bologna: OECD.

Organisation for Economic Cooperation and Development (OECD) (2000b), *Workshop 2: Local Partnerships, Clusters and SME Globalisation*, Bologna: OECD.

Pratten, C. (1991), *The Competitiveness of Small Firms*, Cambridge: Press Syndicate of the University of Cambridge.

Raby, P. (2000), 'Show Me the Money', *Australian CPA*, **70** (4), available at <//global.umi.com>.

Report of the House of Representatives Standing Committee on Industry Science and Technology (1990), *Small Business in Australia: Challenges, Problems and Opportunities*, Fyshwick: Canberra Publishing and Printing Co.

Surry, M. (2000), 'Love It, or Hate It', *Asian Business*, **36** (12), available at <global.umi.com>.

12 Japan: The Role of SMEs in the Mature Economy

Keishi Sugiura

12.1 INTRODUCTION

Relative to the situation in the other economies studied in this volume, assessing the impact of the Asian financial crisis on SME performance is a somewhat complicated exercise in Japan. Japanese SMEs, as well as large enterprises, have been facing structural problems since the early 1990s. These problems include global competition with low-wage countries, the legacy of the economic bubble and its collapse in the late 1980s, the rapid ageing of the population pyramid, and a mismatch between information technology and business customs. The financial crisis in 1997, when a number of financial institutions including some of the largest collapsed, could have taken place due to domestic reasons, regardless of conditions in other Asian countries.

Recent industrial policy appears to have been formulated in the expectation that SMEs will break through this stalemate. They are no longer allowed to wait for trickle-down benefits from large enterprises or bailout packages from the government, but instead are expected to provide the innovative drive necessary to deliver the Japanese economy from its current state of malaise.

In this chapter, the current situation and future prospects of Japanese SMEs are presented, together with some policy implications. The structure is as follows. First, an overview of Japanese SMEs is conducted in Section 12.2 and is followed in Section 12.3 by an analysis of the direct impacts the financial crisis had on their performance. The impacts include (i) an export slump from Japan and (ii) capacity underutilisation and exchange rate losses inflicted on their Asian subsidiaries. Section 12.4 analyses the repercussions of the credit crunch, which intensified at around the same time as the financial crisis. In the author's opinion, however, the above two factors are not the fundamental causes of SME difficulties. More serious concerns are the aforementioned structural problems, manifesting themselves prominently in the automobile industry most recently. Section 12.5 discusses the changing nature of inter-firm relationships in Japan, involving a movement away from the traditional one between small and large enterprises, within the context of a *keirestu*, towards the promotion of inter-firm relationships between SMEs within the context of industrial agglomerations. Recent experience suggests that some types of industrial agglomerations in Japan have demonstrated a resilience to changing market conditions. Section 12.6 identifies developments in the entrepreneurial spirit of the Japanese in the face of shrinking markets, and uses, as an example, the take-up of business opportunities arising from the adoption of e-commerce. The available evidence suggests that, thus far, e-commerce has made only a limited contribution to SME rejuvenation. Finally, Section 12.7 presents a summary of the major issues arising from this chapter, and the major policy implications.

12.2   SMES AND THE JAPANESE ECONOMY

12.2.1   Macroeconomic Contribution of SMEs

Measuring the relative contribution of SMEs to the country's macroeconomic performance is a complicated exercise, in part because of the varying definitions in use. The SME Basic Law adopts two separate criteria – workforce and capital. As might be expected, applying the two criteria produces different results. As shown in Figure 12.1, in 1996, 74 788 firms met the capital criterion (that is, were classified as SMEs by this criterion) but not the workforce criterion; at the same time, 15 520 firms met the workforce criterion but not the capital criterion. Second, branches are included in the term establishments but excluded from enterprises due to the lack of independent status. In other words, branches are not classified as SMEs. Third, there were twice as many 'personal enterprises' as legal entities. Altogether there were 5 072 922 enterprises satisfying at least one of either the workforce or the capital criterion as SMEs. This is indicated as the shaded area in Figure 12.1. Small enterprises, which are classified only by the workforce criterion, numbered 4 483 576 firms.

This intricate classification, if taken over time, shows the changing nature of business organisation in Japan. The numbers of both small and medium sized establishments and small and medium sized enterprises have been decreasing, and the latter at a higher rate. A growing proportion of new establishments are company branches, whereas personal enterprises shut down faster than they open up. The issue of business birth and mortality rates is discussed in more detail in Section 12.6. Moreover, the average number of workers employed by an establishment is increasing, but the figure for legal enterprises is declining. Such a contrast implies that large enterprises tend to divide themselves into small subsidiaries.

Among government agencies, several authorities – for example, the Ministry of International Trade and Industry (MITI), the SME Agency, the Management and Coordination Agency, the Ministry of Finance, the Ministry of Labour and the Bank of Japan – have devised different criteria for their specific purposes. For instance,

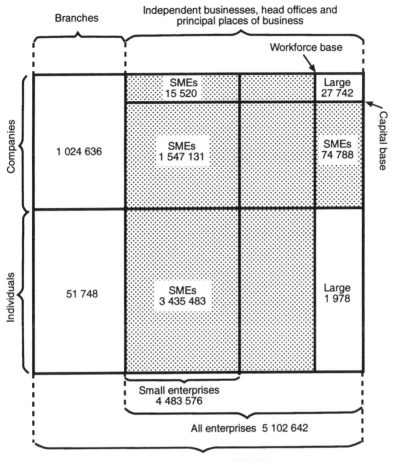

Note: The shaded area is defined as SMEs.

Source: SME Agency White Paper (1999, p. 24).

Figure 12.1   *Legal Definition of SMEs, 1996 (excl. agriculture and forestry)*

MITI defines SMEs as establishments with fewer than 300 employees in order to make use of the Census of Manufactures data. Comparisons between SME statistics produced by different authorities of the Japanese government must therefore be treated with care.

Trade statistics cannot be easily matched against firm-size data. Therefore, MITI arranged the Customs' commodity classification into three groups: typical SME

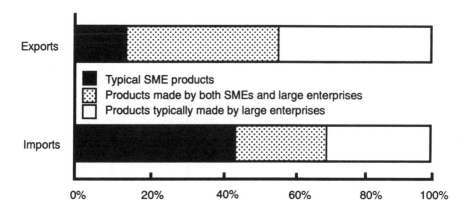

(a) Exports and Imports by Firm Size (1998)

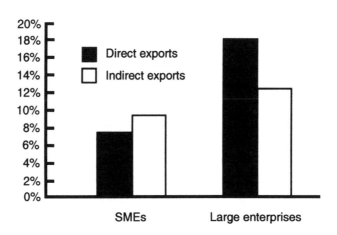

(b) Significance of Indirect Exports (1995)

Source: SME Agency White Paper (1999; p. 395).

Figure 12.2   *SMEs' Contribution to Exports*

products, products made by both SMEs and large enterprises, and products typically made by large enterprises. Typical SME products are 14 per cent of export value and 43 per cent of import value (Figure 12.2). According to the input–output table by firm size, however, SME products are more often exported indirectly as a component of large enterprise exports.

A caveat for international comparisons of SME contributions is that Japanese SMEs tend to be much larger than those in, say, Thailand and the Philippines in terms of value. In Japan, manufacturing SMEs are classified as those with up to 300 employees or capital of 300 million yen (US$2.8 million). Both Thailand and the Philippines define SMEs as firms with up to 200 employees, smaller by one-third than for Japan. However, their definitions in terms of fixed assets are up to 100 million baht (US$2.4 million) in Thailand and 60 million pesos (US$1.3 million) in the Philippines. It is not easy to compare capital and fixed assets directly, but the fact that the capital of Japanese SMEs exceeds fixed assets of ASEAN[1] SMEs suggests that the technological level of these varies considerably. Therefore, initiatives directed at encouraging the networking of SMEs beyond national boundaries in Asia, such as that promoted by APEC, could be doomed to failure due to a basic mismatch in the levels of technological competence.

12.2.2   Recent Trends in the SME Sector

Comparing the production trend between SMEs and large enterprises (see Figure 12.3) suggests that there has been a broad discrepancy since the beginning of 1997. While large enterprises enjoyed a production peak until January 1998, SMEs suffered from a downward trend in production throughout 1997 leading to a much deeper trough in 1999. In addition, the level of SME production in 2000 was still below the 1995 average, while that of large enterprises almost reached the post-bubble peak. It

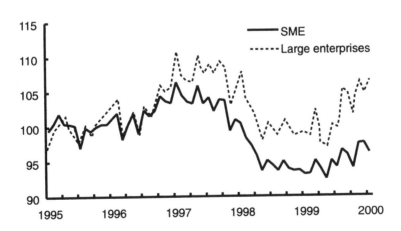

Source: SME Agency (2000).

Figure 12.3   *Changes in Production Indices (1995 = 100)*

is apparent from this that Japanese SMEs are struggling hard to recover their previous rates of growth and production levels.

Sectoral performance has not been uniform under this general trend. Fiscal cutbacks in 1997 directly hit public works and housing construction, with a severe blow to metal products and ceramic/masonry articles. The failure of a number of large financial institutions then upset consumer confidence, slashing demand for transport equipment and textiles/apparels. In early 1998, in the aftermath of the Asian financial crisis as well as the consumption slump in Japan, the market for non-electrical machinery and industrial materials (for example, metal products and chemicals) was devastated. On the other hand the adverse impact on the electrical machinery and precision equipment sector was relatively mild, and this contributed to the initial stage of recovery. Conditions in the industrial materials and wood/paper products sectors also improved in 1999, and in 2000 a wider range of manufacturing activities showed signs of recovery.

Diffusion indices (DIs) showing the net percentage of survey respondents who reported positive answers are presented in Figure 12.4, to examine the trends in SMEs'

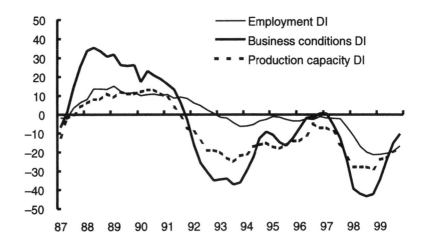

Notes: SME definition is different between the SME Agency and the Bank of Japan.
Business Conditions DI = Improved % – Deteriorated %.
Employment DI = Increase % – Decrease %.
Production Capacity DI = Insufficient % – Excessive %.

Sources: Employment and Business Condition DIs (all industries) from SME Agency and Japan Small and Medium Enterprise Corporation (2000); Production Capacity DI (manufacturing only) from Bank of Japan (2000).

Figure 12.4   Trends in Three SME Diffusion Indices (DIs)

facility utilisation and employment. A number of observations can be made. First, the indices have generally been negative since the bubble burst, except for the Business Conditions (respondents' judgement of general business conditions primarily in the light of individual current profits) DI during 96Q4–97Q1 which was marginally positive. Second, the trough in the post-crisis period was even deeper than that immediately after the bubble. This has implications for the recovery process of the economies of Asia. Third, the Production Capacity DI shows a closer correlation with the Business Conditions DI than the Employment DI does.

It is often maintained in the policy debate in Japan that SMEs are chronically short of an available workforce so that they continue to hire additional labour even in a recession. Some SME owners have argued that they can recruit superior human resources only in a recession when big companies do not skim off the cream. In contrast, large enterprises reduced their workforce in the business upturn of 1994–96 (see Figure 12.5). They could not generate profits without human resource adjustments.

Nevertheless, the correlation between the Business Conditions DI and the Employment DI has become much closer in the latest trough than previously. SMEs' capacity for labour absorption, which was a primary *raison d'être* of SME policies, declined, hitting a historic low in the recent economic stagnation. Non-manufacturing SMEs, which as a group have never reduced their workforce, appear also to have felt the same constraints on hiring as did the manufacturing SMEs.

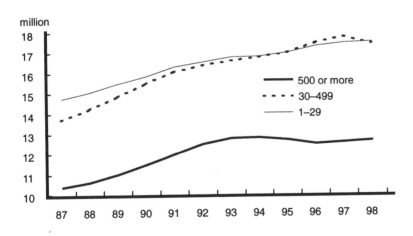

Source: Management and Coordination Agency (1999).

Figure 12.5   *Number of Employees by Firm Size (excl. agriculture and forestry)*

12.3   IMPACT OF THE FINANCIAL CRISIS ON SME PERFORMANCE

Two types of direct impact which the Asian financial crisis had on Japanese SMEs can be identified: (a) a slump in exports to countries which had agreed to terms imposed by the International Monetary Fund (IMF) in order to qualify for financial assistance, and (b) hardship imposed on SMEs with subsidiaries operating in other Asian economies.

12.3.1   Export Slump

Figure 12.6 shows that the impact of the crisis on exports from Japan varied between typical SME products and products usually made by large enterprises. A slump in exports to countries operating under IMF conditionality was much harsher for SME products than large-enterprise products. Moreover, SME products did not enjoy a buffer such as through increasing exports to the United States. The slump was especially deep for exports of non-electrical machinery, indicating capacity underutilisation and investment suppression in the troubled countries. Nevertheless, it should be borne in mind that a large proportion of Japanese SME exports is indirect in the sense that they are incorporated into the final products of large enterprises in Japan before being exported (see Figure 12.6b).

12.3.2   Hardship of SME Subsidiaries in Asia

Figure 12.7 shows that SME subsidiaries in Asia suffered from larger sales losses (in yen terms) at an earlier stage of the crisis, compared both with SME subsidiaries in total and with all subsidiaries in Asia.

There are two aspects of difficulties in SME operations in Asia: real and financial. Real difficulties mean that, despite increasing competitiveness thanks to the exchange rate depreciation, stagnant regional and local markets did not result in an increase in sales. In addition, rising procurement costs due to the high import ratio have offset much of the increased price competitiveness. Financial difficulties were caused by exchange rate volatility and banking-system fragility. The Japan Finance Corporation for Small Business (JFS) conducted a questionnaire survey in September 1998, to which 268 SME subsidiaries were effective respondents. Of particular interest is the source and the currency of finance (Table 12.1).

According to Table 12.1, SME subsidiaries in Asia depend on two potentially risky methods of finance. First, and more prevalent in the ASEAN4 countries, were loans in non-local currency from their parent companies. The latter easily acquired funds from closely connected banks in Japan at very low interest rates. Similar financial sources were foreign-exchange loans from branches of Japanese banks in the offshore market. However, the unprecedented pace of depreciation of the local currency swelled

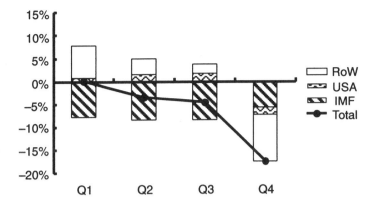

(a) Typical SME Products

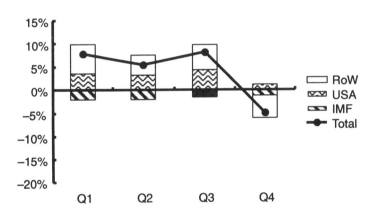

(b) Products Typically Made by Large Enterprises

Notes: IMF = exports to the three countries under IMF conditionalities, that is, Indonesia, Korea and
          Thailand.
          RoW = exports to the rest of the world.

Sources: SME Agency White Paper (1999, p. 397).

Figure 12.6   *Export Growth Rates in 1998 by Destination (year-on-year)*

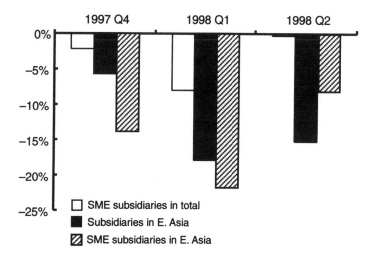

Source: SME Agency White Paper (1999 p. 401).

Figure 12.7   Changes in Sales of Overseas Subsidiaries (year-on-year)

Table 12.1
Finance of SME Subsidiaries in Asia (multiple choice)

	Source							
	Parent company in Japan		Financial institutions in Japan		Local branches of Japanese bank		Local financial institutions	
	Currency							
Location	Japanese yen	Foreign exchange	Japanese yen	Foreign exchange	Japanese yen	Foreign exchange	Japanese yen	Foreign exchange
ASEAN4	81%	45%	2%	1%	15%	10%	12%	3%
NIES4	35%	37%	0%	0%	32%	1%	22%	0%
Total	68%	43%	1%	0%	20%	7%	15%	2%

Notes: ASEAN4 = four ASEAN countries (Indonesia, the Philippines, Malaysia and Thailand); NIES4 = four newly industrialising economies (Hong Kong, Korea, Singapore and Taiwan).

Source: JFS Report No.99 –2 (1999a, p. 25).

the amount of repayments in local currency terms. Most of such loans had not been hedged at all, taking the fixed exchange rate system operative in many of these countries for granted.

Second, and more often seen in the NIES4 countries, were loans in local currency from either branches of Japanese banks or local financial institutions. In the face of an ever-rising ratio of non-performing loans, local financial institutions became extremely hesitant lenders. Moreover, Japanese banks were increasingly being subject to the need to engage in asset restructuring at home, and to reduce their overseas loans. They were subject to a so-called 'Japan spread' added to their cost of foreign-exchange procurement, in addition to Prompt Corrective Action in the case of violating capital-adequacy-ratio (CAR) regulations.[2] Both of these contributed to reluctance to lend by Japanese banks to regional economies. None the less, this adversity did not prevent most of the surveyed respondents from being determined to remain in their host countries. Interestingly, SME subsidiaries in the ASEAN 4, including those located in Indonesia, on balance, appeared to be more optimistic about the future (see Figure 12.8).

In fact, quite a few subsidiaries of Japanese SMEs in Asia employ over 500 workers, far more than their parent companies. Nearly 80 per cent of the respondents are equipped with production facilities at least as new as those of their parent companies, and more than 30 per cent boast of technological capability no lower than in Japan. The potential of enhancing productivity is also high, as the recession has encouraged workers to stay longer in the same plant for training. Market access is also promising after local competitors no longer enjoy preferential treatment, and, under IMF lending

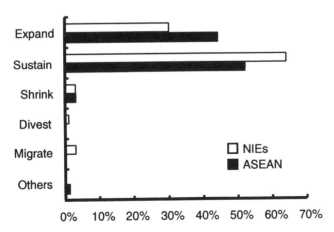

Note: Measured by percentage of survey respondents.

Source: JFS Report No. 99–2 (1999a, p. 37).

Figure 12.8   *Outlook of SME Subsidiaries in Asia*

requirements, local markets are opened up. Finally, surveyed respondents believed in an early recovery of the Asian economies to a sustained growth trajectory. For all these reasons parent companies were willing to issue new stocks to pay back high-interest loans, or swap loans with new stocks to mitigate foreign exchange losses.

Therefore, it can be said that the financial crisis in East Asia was not a primary reason for the current weakness of Japanese SMEs. The majority of SMEs are neither exporters nor overseas investors. Compared with the rapid pace of the recent recovery in some troubled economies, domestic SMEs have been extremely slow to show signs of growth. It is necessary therefore to look into the domestic aspects of the weak performance of SMEs in Japan.

12.4   CREDIT CRUNCH

The term credit crunch (*kashi-shiburi* in Japanese) was a catchphrase in 1998 to express the depth of the recession. It was believed that innumerable SMEs were being forced into bankruptcy due to the self-interest of banks. In fact, the number of 'credit-crunch bankruptcies', classified by a credit-research house, was not particularly large in the context of a total of 18 749 SME bankruptcies in 1998 (see Figure 12.9).

Note: 'Credit-crunch bankruptcy' does not mean all bankruptcies due to lack of funds but only those mainly caused by an attitudinal change of the financial institutions, such as 'reduction in loan value', 'more detailed inspection of financial conditions' or 'demand for additional collateral'. The above number includes large enterprises.

Source: Teikoku Data Bank.

Figure 12.9   Number of So-called 'Credit-Crunch Bankruptcies'

12.4.1   Causes of the Credit Crunch

At the height of the economic bubble in the late 1980s, financial institutions poured easy money into risky real-estate developments and unjustifiable business expansions. Once the bubble burst, however, a large proportion of these projects became untenable and, consequently, were unable to repay their debt. Such developments increased the number of non-performing loans and bad debts held by the overextended banking sector. The Bank for International Settlements (BIS) has stipulated that bank supervisory agencies should apply remedial measures to banks whose capital adequacy ratios fall below 8 per cent. The government of Japan, concerned with the steady erosion of the capital base of the banking system due to increasing bad debts, decided to apply, from April 1998, Prompt Corrective Action[3] to international banks whose CARs were below 8 per cent and domestic banks whose CARs were below 4 per cent. Consequently, the banks rushed to improve their CARs either (i) by reducing the level of risky assets or (ii) by augmenting equity capital. In order to facilitate the latter measure, the government allotted as much as 13 trillion yen in public funds. In the event the financial institutions were reluctant to utilise such public funds, preferring instead to reduce the level of their risky assets. Some of them were so desperate to do so that they declined to roll over loans even to creditworthy borrowers. These developments also contributed to Japanese banks withdrawing loans to regional economies, and contributed to the significant capital flight from the crisis-afflicted economies.

12.4.2   Disproportional Impact on SMEs

The credit crunch has tended to have a more pronounced impact on SMEs, as they are more dependent on bank loans for their finance. Traditionally, large enterprises enjoyed easier access to bank loans, whereas SMEs had to resort to trade liabilities (notes, bills and trade accounts payable). More recently, however, large firms have shifted their financing needs from bank loans to equity capital and debentures on the capital market (see Figure 12.10a). SMEs, however, still depend to a considerable degree for their finance from bank loans (long or short). Consequently, the banks have paid increasingly more attention to the needs of SMEs. Such a switch can be seen more drastically from the structure of the net increase/ decrease in the finance of capital investments (see Figure 12.10b).

The financial condition of Japanese banks remains unclear. The self-assessment of non-performing loans conducted by weak institutions may not provide reliable information. It can be argued, however, that the credit crunch that afflicted the economy during the 1997–98 period, in particular, has been ameliorated since the system of public credit insurance/guarantee was strengthened in October 1998. The recovery of the stock market is also providing a breathing space for private banks with unrealised profits on their loans to date. However, the situation remains volatile.

Although the credit crunch is no longer a general phenomenon across the board,

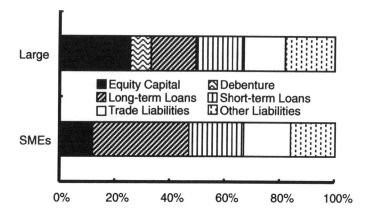

Source: SME Agency White Paper (1999, p. 72).

(a) Outstanding balance at year end (1997)

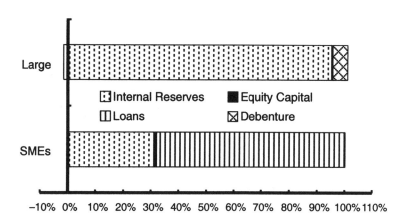

Source: SME Agency White Paper (1999, p. 365).

(b) Net annual change in capital investments (1998)

Figure 12.10   Contrasts in Financing Structure

the conditions of lending are heavily dependent on borrowers' performance. The surge in business bankruptcies was not generated by the credit crunch in its strict sense, but, rather, by their poor performance and business prospects. Businesses, including SMEs, that did go into bankruptcy were those unable to adapt to structural changes which had already been taking place long before the credit crunch, and indeed the financial crisis, appeared.

12.5 INTER-FIRM RELATIONS AND INDUSTRIAL AGGLOMERATIONS

The key characteristics of the Japanese business environment in the late 1990s can be summarised as follows: a consumption slump attributed to a rapid ageing of the population and an associated desire to provide for retirement, and uncertainty about future economic developments; excessive production facilities constructed during the period of the 'bubble' economy of the late 1980s; a banking sector credit crunch as discussed in the previous section; a one-way transfer of production sites from Japan to other Asian economies; and a global alliance between large firms to finance huge R&D expenditures.

These features have had both grave implications for SMEs in Japan as well as presenting new business opportunities, through changing the nature of inter-firm relationships between them and large enterprises. On the other hand, mass customisation and information technology (IT) has promoted a different type of inter-firm relationship, this time between SMEs. This section deals first with the demise of *keiretsu* in the Japanese automobile industry and then, second, with an emerging trend towards new industrial agglomerations.

12.5.1 Meltdown of the Automobile *Keiretsu*

Keiretsu is an inter-firm relationship identified not just in Japan but also in some other late-industrialising countries such as, most notably, South Korea. It is (i) more stable, (ii) more intimate and (iii) more closed than ordinary arm's-length inter-firm relationships. Western countries, the United States in particular, have regarded *keiretsu* both as a barrier to market access and as a source of international competitiveness. However, its terminology is ambivalent and extremely versatile. It can be horizontal among ex-*zaibatsu* (family-owned) large enterprises, or vertical between assemblers and suppliers, or between manufacturers and dealers. It can be financial as in the main-bank system and mutual shareholdings, or commercial with business transactions.

Although *keiretsu* is still seen as omnipresent in Japan, both financial and commercial aspects are rapidly collapsing. The banking crisis and subsequent CAR regulations significantly reduced the merits of the main-bank system and mutual shareholdings. The commercial relationship is also getting thinner, arising from an expansion in the degree of industrial globalisation. Automobile assembly is much more characterised by *keiretsu* than electronics but still less so than the distribution of automobile or petroleum products. It is the automobile industry, a successful model in organising an effective *keiretsu* in the past, that is in the midst of drastic change now. Both automobile assemblers and autoparts suppliers are conducting a comprehensive review of their relationship with each other for two major reasons.

First, domestic demand for automobiles has continued to shrink while overseas demand is increasingly being satisfied by local production rather than by exports from Japan. These reflect changes in the domestic population pyramid and in the global market that are structural in nature, unlike cyclical fluctuations of business conditions and exchange rates. The capacity utilisation of all assembly plants in Japan was only 74.6 per cent in the fiscal year 1998. Moreover, US and European assemblers, who are increasingly winning the global game of market integration, are interested in entering the Japanese market. Consequently, Japanese assemblers can no longer guarantee order sizes sufficient for their *keiretsu* suppliers.

Second, major technological changes under way, such as clean-energy cars, the Intelligent Transport System (ITS) and recycling systems, require a huge amount of investment. Other types of technological change, such as the use of new materials (for example, aluminium and plastic resin), are also generic in nature and thus cannot be adequately utilised simply through incremental improvements by incumbent (for example, iron-casting) suppliers. Moreover, the introduction of the modular system and standardisation of inter-firm communications has reduced transaction costs, and consequently enabled assemblers to pick non-*keiretsu* suppliers and for suppliers to approach non-*keiretsu* assemblers.

Automotive assemblers have not been passive in the face of these challenges. They first integrated platforms and applied common parts to different models. Next, they reviewed their *keiretsu* to optimise their procurement system on a global scale. They then slimmed the product line-up through OEM (original equipment manufacturing) agreements with domestic and overseas competitors. Finally, after all these efforts, they rationalised assembly plants and shut down the least efficient ones.

Suppliers also brushed up their core competence and persuaded non-*keiretsu* assemblers to use their products. Those with overseas plants reshuffled their division of labour, allowing them to make and export higher-end products. Some restructured their product line-up through strategic alliances with non-*keiretsu* competitors. Secondary/tertiary subcontractors organised themselves into cooperative associations so that they could package their competences (such as stamping, machining, and surface treatment).

The dissolution of a *keiretsu* takes place in the most violent form when assemblers are obliged to invite their overseas competitors to provide finance. Mazda (from Ford) and Nissan (from Renault) are cases in point. The Nissan Revival Plan, announced in October 1999, surprised the nation by its thorough overhaul of previous modes of operation. According to the Plan, five domestic plants were to be closed down with the loss of 21 000 group employees (15 per cent of the total). With regard to suppliers, the existing *keiretsu* is to be dismantled by selling stocks held in 1 390 affiliated companies (excluding the four most important subsidiaries) and by reducing its 6 900 suppliers by half. Its ambitious target is to achieve a 20 per cent cost reduction within three years.

The *keiretsu* will be replaced by a system called OPTIMA, which designates just a single supplier per component based on quality, cost, delivery and R&D capability rather than capital affiliation or historical relationship. OPTIMA suppliers are likely to be selected from the 100 largest suppliers in the world, so that Nissan's overseas plants can procure the same component from the same supplier wherever they are. Once the number of suppliers is halved, the order lot per supplier could be twice as large. Resultant cost savings can be further enhanced by design modifications to use the same parts as Renault. Fragile Nissan also no longer supports suppliers' R&D activities.

The initiative in reorganising *keiretsu* suppliers is in the hands of Nissan, as the latter sells its share in affiliates to whoever is appropriate. Nissan also forces them to merge or ally with each other, otherwise they are subordinate to global suppliers. Global suppliers are interested in acquiring them so that they may build production capacities and marketing channels as quickly as possible. A similar principle applies to the stage of module subassembly, where first-tier suppliers choose subcontractors free from Nissan's intervention. Those left out of the Nissan *keiretsu* cannot help but approach other assemblers. Consequently, this brings about a chain reaction and leads the automobile *keiretsu* to an industry-wide meltdown.

12.5.2   Metamorphosis of Industrial Agglomerations

Keiretsu SMEs in the automobile industry are usually located close to one another around assembly plants. Such geographical concentrations of SMEs are called industrial agglomerations. They have been intensively studied both as a source of industrial dynamism and regional imbalance. The SME Agency White Paper in 1997 classified industrial agglomerations according to their birth mechanism: (i) castle-town agglomerations, (ii) specialty agglomerations and (iii) municipal agglomerations. There are advantages and disadvantages with each of these types of agglomeration.

Industrial agglomerations related to the automobile industry are typically of the first type. This type of agglomeration appeared after assembly plants of large enterprises had been attracted by investment incentives, for example, to industrial estates. As the nearby SMEs entirely depend upon a small number of such plants in relatively remote areas, closure of the latter is likely to cause devastating effects to the regional economy and to SMEs.

With the second type of agglomeration there are no dominant actors, as in the castle-town agglomeration. Instead, a large number of SMEs in the specialty agglomeration restrict themselves to the role of producers, leaving the merchandising function to local trading houses. This type of agglomeration can result in a quite rigid division of labour. Should wholesalers become incapable of responding to, or oblivious of, changing tastes, shrinking markets can result in SMEs in the agglomeration engaging in cut-throat competition with each other instead of engaging in innovative initiatives. In the end, this rigid division of labour can result in distress for all the participants due to an information gap and technological lapse.

On the other hand, the third type of agglomeration often exhibits contrasting dynamism. Such agglomerations are located on the outskirts of municipal areas so that SMEs can collect a diverse range of small orders. Unlike the other two forms of agglomeration, there are neither dominant actors nor a rigid division of labour. The functional variety of participant SMEs and the flexibility of inter-firm relationships allow them to cope with special requests and ephemeral trends. SMEs in the other types of agglomerations are stimulated by their success to reduce their dependence on specific customers but usually with mixed results due to the absence of variety and flexibility. SMEs in this third type of agglomeration often organise a voluntary group to function like a multidivisional company. Such an organisation does not stick to fixed membership but invites members depending on the nature of tasks. Business transactions within the group are nothing like hierarchical subcontracting; that is, they could be both suppliers and customers. Members are expected to make a contribution to the planning and design process of new products from their own functional point of view. In this way, SMEs' ability to get through market fluctuations is enhanced.

Some local governments play an important role in encouraging them. Such groups usually have a 'gate-keeper', who is at the centre of in-coming and out-going information and who disentangles a single but complex order into individual processes and allocates them to appropriate SMEs. As gatekeepers run their own businesses, public support for arranging an administrative function with a group database could save their time. This measure also augments procedural and accounting transparency to the group activity. Local R&D institutes should also be oriented to provide them with customer-oriented problem-solving consultancy.

Group participants visit each other to understand their production facilities and expertise. They try to generate mutual trust through frequent communications and social events. In other words, geographical proximity is the very foundation of their dynamism. This point leads us to an interesting question as to whether there could be a fourth type of agglomeration in Japan, that is a virtual one through the Internet. Those in the affirmative present examples of SOHO (Small Office, Home Office) networks which carry out digital transactions on the Net without physical distribution. Nevertheless, identifying a trustful partner in the Internet community is not easy, and this may require the presence of accreditation organisations.

12.6   SMES RUNNING OUT OF STEAM

A wide variety of SMEs and their functional division of labour, coupled with other supporting services, make new business launches relatively painless. New entrants are more interested in new business frontiers, such as e-commerce, where large enterprises have not yet established themselves as dominant players. A new frontier is also where business opportunities expand rapidly in the midst of a prolonged recession. How does Japan fare, in general, in terms of the establishment of new businesses, and especially in the area of e-commerce?

12.6.1   Dwindling Metabolism

New business entrants, together with old exits, bring about metabolic rejuvenation for the economy. There is a very strong correlation between the rate of start-ups and closures. Moreover, a larger proportion of employment gain (loss) has been generated by entrepreneurial entrance (exit) than expansion (downsizing) of operative business units. Therefore, a declining start-up rate is a serious problem for the economy. According to Figure 12.11, the start-up rate for businesses in Japan declined gradually during the last decade, and so did the gap between this and the closure rate (that is the net growth rate of company numbers declined). Some people argue that this is the destiny for a mature economy as the denominator for the start-up ratio (the total number of companies) gets increasingly larger. However, in Japan both the start-up and closure rates are far lower than those in the US, as shown in Figure 12.11.

Worse still, the statistics do not contain establishments without full-time employees. Data from the Management and Coordination Agency, although containing some defects, show that the start-up rate is below the closure rate, as far as personal businesses are concerned. The same data presents bad news for those who believe in the manufacturing supremacy of Japan, because the start-up rate is 2.5 per cent lower than the closure rate in that sector from around 1995.

Why has the entrepreneurial spirit become so weak in Japan? This is not the case because of declining numbers of would-be entrepreneurs and entrepreneurs in preparation, as both increased significantly in the late 1990s. Despite this a declining trend of businesses in operation, and personal businesses in particular, can be identified from Figure 12.12. In addition, the ongoing economic recession and increasing unemployment might have been expected to drive more Japanese to think about establishing their own ventures. Nevertheless, Figure 12.13 unmistakably points out an enormous demographic discrepancy between actual and aspiring entrepreneurs.

There is room for different interpretations of the discrepancy. Firstly, aspirants may not be able to realise their dream due to the lack of a supportive environment. The SME Agency White Paper (1999, p. 306) pointed out that the biggest problem is an inadequate social mechanism for encouraging the birth of start-ups in their formative stage of business. The paper criticises the incompetence of Japanese venture capitalists,

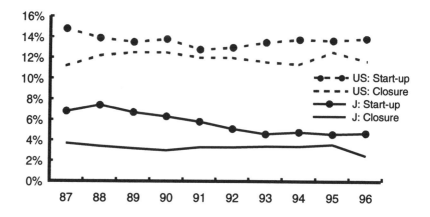

Note: The rates are calculated on the notification basis of unemployment insurance by enterprises with full-time employees.

Source: SME Agency White Paper (1999, pp. 213–14); and US Small Business Administration (1999)

Figure 12.11   Changes in the Start-up and Closure Rates – Japan and the United States (excl. the primary sector)

arguing that they come from *keiretsu* financial institutions and that their period of secondment as venture capitalists is far too short. In addition, they take charge of so many projects that they cannot provide individual ventures with much-needed managerial support. A stark contrast can be drawn with American venture capitalists who often appoint themselves as external board members.

As will be referred to in the next subsection, uncertainty characterises the emerging industrial structure symbolised by e-commerce. The capital markets and venture capital will play a more dynamic role in providing risk money. For the time being, however, most of the start-up capital still comes from entrepreneurs themselves or bank loans. Therefore, bank credit analysts, SME management consultants, tax accountants, lawyers and others need also to be trained as managerial advisers.

The second interpretation is that would-be entrepreneurs are not really ready, as they are: short of experience; lacking in basic accounting knowledge; and lacking in entrepreneurial determination. Regrettably, this argument seems to be more valid. For example Korea, a country with a similar lack of venture support mechanisms, has experienced considerable post-crisis venture activity.

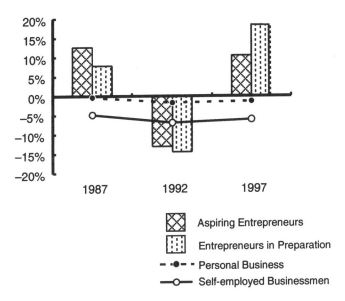

Source: SME Agency White Paper (1999, pp. 210, 266 and 276).

Figure 12.12   *Entrepreneurial Aspiration and Realisation (rate of change in the previous five years)*

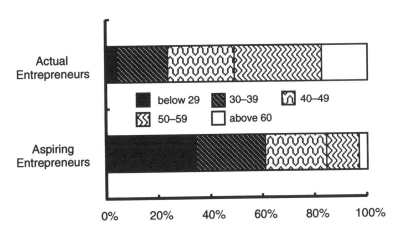

Note: Actual entrepreneurs are those who established business during 1996–98. Aspiring entrepreneurs are those who wished to establish a business in 1997.

Source: SME Agency White Paper (1999, pp. 267 and 277).

Figure 12.13   *Age Structure of Actual and Would-be Entrepreneurs*

12.6.2   E-commerce Myths

E-commerce has been envisaged as a new business field particularly suitable for SMEs. Triumphant ventures, having started with nothing but ideas, reached incredible asset values above those of many large traditional enterprises. Not all ventures were that successful, but it opened the way for average SMEs to sell their niche products/ articles to distant customers without geographical constraints. It therefore presents many potential business opportunities for SMEs in Japan. But have they taken advantage of these opportunities?

Analysts usually separate e-commerce into BtoB (Business-to-Business) and BtoC (Business-to-Consumer), as they are quite different in terms of user motivation. BtoB is introduced by large enterprises to make their supply chain more efficient. Suppliers and dealers are thus forced to adopt it, otherwise they might be left out of business. On the other hand, BtoC is introduced by SMEs and large enterprises to approach consumers directly. However, consumers do not have to choose e-commerce where traditional commerce is more attractive or e-commerce is less friendly. Therefore, the diffusion of e-commerce is much faster in BtoB than in BtoC. This is clearly indicated in the market estimates of BtoB and BtoC e-commerce in Japan and the United States (see Figure 12.14). It must be noted that the market size of e-commerce depends on its definition. According to MITI, e-commerce is commercial transactions of which order or settlement, or pre/post-order data communication related to order or settlement, is conducted through electronic media based on Internet technology. The estimates below aggregate sales value of goods and services (except for medical services, education and telecommunication) for which customers pay directly; that is not counting the market size of e-commerce-related applications and infrastructure.

Taking BtoB first, this has been promoted most vigorously by large electronic/IT-related or automobile/autoparts enterprises due to ever-intensifying global competition. E-commerce is an effective tool not only to simplify administrative work but also to synchronise each stage of the production process, squeeze inventories and adjust production planning to consumer demand (BTO: Build to Order). It is expected that the next wave will come to the construction sector, where SMEs exchange blueprints frequently, and to transport/distribution to integrate supply-chain management (SCM) with manufacturing.

The above BtoBs were those organised by specific large enterprises. In addition, there are several market sites where buyers meet sellers voluntarily as if it were BtoC. General-purpose products such as steel, chemicals and standardised metal/electronic components are amenable to the service. However, most of these sites are also operated by large trading houses thus far.

SMEs, especially those operating in the electronic and automobile industries, are likely to be impacted to a significant degree. Unlike traditional electronic data interchange (EDI) using customer-specific equipment and converting software, Web-based e-commerce is easier to accept. Although suppliers must respond to frequent requests for estimates and discounts, they can reduce inventories by synchronising

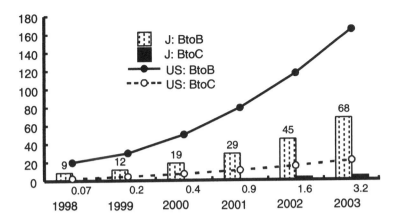

Sources: MITI and Andersen Consulting (1999); ECom and Andersen Consulting (2000).

Figure 12.14   *Market Estimates of E-commerce (trillion yen)*

their production processes with their customers. Tool makers can ask customers to assess their designs before proceeding. Therefore, those who are technologically superior, but have been excluded from business due to high transaction costs, can take this opportunity to expand their market. The consequence will be the aforementioned meltdown of the automobile *keiretsu*.

Compared with BtoB, a wider range of SMEs are launching out into BtoC. They tend to see it as doing on the Net what they were doing without the Net, but can save on costs in regard to customer dealings. Nevertheless, most sites are experimental in nature, and not intended to become a serious business. Mediocrity, or the lack of a well-thought-out business site is a serious problem above all. In contrast, sites with eye-catching success have gone beyond an extension of traditional business. They specialise in adding value to information rather than selling articles. Their income sources are more stable and varied between membership fees, commissions and advertisements. An example of this kind of service is a cyber mall. It is not easy for an SME to induce customers to visit its site for the first time, however unique the site is, unless customer recognition is improved by other advertising media. Malls frequently offer services such as regular auctions to attract consumers repeatedly. Operational costs are kept to a minimum level. In addition, participants are often provided with support to update their sites with minimum hassles. All these measures have contributed to the expansion of such malls with the result of increasing economies of scale.

It is vital for ambitious ventures to grow fast and secure market control, but bank loans are not an appropriate means to satisfy their financial needs. E-commerce millionaires play the role of an angel or an incubator in nurturing the next generation of e-commerce ventures. Initial public offerings (IPOs) of the next generation provide the first generation with cumulative opportunities to amass their riches. The riches are then used to compete with traditional large enterprises, and thus serve to diffuse the e-commerce culture into the entire economy. Nevertheless, the entire process depends on the stock market. During 2000 the share prices of unprofitable Net ventures plummeted. In order to keep the 'multiplier effect' alive, they sometimes do whatever they can to raise the share price, including dubious internal transactions through their finance company.

Large enterprises had been lagging behind these moves due to fear of 'cannibalisation'; namely, BtoC might demolish profitability of their traditional marketing channels. The purpose of their websites was limited to listening to consumers' opinions but never to selling by discounting the price. More recently, however, they have started to consider that their marketing channel is not a liability but an asset to their e-commerce strategy ('clicks and mortar'). For example, shops enhance customer satisfaction by resorting to a sense of 'seeing is believing', while terminals in the shop provide such exclusive services as virtual product coordination.

Although BtoC has opened windows of opportunity for Japanese SMEs, most of them have been slow to implement it. A number of ventures imitating recent American businesses have made a successful entry without generating profits, while the stock market remained bullish solely based on profit expectations. More recently, however, stock market developments suggest a retreat from such optimism.

12.7   CONCLUSIONS: PROSPECTS AND POLICY IMPLICATIONS

To sum up, the prospects for Japanese SMEs are likely to remain grim. The fundamental reason for this prognosis is based on neither such temporary issues as the Asian financial crisis and the domestic credit crunch, nor such cyclical factors as business trends and exchange rate fluctuations. Rather, SMEs are confronted with challenges arising from long-term changes – the rapid ageing of the population and the global integration of business activities – and it is not clear that they will be able to adapt successfully to these developments. Japanese SMEs on the whole are losing entrepreneurial 'spirit' and have suffered indigestion with e-commerce. Despite this, however, expectations about the role of SMEs in this mature economy are high. It was SMEs that introduced BtoC when large enterprises were still holding back for fear of 'cannibalisation'. A number of SMEs did not hesitate to close old businesses and establish new ones, thus driving the structural change. It is SME agglomerations which attempted brave entry into the development and merchandising of new products, organising an *ad hoc* team on their own initiative to supplement their weaknesses and gather their strengths.

It is important to point out that SMEs are no longer a uniform group to be protected from voracious large enterprises. Even within the same agglomeration, some prefer deregulation and competition, while others do not. Some are forward looking but others backward looking in the face of difficulties. Agglomerations in the municipal area have advantages which the other types of industrial agglomerations cannot imitate easily. Recognition of this simple fact has brought about a Copernican change in the philosophy of SME policies in 1999.

The gist of Japanese SME policies had long been income redistribution from metropolitan to remote areas and welfare treatment to losers. The promotion of SMEs was applied equally to all definitional SMEs in the designated industries and geographical areas. The image/model of desirable development was always drawn by bureaucrats, which stifled the initiative of forward-looking SMEs and extended the life of backward-looking SMEs. Now that globalisation has proceeded to such an extent that competitors are beyond Japanese jurisdiction, the most generous policies can no longer reinvigorate backward SMEs and regions.

The new SME policy identifies, or rather asks, firms to select themselves as forward-looking enterprises as their first step. Forward-looking enterprises are those which have a business strategy and core competence to achieve their goal, including that of obtaining outside resources for that purpose. Policy targets are then defined not just based on their scale, but on the gap between what is necessary to carry out the plan and what is available on the market. The nature of the gap varies according to the life cycle of SMEs, that is from the start-up to rapid growth and rejuvenation of stagnant firms. Implementation of the new policy will require support from public funding sources to achieve desired objectives.

This reorientation of policy towards SMEs is a step forward, although the actual redistribution of public funding or review of policy tools will not occur overnight. For the time being, neither public administration nor business associations possess sufficient experts who understand the degree of change. It may take a rather long time for SMEs to lead the structural change of the Japanese economy. The author believes that the key component of policy should be the continuous training of mature people in the most-needed skills. Japan has been relying for much of its human resource development on the internal firm-specific curricula of large enterprises or otherwise on-the-job training. Therefore, development of an accessible retraining system with an attractive and practical content is urgently required. Once employees in the new industries exceed a certain threshold, they should be encouraged to start a new business and accelerate the structural change.

NOTES

1   Association of South East Asian Nations.
2   See the following section.
3   Measures to restore the capital adequacy ratio to the stipulated minimum.

REFERENCES (IN JAPANESE)

Bank of Japan (2000), *Tankan: Short-term Economic Survey of Enterprises in Japan*, Tokyo: Bank of Japan.

Electronic Commerce Promotion Council of Japan (ECom) and Andersen Consulting (2000), 'BtoC Electronic Commerce Market in Japan', January.

Japan Finance Corporation for Small Business (JFS) (1998), 'Challenges to New Inter-firm Networks', JFS Report No. 98–5, June.

Japan Finance Corporation for Small Business (JFS) (1999a), 'Japanese SMEs are Overcoming the Asian Economic Crisis', JFS Report No. 99–2, July.

Japan Finance Corporation for Small Business (JFS) (1999b), 'The Automobile Industry in the midst of International Restructuring and the Current Situation of the Japanese Autoparts Industry', JFS Report No. 99–3, August.

Japan Finance Corporation for Small Business (JFS) (1999c), 'Transformation of the Japanese Automobile Industry and Competitive Strategy of the Autoparts Industry', JFS Report No. 98–6, February.

Japan Finance Corporation for Small Business (JFS) (2000), 'Expected Growth of E-Commerce and the Business Chance for SMEs', JFS Report No. 99–4, March.

Management and Coordination Agency (1999), *Labour Force Survey 1998*.

Ministry of International Trade and Industry (MITI) and Andersen Consulting (1999), 'Research on Market Size of E-Commerce in Japan and the United States', March.

Small and Medium Enterprise (SME) Agency (1997–99), *The White Paper on Small and Medium Enterprises in Japan*.

Small and Medium Enterprise (SME) Agency (2000), *Survey of Indices of Industrial Production for Manufacturing Industries by Scale*.

Small and Medium Enterprise (SME) Agency and Japan Small and Medium Enterprise Corporation (2000), *Survey of Business Conditions in the Small Business Sector*.

US Small Business Administration (1999), *The State of Small Business: A Report of the President 1997*.

'Net Shares are Risky', *Nikkei Business*, 7 February 2000, pp. 32–9.

'Smashing! The E-Revolution in Asia', *Nikkei Business*, 1 May 2000, pp. 26–40.

'The Nissan Revival Plan: Shocks of Chopping Off the *Keiretsu*', *Diamond*, 30 October 1999, pp. 17–19.

'What's Happening in the Collapse of the Nissan *Keiretsu*?', *Diamond*, 13 November 1999, pp. 138–44.

13   Small and Medium Sized Enterprises in New Zealand

Heather Wilson and Nigel Haworth

13.1   INTRODUCTION

Small and medium sized enterprises are a very important part of the New Zealand economy, comprising the majority of business enterprises and accounting for a substantial proportion of employees in the country. This chapter will highlight the critical role of the SME sector in New Zealand, as well as presenting issues pertinent to its future development. However, a preliminary step is to provide a definition of the New Zealand SME in order to place the information of this chapter in context.

There is no official definition of the New Zealand SME. A recent academic publication used a measure of up to 100 employees (Cameron and Massey 1999), while a recent government report adopted a definition of fewer than 20 employees (Ministry of Commerce 2000a). Generally speaking working New Zealand definitions are lower than the official definitions of other OECD nations, which can range up to 500 employees or less (OECD 1997). However, there is growing recognition that such definitions fail to capture the dynamics of the smaller firms within the 0 to 20 employee range, where new firm births and deaths are likely to be highest (Storey 1994). This observation has strong implications for the volatility of New Zealand SMEs, since 96 per cent of New Zealand enterprises employ 19 or fewer people (Ministry of Commerce 2000a). Given this, we shall focus on the 0 to 19 employee size category, as per the recent government publication, unless otherwise stated.

The chapter proceeds as follows. In Section 13.2 an overview of the macroeconomic contribution of SMEs to the New Zealand economy is conducted. The impact of the regional financial and economic crisis on the SME sector is discussed in Section 13.3. The SME sector's access to finance is discussed in Section 13.4 while in Section 13.5 the significance of culture/ networking in the conduct of business in New Zealand is discussed. Section 13.6 focuses upon the SME sector's access to technology and the use of information technology. Section 13.7 specifically focuses upon developments in electronic commerce and its promotion in the SME sector.

Section 13.8 identifies human resource development issues and needs within this sector, while Section 13.9 emphasises key policy issues and the role of government in the promotion of SMEs. Finally, Section 13.10 presents the major conclusions from this chapter and prospects for the SME sector in New Zealand.

13.2   OVERVIEW OF THE MACROECONOMIC CONTRIBUTION OF SMES

This section provides a summary of the macroeconomic contribution of New Zealand SMEs and, as far as possible, these data are presented using historical, larger firm and/or other OECD nation comparisons in order to provide context. However, it should be noted that the presented information is necessarily limited at times due to the available data not always being disaggregated by firm size.

13.2.1   Output

As of February 1999, SMEs accounted for 35 per cent of total sales and other income in the economy, up 2 per cent on the previous year (Ministry of Commerce 2000a). This increase was accounted for by micro enterprises, comprising 0 to 5 employees, at the expense of businesses employing 20 to 49 staff. It is difficult to assess the current contribution of SMEs to GDP, as these data are not disaggregated by firm size. However, we have some historical figures for the 1987–91 period, which show the contribution of New Zealand SMEs (generally fewer than 20 employees) relative to other OECD nations. At 35 per cent, New Zealand SMEs accounted for a greater percentage of GDP than SMEs in Australia and the United Kingdom (Ministry of Women's Affairs 1991), but this figure was almost half of that recorded for many continental European nations (OECD 1996). More up-to-date national figures for 1999 indicate that New Zealand's GDP per capita is lower than the figures recorded for both Australia and the United Kingdom and, of those countries where comparative information was available, exceeded only Chile and the Republic of Korea (Statistics New Zealand 2000).

13.2.2   Employment

The SME sector accounts for 42 per cent of all employees, compared with around 40 per cent employed by large firms (100+ staff) and firms of 20 to 99 employees covering the remaining 18 per cent (Ministry of Commerce 2000a). Micro enterprises, comprising 0 to 5 employees, contributed the greatest net growth in employment over the 1995–97 period. According to the OECD (1996, p. 44), 'many countries reveal the same pattern: net job creation rates tend to be greater in smaller firms'. In addition, since micro enterprises are normally distributed across the regions of New

Zealand compared with other size categories (Cameron and Massey 1999), they play an important part in regional development. However, this has to be tempered with the data that indicate that micro enterprise job security is not great – although 156 700 new jobs were created by these firms between 1995 and 1997, 100 600 jobs were lost during the same period (Ministry of Commerce 2000a).

13.2.3 Investment

The data on investment are not available at the level of the SME, but there are some indicators to understand what is happening at a country level. Historically, New Zealanders have a poor savings record, borrowing money for what could be considered unproductive investments – consumption and house purchases (Flinn 1998). The national accounts for the last financial year highlight the problem:

> These [national] savings declined ... from NZ$5 100 million in 1997/98 to NZ$2 104 million in 1998/99. That's a whopping decline of 59 per cent, rapidly accelerating a declining trend over the past years when the decline was 73 per cent. But weren't we investing in our economy to build economic growth and profitability and to rebuild our savings? Alas, no. While current spending by both households and government was up, investment was down. (Edlin 1999, p. 16)

In addition, what investment there has been had to be financed largely by offshore investors reflecting the fact that in New Zealand 'savings have slumped to a level not recorded since the 1970s' (Edlin 1999, p. 16).

13.2.4 Exports

Based on a favourable definition of firms employing up to 100 staff, approximately 2.5 per cent of all eligible enterprises are involved in exporting (calculated from figures supplied in Ministry of Commerce 2000a, and Anderson 1999). This figure is comparatively low, with 5 to 10 per cent of Australian SMEs involved in export markets based on the same employment definition (OECD 1997). Although other OECD nations employ different employment definitions of SMEs, the roughly comparable data indicates that New Zealand is bottom of the SME exporting scale. However, over the period from 1997 to 1999, New Zealand SMEs increased their share of total exports from 12 per cent to 23 per cent (Anderson 1999). Nevertheless, at an aggregated level, only 4 per cent of all New Zealand enterprises are involved in exporting, with 80 per cent of export earnings due to only 33 firms (Anderson 1999). These figures give lie to the rhetoric that New Zealand is an export-led economy.

13.2.5   Taxation Contribution

Again, there are no statistics on the taxation contribution of different size classes of firm in New Zealand. However, we can provide a general and comparative picture of the current situation in terms of tax compliance costs. SMEs in New Zealand relative to their larger counterparts incur higher PAYE (Pay As You Earn) and GST (General Service Tax) costs. Small firms employing 20 or fewer staff pay up to 150 times the compliance costs of firms employing 500 staff or more (Gouwland 1998). In a 1992 study, this amounted to a PAYE compliance cost of NZ$744 per employee for small firms versus NZ$5 per employee for larger firms (Gouwland 1998). Likewise, for every NZ$1 000 of revenue, GST compliance costs amounted to NZ$26 for businesses with less than NZ$30 000 turnover, NZ$16 for firms with NZ$30 000–NZ$100 000 turnover, and only 5 cents for companies turning over more than NZ$50 million (Gouwland 1998).

13.2.6   Globalisation

New Zealand is one of the most deregulated economies in the world, with no quota restrictions and 90 per cent of imports tariff free. In addition, New Zealand's export earnings are heavily dependent on commodities that are subject to both long-term declining prices and external shocks, like the Russian and Asian financial crises (see Section 13.3 for more detail) and the more recent increases in the price of crude oil. Therefore, not surprisingly, growth in export volumes generally lags behind growth in import volumes (Statistics New Zealand 1999), as indicated by a growing current account deficit (Edlin 1999) and declining international competitiveness rankings (Hunt 1998). This has led to calls for New Zealand firms to become increasingly sophisticated in international markets, in terms of focusing both on more value-added products (Cameron and Massey 1999) and more diversified markets (Campbell-Hunt and Corbett 1996). In this regard, debate has raged in New Zealand about the merits of the producer boards or single marketing desks that represent many agricultural and pastoral SMEs in global markets. On the one hand such monopsony structures are argued to inhibit entrepreneurship and innovation (Scrimgeour and Sheppard 1998), while on the other hand they are argued to increase the bargaining position of New Zealand SME producers relative to larger international purchasers (Gibson et al. 1995).

In sum, in macroeconomic terms, the general consensus is that the free market experiment, that was New Zealand from 1984–99, has not worked. Currently, New Zealand is supporting a large national current account deficit, national debt in excess of GDP by 100 per cent, poor export growth, reliance on commodity production, low savings rates and poor per capita growth rates. Having swung from the protected economic extreme of the 1960s and 1970s to the liberal economic extreme of the 1980s and 1990s, New Zealand is entering an era of more moderate politics with the election of the 'New' Labour/Alliance government in coalition with the Green Party (see Section 13.9). Time will tell if the change of government has an impact on New

Zealand's macroeconomic performance and, by implication, the performance of New Zealand SMEs.

13.3 IMPACT OF THE FINANCIAL CRISIS ON THE SME SECTOR

As indicated above, New Zealand's economy is not well insulated from external environmental shocks, and the Asian financial crisis is a case in point. Following the crisis, world economic growth figures were reviewed, resulting in a relatively modest 0.5 per cent reduction for New Zealand (Amor et al. 1998). In addition, the New Zealand currency did not go into freefall in response to the crisis but, in tandem with the Australian dollar, fell in a 'very orderly fashion' (Thompson 1998). Interpreted at a national level the crisis does not seem so significant; however, New Zealand is particularly exposed to Asia in certain export markets, principally forestry and tourism (Treasury 1998), and to certain countries, principally Japan and Korea (Hlavac 1998). In addition, it is not possible to determine the effect of the crisis on New Zealand SMEs directly, although it is possible to draw inferences given the level of SME exposure to certain sectors of the economy and, in turn, the sectors' exposure to certain Asian markets. Thus, this section will take a sectoral and country approach to the interpretation.

In terms of SME exposure in, first, the primary sector, over 90 per cent of the businesses in the agriculture, forestry and fishing industries have fewer than 6 employees and this figure rises to 97 per cent when focusing on firms of fewer than 20 employees (Ministry of Commerce 2000a). Second, in relation to the financial crisis, Asia represents the largest market for many of New Zealand's primary products, such as fish, wood and wood products, accounting for between 50 and 75 per cent of earnings (Amor et al. 1998). In the wake of the financial crisis, New Zealand primary exporters experienced both lower world prices for their commodity products, although the depreciation of the dollar compensated somewhat, and lower demand from all Asian nations with the exception of Singapore (Treasury 1998). However, projected earnings for the forestry industry, hit hard by the Asian financial crisis (Statistics New Zealand 1998), indicate that exports to Asia will bounce back quickly in response to volume growth for log, lumber and panel products (Ministry of Agriculture and Fisheries 1999). This is, perhaps, a reflection of the fact that most of New Zealand's exports comprise inputs to Asian exports (Amor et al. 1998), which have become increasingly competitive due to the fall in Asian currencies (Thompson 1998).

In terms of the secondary sector, just over 90 per cent of manufacturing enterprises employ fewer than 20 employees (Ministry of Commerce 2000a), focusing solely on the manufacturing category under the ANZSIC (Australia and New Zealand Standard Industry Classification). However, the New Zealand Manufacturers' Federation predicted a dichotomous effect of the crisis on the manufacturing sector based on exposure to 'at risk' countries. Indonesia, Malaysia, South Korea and Thailand were considered to be most risky, due to negative growth forecasts, while the market growth forecasts for China, Japan, Singapore, Hong Kong and the Philippines were predicted to still offer export opportunities (Amor et al. 1998). Industries most exposed to the 'at risk' nations were industrial chemicals and non-ferrous metals, industries that traditionally involve a larger scale of operations and, hence, SME exposure may have been low. However, indirect exposure to the Asian market through other export markets was expected to negatively impact on New Zealand's manufacturing sector, most noticeably for the Australian market where a full 1 per cent reduction in the rate of growth was predicted (Amor et al. 1998). The 1998 Annual Enterprise Survey revealed that the manufacturing industry maintained a steady state in the year following the financial crisis (Statistics New Zealand 1998).

New Zealand's indirect exposure to the financial crisis was also evident in the tertiary sector, but to New Zealand's advantage. The depreciation of New Zealand's dollar relative to the currencies of the US and other major countries resulted in a comparative cost advantage for New Zealand services. However, this comparative advantage depended on enough Asian consumers switching to New Zealand service providers to offset the decline caused by the crisis. However, the fall in international student numbers from Asian countries in 1998 resulted in a NZ$33.5 million loss in foreign exchange earnings across the secondary school, tertiary level and English language sectors (Amor et al. 1998). Nevertheless, SME exposure in the education sector is comparatively limited, with under 80 per cent of enterprises consisting of fewer than 20 employees, whereas the 97 per cent of SMEs in the tourism sector could be hit harder. In the three months to January 1998, visitor numbers from Asia were down by one-third, with the Korean market registering a 70 per cent fall (Thompson 1988), and many flights to New Zealand were cancelled.

Given that New Zealand is a nation of SMEs, it is safe to assume that the SME sector was adversely affected by the Asian financial crisis. However, the impact was short term and this was no doubt facilitated by New Zealand's currency depreciation. Of much greater concern is New Zealand's current account deficit, which has attained the level of many Asian nations prior to their financial crises. While the financial and commercial sector may be comparatively sound, the current account is expected to remain in deficit for some time yet (Bollard 1998).

13.4   ACCESS TO FINANCE FOR SMES

Any treatment of the financial environment for SMEs would be incomplete without a historical discussion about the developments in banking and venture capital provision. Four phases of development can be observed in both industries. During the first phase, before 1984, institutional sources of debt and equity capital were limited to eight banks (Austin et al. 1996) and one publicly owned venture capital agency, namely the DFC or Development Finance Corporation (Brown and Cameron 1995). Thus, SMEs suffered from a constrained source of finance supply during this period. In the second phase, between 1984 and 1987, both industries grew rapidly in the context of economic policy reforms that allowed new activities and freed access to financial markets (Brown and Cameron 1995). Over 16 venture capital investment agencies recorded NZ$90 million in investments in 1987 alone (DTI 1998), with the DFC being a dominant player (Brown and Cameron 1995). However, this period saw the rise of large-scale investments chasing short-term returns, for example highly leveraged management buy outs (Wilson 1995). Thus, although the supply of finance had been expanded, it was not particularly targeted to SMEs.

The third phase, in the wake of the October 1987 share market collapse, saw the financial industries decline rapidly. By mid-1989 no institutional sources of venture capital existed (Brown and Cameron 1995), the DFC having been privatised and going into receivership soon after, and it was estimated that only NZ$30 million remained invested. The banks suffered from significant bad debts and poorly performing loans. SMEs that were fortunate enough to raise funds from institutional sources in the late 1980s, and survive the 1987 crash, faced rising interest rates and restricted lending and refinancing policies (Austin et al. 1996). The fourth phase, the early to mid-1990s, saw the recovery of the New Zealand financial sector. In 1994 the government and the private sector, in collaboration, established the Greenstone Fund. The fund's original remit was to make investments of as little as NZ$50 000. However, once established, the minimum investment was revised to NZ$500 000, effectively putting it out of range of most SMEs. Nevertheless, around about the same time the banks were rediscovering the SME sector, with innovative services on offer such as mobile bank managers, and lower lending rates, with the use of housing loans to finance business needs (Austin et al. 1996).

The overall impression of the above historical review is that funding for the SME sector is extremely volatile, although this would not be a situation unique to New Zealand (Wilson 1993). Much of the equity capital on offer was outside the range of most SME requirements, leading to an observable equity gap for amounts of up to NZ$500 000 (Austin et al. 1996). In a number of other countries, notably the UK and the US, business angel or informal equity investors address this equity gap, given the information constraints of matching available angels to suitable SMEs (Wilson 1995). Although retired business people and philanthropists are likely to have made such investments in New Zealand, they are so few and far between as to conclude that business angel activity is not significant (Austin et al. 1996). However, on a positive note, a 1996 survey of the financial environment for SMEs concluded that 'while sources of institutional equity remain limited, there has been considerable innovation for the supply-side of the market, particularly from within the banking sector' (Austin et al. 1996, p. 44).

In addition, over the last two years there has been a surprising growth in venture capital firms and similar initiatives. In the recent sources of capital directory for

SMEs (Ministry of Commerce 2000b), 30 out of 38 of the equity providers listed are new, while 19 of 21 debt providers listed are new. Twenty-four of the equity and debt providers also indicate that they are prepared to consider minimum investments of under NZ$500 000, so potentially addressing the equity gap highlighted above. Some of these initiatives are from offshore, particularly from the US, where, it is argued, a glut of venture capital resources has resulted in the identification of Australia and New Zealand as potential investment destinations. Others are domestic initiatives recognising not only the funding difficulties facing new and growing companies but also the potential returns available to early investments in growth-oriented ventures (Wilson 1995).

An environment in which venture capital funding can mature is emerging in New Zealand, albeit late in the day in comparison with competitor economies. As a supply of funds builds up, it is clear that the key concern is the capacity of potential projects to, first, present themselves to potential funders in an effective way and, second, allow the investors a means of exit. Capacity building in this area is a priority for New Zealand. To that end the New Capital Market (NCM), introduced in early 2000 alongside the existing New Zealand Stock Exchange and aimed at SMEs requiring up to NZ$1 million, should support further venture capital industry development (Gaynor 2000).

13.5   SIGNIFICANCE OF CULTURE/NETWORKING IN THE CONDUCT OF BUSINESS

Three broad ethnic groups can be seen to make up the culture of New Zealand – the indigenous Maori people, European settlers of the New Zealand colony and, more recently, Asian immigrants. With a key focus of colonisation on assimilation, the European culture dominated. New Zealand's education, legal and political systems are English in origin. The values required by the early settlers to turn a wilderness into Britain's market garden included physical strength, practical skills and inventiveness. The symbols of the culture reflect these values and include agricultural icons such as sheep, gumboots and No. 8 fencing wire, which can be used to solve any problem down on the farm. The physicality of the culture is reflected in the national sport of rugby. The necessities of labour on the land removed any barriers of class distinction and the culture evolved as one that is strongly egalitarian and practical. People are valued who do, rather than think. New Zealand is a young country with little tradition in the arts.

New Zealand enjoyed a high standard of living as Britain's market garden prior to the UK joining the then European Community. This allowed a relaxed lifestyle with a focus on family and outdoor pursuits, taking advantage of New Zealand's natural harbours, beaches, rivers and mountains. Even though New Zealand's comparative standard of living has declined (Crocombe et al. 1991), a strong orientation to lifestyle considerations prevails. In business terms, although New Zealand has a substantial innovative tradition on which companies can be built, the growth of these companies is often stymied by the even stronger concern for lifestyle. As Crocombe et al. (1991) found in their study of New Zealand's national competitiveness:

> Lifestyle considerations limit the success of some of our companies. One software entrepreneur, for example, when asked why his company had not attempted to export a product that was highly successful in New Zealand, said that he earned an acceptable living and would rather spend his weekends sailing than adapting his products for overseas markets. Such choices, though personal and understandable, constrain a company's potential to grow and develop world-class competitive advantage. It also limits the jobs and income such operations can generate for New Zealand. (p. 124)

The last two decades have seen the renaissance of the Maori language and culture and a growing sense of New Zealand's multicultural heritage. This may be a reflection of the population growth rates of Maori and Pacific Islanders relative to those of European origin, and the migration rates of people from Asian nations relative to European countries. Slowly, legal and political processes are changing to reflect the new relationship between the indigenous peoples, colonisers and recent immigrants. For example, the agreement between Maori and European settlers, the Treaty of Waitangi, has been incorporated into New Zealand's legal framework, recognising land and other natural resource rights of Maoris. New Zealand's proportional representation system of government (MMP) has resulted in broader representation of the populace, both culturally and in gender terms. However, despite these changes, it is safe to say that New Zealand's colonial heritage still dominates its business values, a case in point being networking in the conduct of business.

New Zealand business people are not culturally predisposed to employing network business practices, perhaps reflecting the independence required as a remote colony. An exploratory survey across a random sample of all firm sizes and business sectors found a preoccupation with self-sufficiency and competition (Benson-Rea and Wilson 1994). Likewise, the Danish Technological Institute (DTI), in an advisory role on the development of networks, conducted a study on the New Zealand business environment and concluded that there was 'a lack of adjustment to the situation of international competition' (DTI 1994). Deficiencies in this regard included: the failure to recognise that international competition occurs in the domestic as well as in the export markets; the tradition of strong domestic protection; strategic planning to expand into international markets occurring in only a small proportion of New Zealand's manufacturing base; and the heavy reliance on exports of unprocessed agricultural goods rather than sophisticated manufactures. An earlier study, chaired by Michael Porter, on New Zealand's competitiveness concluded that the lack of strong regional clusters of successful firms and industries hindered international competitiveness (Crocombe et al. 1991).

Such observations led to the conclusion that some government intervention was required to encourage, in particular, SMEs to work together to generate the critical mass to exploit opportunities that individual companies could not (McNaughton and Bell 1998). Forcing the issue, the New Zealand Trade Development Board, the government body concerned with export promotion, concluded that its 'services can be more effectively delivered to collectives of businesses rather than to individual businesses' (TRADENZ 1996, p. 7). Two New Zealand Trade Development Board schemes will be outlined here, Joint Action Groups (JAGs), or so-called soft networks, and the Hard Business Network (HBN) program, now called Export Networks.

JAGs consist of groups of firms from the same industry cooperating to increase their relative export earnings (TRADENZ 2000). Two principal approaches are employed by JAGs, 'undertaking generic market development programs in priority export markets, and addressing infrastructure obstacles that inhibit their export development, such as skills shortages, quality requirements, finance issues, and technology transfer' (Brookes et al. 1997, p. 255). The firms participating in the JAGs provide 50 per cent of the required funding while the New Zealand Trade Development Board supplies the other 50 per cent for a limited period of time. To date, more than 1 000 New Zealand enterprises have participated in JAGs, and forty are currently active including COSMEX, a group of SME cosmetic and toiletry exporters (TRADENZ 2000). A case study of the UK Wine Guild JAG illustrates how a small winery was able to enter the UK market by sharing shipping and transportation costs on a pro rata basis with some of its larger New Zealand counterparts (Wilson and Benson-Rea 1998).

The JAG experience highlighted that many exporters and possible exporters lacked the critical mass for tackling export markets (Brookes et al. 1997). The HBN program, now the Export Networks program, was the response, and this initiative allowed for cross-industry and cross-cultural collaboration. Typically involving four to six firms:

> Networked companies commonly commit to shared purchasing, joint export marketing, joint research and development [and/or] shared manufacturing. Each company retains its separate identity and owner control, while at the same time gaining the benefits of critical mass and scale. (TRADENZ 2000)

Modelled on the Danish network program, developed to help Danish SMEs compete under the single market conditions of the European Union, members of the network were able to apply for grants, from the government's (now disestablished) Business Development Boards (BDBs), up to a maximum limit and on a matched funding basis (Brookes et al. 1997). These could be used to employ a broker to help establish and coordinate the network, conduct research and development, investigate new markets, and attend an overseas trade fair. Using a business consultant broker, the Organically New Zealand export network identified that a certified organic vinegar could command a premium price while filling a product niche in the Japanese market

(TRADENZ 2000). Two apple cider companies contributed NZ$5 000, matched by NZ$10 000 from a regional BDB, for planning, market research and trade fairs. Together the apple cider companies have started supplying a Japanese company while continuing to compete in the New Zealand marketplace (TRADENZ 2000). Ten egg producers have formed Sure As Eggs Marketing Ltd, which gives the collective negotiation power that the individual companies did not have in their relationship with large supermarket chains (TRADENZ 2000). Although still domestically focused, their 31 per cent market share and successful product branding has led them to explore export markets.

It remains to be seen whether government-sponsored network initiatives outlive their period of government funding. Certainly, members of JAGs and export networks have seen benefits arise from their network engagement. But the DTI experience, where only one-third of the created networks continued beyond the government subsidies (Brookes et al. 1997), urges caution. None the less, given New Zealand's cultural predisposition to independence and self-sufficiency, even one-third of the networks becoming self-sustaining would represent a significant turnaround in business practice.

13.6 ACCESS TO TECHNOLOGY AND USE OF INFORMATION TECHNOLOGY

Comparative statistics are employed in this section and the next to highlight the level of sophistication of New Zealand's access to technology, use of information technology (IT) and level of electronic commerce (e-commerce). Unfortunately, these data are not disaggregated but, wherever possible, inferences will be drawn to allow us to form an impression of the SME sector. However, it is interesting to note that, despite the stated intention of the new government to recognise the role of the SME in New Zealand's economy (see Section 13.9), a recent government report did not consider firm-size issues when investigating national IT statistics (Ministry of Economic Development 2000).

IT is now generally considered to encompass telecommunications and broadcasting technologies, as well as the more traditional computing and data-processing technologies (Ministry of Economic Development 2000). A brief overview of the wider New Zealand IT environment follows. New Zealand has a well-developed telecommunications infrastructure that appears competitive with Australia in terms of domestic and international service charges (Amos Aked Swift 1997). However, New Zealand compares less favourably with countries possessing a larger population base, like the US, or less geographically isolated nations of similar size, like Sweden. Thus, structural issues rather than competitive issues seem to impact on current telecommunications charges. Likewise, the geographically dispersed population base is implicated in the limited development of cable television in New Zealand

(Information Technology Association of New Zealand 1996). At a consumer level structural issues act in New Zealand's favour with the small physical size of the country and the limited population base resulting in the rapid adoption of new technology consumer products (Apperley 1998), providing they do not require the sort of infrastructure investments as for cable television. The presence of personal computers in homes has been increasing at a rate of 14 per cent per annum since 1986, leading to projections that 43 per cent of households would possess a personal computer in 2000 (Ministry of Economic Development 2000). Actual figures for 1998 indicate that 50 per cent of the household home computers had access to the Internet.

The rate of growth in Internet connections is typically measured by the number of computers directly connected to the Internet. However, this figure does not take into account home or SME connections to the Internet via Internet service providers (ISPs). It has been estimated that the true figure for Internet use could be as much as five times the number for direct Internet connections (Ministry of Economic Development 2000). Over the period from 1996 to 2000, measured by the number of computers directly connected to the Internet per 1 000 people, New Zealand rated more or less in fifth place behind Iceland, Finland, the US and Norway. This placed New Zealand ahead of Australia, Sweden, Denmark, Canada and the Netherlands. However, a 1997 study, which calculated the Internet ratio as the number of Internet hosts plus Internet domains plus Web pages divided by GDP, found that New Zealand ranked sixteenth out of 27 countries, while all of the other aforementioned comparison countries ranked in the top ten alongside Switzerland (Databank Consulting 1997). Thus, while the rankings for the comparison countries are consistent, it seems that New Zealand's ranking is dependent on how the data are cut.

While the above statistics indicate that New Zealand is a relatively well-connected nation in terms of information and communication technologies, this has not been reflected in the country's macroeconomic performance indicators (see Section 13.1). The new government of New Zealand (see Section 13.9) has made the transition to a knowledge economy a top economic priority, and central to this is the development of e-commerce policies with specific reference to SMEs (see next section).

13.7   DEVELOPMENTS IN ELECTRONIC COMMERCE

As an indicator of business activity on the Internet the number of commercial domain name registrations can be used as a proxy measure, especially since the number of overseas companies registering in New Zealand is expected to offset the number not using a .nz domain (Ministry of Economic Development 2000). The total number of New Zealand domain registration names has grown from a few thousand in 1995 to nearly 50 000 in 1999, with almost 90 per cent involving the registration of commercial domains. Relating this at a crude level to the number of private sector organisations in New Zealand, it means that approximately 15 per cent of enterprises could have commercial domain registrations (based on 293 000 private sector enterprises, including the agricultural sector, and 43 000 commercial domain registrations). However, it is likely that the commercial domain registrations overestimate the level of business activity, since companies may have several domain registrations. A better indicator might be websites. Again, growing from a few thousand in 1997, there are now over 25 000 websites in New Zealand, 87 per cent of which are commercially oriented (Ministry of Economic Development 2000). This means that approximately 7.5 per cent of New Zealand private sector organisations could have websites. Another way of cutting these data is to investigate the number of secure websites that incorporate data encryption allowing, for example, Web-based credit card transactions. Relative to the OECD average of 2.1 secure web servers per 1 000 people, New Zealand has a comparatively high level at 2.8 secure web servers per 1 000 people (Ministry of Economic Development 2000). However, given that New Zealand's annual level of growth in secure web servers is only 74 per cent compared to the OECD average of 128 per cent, this comparatively high level may not be sustained for long. Based on these estimates for New Zealand business activity on the Internet, New Zealand involvement in e-commerce at 7.5 to 15 per cent, irrespective of firm size, can be considered to be behind that of Finland (42 per cent, 250 employees), the US (42 per cent, 500 employees), Italy (41 per cent, 250 employees), the UK (37 per cent, 250 employees) and Australia (34 per cent, 20 employees or 65 per cent, 200 employees) (OECD 1998).

A general positive correlation between the adoption of information and communication technologies and firm size (OECD 1998) means that we should not overestimate the involvement of SMEs in e-commerce. The newly-formed Electronic Business Association of New Zealand (EBANZ) observed that SMEs 'are being left behind in the e-commerce race', principally due to the prohibitive costs involved (Bell 2000, p. 25). Indeed, the chairman of the Telecommunications Users Association indicated that the large numbers of SMEs was a contributory factor to the slow development of e-commerce in New Zealand (Bell 2000). Nevertheless, even among the larger organisational members of EBANZ, there was limited engagement in e-commerce activities, such as business-to-business or business-to-consumer transactions, even though the level of website usage was high. A 1998 OECD survey ascertained that the main barriers to the use of e-commerce by New Zealand SMEs were perceived to be lack of awareness, set-up costs, uncertainty of benefits, concern for security and the relative infancy of the technology. However, these concerns were not out of line with the barriers noted for SMEs in other OECD nations.

It is interesting to note the changed government stance since the 1998 OECD survey on SMEs and e-commerce. When this study was conducted, the only noted measures to promote e-commerce to SMEs in New Zealand were provided by the private sector and there were no known government programs. The new Centre-Left government (see Section 13.9) has made a commitment to helping SMEs get involved in e-commerce by promising to convene an e-commerce summit in 2000 (Pullar-

Strecker 2000), author an SME guide to e-commerce and provide financial adoption assistance through industry development programs (Labour Party 1999a; Pullar-Strecker 1999). It is hoped that such measures, if effectively implemented, will overcome concerns that the lack of e-commerce preparedness by New Zealand SMEs will inhibit their ability to compete in the international marketplace (New Zealand Institute of Management 1999).

13.8   HUMAN RESOURCE DEVELOPMENT ISSUES/NEEDS

Human resource development (HRD) issues and needs can be assessed in terms of, first, identification of needs and, second, appropriate HRD capacity building. Needs can be understood in terms of two key dimensions: entrepreneurial and management needs, and employee needs. Capacity building is best defined in terms of public and private capacity building provision.

It is a frequently repeated truism that New Zealand entrepreneurs and managers in the SME sector (that is, the vast majority of New Zealand enterprises) require significant management up-skilling (Campbell-Hunt et al. 1993). The identified needs range from the most basic up to the sophisticated.[1] In new starts, business planning skills are frequently lacking. Good ideas often founder because the commercial groundwork does not underpin the entrepreneurial vision. In many cases, an unwillingness on the part of the technical innovator to create appropriate partnerships with skilled business people has held back potentially successful operations. In SMEs that are up and running, size constraints frequently produce managerial challenges. Key individuals will take on a range of important responsibilities – from production and quality through finance, business planning and regulatory requirements to marketing and distribution. Apart from the obvious possibility of overload, these individuals frequently find it difficult to balance the competing demands within their workload. One important effect of this 'overload and balance' effect is that SMEs plateau in their development at an earlier stage than might otherwise have been the case. The experience of the Business Development Board (BDB) network suggested that many SMEs achieved a level of market success that, while providing the owners with a comfortable living, could be improved substantially given appropriate management development support.

The response of public and private sectors to these challenges is the focus of major debate in New Zealand. As we discuss below, until late 1999, public policy in New Zealand sought to reduce government intervention into the economy (Haworth 1997). Notwithstanding that policy orientation, the government provided a range of support for SMEs, which included a strong capacity building element. Thus, for example, under the BDB scheme, an enterprise could receive, on a dollar-for-dollar basis, financial support to hire the services of an experienced business consultant. The consultant identified strengths and weaknesses in the operation of the enterprise, which in turn could be addressed by further dollar-for-dollar capacity-building activities. It is widely accepted that this simple measure was highly successful as it allowed enterprises to reflect on their operating structures and identify areas where improvement was needed or possible. The BDB was abolished for cost-saving reasons in 1998 and replaced with an information clearing-house model. The BDB scheme was complemented by a range of related government initiatives in areas such as community-based employment creation, technology-based developments and exporting.

Through its education budget, government also supports substantial business education in the tertiary sector. New Zealand's eight universities and their sister polytechnics offer a full range of business-oriented programs, varying from short courses through to MBAs and other advanced postgraduate qualifications. In a policy environment in which government funding to tertiary education has been reduced over a decade, business education in the state-funded tertiary sector has been a significant source of revenue for educational institutions. Since the late 1990s, many of these institutions have begun to address the capacity building needs of SMEs by means of specific SME-oriented initiatives.

The local government sector has also been active in SME HRD capacity building. The larger local authorities have put in place local economic development strategies, sometimes in partnership with the private sector, and frequently offer capacity-building support for new starts and existing enterprises. There is an expectation on the part of the local authorities that the new government, elected in late 1999, will provide further impetus for this type of initiative.

The private sector has been very active in management capacity building for SMEs. Agencies such as the chambers of commerce and the regional employers' organisations have established training and up-skilling programs for SMEs. These have been supported by other developments in the areas of business mentoring, business planning and information and experience exchanges. Banks and accounting firms have also placed increasing emphasis on SME management capacity building as they seek to reduce risks from poor enterprise performance. Similarly, SME performance has become a significant focus in the work of accountancy's professional body. New Zealand's leading newspaper, *The New Zealand Herald*, has also taken a strong lead in the debate about SME management up-skilling.

In terms of management capacity building in New Zealand's SMEs, the paradox is this. Between public and private provision, there is a plethora of opportunities for SME management to gain improved skills. Commentators emphasise the importance of such improvements. For all that, while we have no detailed figures on take-up of opportunity, it is clear that the majority of SMEs in New Zealand are still either unaware of the HRD needs that they may have, or of the opportunities that are available to them to meet these needs, or both. This remains a major challenge for both the public and private sectors.

Turning to employee needs, we have shown above the importance of SMEs for job creation in New Zealand. Employee-related HRD issues in New Zealand SMEs are complex. Between 1984 and 1999 macroeconomic policy focused on liberalisation, including significant deregulation of the labour market. In this model, market forces were expected to be the primary drivers of the price and quality of labour. What followed has been described by Sengenberger (1991) as 'downward restructuring' across much of the economy. Enterprises have generally focused on price advantages, leading to decreased emphasis on training and a subsequent 'upward restructuring' (Maloney 1998). In human capital terms, it is now widely recognised that New Zealand must make a qualitative break from a low-wage, low-growth path to a high(er)-wage, high-growth path. This will require significant shifts, not only in terms of enterprise strategy and behaviour, but also in terms of employee capacities. If New Zealand is to have a future in a technological age, it will need the appropriate human resources.

Employee training in New Zealand is currently a combined function of the education and training system. In the education sector the New Zealand Qualifications Authority (NZQA) is charged with the integration of education provision from senior secondary to postgraduate tertiary levels on a unit standards basis. Both public and private education providers fall under the umbrella of the NZQA. Business plays an important role in establishing the standards that are set in the different levels of the framework, particularly through the activities of the industrial training organisations (ITOs).

The ITOs are jointly funded between the private sector and government (the Industry Training Fund of Skill New Zealand). In over fifty industry groups experts establish training standards, which are then administered by the NZQA. Something over 50 000 trainees are currently in place. In both Skill New Zealand and the NZQA the assumption is made that the involvement of business in the operation of the ITOs and in standard setting will reflect the needs of business, including those of SMEs. Changing political circumstances after the 1999 general election have raised questions about the future of the NZQA and the ITO structure.

Education and training provision should be seen against the background of skill shortages (Haworth and Wailes 1995). This is despite unemployment running at the 6 to 7 per cent rate. Since the mid-1990s employers have noted a changing configuration of skill shortages, particularly in the high technology areas. While not easily quantified, enterprise growth, including the SME sector, may be constrained by skill shortages.

13.9   KEY POLICY ISSUES AND THE ROLE OF GOVERNMENT

A new Centre-Left government assumed office in New Zealand in December 1999 and, as a result, government policy in relation to business has shifted substantially. In many important ways the electoral defeat of the previous Centre-Right government represented popular concern about the dramatic economic reform program first set in train in 1984. Governments since 1984 have been committed to providing a policy environment in which businesses can be successful. While the importance of SMEs to dynamic economic growth was not questioned by prior governments, they maintained that government's role was to provide a stable and sound macroeconomic environment in which SMEs could prosper. Despite copious international data on, and local examples of, market failure in relation to SMEs, especially in the area of finance provision (Aldrich and Auster 1986; Brown and Cameron 1995; Wilson 1995), the governments since 1984 have declined to intervene.

However, before and during the 1999 election campaign it became clear that business did not speak with one voice about its preferred environment. If all business commentary supported lower compliance costs and less regulatory intervention, such unanimity was not found in the business development policy area. Many exporting manufacturers argued that the post-1984 tradition in New Zealand of minimal government intervention in the area of business development was at odds with the active business development policies of competitor nations. Singapore and Chinese Taipei, Ireland and Finland were frequently identified as successful exporting economies in which effective partnerships between government and business had created competitive success. The need for such a partnership in New Zealand was a key theme in the electoral program of the new government, and clearly struck a chord in business circles and beyond.

The new government sees its role as facilitating actively the growth of enterprise, employment and export success. The new government is at pains to establish its pro-growth, pro-enterprise credentials. It has not sought to return to traditional social democratic models of nationalisation and centralisation. Rather, it has adopted the British 'Third Way' approach (Giddens 1998) pioneered by Prime Minister Tony Blair's current government. It has also placed great emphasis on technological change and innovative production methods, and, importantly, on the conditions that support SMEs.

To that end the dominant partner in the new government has promised to establish a small business portfolio and an Office of Small Business within Industry New Zealand, the central delivery agency for industry development (Labour Party 1999b). Its stated aims are to 'provide a strong voice for small business at the heart of Government ... improve the coherence and quality of government support for small business ... and help small firms on regulation issues' (p. 3). Additional SME-focused policy promises include: delivering a range of government assisted financing options; ensuring equal access to tenders for government contracts; restoring the business development program; raising awareness of available assistance; reducing compliance costs; encouraging exports (an export credits and guarantees scheme is under investigation currently); promoting the development of business incubators and industry clusters; encouraging innovation through tax and depreciation revisions; and investing in education and apprenticeships (a scheme has already been established) to improve the skills and knowledge base of the New Zealand workforce.

In terms of government activities in support of SMEs the 1999 election outcome will result in substantial modification of the 1984–99 market-driven policy environment. Interventions by government in support of SME development will increase, but will be carefully assessed in terms of their success. In this assessment the partnership between government and the private sector will play a crucial role.

13.10 CONCLUSIONS AND PROSPECTS FOR THE SME SECTOR

A consensus exists that SMEs are vital for any nation's future economic wellbeing. SMEs are important sources of technical innovation. They are key to the international competitiveness of economies, they are important in job creation and they have important regional significance. The New Zealand government has placed SMEs at the centre of its economic strategy and is bringing forward policy shifts in a host of SME-related areas. New Zealand private sector agencies – chambers of commerce and the like – are equally committed to SME support activities.

Overall, it is useful to gauge the prospects for the SME sector in New Zealand against the best-practice policies for SMEs established by the OECD (1995). Four broad policy areas were identified by the OECD as being most relevant to SMEs, namely financing, the business environment, management capability and access to markets. First, in terms of financing, the OECD report established the need for policy to counter the market failure in the funding of SMEs. The specific policies highlighted as being useful included loan guarantees for start-ups, the promotion of informal equity capital and export financing. While the present government is investigating an export credit guarantees scheme at the moment, New Zealand is deficient in the areas of loan guarantees and informal equity provision. Given that bank loans to SMEs cycle according to the prevailing economic conditions, state-funded loan guarantees may be a means to avoid the harsh lending and refinancing criteria that can cause otherwise viable companies to go into receivership. In addition, while governments are not expected to provide informal equity capital, they have a vital role to play in encouraging such investments, via taxation policies, and in facilitating the marriage of investors and investees.

Second, the business environment can be improved with regard to the regulatory burden experienced by SMEs, information services available to SMEs and government intervention in favour of all businesses (OECD 1995). In New Zealand terms the new government has made a commitment to review the specific disadvantages experienced by SMEs in complying with company legislation. The recently established regionally coordinated BIZinfo network, the result of public and private sector collaboration, is attempting to provide a one-stop information and referral service to help SMEs access government programs and services. The final area of concern, that of government intervention, is a thorny issue in New Zealand. While it is clear that the hands-off policies of the previous Centre-Right government fell out of favour with business people, the current Centre-Left government is steering clear of subsidies, tax breaks and research and development incentives, at least in the short term. Indeed, recent government plans to offer tax breaks for research and development expenditure were shelved without explanation, perhaps because an interventionist stance was considered too extreme in its first year of office. Time will tell if the new government is able to strike a balance between interventionism and neo-liberalism in order to help pump prime the New Zealand economy.

Third, management and innovation capacity building in SMEs has been identified as an area of both OECD (1995) and APEC concern. New Zealand policy in relation to management capacity building is considered to be generally strong. An important issue for New Zealand SMEs is the openness of management to change. Existing capacity-building activities are failing to reach many SMEs that might benefit from advice and support. The recognition that such support is available, and the willingness to seek it out, is for many SMEs a moot point. Innovation capacity building, on the other hand, is weak in both the public and private sectors. New Zealand does not have a national system of innovation. Policy is, at best, haphazard. This is compounded by the lack of value placed in basic research versus applied research. In addition, New Zealanders, while highly inventive, do not have a history of invention commercialisation. Whether policy can address these issues in the short term is debatable, for it seems that many of the barriers lie at the level of the national psyche. That said, an emerging New Zealand focus, albeit late in comparison to competitor economies, is high-technology, 'leading-edge' SME development in areas such as software, bio- and nano-technologies and in the advanced dimensions of the primary commodity sector. We observe an increasing differentiation in SME-related debate, in both the public and private sectors, between what might be called leading-edge developments, perhaps associated with incubation or other support mechanisms, and SMEs bounded by traditional technologies and markets. Emerging venture capital developments seem destined to emphasise this differentiation.

The final area the OECD (1995) highlighted for specific SME policy consideration was access to markets, specifically in terms of government procurement and international trade. Again, the new government has made a commitment, via its Office of Small Business, to review the award of government contracts in relation to SMEs. The aforementioned export credits guarantee scheme is also in train with regard to facilitating SME international trade. However, given the current balance of payments deficit, it is clear that more emphasis needs to be placed on export promotion by the public and private sectors. Nevertheless, public policy initiatives will fail to hit the mark if the impediments relate to the national culture of independence and isolation and the lack of perceived need by management to build capacity in this area. Understanding the impediments to international trade, both real and perceived, is key to developing a stronger international focus.

We have, through this chapter, attempted to take the pulse of the SME sector in New Zealand today. Given that SMEs have recently become a focus of public and private sector attention in New Zealand the data may serve as the benchmark against which to evaluate current and future policy, as well as developments in SME competitiveness. However, to add a note of caution, some of the solutions to the nation's competitiveness might well lie outside the three-year term of New Zealand's governments, since many of the issues lie at the level of the culture and may not be easily solved in the short term or even resolved by policy.

NOTE

1   The following discussion is based on Business Development Board internal documents for the 1988–98 period.

REFERENCES

Aldrich, H. and E.R. Auster (1986), 'Even dWarfs Started Small: Liabilities of Age and Size and their Strategic Implications', *Research in Organizational Behavior*, **8**, 165–98.

Amor, R., M. Fox, M. Hannah, J. Kennedy, R. Lattimore and S. McMillan (1998), 'In the forests of the night: second report of the Asian Economic Crisis Monitoring Group', Lincoln University Commerce Division Discussion Paper No. 52, Canterbury: Lincoln University International Trade Policy Research Centre.

Amos Aked Swift (1997), *An International Comparison of Leased Data Services Pricing*, Wellington: Ministry of Commerce.

Anderson, F. (1999), 'Too Few Companies are Exporting', *The Independent Business Weekly*, 18 August, p. 25.

Apperley, M. (1998), 'Overview of the Information, Computer, and Communication Technologies', in D. McGregor (ed.), *The New Zealand Knowledge Base Reports*, Wellington: Ministry of Research, Science & Technology.

Austin, T.J., M.A. Fox and R.T. Hamilton (1996), *A Study of Small and Medium Sized Business Financing in New Zealand*, Wellington: Ministry of Commerce.

Bell, S. (2000), 'NZ E-businesses Raise their Sights', *The Independent Business Weekly*, 16 February, p. 25.

Benson-Rea, M. and H.I.M. Wilson (1994), *Networks in New Zealand*, Wellington: Ministry of Commerce.

Bollard, A. (1998), *Issues Facing the New Zealand Economy*, Wellington: Treasury, Address by the Secretary of Treasury.

Brookes, R., V.J. Lindsay and I.F. Williams (1997), *Hard Business Networks in New Zealand: An Emerging Strategic Framework*, Auckland: University of Auckland Working Paper.

Brown, K. and N. Cameron (1995), 'Barriers to the Development of a Viable Venture Capital Market in New Zealand', *New Zealand Journal of Business*, **17** (1), 59–74.

Cameron, A. and C. Massey (1999), *Small and Medium-sized Enterprises: A New Zealand Perspective*, Auckland: Addison Wesley Longman.

Campbell-Hunt, C., and L.M. Corbett (1996), 'A Season of Excellence: An Overview of New Zealand Enterprise in the Nineties', Wellington: Ministry of Commerce, Research Monograph 65.

Campbell-Hunt, A., D.A. Harper, and R.T. Hamilton (1993), *Islands of Excellence?: A Study of Management in New Zealand*, Wellington: New Zealand Institute of Economic Research.

Crocombe, G., G.T. Enright and M.E. Porter (1991), *Upgrading New Zealand's Competitive Advantage*, Wellington: Oxford University Press.

Databank Consulting (1997), *Study on the Evolution of the Internet and the WWW in Europe*, Brussels: European Union.

Danish Technological Institute (DTI) (1994), *First Assessment and Recommendation on a Business Network Programme in New Zealand*, Copenhagen: Danish Technological Institute.

Department of Trade and Industry (DTI) (1998), *The New Zealand Venture Capital Market – A Business Perspective*, Wellington: Department of Trade & Industry Discussion Paper.

Edlin, B. (1999), 'Foreign Investment Props up NZ's Weakening Finances', *The Independent Business Weekly*, 17 November, p. 16.

Flinn, R. (1998), 'Unsafe as Houses', *The Independent Business Weekly*, 10 June, p. 32.

Gaynor, B. (2000), 'Canadian Runaway Success Shows Way in Kiwi Market', *New Zealand Herald*, 11 March, p. E5.

Gibson, J., P. Harris and A. Ware (1995), *The New Zealand Dairy Board: A Critical Analysis of the Position of the Business Roundtable*, Hamilton: University of Waikato Centre for Labour and Trade Union Studies.

Giddens, A. (1998), *The Third Way: The Renewal of Social Democracy*, Cambridge: Polity Press.

Gouwland, L. (1998), 'Negotiating the Regulatory Maze', *The Independent Business Weekly*, 30 September, pp. 29–30.

Haworth, N. (1997), 'From Regional Development to Business Development: A Decade of Business Development Boards in New Zealand', Proceedings of the APEC SME Market Development Seminar, Taipei, November.

Haworth, N. and N. Wailes (1995), *Skill, Training and Recruitment in the Auckland Region: Report of a Survey*, Auckland Business Development Board, November.

Hlavac, C. (1998), *A Closeup of New Zealand's Export Statistics: For the Year Ended June 1998*, Wellington: New Zealand Trade Development Board.

Hunt, G. (1998), 'New Zealand Struggles to Retain Competitiveness', *National Business Review*, 24 April, p. 11.

Information Technology Association of New Zealand (1996), *Impact 2001: How Information Technology will Change New Zealand*, Wellington: Ministry of Commerce, Information Technology Advisory Group.

Labour Party (1999a), *Labour Online: Labour's Strategy for Ecommerce*, Wellington: The Labour Party.

Labour Party (1999b), *Labour on Small Business: Labour's 10 Point Plan for Building Stronger Small Businesses*, Wellington: The Labour Party.

Maloney, T. (1998), *Five Years After: The New Zealand Labour Market and the Employment Contracts Act*, Wellington: Victoria University of Wellington Institute of Policy Studies.

McNaughton, R.B. and J.D. Bell (1998), 'Hard Business Network Programmes: Generating Social Capital for Firm Growth and Internationalisation', Dunedin: University of Otago Working Paper.

Ministry of Agriculture and Fisheries (1999), *1999 Post Election Brief – Outlook for Exports and GDP*, Wellington: Ministry of Agriculture and Fisheries.

Ministry of Commerce (2000a), *SMEs in New Zealand: Structure and Dynamics*, Wellington: Ministry of Commerce Firm Capability Team.

Ministry of Commerce (2000b), *Sources of Capital Available to Small and Medium Enterprises 2000*, Wellington: Ministry of Commerce.

Ministry of Economic Development (2000), *Statistics on Information Technology in New Zealand 2000*, Wellington: Ministry of Economic Development, Information Technology Policy Group.

Ministry of Women's Affairs (1991), *The Role of Small Business in the New Zealand Economy*, Wellington: Ministry of Women's Affairs.

New Zealand Institute of Management (1999), 'E-future Looks Bright', *Management Magazine*, August, p. 64.

OECD (1995), *Best Practice Policies for Small and Medium-Sized Enterprises*, Paris: Organisation for Economic Co-operation and Development.

OECD (1996), *SMEs: Employment, Innovation and Growth: The Washington Workshop*, Paris: Organisation for Economic Cooperation and Development.

OECD (1997), *Globalisation and Small and Medium Enterprises (SMEs)*, Paris: Organisation for Economic Cooperation and Development.

OECD (1998), *SMEs and Electronic Commerce*, Paris: Organisation for Economic Co-operation and Development, Working Party on Small and Medium-sized Enterprises.

Pullar-Strecker, T. (1999), 'Labour Says Knowledge Economy a Top Priority', *NZ Infotech Weekly*, 4 October, p. 4.

Pullar-Strecker, T. (2000), 'E-commerce Summit on Track for Mid-year', *NZ Infotech Weekly*, 6 March, p. 4.

Scrimgeour, F. and R. Sheppard (1998), *An Economic Analysis of the Deregulation of Selected Israeli, South African and South American Producer Boards*, Wellington: Ministry of Agriculture and Forestry.

Sengenberger, W. (1991), 'The Role of Labour Market Regulation in Industrial Restructuring', in G. Standing and V. Tokman (eds), *Towards Social Adjustment: Labour Market Issues in Structural Adjustment*, Geneva: International Labour Organisation, pp. 235–50.

Statistics New Zealand (1998), *Annual Enterprise Survey 1998*, Wellington: Statistics New Zealand.

Statistics New Zealand (1999), *Gross Domestic Product: December 1999 Quarter*, Wellington: Statistics New Zealand.

Statistics New Zealand (2000), *New Zealand in Profile 2000*, Wellington: Statistics New Zealand.

Storey, D.J. (1994), *Understanding the Small Business Sector*, London: Routledge.

Thompson, A. (1998), 'Beginners Guide to the Asian Economic Crisis', *Scoop Media*, 7 April, at <www.scoop.co.nz/archive/scoop/stories/66/e7/199804071553. dfe7f8.html>].

TRADENZ (1996), *Stretching for Growth – Two Years into an Eight Year Journey*, Wellington: New Zealand Trade Development Board.

TRADENZ (2000), *Joint Action Groups*, Wellington: New Zealand Trade Development Board.

Treasury (1998), *The Economy of New Zealand*, Wellington: Department of Treasury.

Wilson, H.I.M. (1993), 'An Interregional Analysis of Venture Capital and Technology Funding in the UK', *Technovation*, **13** (7), 425–38.

Wilson, H.I.M. (1995), 'Are the Business Angels of Today the Venture Capitalists of Yesterday?', *Journal of High Technology Management Research*, **6** (1), 145–56.

Wilson, H.I.M. and M. Benson-Rea (1998), 'Coopers Creek and the New Zealand Wine Industry', in G. Johnson and K. Scholes (eds), *Exploring Corporate Strategy: Text and Cases*, London: Prentice-Hall, pp. 756–67.

14 Small and Medium Enterprises in Singapore and the New Economy

Boon-Chye Lee and Wee-Liang Tan

14.1 INTRODUCTION

From its earliest days as a British outpost, Singapore has relied heavily for its economic survival on its position as an entrepôt trading centre. In the first decades after independence in 1965, economic strategy was focused on building infrastructure, attracting foreign direct investment, and export-led growth. The political commitment to openness in both trade and capital – and, more recently, labour – is one of the key features of a strategy that has delivered remarkable returns in terms of the economic well-being of the people of Singapore. Between 1961 and 1996 GDP per capita grew at an average rate of 10.4 per cent a year (Ho and Hoon 2000), vaulting the country into the ranks of the developed economies. However, until recently, the role of small and medium sized enterprises, in so far as they featured in this strategy, has been secondary. They were primarily the local links of the supply chains of the multinational corporations which had set up operations in the country. None the less, in this capacity, they benefited from having largely assured demand for their products, and were often also recipients of technology transfer.

In the late 1980s and 1990s the strategy underwent a significant shift. Following the country's first post-independence recession in 1985, the role of SMEs came to the forefront in the blueprint that was mapped out by the governmental body charged with the task of formulating a strategy for the future. In the wake of the 1997–98 'Asian crisis', a new element was added to this strategy: to gear the skills base and infrastructure of the economy into the 'knowledge-based economy', also known as the New Economy. The knowledge-based economy is perceived as bringing with it a fundamental change driven by two main forces: globalisation and technology. The advent of the knowledge-based economy is rightly viewed as a global development that any nation, particularly one as small and open as Singapore, could ignore only at substantial peril to its competitive position. The government's vision has been widely disseminated by means of various policy documents outlining the vision, as well as wide exposure and discussion in the mass media. Consistent with this, technology-based entrepreneurs[1] have been identified as the enterprises the government is intent on nurturing for the 21st century.

With this drive the role of entrepreneurs and SMEs in Singapore in the official view has undergone a sea change. During the colonial period after the founding of Singapore in 1819 and into the early decades of independence, local entrepreneurs had tended to be regarded with benign neglect. The post-1985 period has seen official recognition of the key role SMEs can play in innovation and in moving the economy up the value chain to higher 'value-added' activities. The initiatives in this respect may be seen as very much part of a comprehensive program to bring about the transformation of the Singapore economy to a knowledge-based economy. The results have been remarkable. The Singapore economy in the 1990s has consistently been ranked by the Swiss-based International Institute for Management Development's *World Competitiveness Report* as among the three most competitive in the world, together with the United States and Hong Kong. The broad strategy which has delivered this outcome relies on a continued concerted effort to upgrade the country's human resource base and physical infrastructure, and continual fine-tuning of economic incentives while moving up the value chain to stay ahead of its regional neighbours. The country has become according to one recent assessment the most globalised nation in the world (*Foreign Policy* 2001), reflecting, *inter alia*, its continuing openness to trade, foreign direct investments and portfolio capital flows, but also the increasing utilisation of information technologies. As a recent report by the International Monetary Fund noted:

> Continued success in shifting to a knowledge-based economy will rely increasingly on the development of a more dynamic and entrepreneurial private sector, through deregulation, privatisation, and upgrading human capital. (IMF 2000)

In this chapter, we outline the role of SMEs in relation to Singapore's economic development, the experience of the SMEs during the Asian financial crisis, and their prospects in the knowledge economy. We begin in Section 14.2 by examining the definitions of SMEs used for policy purposes and the contribution of SMEs to the overall economy of Singapore before moving on to look at in Section 14.3 the role of entrepreneurs and SMEs in Singapore in historical context. An important key to understanding developments in the post-colonial period is the extent to which government is involved in providing initiative and direction, not only to economic activity, but to almost every aspect of social policy, in Singapore. This occurs to a much greater extent than tends to be the case in other market economies. Official attention has turned in recent years to the need to develop a more entrepreneurial culture as a prerequisite if the country is to reap the benefits offered by the New Economy. SMEs are the logical entities to meet this challenge. The extent to which they are able to do so will shape the future of the country and this is discussed in Section 14.4. Section 14.5 looks at the prospects for Singapore's SMEs and Section 14.6 presents a summary of the major conclusions from this chapter.

14.2   SMALL AND MEDIUM ENTERPRISES IN SINGAPORE

For policy purposes, *local* SMEs are defined by the Productivity and Standards Board (PSB) as enterprises with at least 30 per cent local equity; fixed asset investment of up to S$15 million in the case of SMEs in manufacturing; and up to 50 employees in the case of service sector SMEs. The definition is occasionally revised (see Table 14.1).

The contribution of SMEs to the Singapore economy is shown in Table 14.2.

It is clear that SMEs play an integral role in the economy. In 1997, they employed 72 per cent of all workers in the country and contributed 58 per cent of the value added. They augment the economic activities of the larger manufacturing concerns, the multinational enterprises and the larger listed companies. They provide services in the areas of logistics, services and trading.

On the other hand, if they are inefficient, SMEs utilise capacity that could be better utilised in other activities. Hence, a major concern of government agencies has been over the productivity of the SMEs. In 1997, the value-added per worker in SMEs in general was roughly half that of workers in other establishments (S$66 000 compared with S$123 000). The disparity is particularly marked in manufacturing and in services, where SME value added per worker in both these sectors was just 36 per cent that of workers in other establishments. It is less pronounced in commerce, at 70 per cent.

Table 14.1
Definitions of Local SMEs in Singapore, 1994 and 2000

Business sector	Local equity		Fixed assets at net book value		No. of employees	
	1994	2000	1994	2000	1994	2000
Service and commerce	>30%	>30%	S$12 m.	S$15 m.	<100	<50
Manufacturing	>30%	>30%	S$12 m.	S$15 m.	na	na

Table 14.2
Contribution of the SME Sector to the Singapore Economy, 1997

Sector	Establishments		Employment		Value added (VA)		VA/Estb	VA / Worker	
	Number	%	Number	%	(S$bn)	%	(S$'000)	(S$'000)	%
Overall economy									
SMEs	98 156	92.1	801 635	72.2	52 580	58.1	536	66	80.5
Others	8 365	7.9	309 294	27.8	37 905	41.9	4 531	123	150.5
Total	106 521	100.0	1 110 929	100.0	90 485	100.0	849	81	100.0
Manufacturing									
SMEs	3 772	91.8	175 851	48.0	7 442	25.1	1 973	42	52.3
Others	336	8.2	190 845	52.0	22 212	74.9	66 107	116	143.9
Total	4 108	100.0	366 696	100.0	29 654	100.0	7 219	81	100.0
Commerce									
SMEs	52 713	96.0	272 133	77.7	15 602	71.1	296	57	91.5
Others	2 222	4.0	78 202	22.3	6 352	28.9	2 859	81	129.6
Total	54 935	100.0	350 335	100.0	21 954	100.0	400	63	100.0
Service									
SMEs	41 671	87.8	353 651	89.8	29 536	76.0	709	84	84.6
Others	5 807	12.2	40 247	10.2	9 341	24.0	1 609	232	235.2
Total	47 478	100.0	393 898	100.0	38 877	100.0	819	99	100.0

Source: Productivity and Standards Board (2000).

14.3   TRANSITIONS IN THE ROLE OF ENTREPRENEURS AND SMES IN SINGAPORE

14.3.1   Beginnings to 1985

Founded in 1819, Singapore grew quickly as a British trading port along with Penang and Malacca. The indigenous Malay population was augmented significantly by early immigrants who came from Mainland China, India and the Middle East, with the majority being Chinese. The immigrants tended to see themselves as transient visitors to the island, for whom a chief objective was to remit their earnings home. They had a short time horizon on their activities. While they came largely as labourers, inevitably some became entrepreneurs. These early immigrant entrepreneurs were opportunistic entrepreneurs, or 'arbitrageurs', in Kirzner's (1979) terminology, who recognised and exploited the opportunities presented to them in the new British colony. It would be a mistake, however, to regard them with disdain. Yu (1995), in his examination of Hong Kong's economic development, concluded that opportunistic entrepreneurship contributed more significantly to its economic growth than Schumpeterian-type entrepreneurs, who bring about new combinations and inventions.[2] The early Singapore economy had many things in common with the situation in early Hong Kong, including the nature of entrepreneurial activities.

The social backgrounds of the immigrants strongly influenced the nature of their activities when they arrived in Singapore. A large proportion of the Chinese immigrants to Singapore had fled poverty and unemployment in the coastal regions in China. They came with little capital and few business skills and network alliances – not, on the face of it, very promising material or under exactly the best conditions for business start-ups.[3] The Indian immigrants came as British convict labourers and as workers for farms, plantations and construction workers. In Singapore's economic development they have been conspicuous as textile and piece-goods wholesalers and retailers, money-lenders, civil servants and labourers (Sandhu 1993). They also had almost a monopoly of the laundry business in early Singapore (Mani 1993).

A prominent feature of the early entrepreneurs in Singapore was the tendency to establish businesses that were family owned and controlled. These family businesses thrived, a number of them growing into dynamic large businesses well into their second and third generations of successors (Tan and Fock 2001). Some of these family businesses are represented today in the hospitality industry as hoteliers, in the finance industry as bankers and owners of finance companies, in the real estate and construction industry as property developers and in the pharmaceutical industry as manufacturers of Chinese medical products.

After independence in 1965, the Singapore economy experienced two decades of continuous high growth. This growth took place seemingly despite the state of the business cycle and other developments in the rest of the world – global recessions and oil crises – with 5 per cent GDP growth in a 'bad' year and 15 per cent in a boom year (Ministry of Trade and Industry 1986). A key aspect of the government's economic strategy centred on attracting foreign direct investments through a range of incentives, including preferential tax and accounting treatment, and the continuous upgrading of physical infrastructure. The policy was highly successful. Together with the economic incentives, and offering an excellent infrastructure for industry and a well-educated and disciplined English-speaking labour force, the country was an attractive location for multinationals seeking a low-cost base in Asia. In large part, therefore, the multinationals provided the engine for growth during this period, setting the stage for continued growth by the transfer of technology and other expertise. The role of SMEs in generating the remarkable growth of this period was relatively minor by comparison.

14.3.2   1985 to Present

The boom period was interrupted when recession struck in 1985. During the intense official (and non-official) soul-searching that ensued, the importance of entrepreneurs in the economy was realised and rediscovered, as Kent (1984) observed has been the case in many rapidly developing economies. The Economic Committee that was appointed in the same year by the government to review the progress of the economy and to identify new directions for its future growth recommended that attention be paid to entrepreneurship and small- and medium-sized local businesses.

Prior to this there had been little direct emphasis on smaller local enterprises (Doh 1996). It was now felt that the smaller, more nimble local enterprises could provide a buffer to the more ponderous multinational corporations (MNCs). The Economic Committee recommended that the government should take steps to remove impediments and actively encourage the growth of local small and medium enterprises (Ministry of Trade and Industry 1986). This report led to the first *SME Master Plan* (Economic Development Board 1989). The strategy enunciated was to stimulate local enterprises through the creation of a more pro-enterprise environment, providing assistance for self-help, and accelerating the pace of growth with a range of incentives. The government's role was to guide and assist enterprises by setting the direction, improving the business environment and building up a supportive infrastructure (Economic Development Board 1989).

It is interesting to reflect on the changes to the role accorded by policy makers to entrepreneurial activity in Singapore and on their implications. Until the publication of the *SME Master Plan*, there had been an emphasis on MNCs and the development of state enterprises in the areas of manufacturing, shipping, air transport, international trade, long-term finance, marine-related services, technology and defence-related industries. These state enterprises, it has been argued, may be considered to constitute a distinct category of entrepreneurship, what Lee and Low (1990) have termed 'state entrepreneurship'. Thus the implicit belief in the primacy of government in identifying and articulating a strategic vision for the economy extended to undertaking entrepreneurial activities, except that the traditional channels of these activities, SMEs, were not recognised. The recent change in policy would appear to reflect the government's recognition of the central role of SMEs as a source of entrepreneurship and innovation. Government policy is now focused on encouraging and nurturing successful indigenous companies with the potential to grow into companies of global stature. Yet just as there may be a touch of irony in the notion of state entrepreneurship, there may also be irony in government identifying and setting the direction (technological innovation) for entrepreneurs to take. Given the government's record of success, however, it would be unwise to scoff at this approach.

14.3.3 Impact of the Asian Financial Crisis

The economy of Singapore is extraordinarily open and dependent on trade (see Table 14.3). Given this, it would be surprising if it had escaped the Asian financial crisis unaffected. What is remarkable is that it was not more seriously affected than it was, and the speed with which the economy recovered. The impact of the crisis was less pronounced than in the other countries of the region. The economy slid into a recession in early 1998 but GDP growth in 1998 overall was 0.4 per cent, rebounding to 5.5 per cent in 1999. During that time the unemployment rate reached a peak of 4.5 per cent in 1998, dropping to 3 per cent at the end of 1999 and to 2.9 per cent in early 2000.

Table 14.4 shows the impact of the Asian crisis on the country's external trade. Total trade fell by 7.5 per cent in 1998, then recovered by 8.1 per cent in 1999 to the pre-crisis level of $382 billion that was achieved in 1997 (Trade Development Board 2000). The growth reflected a strong 17.3 per cent increase in the second half of 1999, following a marginal decline of 0.9 per cent in the first half of 1999. The significant improvement in the second half of 1999 was supported by the continued recovery of crisis-hit Asian economies, as well as the increasing global demand for certain product segments, in particular, electronics.

The extent of the recovery is shown in the outlook for Singapore's trade in 2000, which is expected to grow by between 11 and 13 per cent (Trade Development Board 2000). The outlook for Singapore trade *vis-à-vis* other countries is shown in Table 14.5.

Table 14.3
Openness of the Singapore Economy

	1961	1966	1971	1976	1981	1986	1991	1996
Exports/GDP	1.42	1.01	0.79	1.12	1.56	1.27	1.35	1.33
Imports/GDP	1.70	1.22	1.27	1.54	2.05	1.44	1.52	1.40
Total trade/GDP	3.12	2.23	2.06	2.66	3.61	2.71	2.87	2.73

Source: Adapted from Ho and Hoon (2000).

Table 14.4
Trade Performance (% and S$bn)

	1997 Annual change (%)	1997 Annual (S$bn)	1998 Annual change (%)	1998 Annual (S$bn)	1999 Annual change (%)	1999 Annual (S$bn)
Non-oil domestic imports	5.3	91.6	0.9	92.4	9.5	101.2
Non-oil re-exports	7.3	77.8	−0.1	77.7	0.1	77.8
Non-oil imports	6.0	178.0	−12.2	156.2	9.5	171.1
Oil exports	−3.0	16.2	−15.9	13.6	12.4	15.3
Non-oil trade	6.1	347.4	−6.1	326.3	7.3	350.0
Total trade	5.7	382.2	−7.5	353.6	8.1	382.4

Source: Ministry of Trade and Industry (2000).

The relatively mild impact of the Asian crisis on Singapore can be attributed to two main factors: strong fundamentals and a flexible and timely policy response (Stone 1999; IMF 2000). The strong fundamentals include responsible and credible fiscal and monetary policy, flexible labour markets and policies, and an open trade regime. The effects of the recession were mitigated by the government's actions to improve enterprise cost competitiveness. A top priority in the crisis was to minimise unemployment and to preserve the production capacity. On a policy level, business cost reductions were engineered through wage cuts and various fees and tax rebates, amounting to US$7.4 billion, or about 7 per cent of GDP. The wage cut was achieved through a reduction in mandatory employers' contributions to workers' Central Provident Fund[4] contributions from 20 per cent to 10 per cent of wages.[5] A fiscal stimulatory package comprising sharply increased development expenditures which brought the budget balance into a deficit of 0.5 per cent of GDP in 1998/99, the first deficit since the recession in 1985, was to have been sustained into 1999/2000. The deficit was expected to widen to 3.5 per cent of GDP (Stone 1999). However, this subsequent fiscal stimulus was withdrawn in view of the strength of the recovery, and a strictly neutral fiscal stance adopted instead.

The immediate impact of the Asian financial crisis on SMEs was on their exports. The export markets of most Singapore SMEs are regional markets in Asia. The financial contagion that affected the region negatively affected sales. The greatest difficulty faced by these SMEs, if not all local enterprises, was securing access to financing to tide over the recession that affected their domestic and international sales.

The findings of a study by Tan and Tan (1998) provide an insight into the manner in which the SMEs coped with the financial crisis as well as into the impact of the crisis on SMEs. The study was a longitudinal one involving two samples of SMEs –

Table 14.5
Singapore's Outlook for Trade in 2000 *vis-à-vis* Other Countries

	1998	OECD[a]				IMF[b]		Singapore government	
		1st half 1999	2nd half 1999	1999	2000	1999	2000	1999	2000
World	2.5	na	na	3.0	3.5	3.0	3.5	na	na
US	3.9	3.8	3.8	3.8	3.1	3.7	2.6	3.2	na
EU	2.8	1.6	3.1	2.1	2.8	2.0	2.7	2.1	3.0
UK	2.1	1.1	3.1	1.7	2.7	1.1	2.4	1.5	2.75
Germany	2.8	0.7	3.3	1.3	2.3	1.4	2.5	1.4	2.7
Japan	−2.8	3.3	1.2	1.4	1.4	1.0	1.5	0.63	1.0[c]
Indonesia	−13.7	na	na	−0.5	2.5	−0.8	2.6	0.0	3–4
Thailand	−8.0	na	na	3.8	5.0	4.0	4.0	4.1	4.4
Malaysia	−6.8	na	na	4.5	5.5	2.4	6.5	4.3	5.3
Philippines	−0.5	na	na	3.2	4.5	2.2	3.5	2.6–3.2	4.0
Taiwan	4.9	na	na	na	na	5.0	5.1	5.48	6.04
Hong Kong	−5.1	na	na	0.0	4.0	1.2	3.6	1.8	4.5
Korea	−5.5	na	na	9.0	6.5	6.5	5.5	8.8	6.4
China	7.8	na	na	7.1	6.8	6.6	6.0	7.0	7.0
Singapore[d]	−7.5	−0.9	17.3					8.1	11–13

Notes:
a   OECD, *Economic Outlook*.
b   IMF's *World Economic Outlook*.
c   Refers to fiscal year, that is, April current year to April subsequent year.
d   Trade Development Board, *Review of 1999 Trade Performance and Outlook for Year 2000*.

one sample of 132 SMEs in 1996 (a 'good year'), and the second sample of 82 SMEs in 1998 (a 'bad year'). They defined SMEs as enterprises with fewer than 200 employees. The study was conducted in the first quarters of 1996 and 1998. In 1996, the year before the onset of the crisis, the country enjoyed GDP growth of 9.5 per cent. The 1998 survey was taken six months into the crisis, when its effects had started to bite. The SMEs were asked to rate the importance of 16 generic strategies to improving their profitability on a 5-point scale with 1 being 'extremely undesirable' and 5 being 'extremely desirable' in priority.

    The authors found differences in the importance placed by the SMEs on different strategies in the two periods. The differences in the means for each of the strategies in both years were analysed using analysis of variance. The results of the analysis are summarised in Table 14.6.

Significant differences were found between the mean scores of several strategies between the two surveys. The findings indicated that the SMEs placed greater emphasis on financial control and better working capital management in 1998, after the onset of the crisis. Cost-reduction strategies were also foremost in their minds as indicated by the change in the mean for reduced borrowing and for staff reductions. The results also indicated a significant decrease in the importance attached to advertising and to becoming more environment friendly. In general, the SMEs' focus on cost-reduction strategies reinforced the government's policies. While staff reductions were regarded as more important in 1998, the desirability of redeploying staff was rated as significantly more important for profitability, perhaps indicating that the SMEs were mindful of not decimating the core competencies represented in their human resources.

Table 14.6
Comparison of Strategies for Improving Profitability in 1996 and 1998

Strategy	1996	1998	*F* statistic	*p*
Redeployment of staff	3.1468	3.5000	3 616.79[d]	0.00[d]
Greater financial control	3.9541	4.1866	7 406.99[c]	0.01[c]
Better working capital management	3.9083	4.1493	6 060.06[b]	0.02[b]
Staff reductions	2.6514	2.8731	2 343.06[b]	0.05[b]
Increasing advertising expenditure	2.9358	2.7239	2 462.11[a]	0.06[a]
Reduced borrowing	3.2064	3.4179	2 642.69[a]	0.10[a]
Becoming more environment friendly	3.4128	3.2239	3 456.55[a]	0.10[a]
Increased turnover in reduced prices	2.9817	3.1940	2 003.66	0.12
Divesting non-core business	3.0092	2.8433	20 399.95	0.20
Curtailing training expenditure	2.2018	2.3284	1 770.57	0.24
Contracting in/out	3.0321	3.1418	2 733.15	0.35
Curtailing management development	2.2156	2.2985	1 578.64	0.47
Improved management of quality	4.2615	4.2388	6 893.35	0.82
Increased product focus	4.0321	4.0075	4 269.03	0.84
Targeted marketing	4.0780	4.0672	5 235.45	0.92
Curtailing R&D expenditure	2.2890	2.2985	1 355.82	0.94

Notes: a $p = 0.10$; b $p = 0.05$; c $p = 0.01$; d $p = 0.00$.
Source: Tan and Tan (1998).

The fact that significant differences were found in the means for greater financial control, reduced borrowing and better working capital management would appear to indicate difficulties with liquidity, and that one of the impacts of the crisis on SMEs was reduced access to financing. An interesting aspect of the findings, as Tan and Tan (1998) noted, was that the SMEs appear to have differentiated between short-term contingency actions and longer-term strategic imperatives. Thus, for example, there were no significant differences in the means for curtailing R&D expenditure, reduction of training expenditure and curtailing management development, reduction strategies which would affect a firm's long-term development plans and human resource strategies.[6]

14.4   TRANSITION TO THE NEW ECONOMY

14.4.1   Infrastructure and Use of Technology

In general, the infrastructure in Singapore to cater to the requirements of the knowledge-based economy is comprehensive and as developed as it is anywhere else in the world. The foundations of the information highway were laid in the 1980s, and the physical infrastructure is of an excellent standard. The country is among the front runners of Asian countries in terms of the widespread availability and use of technology (see Table 14.7), while the population is well-educated and technically literate. Access to the Internet is relatively widespread, with 42 per cent of households linked to the Internet, compared with 22 per cent in Australia and 13 per cent in Japan.[7]

Typically, the government has provided the lead and vision in the transition to the New Economy. The IT2000 Masterplan, the blueprint for the use of IT in every government department, has been largely implemented (*The Economist* 2000).

Table 14.7
Use of Technology, Selected Countries

	Singapore	Australia	Hong Kong	Japan	Korea	New Zealand
Personal computers per '000 pop	399.5	362.2	230.8	202.4	150.7	263.9
Telephone main lines per '000 pop	543	505	565	479	444	486
Mobile phones per '000 pop	273	264	343	304	150	149

Source: World Bank (2000).

Singapore ONE ('One Network for Everyone'), a national broadband high-speed network established in 1997, delivers interactive multimedia applications and services to almost every home, school and office in the country (Tan 1999). Since then, other broadband offerings by other providers – for example, cable modem access provided by Singapore Cable Vision – have established a presence in the market. The government is putting together the next blueprint, the ICT21 Masterplan, with the express aim of transforming the country into a fully-fledged New Economy by 2010.

It has pursued its vision with typical single-mindedness and thoroughness. The 'eCitizen Centre' which was launched in 1999, for example, is a comprehensive government web portal with links to the various government agencies, and that allows Singaporean residents to conduct the full range of transactions with government agencies on the Web. These include matters relating to business, defence, education, employment, family, health, housing, law and order, and transport, with the site thoroughly integrated and organised by function rather than government agency. Singaporean residents are able to register births and deaths, apply for licences, search for jobs, apply for telephone services and utilities, file for bankruptcy and so on through the portal. The US General Services Administration, in an international survey of sites offering integrated service delivery in 1999, noted that 'Singapore's eCitizen Centre is the most developed example of integrated service delivery in the world'.[8]

One of the key benefits of this approach is that it helps create a population that is comfortable with carrying out transactions on the Internet and with information technology in general, overcoming an important psychological barrier. As a government official has noted: 'The development of electronic public services is critical to setting the pace in proliferating the use of IT and creating an IT-savvy culture in Singapore. It will enhance the ability of the public to be increasingly familiar and comfortable with IT, which has become a critical component in the knowledge economy. Our people's openness to and skill with IT can offer a distinctive competitive edge to Singapore'.[9]

In terms of the legal framework, the Electronic Transactions Act, which provides a legal foundation for electronic transactions and is based on the United Nations Commission on International Trade Law (UNCITRAL) Model Law on Electronic Commerce, was enacted in 1998. It is backed up by the Computer Misuse Act, which was amended to provide greater protection to critical computer systems. In addition, copyright laws were updated to protect multimedia works, and a Privacy Code to safeguard consumer data was drafted for industry self-regulation (National Computer Board 1998). In 1999, the Electronic Transactions (Certification Authority) Regulations 1999 came into effect. The resulting legal infrastructure is designed to provide greater certainty to individuals and businesses conducting electronic commerce, and to encourage the growth of electronic commerce.

The government has declared its intention to increase the use of some form of e-commerce by SMEs to 25 per cent by 2003.[10] However, while access to the Internet is widespread, the number of businesses utilising electronic commerce is low. A survey of businesses in the country, broken down by establishment size as measured by number of employees, indicated that while more than 80 per cent of businesses had access to the World Wide Web, less than 31 per cent had a business home page (see Table 14.8). The groups with the highest proportion of business e-commerce users were the larger businesses.

Another survey of Internet-based business-to-business (B2B) electronic commerce in Singapore, conducted in January 1999, revealed that while more than 16 per cent of large companies were using the Internet for B2B electronic commerce, less than 8 per cent of small and medium companies were doing so (National Computer Board 1999b).[11]

Table 14.8
Access to the World Wide Web by Business Size, 1998

Business size (no. of employees)	% with access to the Web	% with home page
<25	80.0	28.8
25–99	86.5	46.3
100–199	99.7	63.7
200–499	97.7	77.6
>500	100.0	85.6
All businesses	80.8	30.8

Source: National Computer Board (1999a).

14.4.2 Policy Measures

In January 2000 the government issued its second major policy document on SMEs, *SME 21: Preparing SMEs for the 21ˢᵗ Century*. This report, a 10-year plan for the development of the SME sector, expands on the 1989 SME Master Plan and focuses on the outlook for SMEs in the twenty-first century. Developed collectively with representatives from SMEs, industry and trade associations, chambers of commerce and industry, financial institutions and government agencies, the plan recommends key strategies and programs to realise the vision of creating vibrant and resilient SMEs in order to enhance the economy's competitiveness and economic growth.

A comprehensive network of government agencies charged with various aspects of SME policy and assistance programs has been put together since the focus on SMEs was first articulated. The lead agency for administering SME policy is the Singapore Productivity and Standards Board (PSB). There are some 80 assistance programs that address the needs of SMEs. It is instructive to examine these because they reflect the key areas of perceived need of SMEs. The discussion here adopts the framework of the APEC SME Ministerial Meeting in Osaka in 1994, which identified the four key problem areas of SMEs as being access to technology, access to manpower, access to finance and access to markets.

Access to technology

The relative lack of size of SMEs often tends to be a disadvantage when it comes to access to technology. This is an important factor given the critical reliance of a knowledge-driven strategy on access to technology. The key issues relate to the areas of awareness of the need for new technologies, identification, evaluation of the technical and commercial feasibility of new technology and prototyping. Closely related to these considerations is the issue of encouraging and accelerating the diffusion of technology to SMEs generally.

SME 21 (Productivity and Standards Board 2000) has attempted to address this with two proposals. *SME 21* has proposed a Technology Network (TechNet) Program to facilitate connections to researchers, experts and venture capital funds. Researchers with potential research ideas can register their interest with the program and be matched with prospective SMEs or investors. Incentives can be provided to encourage such collaborations.

The technology matching program could be carried out through a physical centre or the Internet. Facilitators can also help prepare the business proposals and seek funding from venture capitalists and business angels. A mechanism can be set up to gather the latest technology trends and market intelligence through the government-linked offices. The TechNet Program will:

- Organise overseas technology missions to study new technologies.

- Foster partnerships with foreign research organisations and patent holders and assist in the application of patents and trademarks.

- Conduct research into technology trends and forecasting.

- Develop a database on best practices in technology management, technology trends and market intelligence.

- Develop a listing of venture capitalists and business angels.

The second proposal under *SME 21* is business fusion. The term is used in the document to refer to a process whereby a group of related companies come together to share knowledge, experience and ideas. It can provide a platform to spur the development of new and innovative products, services and business formats. The government's intention is to provide access to internally developed technology through business fusion, drawing upon the Japanese experience. In Japan, the Small Business Fusion Foundation actively encourages business fusion activities and promotes new ideas, products and services developed from such interactions.

The PSB is charged with spearheading the development of business fusion groups together with the SMEs, trade chambers and industry associations. SMEs under the Business Fusion Program can be supported by technical specialists, facilitators and

R&D centres which will test the viability of the participants' ideas and innovations, and be funded by the Local Enterprise Technical Assistance Scheme (LETAS).

LETAS is intended to help local enterprises defray the costs incurred in modernising and upgrading their operations through the engagement of an external expert for a limited period of time. The scheme generally grants support of up to 70 per cent of the cost of engaging external experts for an approved short-term assignment. The areas of assistance that may be supported include the identification and solving of technical problems, technical improvements to present operations or processes, mechanisation, automation or computerisation of operations or processes, quality management systems, business development, financial development, market development, management information, human resource management, product development, and franchise feasibility study and development.

Access to manpower

At the non-managerial level, SMEs have tended to have difficulties in recruiting staff. The fact that the economy was in a state of full employment prior to the Asian financial crisis meant that recruiting employees at non-managerial level was particularly acute. The Asian crisis led to an easing of the labour shortage but this was merely a temporary reprieve.

The problem is worse with regard to graduate-level and professional staff. The widely-held perception that SMEs are not good paymasters, and that they are less dynamic in terms of rewards and professional development, has meant that SMEs have tended to experience difficulty attracting young graduates and managerial staff. Some of the motivations of professionals are highlighted in a recent study of professional managers in Singapore family businesses (Tan and Zutshi 2000). Tan and Zutshi (2000) found that while the professionals surveyed did choose to work in SMEs, all of them did so with the hope of a reward in being responsible for taking the firm to a public listing. It was even highlighted as a means to impress their contemporaries who may be serving in larger corporations: to be a success in the corporate world. It also offered some the opportunity to serve as general managers or chief executive officers in corporations when they otherwise may not have had the chance in a large multinational.

Since 1997 government policy has attempted to assist local enterprises in professionalising their management by providing scholarships tenable at the Economic Development Board, but served at a 'promising local enterprise' under the EDB-PLE scholarship scheme. The scheme serves to attract scholars to work for the local enterprises under the auspices of the EDB. The scholars would be able to pursue a career with the EDB after their stint with the local enterprises should they not be satisfied with the opportunities there.

Under *SME 21*, the PSB will work with the chambers of commerce, industry associations and innovative high-growth firms, such as promising SMEs, to design more of such scholarships or human resource development program for local talent, on a cost-sharing basis. The promising SMEs can provide tertiary scholarships and internships or industrial attachment programs to undergraduates. Training institutes and polytechnics can also offer apprenticeship programs to workers in SMEs.

SMEs are in the same position as other employers in that they have access to incentives under the Skills Development Fund. This fund not only serves to motivate the employers to engage in training of their staff but also the training providers as well. They are motivated to have their training programs accredited so that the employers will be entitled to reimbursement for part of their employees' training costs. A training provider, initiating a new training program, will not be able to advertise that its participants who are employees qualify for funding from the Skills Development Fund, unless it has successfully conducted the program on two prior occasions. It needs to submit its program outline and the participant evaluations of the programs to the Skills Development Fund for its consideration. Upon obtaining its accreditation, the provider may include in its announcements the availability of Skills Development Fund funding, which is up to 50 per cent of the training costs. To be eligible, the employing companies have to be registered in Singapore, with training being fully sponsored by the companies. Workers also have to be Singapore citizens or permanent residents, or those with three-year work permits (Productivity and Standards Board 1999).

Access to manpower does not merely refer only to the availability of manpower but the availability of skilled manpower. Structured on-the-job training (OJT) is a cost-effective means of training encouraged by the Singapore government. It helps to develop the job-specific skills of employees as business requirements change. PSB has developed OJT blueprints for specific jobs in different industries. There is obvious potential for these to be adapted for use by SMEs.

Structured OJT can benefit the organisations and their workforce in a number of ways. Organisations that have a structured OJT system will be able to train staff more quickly and respond swiftly to constantly changing technology and new demands. They will be able to reduce their time-to-market. As organisational and task analyses are involved in the development of structured OJT, there will be better workflow and improved work processes as well as more effective staff deployment. As OJT is one-to-one training, it allows for individual difference in learning and helps strengthen the bond between staff and supervisors resulting in better staff performance. OJT can reduce training costs by as much as 75 per cent as employees need not be released from their jobs for training, which forms an integral part of their work. OJT at the same time partially addresses the needs of SMEs affected by the turnover of staff. A high turnover of staff may render it difficult to have new staff trained when they are required to cover the responsibilities vacated by their predecessors.

To provide access to manpower, the Ministry of Manpower has a service for employers and employees. Employees can submit their details to the MOM. This is particularly relevant to retrenched workers. The employers may use the service to recruit suitable manpower without advertising or relying on human resource specialists.

Access to finance

As in other countries, this is a particular area of difficulty for SMEs in Singapore. The venture capital market is relatively undeveloped, although efforts have been made by the government to encourage such a market.

Two related initiatives are planned under *SME 21*, business angel networks and working capital matching. Business angels can be a catalyst in starting a business. These informal investors are wealthy individuals who are prepared to use their financial resources to make risky investments based on their business acumen, experience and interests. They are often retired senior executives of big enterprises, or people who have sold their companies and now intend to reinvest their money. Besides providing financial support, business angels can provide expertise and connections, as they tend to invest in industries with which they are familiar. There is a need to formalise a network as these angels are known in their respective circles but the SMEs may not be aware of their existence. No such formal network exists at present, although informal networks do exist and a new start-up may need to grope in the dark to locate them. It would be fruitful to initiate these networks as experience in the US and Europe demonstrates.

SMEs have working capital needs which careful planning of their business operations may fail to anticipate. Mismatches in the timing of purchases and collections may occur leading to cash shortages that are usually short term and urgent in nature. The usual recourse for SMEs is to seek financing from banks but the approval of working capital loans may take some time. It was the credit crunch that resulted from the Asian financial crisis that saw a number of SME failures in Singapore. This prompted an expansion of the rules under the government's Local Enterprise Financing Scheme.

A proposal under *SME 21* is to provide working capital to SMEs through a Working Capital Matching Service, functioning as a business-to-business capital-matching service to help SMEs in need of working capital to purchase raw materials for production or to fulfil a contract. Under the proposal a listing of companies interested in partnering SMEs with such working capital needs would be created. In addition to financing, the partnership can also involve supply of raw materials and joint involvement in a specified project. SMEs that need working capital funds can approach the companies interested directly.

The Local Enterprise Financing Scheme, which is administered by the Singapore Productivity and Standards Board, represents an attempt to address the problem of lack of access to finance. The scheme provides a fixed interest rate financing program designed to encourage and assist local enterprises to upgrade, strengthen and expand their operations. It is offered through 27 participating financial institutions and facilitates factory term loans, finance leases, machinery term loans, working capital loans, hire purchase loans and factoring loans. The maximum limit on loans is S$15 million.

Access to markets

The lead agency responsible for trade is the Trade Development Board (TDB). It was established in 1982 by an Act of Parliament as a fully-fledged autonomous agency that could effectively represent and promote the country's international trade interests and exports. Its formation was prompted by the perceived threat to the country's trade at the start of the 1980s from global protectionist trends, changes in world trade patterns, and the weakening of Singapore's markets under the stresses of global recession. The main aspects of the TDB's work that have an impact on SMEs revolve around trade promotion, trade facilitation, business marketing, information on trade procedure, and information on foreign markets.

To facilitate trade, the TDB showcases Singapore products and services through its online Singapore Products & Services Directory. This directory was created with the purpose of allowing collaborations between Singapore-based companies and overseas corporations. The directory allows companies to advertise their products and services, with the purpose of establishing contacts with buyers and/or sellers from around the world. The TDB also showcases Singapore companies through its annual awards and by posting details of the award winners on the TDB web page. To promote trade, SMEs are given tax incentives for participating in international trade fairs and exhibitions. The government at the same time encourages the development of credible regional trade fairs and forums in Singapore. The incentives under this program include endorsement and marketing assistance through tax incentives and grants offered by the TDB. Singapore-based exhibition organisers are also encouraged to stage new trade shows in Singapore as well as to market existing shows under the approved exhibition organiser. This is achieved through a concessionary tax rate of 10 per cent on incremental income derived by approved exhibition organisers. The trade shows and exhibitions not only serve to export services but facilitate trade promotion and new business alliances. The Productivity and Standards Board and the Trade Development Board regularly lead groups of Singapore small and medium enterprises to seek out business opportunities in and beyond the region. They have, for example, ventured to Canada, Chile, Germany and Australia.

There are also specific government assistance schemes to develop SMEs' export market potential through branding, franchise development, product design, packaging design, and the licensing of technology developed by local SMEs. The new initiative under *SME 21* is the promotion of Singapore as a hub for SMEs to help the SMEs plug into the global network quickly. There is a German SME centre and a French SME centre in Singapore. A Nordic centre is being planned. The presence of foreign SMEs in Singapore will encourage the cross-fertilisation of best practices, expertise and ideas, and help local SMEs to upgrade and find new markets. The aim is for Singapore SMEs to venture overseas through strategic alliances.

The Internet revolution presents both threats and opportunities to businesses. The government's declared aim is to 'dot.com' the entire country – transforming Singapore into 'Singapore.com', a competitive, vibrant knowledge-based economy. The key challenge is to find ways to help as many of the SMEs as possible to be part of this movement to dot.com Singapore with a view to harnessing the Internet for e-commerce.

14.5   PROSPECTS FOR THE FUTURE

In the previous section we highlighted the main elements of the government's strategy to provide what Tan et al. (2000) term the 'entrepreneurial infrastructure' in Singapore. By entrepreneurial infrastructure, Tan et al. (2000) refer to the public and private sector elements intended to assist SMEs in the areas of assistance with tasks, resources, knowledge (training, development and education) and information. As Tan et al. (2000) point out, merely providing the infrastructure is insufficient. There are also the issues of communication, publicity, availability and perceptions. Access to the infrastructure requires awareness of the policy instruments – for example, an SME may not use the patent search service unless the entrepreneur is aware of this service. The need for the service may only be invoked when there is awareness of the availability of a resource: the element of latent demand.

The need to develop a more entrepreneurial culture as a prerequisite if the country is to reap the benefits offered by the New Economy has driven the government's initiatives in this area. As part of its continuing drive to channel enterprises towards higher-value-added activities, the government has recognised that SMEs are the logical vehicles for entrepreneurs to meet the challenges posed by the New Economy.

It is by no means certain, however, that they are capable of taking up the challenge. The success of Singapore, one of the most remarkable economic success stories of the second half of the twentieth century, has been built on the creation of an environment conducive to attracting foreign direct investors and multinational corporations. As Dr Goh Keng Swee, who has been described as 'Singapore's early economic architect' (Ho and Hoon 2000), noted in his Budget Statement to Parliament in 1970:

> We have made long and strenuous efforts to attract foreign investment into Singapore, but not because we need the money. The high level of our overseas assets shows that we have more than we can usefully spend in Singapore. We welcome foreign investors for the two things they bring with them – technology and markets. (Quoted in Ho and Hoon 2000)

The evolution of a highly professional and efficient civil service, to whose ranks have been drawn many of the brightest minds of the country, has supported these developments in vital ways. In turn, the top ranks of government-linked corporations have been filled by transfers from this elite corps of professionals. The result has been a virtual monopolisation by the government of much of the cream of the country's human capital. The multinational corporations, with their attractive employment conditions, absorbed most of the remaining pool of talent (Lian 2001).

It may be conjectured that successful entrepreneurs in the New Economy are likely to be educated and technically literate and numerate as basic prerequisites, given the knowledge-intensive nature of the IT industry. In addition, these people will need to possess Schumpeterian entrepreneurial qualities, the class of innovators known as technopreneurs. Thus, as Lian (2001) has argued, the very people likely to enjoy the attributes necessary for success as entrepreneurs in the New Economy have tended to be absorbed by the apparatus that has delivered success in the Old Economy. It therefore remains to be seen whether the efforts of the government in bringing about a drastic change in the mindset and economic culture built up painstakingly over three decades will succeed in channelling talent in the desired direction and bring about a successful transition.

14.6   SUMMARY AND CONCLUSIONS

The role and development of SMEs in Singapore cannot be fully understood without referral to the pervasive influence of government in the country and the crucial role it plays in setting directions, marshalling resources, and coordinating the overall strategy of the different players in the economy. The goal of the knowledge-based economy holds great promise for the country, as indeed it does for other countries. What sets the country apart from most others is the scale of its government's ambition and the thoroughness and single-mindedness with which it pursues it. At the same time, there is a certain efficiency in the approaches taken. The policy of identifying 'promising local enterprises', for example, may be regarded as an adaptation of the government's favoured approach of picking winners, except that at the earlier stages of development the enterprises most likely to 'win' are allowed to sort themselves out from the others before being singled out for special attention.

While the existing SMEs cope with change, new entrants in this state of disequilibrium will be what Schumpeter called 'entrepreneurs' in his theory of economic development. These enterprises will be the ones for whom the new technopreneurship initiatives have been crafted.

Official attention has turned in recent years to the need to develop a more entrepreneurial culture as a prerequisite if the country is to reap the benefits offered by the New Economy. The government has highlighted certain industries that it hopes to foster in the next ten years in the area of e-commerce and life sciences. SMEs are the logical entities to meet this challenge. The extent to which they are able to do so will critically shape the future of the country and may well determine its economic survival.

NOTES

1   The somewhat unwieldy term 'technopreneurship' has been coined to refer to this form of entrepreneurship.
2   See also Cheah and Yu (1996).
3   This contrasted with the situation in Hongkong after the 1949 Communist takeover of the mainland. The British colony received entrepreneurs fleeing the Communists from Shanghai and elsewhere on the mainland. These people possessed business experience, expertise, capital and technical skills (Sit et al. 1991).
4   The Central Provident Fund scheme is essentially a state-administered superannuation scheme covering all workers in the country. It has proved a powerful tool of economic policy for the government, allowing it to fine-tune wages, and delivering a degree of flexibility not available to most other governments.
5   The cuts were partially restored; as of April 2000, employer contributions to their employees' CPF were increased by 2 per cent to 12 per cent.
6   This view is weakly reinforced by the fact that the study also found a non-significant increase in the importance attributed to improving the management of quality.
7   Figures reported in the *Sydney Morning Herald* ('Web of Intrigue'), 29 April 2000 [no page numbers given].
8   Quoted in *The Economist* (2000, [no page numbers given]).
9   The Education Minister, Peter Chen, quoted in *The Economist* (2000, [no page numbers given]).
10 Raj (2000), reporting on an address by the Minister of State for Communications and Information Technology, Lim Swee Say.
11 The National Computer Board was renamed the Infocomm Development Agency in 2000. For the purpose of the survey, small companies were defined as those with fewer than 10 employees, medium companies as those with between 10 and 99 employees, and large companies as those with 100 or more employees.

REFERENCES

Cheah, H.B. and T.F.L. Yu (1996), 'Adaptive Response: Entrepreneurship and Competitiveness in the Economic Development of Hong Kong', *Journal of Enterprising Culture*, **4** (3): 241–66.

Doh, J.C. (1996), 'The Strategy of SME Development in Singapore', in A.M. Low and W.L. Tan (eds), *Entrepreneurs, Entrepreneurship and Enterprising Culture*, Singapore: Addison-Wesley, pp. 235–43.

Economic Development Board (1989), *SME Master Plan: Report on Enterprise Development*, Singapore.

Economist, The (2000), 'Island Site', *The Economist*, 22 June, at <www.southampton-institute.ac.uk/library/>.

Foreign Policy (2001), 'Measuring Globalization', *Foreign Policy*, January/February, 56–65.

Ho, K.W. and H.T. Hoon (2000), 'Assessing Export Platforms: The Case of Singapore', Consulting Assistance on Economic Reform (CAER II) Project Discussion Paper No. 72, Harvard Institute for International Development, April.

International Monetary Fund (2000), 'IMF Concludes Article IV Consultation with Singapore', Public Information Notice No. 00/46, June.

Kent, C.A. (1984), 'The Rediscovery of the Entrepreneur', in C.A. Kent (ed.), *The Environment for Entrepreneurship*, Lexington, MA: Lexington Books, pp. 1–19.

Kirzner, I. (1979), *Perception, Opportunity and Profit: Studies in the Theory of Entrepreneurship*, Chicago: University of Chicago Press.

Lee, T. Y. and L. Low (1990), *Local Entrepreneurship in Singapore: Private and State*, Singapore: Singapore Institute of Policy Studies and Times Academic Press.

Lian, D. (2001), 'Singapore: New Economy Proletariat or Bourgeoisie', Morgan Stanley Dean Witter Global Economics Team, 16 January.

Mani, A. (1993), 'Indians in Singapore Society', in K.S. Sandhu and A. Mani (eds), *Indian Communities in Southeast Asia*, Singapore: Institute of Southeast Asian Studies, pp. 789–810.

Ministry of Trade and Industry (1986), *The Singapore Economy: New Directions*, Report of the Economic Committee, Singapore: Ministry of Trade and Industry.

Ministry of Trade and Industry (2000), *Economic Survey of Singapore Second Quarter 2000*, Singapore: Ministry of Trade and Industry.

National Computer Board (1998), 'Singapore Launches Electronic Commerce Masterplan', at http://www.ec.gov.sg.

National Computer Board (1999a), *Key Findings of ICT Usage Survey 1999 on the ICT Adoption of Business in Singapore*, Singapore: National Computer Board.

National Computer Board (1999b), 'Key Findings of NCB Survey on Internet-based Business-to-Business Electronic Commerce in Singapore', at http://202.42.217.232/11061999/ 11061999_1.html

Productivity and Standards Board (1999), *Annual Report*, Singapore: Productivity and Standards Board.

Productivity and Standards Board (2000), *SME 21: Preparing SMEs for the 21st Century*, Singapore: Singapore Productivity and Standards Board.

Raj, C. (2000), 'Singapore to Pump Up SMEs Doing E-Commerce', *Business Times*, 11 April.

Sandhu, K.S. (1993), 'Indian Immigration and Settlement in Singapore', in K.S. Sandhu and A. Mani (eds), *Indian Communities in Southeast Asia*, Singapore: Institute of Southeast Asian Studies, pp. 775–88.

Sit, V.F.S., R.D. Cremer and S.L. Wong (1991), *Entrepreneurs and Enterprises in Macau: A Study of Industrial Development*, Hong Kong: Hong Kong University Press and API Press.

Stone, M.R. (1999), 'Fundamentals, Timely Policy Measures Help Singapore Weather Asian Crisis', *IMF Survey*, 26 April, 127–28.

Tan, K.Y.T. (2000), 'Moving From the Old Economy to the New Economy: Implications for the Formulation of Public Policies', speech of the Deputy Prime Minister and Minister for Defence, delivered at the administrative service dinner and promotion ceremony on 27 March, Singapore.

Tan, M. (1999), 'Creating the Digital Economy: Strategies and Perspectives from Singapore', *International Journal of Electronic Commerce*, **3** (3), Spring, 105–22.

Tan, T.M., W.L. Tan and J.E. Young (2000), 'Entrepreneurial Infrastructure in Singapore; Developing a Model and Mapping Participation', *Journal of Entrepreneurship*, **9** (1), 1–33.

Tan, W.L. and S.T. Fock (2001), 'Coping with Growth Transitions: The Case of Chinese Family Businesses in Singapore', *Family Business Review* (forthcoming, June).

Tan, W.L. and L.B.L. Tan (1998), 'Strategies Adopted by SMEs in Hard Times', *Asian Small Business Review*, **1** (1), October, 115–28.

Tan, W.L. and T.M. Tan (1999), 'The Implications of the Knowledge Economy for Venture Promotion Policies', *The Role of Venture SMEs in the Knowledge-based Economy: A Challenge for the Asia–Pacific Countries*, Proceedings of the Third Annual Asia-Pacific Forum for Small Business, 15 October, Seoul, Korea.

Tan, W.L. and R. Zutshi (2000), 'Family Businesses and Professional Managers: Recruiting the Professionals is Only the Beginning', *Zeitschrift für Klein-und Mittelunternehmen* (Journal published by the Swiss Research Institute of Small & Business Entrepreneurship), **48**, 220–36.

Trade Development Board (2000), 'Meeting Challenges of the Future: Opportunities and Potential in the New Economy', *Singapore Trade Development Board Annual Report 1999/2000*, Singapore: Trade Development Board.

World Bank (2000), *Entering the 21st Century: World Development Report 1999/2000*, New York: Oxford University Press.

Yu, T.F.L (1995), 'Adaptive Response: Entrepreneurship and Economic Development in Hong Kong', unpublished PhD thesis, University of New South Wales.

Index